A Different Face

HARPER & ROW, PUBLISHERS

New York, Evanston, San Francisco, London

1817

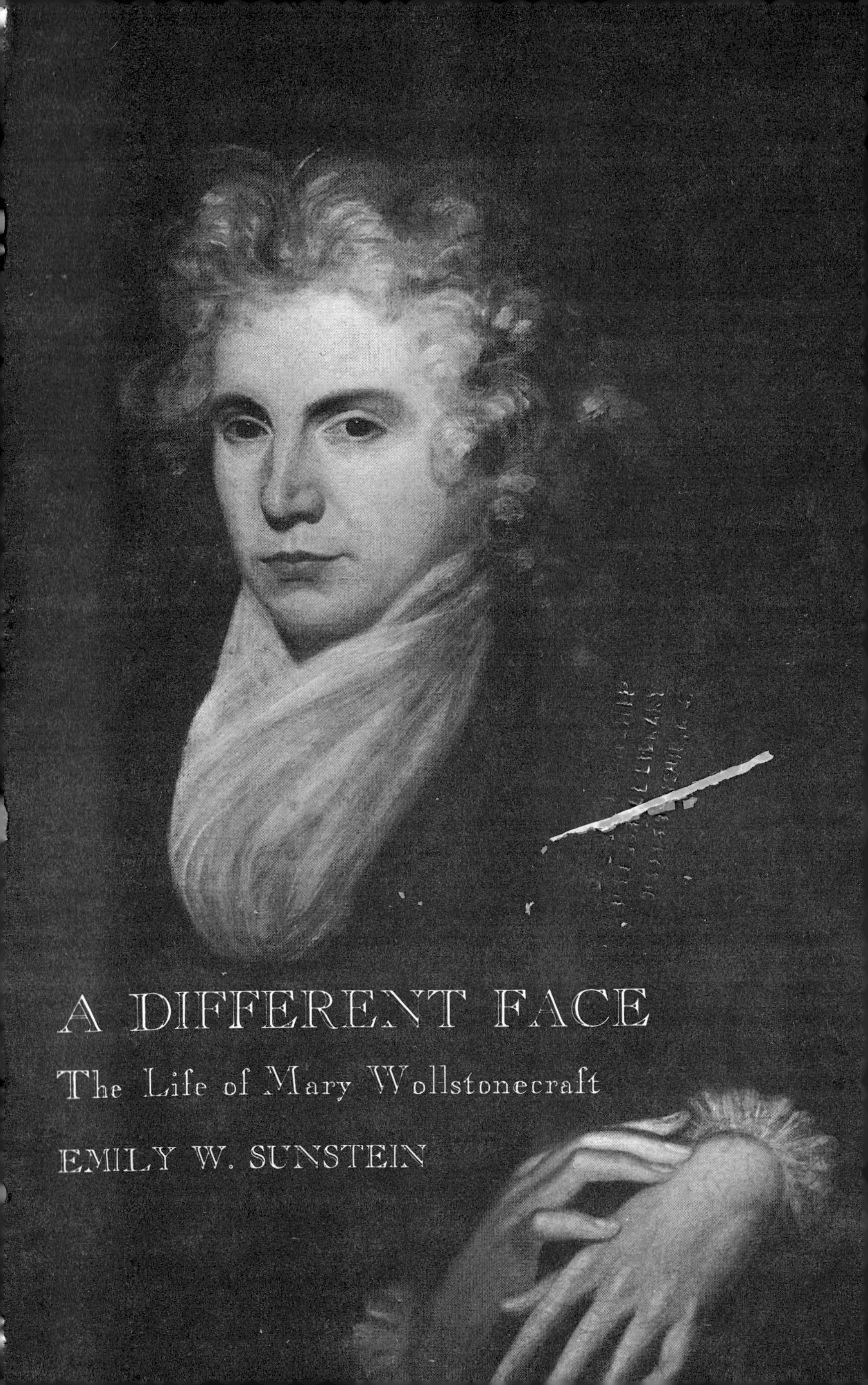

A DIFFERENT FACE

The Life of Mary Wollstonecraft

EMILY W. SUNSTEIN

For Lee

 For information address Harper & Row, Publishers, Inc., 10 East 53rd Street, New York, N.Y. 10022. Published simultaneously in Canada by Fitzhenry & Whiteside Limited, Toronto.

FIRST EDITION

Designed by Dorothy Schmiderer

Library of Congress Cataloging in Publication Data

Sunstein, Emily W
A different face.
Bibliography: p.
"Works by Mary Wollstonecraft": p.
Includes index.
1. Wollstonecraft, Mary, 1759–1797—Biography.
I. Title.
PR5841.W8Z79 828′.6′09 [B] 74-15856
ISBN 0-06-014201-4

---

75 76 77 10 9 8 7 6 5 4 3 2 1

Contents

	Acknowledgments	*ix*
	Author's Note	*xi*
	Works by Mary Wollstonecraft	*xiii*
I	THE ORIGINAL DEFECT	*1*
II	THE BITTER BREAD OF DEPENDENCE	*49*
III	THE FIRST OF A NEW GENUS	*149*
IV	LEANING ON A SPEAR	*227*
V	HOME, TO DEPART NO MORE	*301*
	Bibliographical References	*357*
	Notes to Chapters	*359*
	Index	*373*

Illustrations

These photographs will be found in a separate section following page 144.

Joseph Johnson, by Moses Haughton. (*The British Museum*)

St. Paul's Churchyard. (*The British Museum*)

"Indeed We Are Very Happy!" Engraving by William Blake. (*Library of Congress, Rosenwald Collection*)

"Look, What a Fine Morning It Is." Engraving by William Blake. (*Library of Congress, Rosenwald Collection*)

"An Establishment for Young Ladies," by Edward F. Burney. (*Victoria and Albert Museum—Crown Copyright*)

Henry Fuseli, by Moses Haughton. (*The British Museum*)

Self-portrait by Henry Fuseli. (*Victoria and Albert Museum—Crown Copyright*)

"The Debutante," by Henry Fuseli. (*The Tate Gallery, London*)

Portrait of Mary Wollstonecraft by unknown artist. (*By permission of the Walker Art Gallery, Liverpool*)

Mary Wollstonecraft, by John Opie. (*The Tate Gallery, London*)

Portrait of Sophia Fuseli, by Henry Fuseli. (*Auckland City Art Gallery*)

"Satan's First Address to Eve," by Henry Fuseli.
(*Auckland City Art Gallery*)

William Godwin, by Sir Thomas Lawrence. (*The British Museum*)

Mary Wollstonecraft, by John Opie. (*National Portrait Gallery, London*)

Three letters of Mary Wollstonecraft:
A. To Everina Wollstonecraft from Dublin, May 11–12, 1787.
B. To George Dyson, 1795–1797. Signed "Mary Imlay."
C. To Maria Reveley, June 26, 1797. Signed "Mary Godwin."
(*By permission of the Carl H. and Lily Pforzheimer Foundation, Inc., on behalf of the Carl H. Pforzheimer Library*)

The jacket photograph is of the last portrait of Mary Wollstonecraft, painted by John Opie. (*National Portrait Gallery, London*)

Acknowledgments

Lord Abinger of Clees Hall, Bures, Suffolk, very generously gave me permission to read and to quote from letters of Mary Wollstonecraft and her circle in his remarkable collection. These I read on microfilm by courtesy of the Carl H. and Lily Pforzheimer Library in New York, which has the only set of such films in the United States. I wish to thank the Carl H. and Lily Pforzheimer Foundation, Inc., for permission to quote extensively from its manuscripts as published in the magnificent *Shelley and his Circle,* edited by Kenneth Neill Cameron et al. I wish also to thank Dr. Cameron for his encouragement and the staff of the Pforzheimer Library for their interest and assistance.

In addition I am grateful to the following for permission to quote from material in their collections: the Liverpool City Libraries for Letters of Mary Wollstonecraft to William Roscoe in the Roscoe Papers; the Houghton Library of Harvard University for the letters of Joel Barlow to Ruth Barlow, by permission of the Harvard College Library; the Henry W. and Albert A. Berg Collection, the New York Public Library, Astor, Lenox and Tilden Foundations, for quotations from portions of the Diary of Fanny Burney (Fanny Burney's conversation with "Miss White" of Wednesday, June 8, 1780). The letters of Mary Wollstonecraft, originally published by the University of California Press as *Four New Letters . . .* , edited by Benjamin P. Kurtz and Carrie C. Autrey, are reprinted by permission of the Regents of the University of California. I am thankful to Columbia University Press for material quoted from *New Letters of Robert Southey,* edited by Kenneth Curry; to Coward, McCann, and Geoghegan, Inc., for permission to quote

Mary Wollstonecraft's letter to Von Schlabrendorf, as used in Eleanor Flexner's *Mary Wollstonecraft: A Biography;* and to the University of Kansas Press for permission to reprint letters in *Godwin & Mary,* edited by Ralph M. Wardle.

I am greatly indebted to the following institutions and individuals: the Library Company of Philadelphia, Edwin Wolf II and Lilian Tonkin; the libraries of the University of Pennsylvania, the Philadelphia College of Physicians, and the Pennsylvania Historical Society; the New York Public Library; the Lehigh University Library; the Bath Municipal Library; the Beverley Area Public Library, Mr. G. P. Brown; the Guildhall Library; the Greater London Record Office; the Public Record Office; the British Museum; the Greater London Council; the Hackney Library; the London Borough of Tower Hamlets; and the Wellcome Trust.

I would also like to acknowledge the help of the late Catherine Drinker Bowen; Miss Mary Woodworth; Joyce Hemlow, editor of the Burney papers; Mr. Warren Darry of Bath; Peter S. Harrison, Vicar of Beverley Minster; Mr. R. Sygrove, Verger of St. Mary's in Beverley; Mr. C. A. Arden, Knaresborough, Yorkshire; Dr. F. G. Emmison, formerly of the Essex County Record Office and K. C. Newton of that office; Margaret Crum, Dept. of Western MSS, Bodleian Library; Dr. Paul Sloane; Dr. Louis A. Wikler; Kay Sunstein Hymowitz; Lauren Sunstein; John Hellebrand; Andrea Nettl; Jennifer Seder Frosh; and the late Wayne A. Wilcox and Pauline C. de I. McHarg.

Joan Younger Dickinson read the original draft of this book; it could not have been produced without her skillful and generous assistance.

I am grateful for three years of the exceptional, even for him, understanding, patience, and fortitude of Leon C. Sunstein, Jr.

E. W. S.

Author's Note

My interest in Mary Wollstonecraft originated many years ago with Virginia Woolf's essay in *The Second Common Reader* and with W. Clark Durant's edition of Godwin's *Memoirs,* with Durant's splendid *Supplement.* In preparation for this book I read most of the work pertaining to Mary Wollstonecraft. Anyone interested in her can now obtain a complete bibliography by subscribing to the *Mary Wollstonecraft Journal,* edited by Janet Todd of Rutgers University. Of recent books, Ralph M. Wardle's *Mary Wollstonecraft* (1951) is a substantial, thorough work of scholarship. In editing *Shelley and his Circle,* Kenneth Neill Cameron, Eleanor L. Nicholes, and Eleanor Flexner made important new contributions. Margaret George's *One Woman's "Situation"* (1970) is a brilliant short study, although in my opinion limited as well as illumined by George's particular feminism. Edna Nixon's 1971 biography not only retains old errors but adds her own. Eleanor Flexner's *Mary Wollstonecraft* (1972) presents fine new research. Claire Tomalin's *The Life and Death of Mary Wollstonecraft* (1974) contains some colorful new details, but I feel the interpretation lacks balance as well as sympathy.

Although beholden to many biographers, I have attempted not to allow anything to come between this study and the sources: the events of Mary Wollstonecraft's life and everything she wrote, public and private.

Works by Mary Wollstonecraft

Since Mary Wollstonecraft's major books are used freely and not in chronological order in this work, the following list may be useful.

Age

27 *Thoughts on the Education of Daughters: with Reflections on Female Conduct, in the More Important Duties of Life:* the title is an accurate description; written in the spring of 1786, when Mary was mistress of a school, living with her sisters at Newington Green.

27–28 *Mary, a Fiction:* a novel based on her ardent friendship with Fanny Blood and an unfortunate, probably fictional love affair; completed in the first half of 1787, while she was a governess in Ireland and Bristol.

28 *Cave of Fancy:* uncompleted fantasy, laid aside in late 1787.

28 *Original Stories from Real Life; with Conversations, Calculated to Regulate the Affections, and Form the Mind to Truth and Goodness:* a book for children, written in the last half of 1787 while she was working for the London publisher Joseph Johnson.

31 *A Vindication of the Rights of Men:* her first political work, written in November, 1790.

32 *A Vindication of the Rights of Woman:* the famous controversial work that established her reputation, written in the last quarter of 1791.

34 *An Historical and Moral View of the Origin and Progress of the*

French Revolution: begun in 1793, completed in 1794, while she was witnessing the Revolution in Paris and Havre.

34–37 Letters to Gilbert Imlay: letters to her lover, written in France, England, and Scandinavia, 1793–1796, published in her *Posthumous Works.*

37 *Letters Written during a Short Residence in Sweden, Norway, and Denmark:* the account of a journey for Imlay, written at the end of her relationship with him, in late 1795.

37–38 *The Wrongs of Woman: Or, Maria:* a novel dramatizing her experience with Imlay and her perception of women's plight, unfinished at her death in September, 1797.

MARY

. . .

Mary moves in soft beauty and conscious delight,
To augment with sweet smiles all the joys of the night,
Nor once blushes to own to the rest of the fair
That sweet love and beauty are worthy our care.

. . .

Some said she was proud, some call'd her a whore,
And some, when she passed by, shut to the door . . .

'O, why was I born with a different face?
Why was I not born like this envious race?
Why did Heaven adorn me with bountiful hand,
And then set me down in an envious land?'

. . .

She went out in mourning attir'd plain and neat;
'Proud Mary's gone mad,' said the child in the street;
She went out in mourning in plain neat attire,
And came home in evening bespatter'd with mire.

She trembled and wept, sitting on the bedside,
She forgot it was night, and she trembled and cried;
She forgot it was night, she forgot it was morn,
Her soft memory imprinted with faces of scorn;

. . .

And thine is a face of sweet love in despair,
And thine is a face of mild sorrow and care,
And thine is a face of wild terror and fear
That shall never be quiet till laid on its bier.

—William Blake, c. 1801–1803

I

The Original Defect

Chapter 1

Mary Wollstonecraft was born in mid-eighteenth-century England into a society that believed women to be inferior morally and intellectually, and into a class whose ideal women were the sheltered, submissive, lifelong wards of fathers or husbands—decorative, domestically useful sex objects. The system, maintained by church and state law, normally protected and rewarded its dependents. However, it did not work for Mary Wollstonecraft. She could not depend on her family, which failed her in every way; she would not marry for security; she had intellectual ambitions; she rebelled against injustice and defied the presumption of inferiority. Educated as few women were, and solely on her own initiative, she made herself independent, became an educator, a pioneer career writer, a political radical, and, at thirty-two, produced what one historian has called perhaps the most original book of her century, *A Vindication of the Rights of Woman,* rights which she alone gave equal weight with Rights of Man proclaimed in the two revolutions through which she lived. She was so far ahead of her time as to be isolated and reviled, but posterity has paid her the tribute—given only to authentic revolutionaries—of taking for granted her substantive insights while continuing to debate their exact application.

Mary Wollstonecraft was particularly modern in another sense: she demanded happiness. At thirty-three, when she was at last able to free herself of personal and social inhibitions, she had a passionate love affair that resulted in an illegitimate child, and having added that fulfillment to her perception of women's rights, she went on to fall in love with—and marry, while pregnant with his child—William Godwin, the most prominent English radical philosopher of the time. With him she launched an experiment in coordinate marriage, cut short when she died in childbirth. Their daughter married Percy Shelley, and like her mother wrote a classic work, *Frankenstein.*

Mary Wollstonecraft's whole existence was an attempt to make life conform to her needs, and her expectations and demands were so unrealistic as to be self-defeating. "There is certainly an original defect in my mind," she said at thirty-eight, "for the cruelest experience will not eradicate the foolish tendency I have to cherish, and expect to meet with, romantic tenderness." She sought ideal men and women, individual and systemic justice. Inevitable disappointment could not reach her resignation; she continued to search for happiness and justice with inextinguishable hope but also with great anger. She spent her life looking for a peace of mind her own ambivalence made difficult. In 1797, when she died, she had almost found it.

> Mary Wollstonecraft was born on the 27th of April 1759. Her father's name was Edward John, and the name of her mother Elizabeth, of the family of Dixons of Ballyshannon in the kingdom of Ireland: her paternal grandfather was a respectable manufacturer in Spital-fields, and is supposed to have left his son a property of about 10,000*l.* . . .
>
> I am doubtful whether the father of Mary was bred to any profession, but, about the time of her birth, he resorted . . . to the occupation of farming . . .

This is the brief account of Mary Wollstonecraft's origins in her *Memoirs,* written immediately after her death by her husband, William Godwin. The biographer of a great figure, he said, should "record the fragments of progress and cultivation that may have come down to him," however imperfect, and this Godwin conscientiously did. However, the *Memoirs* are particularly illuminating not only because Godwin was candid in almost every instance, but because he was passing along Mary Wollstonecraft's own highly subjective version of her life; the hand is Godwin's, the narrative voice to a great degree is Mary's.[1*]

* Notes to chapters begin on page 359.

The information he had from her in this initial passage is immediately interesting for its meagreness and error. Her mother's maiden name was Dickson. Her father was brought up to be a master weaver like her grandfather and worked at that profession, which the family conveniently forgot, during her early childhood. Although she was not sure precisely where she was born, it was in London, where she lived until she was over four years old.

Her paternal grandfather, Edward Wollstonecraft, was born in 1689, into Defoe's England. By the middle of the eighteenth century London directories listed him as Citizen and Master Weaver living in Primrose Street where he owned "several brick messauges or tenements." In 1756 he built a house on the north side of Hansbury Street, or Brown's Lane as it was then known, including a shop, warehouses, and stables for which he obtained a building lease as Edward Wollstonecraft, "gentleman," an appellation which indicates he built the family status as well as its fortune. He outlived two wives and had only three children who lived to maturity; of them, one, Charles, died before his father and left a widow, Mary. Another, Elizabeth Ann, married Isaac Rutson, probably a widower, and produced three children: Edward Woodstock, Sarah, and Mary. The year Mary Wollstonecraft was born, another Mary Wollstonecraft died at the age of thirty-eight; her relationship to the family is not known. Nowhere in Mary's extant letters or those of her sisters is there any mention of these relations. Her father, Edward John, was born about 1736. He was his father's Benjamin, for the older Wollstonecraft would then have been forty-eight.[2]

Judging from his lengthy and elaborate will, drawn up when Mary was five, her grandfather was prosperous, for in addition to his London properties he held shares in the East Indiaman, *Cruttenden,* £1700 worth of Bank of England stock, and substantial plate, household goods, and furniture. He was pious. The will began with a lengthy invocation: "I commend my soul to the hands of Almighty God," etc. Perhaps he had known poverty and bad luck; he left £5 to "confined debtors" in three London jails and a small amount to paupers in the parish workhouse. He did his duty by his dependents judiciously—Isaac Rutson's married daughter he left "the sum of one shilling, she having already shared sufficiently of my bounty." He also made sure Elizabeth Ann Rutson would keep what he left her "separate of her husband, and with which he is not to intermeddle." Without this provision, her property would have been completely under her husband's control, according to the law of the time.

A master weaver like Wollstonecraft flourished under the domestic system, buying prepared thread and farming it out to skilled journeymen who usually worked in their own homes and returned the finished goods to the master. "Some of the masters only keep a loom or two at work . . . but there are others who are great dealers and employ from £500 to £50,000 in trade . . . with an apprentice who will be chiefly employed in the counting-house." So reads a contemporary vocational guide.

The elder Wollstonecraft was a religious, benevolent, businesslike, solid middle-class citizen. He intended that his son should carry on the family name and trade. Young Edward John at about fourteen was formally apprenticed to his father and spent his adolescence in Spitalfields learning the business.[3] Hogarth's "Industry and Idleness" series illustrates what young Wollstonecraft's apprenticeship must have been like. In the fourth etching of the series, Francis Goodchild is working in the office, as befits the master's son, while the master leans affectionately on the son's shoulder and points to the looms in the background that someday will be his. Whether or not the real life relationship between father and son was so ideal is another question. Edward John was high-spirited, wild, puerile, lacking judgment and self-control; he may have been simply a spoiled brat or father-dominated or both. The young man was released from his apprenticeship after the usual seven years, on May 2, 1757, when he was twenty or twenty-one years old. Whatever he was supposed to have learned about balancing books does not seem to have taken root; he had uncommonly bad sense about money and business, as did his children.

His marriage to Elizabeth Dickson apparently took place about the time of his majority, when his father moved to Brown's Lane. It could have been a love match or the more usual marriage for property advantage. Parents could and did control the matches their children made, hopefully for the sake of solid bargains. An advanced political and moral writer of the time, James Burgh, in his *Youth's Friendly Monitor*, advised his pupils with shattering realism: "You may be as sure of a Woman of Merit with a moderate fortune, as with nothing; and if you get a Fortune in Marriage, you make sure of Somewhat."[4] Whatever fortune Elizabeth Dickson brought to her marriage belonged to her young husband, for a wife had no civil existence in law, although she could make some provision for herself and her children in her marriage settlement.

Edward John Wollstonecraft, then, only son of a man of means, married, educated to take over a trade, was set for a fine and even splendid future. Young men of his class at a time of prosperity, expansion, and upward mobility in England had opportunities to become magnates in the city or gentlemen of means in the counties. For the first years of his marriage Edward John Wollstonecraft lived in London at his father's property on Primrose Street. By 1759 London street directories listed the son rather than the father as master weaver.[5] Possibly the older man, then past seventy, had turned the business over to the younger. Elizabeth Wollstonecraft promptly produced a son and heir. There must have been great rejoicing in Primrose Street, for this direct male descendant would be particularly meaningful to the patriarch. The baby was named Edward, third in series of which there were to be four. The old man as well as the child's mother doted on him.

This was the household into which Mary Wollstonecraft was born on April 27, 1759, about three years after her young parents' marriage, a year or more after the birth of her older brother. She was baptized May 20, at St. Botolph's Bishopsgate, the family's parish church. On February 1, 1761, a second son, Henry Woodstock Wollstonecraft, was baptized in the same church. (This son is not mentioned in the *Memoirs*.) July 24, 1763, another daughter, Elizabeth, was duly christened in St. Botolph's.[6]

Until mid-1763, therefore, the Wollstonecraft family lived in London, and here Mary Wollstonecraft spent the first four-odd years of her life. The typical area merchant's house was brick or stone, three or four stories high, built on the street end of a narrow but deep plot, with a garden or court behind it and beyond perhaps a stable or outbuilding. The offices were on the ground floor, warehousing in the cellar. Outside, all the stir and noise of city street life: cries of vendors peddling fragrant food or notions; geese or cattle occasionally driven into town from the country; coaches, carts, and wagons grating along the pavement; filth in the gutters; passing workmen, beggars, and burghers. Inside, business transacted and discussed, an impressive grandfather visiting, and three or four children in close quarters. Mary Wollstonecraft had only vague memories of this scene, so thick with character, sound, and smell, so different from the serenity of the countryside that was the first definite place memory of her childhood.

Far from being treated as a crucial formative stage, infancy at this period was only beginning even to evoke much interest. The infant mortality rate was staggering but acceptable; physicians, according to one medical man, "have refused to visit infants, even when sick." In the month of Mary Wollstonecraft's birth, 1,107 babies were baptized in London and 669 buried, not counting those disposed of informally on garbage heaps. Although parents had to keep some emotional distance from babies who were as likely to die as to live, they were also indifferent or at best unwittingly callous. It was still common for babies to be farmed out to a wet nurse for the first two years. An infant was called "little animal" or "brat" (little angel was a nineteenth-century term). Control was the parents' first concern. The infant was usually immobilized by stays and wrappings, tossed for exercise, and doused in cold water, "the colder the better," for stimulation. Parents, said one expert, James Nelson, "may be surprised" to learn that there was a definite connection between their method of handling babies and how the babies' habits developed, and he expounded on the paramount task, subjugating "wilfulness" and "passions" in children even at six months of age. By six years they were to be effectually broken in. The attitude retained something of the older concept of innate evil which had made it possible to beat babies for crying while highlighting the period's increasing emphasis on the importance of environment. Mary Wollstonecraft was to become an advocate of a freer, more empathetic child care. She was motivated by lifelong resentment of her unfortunate family experience, a repressive system carried out by an unloving mother and an unstable father, as evidenced promptly on the second page of the *Memoirs:*

> She experienced in the first period of her existence, but few of those indulgences and marks of affection, which are principally calculated to soothe the subjection and sorrows of our early years. She was not the favourite of either her father or mother. Her father was a man of a quick, impetuous disposition, subject to alternate fits of kindness and cruelty. . . . The mother's partiality was fixed upon the eldest son, and her sys-

tem of government relative to Mary, was characterized by considerable rigour.[7]

Elizabeth Wollstonecraft did not send her children out to nurse and apparently breast-fed only her oldest, which Mary felt would partially account for her mother's preference for him. Junior to this indulged brother, nursed without devotion and even with "rigour," Mary never outgrew her anger. Elizabeth Wollstonecraft's neglect may account for Mary's uncertainty about her birthplace, for the child did not have the kind of maternal care that delights in loving tattle, reminiscences, and infantile accomplishments. Mary herself, according to the *Memoirs,* attributed her ignorance of the matter, infinitesimal as it was on the scale of her resentments, to her father's character:

> He was of a very active, and somewhat versatile disposition, and so frequently changed his abode, as to throw some ambiguity upon the place of her birth. She told me, that the doubt in her mind in that respect, lay between London, and a farm upon Epping Forest, which was the principal scene of the first five years of her life.[8]

Actually, Mary was over four when Edward John Wollstonecraft left the silk business and moved to Epping in 1763. Silk weaving had flourished during the Seven Years War, but after the Peace of Paris in 1763, a depression set in, profits declined, and master weavers squeezed their workers or began to leave London. London journeymen rioted and petitioned; in October, 1763:

> Several thousand journeymen weavers assembled in Spitalfields, and, in a riotous and violent manner, broke open the house of one of their masters, destroyed his looms, and cut a great quantity of rich silk to pieces, after which they placed his effigy in a cart, with a halter about his neck . . . and hang'd it to a gibbet, then burnt it to ashes."[9]

Edward John Wollstonecraft had another reason to leave Spitalfields and his trade. The social frontier for the bourgeois of means was in owning land, whereby a man could buy the perquisites of the upper class and see his son in Parliament with luck and a proper marriage. Land ownership had prestige; trade was socially impossible unless accompanied by great wealth. Thus Mary Wollstonecraft had contempt for businessmen all her life and either did not know or did not want to bring up her father's career in Spitalfields. She was reared as the daughter of a gentleman, and she and her family took pride in that status.

There was a brisk demand for estates in the home counties around London, by merchants and tradesmen who wanted the air and the social standing. The properties available were usually small, with old-fashioned houses advertised as suitable for remodeling by a gentleman. Wollstonecraft moved to a "genteel old house with a court-yard before it . . . near the Whalebone, on Epping Forest." The Whalebone is mentioned by Defoe as "a place so called because a Rib-bone of a large Whale, taken in the River of *Thames* the Year that Oliver Cromwell died, 1658, was fixed there." The eighteenth-century Sun and Whalebone public house at Latton, named for the vanished landmark, is still in business three miles beyond Epping Village, at the fork of the old London road and the turnoff to Chelmsford. Driving north on the new A 11 one can see it, the same site and possibly the same building.[10] The farmland is open and rich; during the eighteenth century the area was noted for dairy farms that produced the famous Epping butter.

This was the countryside Mary Wollstonecraft first remembered distinctly. She lived there from age four until she was over six, and here another sister, Everina, was born. In 1765 her father became richer by his share of the £10,000 left by his father. On February 5, 1765, Mary's grandfather was buried at the age of 76 in London at St. Botolph's. His estate was divided. His daughter, Elizabeth Ann Rutson, was left £1,700 in trust. Edward John got the leasehold of the Primrose Street properties, with their profitable rentals, and £3,000 from a mortgage debt. Edward Bland Wollstonecraft, his grandson, then about eight years old, was left the Brown's Lane property, the East Indiaman shares, and the grandfather's "own picture." Primogeniture was accepted practice, but the fact that the old man left his grandson's portion to be managed until his majority by Edward John rather than in trust indicates that he did not understand his son's character.

Edward John Wollstonecraft moved after his father's death to a house behind the ancient town of Barking, some eight miles east of London on the river Roding, which runs into the Thames. Around the town were prominent manor houses and market farms of varying size; in 1762 the area contained 563 houses, 283 mansions, 180 cottages, and

36 alehouses. The Wollstonecraft home was in Ripple Ward, bounded by the Roding on the west and the Thames on the south. Wollstonecraft's poor-rate assessment was £291.0.9; his house and land were substantial. He was received in Barking as a responsible, respectable gentleman. In May of 1766 he was one of a committee to review the questionable accounts of the workhouse overseer; a year later the committee reported the expenses "very grievous and burdensome." They did not answer "the intention for which rates are made, nor relieve in such manner as could be wished." To help reform this situation Wollstonecraft was chosen an overseer in 1767, responsible for the administration of the workhouse and the madhouse, the disposition of pensioners, and other activities on behalf of the poor.[11]

Wollstonecraft's decision to become a gentleman farmer was realistic and could have been most advantageous. His friend and neighbor in Barking was Joseph Gascoygne, brother of Bamber Gascoygne, the local bigwig, Member of Parliament, verderer of Epping Forest, owner of a landmark mansion, Bifrons. The Gascoynes exemplify the kind of success transplanted London tradesmen sometimes achieved; the father had been a brewer in Houndsditch; Bamber ended as Lord of the Admiralty, and his daughter married the Marquess of Salisbury, to whom she brought a fortune of £12,000 a year.[12] Farm income was steadily rising. While the accelerating enclosure of land drove out small farmers, it created opportunity for greater profits for those skilled and wealthy enough to employ efficient and advanced techniques, which, however, required large outlays in equipment and labor per acre. Gentry without sufficient financial cushion could get into trouble.

Wollstonecraft made a good start in Barking but in the course of the next ten years his career plunged him into failure and all but destroyed his family. He was neither rich nor steady enough for success, being unstable, extravagant, and self-indulgent. His children grew up witness to the degeneration of the man who should have been their model of stability, effectiveness, and constructive power. Mary Wollstonecraft was, according to the *Memoirs,* a child of "exquisite sensibility, soundness of understanding, and decision of character." Out of her early dependence on a man of little dependability and a woman of little affection came a determination to survive through personal strength, as well as a lifelong obsession with her misfortunes. "So ductile is the understanding," she said, "yet so stubborn, that the associations which depend on adventitious circumstances, during the period that the body takes to arrive at maturity, can seldom be disentangled by reason."[13] She spent her life reworking her early experience; everything she wrote was intensely subjective and often literally descriptive.

The Wollstonecraft family was an unhappy one, and its way an interplay of violence and submission, harshness and guilt, love and anger. Mary Wollstonecraft often said her life was a warfare. The original field of battle was her home. As the *Memoirs* describe her father:

> In his family he was a despot, and his wife appears to have been the first, and most submissive of his subjects . . . The conduct he held towards the members of his family, was of the same kind as that he observed toward animals. He was for the most part extravagantly fond of them; but when he was displeased, and this frequently happened, and for very trivial reasons, his anger was alarming.

In her first fiction, *Mary,* Mary Wollstonecraft described the heroine's father as "very tyrannical and passionate, indeed so very easily irritated when inebriated, that Mary was continually in dread lest he frighten her mother to death." In her last book, *Maria,* he was the martinet captain of a man-of-war. When enraged or drunk, Wollstonecraft sometimes beat his wife and slapped his children, after which he was sobbingly remorseful. Elizabeth Wollstonecraft, whom her daughter characterized as "the humble dependent of her husband," submitted to his moods, but the whole household was in a state of constant anxiety, never knowing whether its master would inordinately adore or violently abuse them. Mary Wollstonecraft never forgot: "Children will never be properly educated till friendship subsists between parents," she wrote in her famous *Vindication.* "Virtue flies from a house divided against itself—and a whole legion of devils take up their residence there."[14]

Neither of her parents were a source of security. "The weakest," Mary observed, "have it in their power to do most mischief." Elizabeth Wollstonecraft, the weaker parent, withheld from her oldest daughter "the grand support of life—a mother's affection," as Mary wrote with bitterness in *Maria.* Elizabeth Wollstonecraft was not only unable to love Mary, but seems to have needed to make the child suffer. "I wish to remark," Mary wrote in *Thoughts on the Education of Daughters,* "that it is only in the years of childhood that the happiness of a human being depends entirely on others—and to embitter those years by needless restraints is cruel." Her mother's governance was harsh for harshness' sake: "Continual restraint in the most trivial matters; unconditional submission to orders, which, as a mere child, she soon discovered to be unreasonable, because inconsistent and contradictory; the being obliged to sit, in the presence of her parents for three or four hours together, without daring to say a word," as the *Memoirs* relate. At the height of her own success, the daughter could not forgive:

> [Dependent women] make their children and servants endure their tyrannical oppression. As they submit without reason, they will . . . be kind or cruel, just as the whim of the moment directs; and we ought not to wonder if sometimes, galled by their heavy yoke, they take a malignant pleasure in resting it on weaker shoulders.[15]

Although she could not love her daughter, Elizabeth Wollstonecraft adored her eldest son, whom the family called Ned. In *Maria* the eldest son was

> a being privileged by nature—a boy, and the darling of my mother, he did not fail to act like an heir apparent. Such indeed was my mother's extravagant partiality, that, in comparison with her affection for him, she might be said not to love the rest of her children. Yet none of the children seemed to have so little affection for her.

Mary Wollstonecraft hated her brother; the injury of his sex and seniority, the insult of overt favoritism made even more damaging by the fortune he received from his grandfather. "Who can recount," she wrote, "all the unnatural crimes which the laudable, interesting desire of perpetuating a name has produced? The younger children are sacrificed to the eldest son [for] the *family* estate."

As a female child she was expected to submit to "the idol of his parents, and the torment of the rest of the family," as she wrote in *Maria*. "Such indeed is the force of prejudice, that what was called spirit and wit in him, was cruelly repressed as forwardness in me." In *Mary*, she conveniently killed off the heroine's brother (who in real life she must ardently have wished to see dead—and his adoring mother with him), and the heroine became the heiress. Mary Wollstonecraft put most of the blame for her brother's arrogant egotism on her mother, who, she claimed, spoiled him with "the brutal affection of some weak characters. They think it a duty to love their relations with a blind, indolent tenderness, that *will not* see the faults it might assist to correct, if their affection had been built on rational grounds."[16]

It may be that Elizabeth Wollstonecraft, disappointed by her husband's failures and her difficult marriage, transferred her hope and love to her son. Mary believed that her mother's relationship to her father was "weakness that loves, because it wants protection; and is forebearing, because it must silently endure injuries; smiling under the lash at which it dare not snarl."[17] Perhaps the wife's revenge was in her silence—itself an accusation. Or perhaps she loved her husband and found her own gratification in submitting to him.

Mary Wollstonecraft could not accept the irrationality of love: "Of what materials can that heart be composed, which can melt when insulted, and instead of revolting at injustice, kiss the rod?" Nor could she accept lack of love. Unable to depend on her mother's spontaneous affection, she tried to win approval by submitting to her orders, only to be met with indifference, withdrawal, and rigidity. Elizabeth Wollstonecraft softened her regime with the daughters born after Mary, but the older child's resentment was only augmented. The situation left her with an enduring sense of injustice and an unappeasable desire to have for herself the singular love bestowed on Ned. She depended on her mother to restrain her hostile impulses and discipline her. "When she felt she had done wrong, the reproof or chastisement of her mother, instead of being a terror to her, she found to be the only thing capable of reconciling her to herself." Godwin said he heard her remark on this "more than once." And in Mary's yearning to make a home and enjoy "domestic comforts," she indicated a normal wish to be in her mother's place. But relations between mother and daughter were always uneasy. Until the last year of her own life, the only credit Mary ever gave Elizabeth Wollstonecraft was to praise the physical rearing she gave her family. "All her children were vigorous and healthy," the *Memoirs* said approvingly.[18]

To turn to her father was like nestling up to a seesaw. The man was a violent child himself all his life. However, he was Mary's major source of love, and, as she told Godwin, except for his tantrums he was demonstratively, inordinately and "extravagantly fond" of his family. Mary may have felt she was not his favorite, but they did have a special closeness. She loved and understood him as she never could her mother, and he reciprocated in his way. The existence of this love appears in major attitudes of her life: her inveterate tendency to expect tenderness from men, which she observed in herself; her abiding religious feelings, originally built on trust in a "Father who will wipe away all our tears," a God who would someday reward his children for the pain his mysterious justice allotted them. She also identified with her father. She was congenitally as emotional as he, and her childhood experience, the examples she saw, did everything to elicit this innate temperament. She knew it. In *Mary* the heroine was "violent in her temper; but she saw her father's faults, and would weep when obliged to compare his temper with her own."[19] Elizabeth Wollstonecraft must have articulated that similarity, situated as she was between passionate father and daughter.

Both parents were neglectful, yet demanding of unquestioning filial obedience as their natural and divinely ordained right. Mary did not believe in indulgence. "I once heard a judicious father say," she wrote approvingly in *Thoughts,* " 'he would treat his child as he would his horse: first convince it he was its master, and then its friend.' " "Filial esteem," she observed, "always has a dash of fear in it." Indulgence meant the kind of preference her brother got. She did believe—stubbornly, and for years—that love should be portioned out in just ratio to the needs and deserts of the object. She also cried out for "uniformity of conduct," and, not receiving it, felt the injustice due in part to her sex; "the irregular exercise of parental authority," she wrote, "first injures the mind, and to these irregularities girls are more subject than boys."[20]

Mary's parents were too agitated by their own troubles to be able to think about beneficial regimes for their children. Witness this harsh yet poignant description of their home life:

> Yoked to a man whose follies and vices made her ever feel the weight of the chain . . . I have seen [my mother] weep . . . lamenting that the extravagance of a father would throw us destitute on the world. . . . After a violent debauch he would let his beard grow, and the sadness that reigned in the house I shall never forget; he was ashamed to meet the

> eyes of his children. This is so contrary to the nature of things, it gave me exquisite pain; I used, at those times, to show him extreme respect. I could not bear to see my parent humble himself before me. . . . He had . . . a childish affection for his children, which was displayed in carresses that gratified him for the moment, yet never restrained the headlong fury of his appetites.[21]

It was characteristic of Mary Wollstonecraft to be able to show tenderness for people in trouble. "I think I love most people best when they are in adversity—for pity is one of my prevailing passions," she said. But she was also threatened and infuriated by deprivation and uncertainty, then ridden with guilt for the resulting anger and fearful of its consequences. "Mary," said Godwin, from intimate knowledge, "was a very good hater." Such ambivalent people are overcome by remorse for the suffering of those to whom they are attached and from whom they constantly need love. This was the source of Mary's precocious interest in charity and benevolence.

By this route she developed a protective love for her mother. When her father beat Mary, she stood up to him with contempt and defiance. But when he attacked his wife, "Mary would often throw herself between the despot and his victim, with the purpose to receive upon her own person the blows that might be directed against her mother." She hoped she would earn her mother's love, but felt she had managed only "to extort some portion of affection from her mother."[22] Her very words betray her bitterness.

The role Mary assumed in this trio was also gratifying and stimulating for the child. Violence and sex became closely associated for her. Her father's outbreaks gave her an excuse to do what every child wants, and many actually do. She listened outside her parents' door, fearful and curious. She could justify it to herself and to Godwin with perfect faith in her innocent desire to protect her mother. "She has even laid whole nights upon the landingplace near their chamber door, when, mistakenly, or with reason, she apprehended that her father might break out in paroxysms of violence." His brutality was a sexual stimulant which gave her all the more reason to defy him. On one terrible occasion Wollstonecraft, in a mad rage, apparently hung one of his dogs by the neck until it died. Mary saw it in an "agony of abhorrence" that must have been close to hysteria.[23] Such a father is dangerous, confusing—and unforgettable.

In Mary Wollstonecraft's fiction her family situation was repeated over and over. The father's character is consistent in all. In *Mary* and *Maria* the heroine is rejected by a victimized mother who adores her older son. In *Mary* the heroine finds relief from her anger in caring for her ailing mother. There is a curious episode in the latter book. The heroine's mother dismisses an ill child servant, who then stabs herself in a delirium. The heroine is tortured by nightmares and vows "that if she was ever mistress of a family, she would herself watch over every part of it. The impression that this incident made was indelible."[24] Mary's identification with the child is clear, and the daughter knows she is a better potential parent than her mother—that is also clear. Of course, the use of such childhood situations and fantasies is common; what is uncommon is their tenacity, specificity, and obsessive repetition. Mary Wollstonecraft was never able to resolve and transform the childhood experiences most girls work out of as they mature.

Nevertheless, Mary wanted very much to be a loving member of her family; it was one of her ideals. From her early letters it is apparent that she had substantially repressed her anger and believed in her own filial reverence and familial dutifulness. It was only around the age of twenty-six, when she first wrote professionally, that she began to express these hostilities openly. With each subsequent year, each succeeding book, more bitterness came to the surface. One must work backward at least from *A Vindication of the Rights of Woman* to see the layers of profound resentment as they were uncovered, and to understand the extreme conflict between young Mary's awareness and actions and the anger she actually felt.

This is the darker side of Wollstonecraft family life. All the children were damaged by it, the favorite Ned with the rest, although Mary was convinced she suffered the most. But family life was not all unhappy, as she herself conceded in *Maria:* "The circumstances which, during my childhood, occurred to fashion my mind, were various; [I can] revive the fading remembrance of new-born delight . . . youthful hopes . . . I almost scent the fresh green of spring."[25] The girl grew up in the country, which she always loved. Rustic life was healthy and delightful; country fairs, the changing seasons, farm animals, traveling packmen who sold books at farmhouse doors, fiddlers who came to play for parties, strolling players. There was much socializing among the families of the gentry. Wollstonecraft, who loved hard riding and drinking, did his share in style, and must have seemed a dashing character to his children.

Then, too, the very negligence and indolence for which Mary reproached her mother gave the children a degree of freedom and independence. Preoccupied and peevish with household cares, her husband's moods, and in 1786 with a sixth baby, James, Elizabeth Wollstonecraft did not have the energy to insist that her eldest daughter keep to the behavior of genteel female children, restricted mostly to sedentary and indoor activity, "fondness for dolls, dressing, and talking . . . cramped with worse than Chinese fetters," as Mary herself said. It was a time during which conscientious parents attempted intrusively to conquer and model their children's characters and even their bodies; children were sometimes strapped into backboards, iron collars, and similar devices to insure good posture. Mary shared the active hardy sports of Ned and Henry and was allowed to run off steam with them along the wharfs of Barking. "The healthy breeze of a neighboring heath, on which we bounded at pleasure . . . to enjoy open air and freedom, was paradise, after the unnatural restraint of our fire-side," she recalled. She always needed and loved exercise, especially walking. "A girl," she maintained, "whose spirits have not been damped by inactivity, or innocence tainted with false shame, will always be a romp, and the doll will never excite attention unless confinement allows her no alternative." All the intelligent women she knew, she said, had been allowed to run wild as children.[26] In truth, little in her mother's position or actions made female accomplishments attractive to the child.

Moreover, the Wollstonecraft marriage, bad as it seems, has to be judged in terms of the times. Women were considered almost an intermediate category, somewhere between men and children. Sexual mores were very clear. Men were dominant, women submissive; or as Rousseau said, "*La femme est faite pour plaire et pour être subjugée.*" Marriott's *Female Conduct* of 1760, a volume of page after page of doggerel designed to confirm women in their duty, could have been written for Elizabeth Wollstonecraft:

Imperial man drives his Claim from Heav'n . . .
The Woman was doomed subject to her Mate,
E'er since *Eve* first, the Fruit forbidden, eat;
Hence ev'ry Wife her Husband must obey . . .
To what-so'er opinion he's inclined,
Conform your Judgment, to his Changing Mind . . .
In mild Deportment, study to excell,
Let sweet Good nature, in your gestures dwell . . .
In all Disputes, the wiser Wife will yield,
And leave her Husband Master of the Field . . .
Be silent, while you feel Resentment warm,
Silence can speak, and is a female Charm . . .
If Wine, the Solace of each human Care,
Oft to excess, your consort should ensnare,
By frown, or Clamor, ne'er disturb his Bliss . . .
If sudden Sallies of impetuous Ire,
Your Consort's youthful Blood, should often fire;
You by soft Words, conveying healing Balm,
May sooth his stormy Passion, to a calm . . .[27]

Edward John Wollstonecraft was brutal at times—but in a period when callous indifference and cruelty was still acceptable, particularly when it could be rationalized. Public executions of criminals were popular entertainment, as they had been for generations. The last legal burning at the stake in England was in 1784; the criminal was Mary Beyley, who had killed her husband. Petty thievery and forgery were hanging crimes even for adolescent offenders. Compassion and humanitarianism in English society became standard, articulated values only during Mary Wollstonecraft's lifetime.

Enlightened intellectuals supported proper subordination, by rank —Richard Price was indignant that the lower classes were beginning to use refined sugar in their tea—and by family status as well as sex. Children did not dispute authority, and drastic punishment, physical and otherwise, was common. Although there were complaints that children were overindulged, parents had substantial practical and psychic dominion over them, particularly daughters, and often far past childhood. In *Clarissa*, Richardson's strong-minded, independently wealthy heroine was treated like a criminal by her family when she refused to marry the man of their choice, a reaction considered harsh but not unwarranted.

The celebrated author Fanny Burney, in obedience to her father, spent five wretched years as lady-in-waiting at court before, at the age of thirty-nine, she found the courage to beg him to permit her to resign.

The Wollstonecraft family was a conventional one. Many of the circumstances of Mary's upbringing were duplicated in other households. But the parental flaws of Elizabeth and Edward John Wollstonecraft and the influences of Mary's early life, instead of training her to acceptance, brought about a protest unusual in degree and kind that dominated the rest of her life.

Chapter 2

In 1768, when Mary was nine, Edward John Wollstonecraft moved his family from Barking to a farm at Walkington in the Wolds of East Yorkshire, three miles southeast of the town of Beverley. The seventh and last Wollstonecraft child, Charles, was born here in the summer of 1770. The terrain and climate were harsher than in the south, and the land was hard to work; "the winds, as they sweep over this plain and unbroken surface, being extremely violent and penetrating . . . on a small property no one could gain a livelihood," an agriculturalist wrote. Moreover, Wollstonecraft compounded his problems by neglecting his lands; in 1771 he moved into the town of Beverley, perhaps to be closer to the social life he loved.[1]

Beverley was not large, its population probably about 5,000, but twelve-year-old Mary was impressed and found it "very handsome, surrounded by genteel families, and with a brilliant assembly." Her father's house was in the Wednesday marketplace, one of two such squares for the sale of farm products, leather, and other goods produced in the area around the town. The red tile-roofed brick Georgian houses have a Dutch cast, for there were associations with the Netherlands across the Channel. The great Gothic Minster of St. John the Evangelist towered above the town; its magnificent interior and organ festivals were famous. There was a theater where traveling companies played, and a circulating library. The assembly Mary thought so brilliant was a meeting place for the gentry. Subscribing families, according to the published rules, for one pound and one shilling got tickets for "the whole Year, Card-Meetings, and Races included." Tea, coffee, chocolate, negus, Bishop, madeira, and cards could be purchased. Doubtless, Edward Wollstonecraft was a formidable customer for the liquors, the cards, and the races. The Assembly rooms were available for private parties and balls. On such occasions the rules provided: "that the Candles be Lighted at Seven O'Clock in the Lustres. . . . That none of the musicians leave the room above Half an Hour. . . . That the Hackney Coachmen take their Turns in Carrying Company and not crowd near the Door."[2]

Outside the town, near the race course still popular in Beverley, is Westwood, a park where Mary Wollstonecraft, too young for Assembly balls, walked on paths between gentle hillocks, through groves, and across the common on which Beverleyians still enjoy kiting, riding and gamboling.

Mary's associations until this age had been centered on her family, but in Beverley she began to make tentative moves outward. She was sent to a local day school for her first and only formal education, which put her in touch with girls of her age. Although it was not easy for her to make friends, she found one girl, Jane Arden, six months her senior, whom she particularly liked. The Ardens were poor but had intellectual standing. Jane's father, Dr. John Arden, lived in Eastgate near the Minster, not far from the Wollstonecrafts. He was seriously religious; born Catholic, he was disinherited by his father for his conversion to Protestantism. Arden was a member of the Royal Society, a lecturer and teacher specializing in astronomy—possibly the first scholar Mary Wollstonecraft had ever known. It was at one of the lectures he gave for adults and interested young people that Mary and Jane met, for Jane was educated at home by her father.

The Arden family's respect for learning must have been one of Jane's recommendations to Mary. Although Mary was an avid reader, she had no structured education, nor did the Beverley day school give her, as the *Memoirs* put it, "any advantage of infant literature." Her schooling was that considered adequate for a gentlewoman; common arithmetic, literature, geography, music, dancing, and even a bit of French. Her letters were well written, full of long quotations from poems she admired, although her spelling, grammar, and handwriting were only fair. Neither of her parents expected or desired more for her than this conventional training. Girls of her genteel status were educated separately from boys and for quite a different purpose, to be graceful companions to the husbands they were to find. They were thought by most educators to lack the innate capacity to reason. As Mrs. Anna Barbauld, herself a bluestocking, said: "Women must often be content to know that a thing is so, without understanding the proof. . . . They cannot investigate; they can remember." Nor, according to Dr. John Gregory, had they any use for education: "the principal end is to enable you to fill up, in a tolerably agreeable way, some of the many solitary hours you must necessarily pass at home."

Seminaries for girls were finishing schools; Jane Austen's novels are full of sarcasms about filigree baskets and embroidered fripperies produced by elegant female students. If, somehow, a girl should get an education, the worldly, intellectual Lady Mary Wortley Montague advised her to observe the principle "caution (which is absolutely necessary) . . . to conceal whatever learning she attains, with as much solicitude as she would hide crookedness or lameness."[3]

But there were girls at this time who had exceptional education, in almost every instance because of their father's initiative. Mrs. Barbauld's father, a teacher, taught her modern languages—she could read at age three. Somewhat taken aback at her accomplishment, he "very reluctantly" added Latin and Greek. Catherine Macaulay, the great historian, "by her father's wish" was educated by masters at home. Hannah More's father taught her classical history, Latin, and mathematics, and then became "frightened at his own success." The learned Elizabeth Carter and Catherine Talbot were educated by clergymen fathers. An accomplished aristocratic young lady like Maria Holroyd (later Lady Stanley of Alderley) was employed by her father, Lord Sheffield, to read him political treatises. But most parents who cared about their daughters were primarily interested in making them into proper young ladies. Maria Holroyd's Aunt Serena, who adored her "Brattikins," wrote the girl frequently on this point: Maria spoke too fast; "deviated from perfect feminine softness and elegance" in her "brusqueries"; and was a "wild original." "Could I but make you quiet," she admonished, "you would be as near my wishes as you well could be."

"Propriety," said Hannah More, "is to a woman what the great Roman Citizen said that action is to an orator; it is the first, and the second, and the third requisite." Propriety dictated that women not study botany, for it was indelicate, nor portrait painting, which entailed "staring at men's faces," as Dr. Johnson put it. Erasmus Darwin, a scientist and radical freethinker, allowed girls to read Sheridan's plays, but could not stomach the idea of amateur theatricals. "The danger consists in this, lest the acquisition of bolder action and a more elevated voice, should annihilate that retiring modesty and blushing embarrassment to which young ladies owe one of their most powerful charms."[4] Elizabeth Wollstonecraft had neither the energy, intellectual framework, or affection, nor Edward John the interest, to model their daughter successfully along these lines.

In *Original Stories* Mary Wollstonecraft described herself as a fourteen-year-old orphaned girl—named Mary—who was educated with her younger sister by a Mrs. Mason. The fictional young Mary had a face "not to be proud of," while her younger sister was very handsome. (Eliza Wollstonecraft was the beauty of the family.) Mary's faults were her temper, "a turn for ridicule," frequent lateness, careless dress, and high spirits that sometimes made her rude. Her virtues were generosity, fortitude, abstemiousness, spontaneity, and judgment; "her lively feelings fixed the conclusions of reason in her mind." And she was brave and compassionate: "There is a just pride, a noble ambition in some minds that I greatly admire," says Mrs. Mason. "I have seen a little of it in Mary . . . she seems to feel more uneasiness, when she observes the sufferings of others, than I could ever trace on her countenance under the immediate pressure of pain."[5]

The transition from this boyish ideal to physical maturity was not easy for Mary Wollstonecraft. Fifteen then being the average age, she probably began to menstruate at this time. A widely-read contemporary physician advised mothers to instruct their daughters prior to their first menstrual period, which, he wrote, "is generally preceded by symptoms which foretell its approach; as a sense of heat, weight, and dull pain in the loins; distension and hardness of the breasts; headache; loss of appetite; lassitude." He recommended a soothing, kind, and affable behavior to young females when they were "out of order." However, it is unlikely that Elizabeth Wollstonecraft initiated her daughter constructively or supported her thereafter. Mary's reaction to her body's functions, even as late as when she was in her thirties, was one of shame and revulsion: "How can *delicate* women obtrude on notice that part of the animal economy, which is so very disgusting?"[6]

Mary Wollstonecraft was a proud, aspiring, avid, passionate adolescent, alternately withdrawn and vivacious. Dissatisfied with her family, needing solace, stimulation, and meaning, she absorbed herself in reading and responded with strong emotion to everything from the trivial to Thomson's *Seasons*, Young's *Night-Thoughts*, and Milton's *Paradise Lost*. In *Mary* she overdramatized the heroine's situation, but the essentials are clear:

> . . . she perused with avidity every book that came her way. Neglected in every respect, and left to the operations of her own mind, she considered every thing that came to her inspection. . . .
>
> . . . her mother had often disappointed her, and the apparent partiality she showed to her brother gave her exquisite pain. . . .
>
> She had once, or twice, told her little secrets to her mother; they were laughed at, and she determined never to do it again. In this manner was she left to reflect on her own feelings; and so strengthened were they by being meditated on, that her character early became singular and permanent. . . .
>
> . . . Could she have loved her father and mother, had they returned her affection, she would not so soon, perhaps, have sought out a new world.

Mary, who considered her mother "lukewarm," experienced ecstatic religious feelings, which she described in *Mary:*

> Enthusiastic sentiments of devotion at this period actuated her. . . . Often did she taste . . . joys . . . ecstasies. . . .
>
> She was now fifteen, and she wished to receive the holy sacrament . . . discussing some points of doctrine which puzzled her, she would sit up half the night, her favorite time for employing her mind. . . .
>
> The night before the important day, when she was to take on herself her baptismal vow, she could not go to bed, the sun broke in on her meditations. . . .
>
> . . . She was indeed so much affected when she joined in the prayer for her eternal preservation, that she could scarcely conceal her violent emotions.[7]

The English Sunday was strictly observed in Beverley—Mary later remembered that the churchwarden would go out during the service to catch the irreverent playing at bowls and skittles—but religious enthusiasm was frowned upon by common-sensical adults. Mid-eighteenth century standards dictated propriety in religion, and educators reproved those, especially girls, "who think to gain the favour of God by senseless enthusiasm and frantic raptures, more like the wild excesses of the most depraved human love, than reasonable adoration."[8]

This passionately emotional girl, with her father's example always before her, felt anger was her major fault. "The governing of our temper is truly the business of our whole lives," she wrote in *Thoughts*. Like the heroine in *Mary*, she struggled for control and writhed over her failures: "artless prayers rose to Heaven for pardon . . . and her contrition was so exceedingly painful, that she watched diligently the first movements of anger and impatience, to save herself the cruel remorse."

She was convinced of her superiority, ambitious without a specific goal. Her brother Ned was to be an attorney. Portionless Jane Arden was preparing to be a governess, and other well-to-do young people like Mary were simply enjoying the pleasant social life to which Mary was attracted. Still she worried about being different, and she turned this alienation into proof of her unique character and gifts. In *Cave of Fancy:*

> The gallantry that afforded my companions, the few young people my mother forced me to mix with, so much pleasure, I despised; I wished more to be loved than admired, for I could love. I adored virtue; and my imagination . . . overlooked the common pleasures of life; they were not sufficient for my happiness. A latent fire made me burn to rise superior to my contemporaries in wisdom and virtue.[9]

The adolescent girl secretly harbored this lofty and inflated concept of herself while outwardly she led a normal life. She helped with the younger children and with suitable household tasks. At fourteen she was relieved of the presence of one major irritant—Ned went away from home to live with the attorney to whom he was articled. The irreducible problems, however, were still in residence: her unloving mother and her father with his alcoholic rages.

With even more intensity and anxiety, therefore, than most adolescents, Mary Wollstonecraft made an attempt to get and fix love with someone of her own age group, and she was interested only in a serious and exclusive relationship. She approached nearer to Jane Arden, an affectionate, reliable girl of mild and amiable temper, to whose good-natured serenity, so different from her own emotionalism, she was drawn. Jane was the kind of well-organized girl who kept everything, including Mary's letters to her, which she still had twenty-six years later. Mary admired Jane's academic achievements and envied her the father who taught and encouraged her. The girls shared an interest in poetry and literature. In the pecking order of Jane's friends, however, Mary came second, for a Miss R. was the best friend. Jane was popular. Through her and supported by her, Mary found her way into Beverley's young social set with less discomfort than she could have on her own. The girls went to parties together, took walks in "my darling Westwood," gossiped, exchanged favorite books, and laughed over beaux, dress, and amusements.

In May of 1773, when Mary was fourteen, Jane went to Hull on a long visit to a Miss C., who had just become engaged. Addressing herself in ladylike form to "Dear Miss Arden"—and in a state of some excitement at being asked to enter into proper correspondence with a friend—Mary wrote Jane three letters. She stayed home from Sunday church services to write the first.

Dear Miss Arden
According to my promise I sit down to write to you

"My promise and my faith shall be so sure
As neither age can change, nor art can cure."

. . . I thought Miss R.– behaved rather oddly on Saturday but I believe I was in the wrong—

"I see the right, and I approve it too—
I blame the wrong and yet the wrong pursue . . .
Impute my errors to your own decree,
My hands are guilty, but my heart is free."

But however I think it very unpolite in Company if all present are unacquainted with the Cause;—you need not tell Miss R– or Miss G– what I have said, but I need not doubt your friendship.—

"A friend should always like a friend indite
Speak as she thinks, and as she thinks sho^{d} write."

Pray make haste and translate the french Song as I have already made a couple of aenigmas one on Beverley, the other on a friend . . .

Pray tell Miss C– that if she can get time to write she may inclose it in your letter.—

I wish you may not be as tired with reading as I am with writing.—

I am, your friend
& humble Servant
Mary Wollstonecraft

Sunday afternoon 4 o'Clock.

P.S. Pray write soon—I have a hundred things to add, but can't get time for my Mama is calling me . . .[10]

Mary enclosed a long poem by an unknown author, "Sweet Beverley," which was popular around town and which Jane had evidently asked for to show her friend in Hull. Jane answered, enclosing verses as well. In Mary's next letter, which included seven stanzas of a current satire on "Sweet Beverley," she referred again to Jane's preferred friend:

> My Papa informs me that Miss R– is gone to York today:—I wish her an agreeable journey—For my part all animosities have ceased, but I was resolved not to make the first concession. . . . I have just glanced over this letter and find it so ill written that I fear you cannot make out one line of this last page, but—you know, my dear, I have not the advantage of a Master as you have, and it is with great difficulty to get my brother to mend my pens.[11]

Jane responded with a lively description of flighty, unfilial Miss C., her incompatible fiancé, and the adventures Jane was having in Hull. Mary answered this letter the day she received it, hastening to encourage Jane's criticism of her Hull friends, particularly Miss C.'s giddiness and disrespect for her parents; "a girl of your delicacy must be disgusted with such nonsense," she wrote, probably hopefully. Mary urged Jane to enjoy herself dancing with Hull's fashionable young men, and she cloaked in sarcasm her own eagerness to try her charms in society. All the world had been at a tea party in Beverley except for the two friends Mary missed. "Don't be jealous," she wrote Jane. "The other is not a lady." She enclosed a long set of popular verses describing the acknowledged beauties of Beverley (fair Champion, graceful Ward, proud Webb, virtuous Smelt, captivating Clubly, sweet Stanhope): "I lament

—I am sorry I am not older to have had my name inscribed in such divine poetry," she added.[12] If there had been such a thing as a Beverley high school football team, Mary would secretly have wanted to be cheerleader and the captain's girl. But she knew Miss Arden, Miss R., Miss C., or Miss J. would have been chosen over her. The problem is clearer in the next letter, written after Jane had come back to Beverley bringing Miss C. with her for a return visit:

> Miss A.– Your behaviour at Miss J–'s hurt me extremely, and your not answering my letter shews that you set little value on my friendship.—If you had sent to ask me, I should have gone to the play, but none of you seemed to want my company.—I have two favors to beg, the one is that you will send me all my letters;—the other that you will never mention some things which I have told you. To avoid idle tell-tale, we may visit ceremoniously . . . You never called yesterday; if you wish to be on the least friendly footing, you will call this morning.—If you think it worth while, send an answer by my sister.
>
> M. W.[13]

Her earlier confidence in Jane's friendship had evaporated, for it was more hope than trust. It is a pattern so woven into her character that the childish incident, which she said had happened to her before, was to repeat itself all her life. As she wrote Imlay in 1795:

> One thing you mistake in my character, and imagine that to be coldness . . . is just the contrary. For, when I am hurt by the person most dear to me, I must let out a whole torrent of emotions, in which tenderness would be uppermost, or stifle them altogether; and it appears to me almost a duty to stifle them, when I imagine *that I am treated with coldness.*

"I do not choose to be a secondary object," she wrote her lover, Imlay, years later when she was in her thirties. The problem was one of dependence and constant need for reassurance. "Disregard can scarcely be borne when there is no internal support," she said in *Thoughts.*[14] It was impossible for her to stifle her feelings, even when she wanted to protect herself. Her vulnerability went hand in hand with a conviction that when she let out the torrent of emotions to loved ones, she would possess them securely. She was needy and deserving; love should follow. So she poured out herself to Jane Arden after her friend had replied to her:

Miss Arden.– Before I begin I beg pardon for the freedom of my style. —If I did not love you I should not write so . . . I have formed romantic notions of friendship.—I have been once disappointed:—I think if I am a second time I shall only want some infidelity in a love affair, to qualify me for an old maid. . . . I am a little singular in my thoughts of love and friendship; I must have the first place or none.—I own your behaviour is more according to the opinion of the world, but I would break such narrow bounds.—I will give you my reasons for what I say; —since Miss C– has been here you have behaved in the coolest manner. —I once hoped our friendship was built on a permanent foundation. . . . I would not have seen it, but your behaviour the other night I cannot pass over;—when I spoke of sitting with you at Church you made an objection, because I and your sister quarrelled;—I did not think a little raillery would have been taken in such a manner, or that you would have insinuated, that I dared to have prophaned so sacred a place with idle chit-chat.

. . . When I have been at your house with Miss J– the greatest respect has been paid to her; everything handed to her first;—in short, as if she were a superior being.—Your Mama too behaved with more politeness to her.

I am much obliged to your Papa and Mama and desire you will give them my complimentary thanks, and as I have spent many happy hours in your company, shall always have the sincerest esteem for Miss A– . . . what I have written flows spontaneously from my pen and this I am sure, I only desire to be done by as I do;—I shall expect a written answer to this,—

and am yours

M. W.

Don't tell C– to you I have told all my failings;—I would not be so mean as to shew only the bright side of the picture;—I have reason to think you have not been so ingenuous to me.—I cannot bear the reflection that when Miss R– comes I should have less of your company.— After seeing you yesterday, I thought not to have sent this—(but you desire it) for to see you and be angry, is not in my power.—I long for a walk in my darling Westwood. Adieu.

Mary Wollstonecraft[15]

Jane Arden responded with realistic reproof and solid affectionate assurance, but, although somewhat relieved, Mary continued to press for commitment. Miss R.'s position was bad enough, Miss C.'s presence was too threatening to bear:

> Dear Jenny
>
> I have read some where that vulgar minds will never own they are in the wrong:—I am determined to be above such a prejudice . . . and hope my ingenuously owning myself partly in fault to a girl of your good nature will cancel the offence—I have a heart too susceptible for my own peace:—Till Miss C– came, I had very little of my own. . . .
>
> Love and Jealousy are twins.—I would allow Miss R– the first place, but I could not bear the thought of C–'s rivalling me in your love.
>
> As to the affair at Miss J–'s I am certain I can clear myself from the imputation.—I spent part of the night in tears . . . I cannot bear a slight from those I love . . . I mean no reflection on your Papa, I shall always think myself under an obligation for his politeness to me.—I should have called this morning but for a hint in your letter which made me think you have told your Mama and sisters.—I shall take it as a particular favor if you will call this morning, and be assured that however more deserving Miss R– may be of your favor, she cannot love you better than your humble Servant
>
> Mary Wollstonecraft
>
> P.S. I keep your letters as a Memorial that you once loved me, but it will be of no consequence to keep mine as you have no regard for the writer.—
>
> There is some part of your letter so cutting, I cannot comment upon it.—I beg you will write another letter on this subject.—Pray send me word by your sister, if you will call this morning.[16]

Mary ended by enclosing and quoting from an essay on friendship which Dr. Arden had lent her, as if to give him as authority for the relationship she wanted with Jane: "the most solemn sacred union, displaying itself in all the offices of true affection and esteem,—Happy beyond expression is that pair who are thus united." Her publisher, Joseph Johnson, later said of Mary Wollstonecraft, "she was incapable of disguise, whatever was the state of her mind it appeared . . . when harassed, which was frequently the case, she was relieved by unbosoming herself."[17] Purgation, however, gave her only temporary relief. She was compelled to repeat the same experience, to hope for impossible devotion, to find fault with the humanly imperfect love object, and to despair in inevitable disappointment. Disappointment was a word constantly on her lips. Even in her thirties, she was only beginning to understand the extent to which she herself was executioner as well as victim.

Mary's friendship with Jane Arden was restored after this episode, and the girls enjoyed a gay and confidential intimacy: Mary attached herself especially to Jane's father, from whom she received lessons "on the globes" and appreciation for her intellectual talents. "Pray tell the worthy Philosopher," she wrote Jane almost coquettishly in November, 1774, "I hope I shall convince him I am quicker than his daughter at finding out a puzzle, tho' I can't equal her at solving a problem." And Mary sent with her note Goldsmith's *Citizen of the World*, a lively social satire, and a copy of a clergyman's letter relating a curious miracle in a graveyard.[18]

Mary's resolve to establish herself securely with Jane Arden and with a father-teacher was one in a series of such efforts she made to develop the particular affection and the intellectual success she craved. Both would bring her independence from her parents. Jane Arden, being poor, expected to make her own living as soon as possible while Mary, the supposedly affluent gentleman's daughter with an anticipated small income of her own, had no apparent reason to want a self-supporting future. But Mary at this age was getting a fix on the kind of life she needed. By 1774 her father's wildness, extravagance, and violent temper had become a subject of common gossip in Beverley, and Mary knew it. "The good folks at Beverley (like those of most Country towns) were very ready to find out their Neighbour's faults, and to animadvert on them," she wrote Jane four years later. "Many people did not scruple to prognosticate the ruin of the whole family, and the way he went on, justified them for so doing."[19] An adolescent's discovery of parental failings is disturbing, even when the faults are minor, and their public exposure can be excruciating. The strain on Mary Wollstonecraft's daughterly role was extreme. In addition to being ashamed and angry, she was beginning to understand what her father was doing to his family with his insistence that they live as if they were wealthy—his debts, his schemes to recoup. "How much domestic comfort and private satisfaction is sacrified to this irrational ambition!" she wrote in her first

Vindication. "It is a destructive mildew, that blights the fairest virtues."[20]

Small wonder Mary Wollstonecraft was so touchy at real or imagined slights to her, as when everything was handed first to Miss J.; in her class- and money-conscious world the leaching away of affluent rank was a dangerous drain on one's value. This was problem enough. Her emotional difficulties were even worse. The Wollstonecraft household must have been a hell. Her mother bewailed their plight but could not control her reckless husband, whose sporadic brutalities increased with his failure. Mary interpreted the situation in her own way. "At fifteen, I resolved never to marry for interested motives, or to endure a life of dependence," she told Godwin. Along with her mother's life she began to reject her father as well. To Joseph Johnson, one who replaced him many years later, she wrote, "I never had a father . . ."[21]

Chapter 3

DESPITE HIS EXCESSES Edward John Wollstonecraft was rational enough to think of his sons' careers. In January of 1775 he apprenticed Henry, then almost fourteen, to Marmaduke Hewitt, surgeon and apothecary, also a churchwarden at St. Mary's near the Bar in Beverley. The term was for seven years. Then, suddenly, Wollstonecraft decided to move again, this time back to the London area. According to the *Memoirs*, "the restlessness of his disposition would not suffer him to content himself with the occupation in which for some years he had been engaged, and the temptation of a commercial speculation being held out to him, he removed to Hoxton near London for the purpose of its execution." Mary Wollstonecraft had lived in Yorkshire from age nine until sixteen, longer than she was ever to be in any other one place. "Those were peaceful days," she recalled to Jane Arden, "merry days we spent together at Beverley, when we used to laugh from noon till night." Even if she was uncomfortable with the fact that her father was a subject of town gossip, she regretted the uprooting. Her associations with Beverley were deep and lasting; she thought of herself as a Yorkshirewoman for many years. Even the distinctive Yorkshire speech with its peculiar caressing inflection was the dialect she fell into in intimate moments; "when my heart is warm," she later wrote her lover, "I must use my Yorkshire phrase . . . pop come the expressions of childhood into my head."[1]

The trip south toward London in 1775 was probably made in the spring, the season when leases in Beverley ended and horse-drawn ploughs could clear the highways of winter debris. Great wagons carried household goods; people went by stagecoach. As a residence Hoxton was an odd choice, one of the least attractive of the suburban villages around London. A contemporary booster claimed it was "inhabited by gentlemen and others, whose business principally lies in the city, but who occasionally retire hither for the benefit of the air." But he admitted that the town was run-down, and neglected to mention, as another author noted, that "this hamlet, has, for many years, acquired a melancholy distinction as the retreat of the insane and the city poor. There are three private establishments, of considerable magnitude and respectability, devoted to the former." As early as the seventeenth century the name "Hoxton" was synonymous with lunacy; clowns at Bartholomew Fair could always raise a laugh by mentioning the place. One of the famous madhouses was called Balmes-house, from which comes our term "barmy." There were, in addition, some forty-two almshouses, several established for the widows of poor weavers.[2]

Mary's family settled in a house in Queen's Row. Their next door neighbors were a clergyman and his wife, Mr. and Mrs. Clare. Like Dr. Arden, Mr. Clare was an intellectual. His bent was literary; he was said to resemble Pope—small, "deformed and delicate"—and to have had an odd sense of humor. He was a lovable eccentric, almost a hermit; one pair of shoes, he said, had lasted him fourteen years. He and his wife were attracted to Mary Wollstonecraft, a "wild, but animated and aspiring girl of sixteen," who was obviously unhappy at home and looking for the combination of intellect and affection the Clares were ready to offer. She attached herself to them; they practically took her into their home. The Wollstonecrafts must have approved the relationship; in effect Mary was getting a free education, and, while within reach, was occupied and less dissatisfied than she would have been at home. She told Jane Arden later, "They took some pains to cultivate my understanding (which had been too much neglected) they not only recommended proper books to me, but made me read to them."[3] She lived happily with them for days and weeks at a time. It was a move toward independence from her family.

Even if her parents had objected, it would have been hard to stop

Mary Wollstonecraft from doing what she had her heart set on. "Let me tell you," she wrote Joseph Johnson over ten years later, "I have never yet resolved to do, anything of consequence, that I did not adhere resolutely to it, till I had accomplished my purpose, improbable as it might [seem] to a more timid mind."[4] Her purpose, although she had not yet fully articulated it, was to satisfy her needs away from her mother's peevishness and her father's fallibility.

In a letter written in 1778, Mary Wollstonecraft told Jane Arden that she would have been very happy studying and living with the Clares "if it had not been for my domestic troubles," and, she continued, "some other painful circumstances which I wish to bury in oblivion." These other unhappy events are unknown, but they may have involved Mary's brother, Henry Woodstock Wollstonecraft.

When Mary wrote Jane Arden the letter of 1778, the first communication between the two friends since the Wollstonecrafts had left Beverley, Mary brought Jane up-to-date on family news since their departure. She accounted for Ned, Eliza, and Everina, but made no mention of Henry.[5] This is a strange omission, for Henry was only two years younger than Mary and Jane and was well known to Jane in Beverley. If he were still there as an apprentice, Mary would have reported that fact, and particularly so because Jane was then a governess in Norfolk and would have welcomed news of her former hometown. It is hard to believe that a boy of fifteen could have committed a crime serious enough to warrant his elimination from the family. Moreover, if Henry were dead Mary would surely have informed Jane. There is no record of Henry's death in parish records of Beverley, and no trace of his adult residence there either.

Nine years later Mary Wollstonecraft wrote in a letter to Everina from Dublin dated May 15, 1787: "I have been considering—a journey would be of great use to you and your presence of the most profound service to Bess [Eliza]. . . . The account you sent about Henry has harried my spirits."[6]

Henry Wollstonecraft, then, was not dead. The "Henry" cited in a section of the letter referring only to family members must be Mary's brother.

Godwin never mentions Henry's existence in the *Memoirs*. One must assume either that Henry's fate between 1775 and 1787 was such that Mary never told Godwin about him or that Godwin deliberately omitted him, as he did Edward John Wollstonecraft's financial chicanery of 1776 and Eliza's postpartum breakdown of 1783, to protect Mary's family. Mary's concern for the other members of her family is prominent in the *Memoirs* and in her letters. Henry was a special case.

A reasonable hypothesis is that Henry may have suffered a serious and permanent breakdown that began in Beverley—perhaps even was the cause of the family's departure and subsequent residence in Hoxton—and which the family concealed. The supporting evidence, while circumstantial, is impressive.

The Wollstonecrafts moved from Beverley to Hoxton, a known center for private insane asylums. Under the circumstances, it is possible that young Henry could have become a patient in one of these institutions. Unfortunately, records from the Hoxton asylums for the period 1775–1787 have been lost, and with them the names of patients confined there.

Mary's documented experience with insanity is limited, yet her writings reveal an acquaintance that is more than slight. In 1783 she went to London to take care of Eliza at her husband's house during her breakdown. None of her letters mention that a physician visited the patient. Her first letter reporting to Everina on Eliza's condition indicated her own familiarity with madness: "One thing, by way of comfort, I must tell you, that persons who recover from madness are generally in this way before they are perfectly restored."[7]

In her *A Vindication of the Rights of Men,* written in 1790, Mary Wollstonecraft violently and for several pages attacked Edmund Burke for supporting the Prince of Wales's effort to take the regency during George III's mental breakdown of 1786. The long passages go far beyond her experience with Eliza's brief illness and actually describe asylums: "those dreadful mansions." She discusses such calamities with emotion that may have been the result of first-hand knowledge:

> Had not vanity or interest steeled your heart, you would have been shocked at the cold insensibility which could carry a man to those dreadful mansions, where human weakness appears in its most awful form. . . .

> You might have been convinced, by ocular demonstration, that madness is only the absence of reason . . . you would have seen every thing out of nature in that strange chaos of levity and ferocity, and of all sorts of follies jumbled together. You would have seen in that monstrous tragi-comic scene the most opposite passions necessarily succeed, and sometimes mix with each other in the mind; alternate contempt and indignation; alternate laughter and tears; alternate scorn and horror.[8]

In 1790, when Mary Wollstonecraft was editorial assistant for *The Analytical Review* and reviewed books in which she had a particular interest, she reviewed B. Faulkner's *Observations of the General and Improper Treatment of Insanity,* noting that "the importance of the subject renders any apology for the length of this extract unnecessary." The extract she quoted discusses the ill effects of injudicious confinement of the mentally ill.[9] Because Mary approved Faulkner's methods, a search for records of his hospital in Chelsea has been made, but no records are now extant.

Mary Wollstonecraft's last novel, *Maria,* opens with the heroine in a madhouse. Her descriptions are graphic:

> What a task, to watch the light of reason quivering in the eye, or with agonizing expectation to catch the beam of recollection; tantalized by hope, only to feel despair more keenly, at finding a much loved face or voice, suddenly remembered, or pathetically implored, only to be immediately forgotten, or viewed with indifference or abhorrence!

In Chapter XVII a trial takes place during which opposing counsel makes the following statement about the heroine. "After the birth of her child, her conduct was so strange, *and a melancholy malady having afflicted one of the family, which delicacy forbade the dwelling on,* she was confined [italics added]."[10]

It may be that Eliza's postpartum illness was the second and less serious or lasting tragedy in the Wollstonecraft family. Mary Wollstonecraft was apprehensive about her own mental condition in 1786–1787, as will be seen. In one letter she actually said, "My reason has been stretched too far and tottered on the edge of madness."[11] Perhaps she had good reason to be afraid.

Mary Wollstonecraft's family situation was unpleasant enough for her to look for satisfaction outside it. The Clares were important, but Mary needed more. As the *Memoirs* relate:

> a connection . . . originated about this time, between Mary and a person of her own sex, for whom she contracted a friendship so fervent, as for years to have constituted the ruling passion of her mind. The name of this person was Frances Blood; she was two years older than Mary. Her residence was at that time at Newington Butts, a village near the southern extremity of the metropolis; and the original instrument for bringing these two friends acquainted was Mrs. Clare . . . who was on a footing of considerable intimacy with both parties.

Godwin was accurate in using the words "contracted" and "passion" to describe this attachment. It was, for Mary Wollstonecraft, a decisive love of her life; Godwin even compared her first sight of Fanny Blood to Werther's first glimpse of his fatal love, Charlotte, and while he meant to refer to the visual aspect of the meeting there is no question that Mary experienced Werther's emotion as well. She described the scene to Godwin twenty years later as if she could still see every detail, and he repeated it in the *Memoirs:*

> She was conducted to the door of a small house, but furnished with peculiar neatness and propriety. The first object that caught her sight, was a young woman of a slender and elegant form, and eighteen years of age, busily employed in feeding and managing some children, born of the same parents, but considerably inferior to her in age.[12]

Mary Wollstonecraft was entranced at this picture of charm and tenderness, and completely captivated by the end of the visit. Fanny was as delightful to know as to look at:

> Her voice is sweet, her manners not only easy but elegant . . . her little ones hang on her hands. . . . Neighbors call her the *Gentlewoman;* indeed, every gesture shows an accomplished and dignified mind, that relies on itself, when deprived of the fortune which contributed to polish and give it consequence.
>
> Drawings . . . ornament her neat parlour; some musical instruments stand in one corner; for she plays with taste, and sings sweetly.
>
> All the furniture, not forgetting a book-case, full of well-chosen books, speak the refinement of the owner, and pleasures a cultivated mind has within its grasp.[13]

This description of Mrs. Trueman in *Original Stories* is undoubtedly Fanny—and, indeed, Mrs. Trueman's little daughter is named Fanny.

Before the first visit was over "Mary had taken, in her heart, the vows of eternal friendship," as the *Memoirs* said. Regardless of the fear of disappointment she had expressed to Fanny's precursor, Jane Arden, Mary threw herself completely into this love, and Fanny, affectionate and needful as well, responded. Mary Wollstonecraft's first novel, *Mary*, is in part the story of this friendship; Fanny is Ann in the book. The heroine of *Mary* is fifteen when she meets Ann; Mary Wollstonecraft telescoped the earlier, less meaningful friendship with Jane Arden into the more important one. Mary named her first child for Fanny. And long after her friend Fanny had died in her arms, in the last year of her own life, she continued to recall Fanny's charms, Fanny's songs. She always wore a ring made of Fanny's hair, which Mary Shelley inherited.[14]

The relationship was one of complementary attributes, but the girls had in common Irish heritage and parental problems. Mr. Blood, like Wollstonecraft, was an extravagant and self-indulgent man who had brought his family to the verge of actual poverty, a state Mary's father had not yet attained. Mrs. Blood, whom Mary later spoke of as "our mother," was very kind but limited, "trivial, uninteresting." Neither girl was companionable with her mother, although for different reasons. Fanny and her mother struggled to maintain their shabby gentility by selling needlework and Fanny's drawings of "exquisite fidelity and neatness." It was a projection of the lot Mary Wollstonecraft and her sisters would face, and she must have pondered the miseries her own father might inflict on the family if he continued in the ways her mother so often bewailed. In *Mary*, Ann is educated by a clergyman to relieve her family in its distress. Fanny had the presence of a gentlewoman quite out of place in her circumstances. She was accomplished and graceful, musical, literary, artistic, and refined. Compared to her, and despite her higher social standing, Mary Wollstonecraft felt clumsy, neglected, and inferior. Fanny Blood was to Mary at first someone to wonder at and reverence. It is interesting that a girl of Mary's force would be so overwhelmed by a young woman whose forte was "ideas of minute and delicate propriety."[15] Fanny was a feminine ideal, loving, maternal, restrained, and Mary felt that her own behavior improved in consequence.

The two girls found it hard to be together as often as Mary wished.

Newington Butts was all the way across London from Hoxton; Fanny was needed for work at home; the Wollstonecrafts were not a family Mary would have wanted her friend to see much of. When not together at the Clares, they wrote each other assiduously. Fanny's letters in her elegant and precise hand shamed untutored Mary, so the older girl offered to be her instructor in grammar, spelling, and general literary form. Soon a course of study developed that went far beyond its original intent. To gain approbation and satisfy her own drive, Mary devoted herself to self-education. "Her ambition to excell was now awakened, and she applied herself with passion and earnestness," the *Memoirs* said. Between Fanny and the Clares, Mary's intellectual interests became a focus for her. But she still suffered, for even with Fanny she was second, as she described in *Mary:*

> She felt less pain on account of her *Mother's* partiality to her brother, as she hoped now to experience the pleasure of being beloved; but this hope led her into new sorrows, and as usual, paved the way to disappointment. Ann only felt gratitude; her heart was entirely engrossed by one object, and friendship could not serve as a substitute.

No one but Mary Wollstonecraft would have expected that it could. Fanny was in love with a prosperous young Irishman, Hugh Skeys, who had "never talked of love; but then they played and sung . . . drew landscapes together, and while she worked he read to her . . . and stole imperceptibly into her heart." Poor Fanny, with no marriage portion, dared not hope for much. Skeys had not proposed marriage, and left Fanny to wait, as it turned out, another eight years. "This disappointment spread a sadness over her countenance, and made it interesting," Mary described Fanny's counterpart, Ann. Adding to Fanny's melancholy was her ill health; she was threatened by consumption. Fanny was devoted to Mary but sometimes absent-minded and sad. Mary, who always wanted first place, played the disappointed heroine over and over again in her novel. It is the equilibrium of the pendulum:

> Mary was often hurt by the involuntary indifference. . . . When her friend was all the world to her, she found she was not as necessary to her happiness. Very frequently has she run to her with delight, and not perceiving anything of the same kind in Ann's countenance, she has shrunk back. . . .
>
> She would then imagine that she looked sickly or unhappy, and then

> all her tenderness would return like a torrent, and bear away all reflection. In this manner was her sensibility called forth, and exercised, by . . . her friend's misfortunes, and her own unsettled mind.[16]

Obviously, Mary Wollstonecraft was not this miserable with Fanny. *Mary* is a dramatization written with all the stops out to prove the unique sensibility of its interesting author, and perhaps to help her handle the conflicts of her "unsettled mind." Fanny could never have put up with incessant reproaches or scenes, and Mary was capable of high spirits as well as low with this "friend whom I love better than all the world beside, a friend to whom I am bound by every tie of gratitude and inclination," as she told Jane Arden. Strangely enough, Mary's first and last loves crossed paths at Hoxton. William Godwin was a student at the Dissenting Academy there during the Wollstonecrafts' residence. He never met Mary, but he speculated in the *Memoirs* on what might have happened if they had known and loved each other when she was seventeen and he twenty. "Which would have been predominant; the disadvantage of obscurity, and the pressure of a family; or the gratifications that might have flowed from their intercourse?"[17]

Mary Wollstonecraft was in Hoxton only a year—probably not long enough to have found out, even if she and Godwin had made contact. Wollstonecraft's speculation failed. In the spring of 1776 he threw it over and decided to go back to being a farmer. For an unknown reason he chose Laugharne in Wales. Mary was distraught but helpless. If she could have stayed somehow with Fanny or the Clares, she would have. There must have been bitter tears and rages between father, mother, and daughter. But there was no stopping Wollstonecraft, and no place else to go. Mary went with her family to Wales, but she must have promised herself and Fanny that it would not be forever. And so another sad uprooting, with less hope than the exodus from Beverley—"a most expensive and troublesome journey that answered no one good end."[18]

Laugharne was the most beautiful place Mary had ever seen, vastly more picturesque than the mundane fields of Yorkshire. But that was its only asset as far as she was concerned. It is a town on the sea, at the mouth of the Taf, Dylan Thomas's home. When the poet lived there, it had not changed much from the eighteenth century: crooked cobblestone streets, the sea, the estuary patterned with flats at low tide, pebbled beach, little fishing boats, cormorants and great flocks of white gulls, and above, the ruin of Laugharne Castle, "a crumbling, dignified thrust of stone covered with ivy . . . invaded everywhere by flora."[19] Some of this landscape appears in *Mary*—cliffs, winds, clouds, and a great cave in the rocks that became a place for her to hide, read, and dream. She turned the cave into the Sage's mysterious abode in her later *Cave of Fancy*, and she used other aspects such as the people, their music, their language, and their famous pride in *Original Stories*. In the shanties beneath the castle the heroine of *Original Stories* had to hide a smile when she "heard the inhabitant of a little hut, that could scarcely be distinguished from the pig-sty which stood in the front of it, boast of their ancestors and despise trade." Mary was also struck by Welsh poverty and took pleasure in small charities. She had some social life, once meeting the John Allen family, two of whose daughters married sons of the famous Josiah Wedgwood. One later became the wife of James Mackintosh, whom Mary also knew in London.[20]

The Wollstonecrafts spent only a year at Laugharne, and a bad year. Edward John Wollstonecraft's decline was gathering speed. He probably bought the Laugharne farm, but he was restless and bored. Mary told Jane Arden that "business or pleasure took him often to London," doubtless carrying long letters to Fanny Blood. When he made up his mind to return permanently to London his accumulated follies came crashing down on his head, battering the whole family. What happened is not clear, for the *Memoirs* do not mention the disaster, and Mary Wollstonecraft wrote Jane Arden only generally about it one or two years later, after the dust had settled.

Wollstonecraft evidently gambled heavily and lost in some financial scheme, and in addition did something almost criminal. Perhaps he appropriated some of his oldest son's inheritance from the grandfather. Or perhaps he demanded some of his son's money to retrieve himself. Three years later Ned was paying off debts, indicating that something must have happened to his own fortune. At any rate, there was a terrible family upheaval. Trapped and furious, Wollstonecraft ran raging over his wife and children, trying to face down his misdemeanors. Mary Wollstonecraft was appalled by the event and the fault of her wretched father. She loved him still; she said he did not vent his wrath on her—an instance of the character of their attachment. Her first reaction was misery, which left her physically weak and extremely depressed. Her second was to find some relief by helping to set matters straight at a price she was glad to pay. In order to save himself, Wollstonecraft asked his children to give him money that had been settled on them. The source or amount of their portions—other than Ned's—is unknown; it could have come from their mother's marriage settlement or perhaps from the Edward Bland Wollstonecraft for whom Ned was named and who may be the uncle mentioned in *Maria*. In any case, Mary readily gave up her share and was left with nothing, whereas Everina apparently retained enough for a small annuity.[21]

To be left penniless under these circumstances was bad enough; Mary's equally difficult problem was how to accept her father's behavior. She found it hard to align her emotional bond with her rational judgment of him; love and deserts were supposed to go together. Her sense of rectitude was strong. "When forbearance confounds right and wrong, it ceases to be a virtue," she wrote in *A Vindication of the Rights of Woman*. And in *Thoughts:* "We should always try to fix in our minds the rational grounds we have for loving a person, that we may be able to recollect them when we feel disgust or resentment." She struggled for relief. "Resentment, indeed, may be felt occasionally by the best of human beings; yet humility will soon conquer it, and convert scorn and contempt to pity."[22] Pity was the path back to love for Mary Wollstonecraft.

But she now felt she had a right to assert herself, and as the oldest child living at home she did so, her natural authority enhanced by her financial sacrifice. She insisted that out of this debacle she at least gain one happiness, to be near Fanny. Her father acceded, and the family settled at Walworth near the Bloods. Her father, frustrated and bitter, was idle. He took it hard, and Mary felt for him. "Dissipation leads to poverty, which cannot be patiently borne by those who have lived on the vain applause of others . . . they are tormented by false shame when by a reverse of fortune they are deprived," she wrote later. Nor was it easy for her mother, who sighed for escape. "Mother's Cottage in the New World," was Elizabeth's dream of emigration to the land of freedom and opportunity, which Eliza recalled years later.[23] Only Mary Wollstonecraft, at eighteen, fully realized she would have to create her own opportunity.

Mary gave her money to her father not only as a duty but as a down payment on her freedom. She could expect her family to contribute nothing to her future, emotional or material, and her inclination to be independent became compulsion. She considered leaving home to make her own living, as Jane Arden, only six months older than she, had done the year before. When the Wollstonecrafts protested, Mary demanded that she be given a room of her own in the Walworth house, a symbol of freedom, and the privacy and books she needed for study. She was determined to be self-reliant. She also knew her chances of making a love match were, like Fanny Blood's, impaired. Although at fifteen she had rejected the idea of marriage for security there is reason to believe her secret alternative was romantic love and ideal wedlock. The change in her family finances was deeply disturbing. The chapter in her first book, *Thoughts,* on "Temper," was immediately followed by one entitled "The Unfortunate Situation Of Females, Fashionably Educated, And Left Without A Fortune." Of such young women Mary declared, "if they are not entirely devoid of delicacy, they must frequently remain single . . . a young mind looks round for love and friendship, but love and friendship fly from poverty, expect them not if you are poor!"[24]

Fanny Blood's was the love and friendship that Mary now concentrated on more than ever. Fanny, still unwell and still unhappy about Hugh Skeys, was lovelier than ever in Mary's eyes, but no longer the ideal she had been. She was helping Mary channel her gifts, to consider form and direction, but the balance of influence was shifting, the younger now surpassing the older girl. In *Mary,* Mary Wollstonecraft wrote of Ann:

> She was timid and irresolute, and rather fond of dissipation; grief only had power to make her reflect. . . .
>
> She often wondered at the books Mary chose, who, though she had a lively imagination, would frequently study authors whose works were addressed to the understanding. . . .
>
> Ann's misfortunes and ill health were strong ties to bind Mary to her, she wished so continually to have a home to receive her in, that it drove every other desire out of her mind.[25]

The idea of having a home some day with Fanny Blood was more than a dream to Mary Wollstonecraft; she meant to make it a reality.

Poor Fanny could only hope Hugh Skeys would eventually provide one. Mary badly needed a love she could count on; possessiveness was her way of attempting to secure it. The relationship, if intense, was not unusual. Since the sexes were strictly separated at this period, and female sexuality unnaturally repressed, what would now be called a crush was then a "friend of the heart," approved and even fostered girlish behavior that protected adolescent and unmarried girls from sexual danger. An author of the period whom Mary admired for her understanding of girls, Mrs. Hester Chapone, devoted half a volume of her *Letters* to a fifteen-year-old to this subject because of its important function. She advised girls how to select and attach themselves for life to a worthy female friend, encouraging devotion and fidelity in "two hearts desirous to perpetuate their society beyond the grave."[26] In the essay on friendship Dr. Arden gave Mary in Beverley, the language of friendship is equally elevated.

Mary Wollstonecraft's love for Fanny Blood was jealous and monopolizing, a not uncommon result of such relationships and one that Mrs. Chapone warned against. In Mary's case it was true of her loves all her life. If in modern eyes, Mary, the firmer character, caring for Fanny the gentle sickly one, seems an obvious homosexual fit, the mores of the times cannot be overlooked—nor Mary's need to control. Yet Fanny held back somewhat, as Jane Arden had, from the passionate commitment Mary made. Fanny was, of course, secretly waiting for Skeys, but she may also have been a little uneasy. Mary, having no male love and having convinced herself she was unlikely to find the kind she thought she deserved, sought from Fanny Blood the emotional gratification she required.

Mary Wollstonecraft was in Walworth for two years. It was a difficult period for her. She was depressed and troubled by "a lingering sickness," as she told Jane Arden, with headaches and pain in her side. It was the first time she reported such symptoms, which were to become chronic reactions to unhappiness, conflict, and frustration, sometimes almost overwhelming her. Godwin said in the *Memoirs* that her misfortunes were, realistically, "not among the heaviest in the catalogue of human calamities," but knowing her intimately as he did, compared her to a female Werther, "endowed with the most exquisite and delicious sensibility . . . almost of too fine a texture to encounter the vicissitudes of human affairs, to whom pleasure is transport, and disappointment is agony indescribable."[27] Sensibility—then comprehending physically sensitive nerves, intense and quick response to stimuli, and emotional susceptibility—was an attribute Mary celebrated in herself with the pride of a hypochondriac. Perception and responsiveness were her chief talents, ones she could exercise with Fanny Blood, the epitome of a more genteel sensibility.

In her family Mary Wollstonecraft protected her sensitivity and needfulness with self-assertion, substituting "the inflexibility of resistance for the confidence of affection," as Godwin said. Her physical symptoms reflected hidden anger at being denied that confidence in her father and affection from her mother. Home was a dead end that brought out the worst in her. "The tender," she said of herself in her family situation, "give way for the sake of peace—yet still this giving way undermines their domestic comfort, and stops the current of affection; they labour for patience."[28] Deeply troubled by this constant conflict between her tender feelings and hostile reactions, she chose independence, control of her own life—a job.

Finding work was no simple matter for a young woman of Mary's upbringing. As she described with bitter realism in her first book, the choices were limited: governess, teacher, or companion. "The few trades that are now left," she said of other female employment, "are now generally in the hands of man, and certainly they are not very respectable." Class distinction in women's jobs was crucial. Lower-class women could not be choosy—they did everything from slop work to match selling, with long hours for less pay. In summer, for example, girls from Shropshire and North Wales came on foot to the market gardens around London, where they worked on farms and carried heavy loads of fruit and produce to Covent Garden. They got five to ten shillings a week compared with ten to twelve for men. A contemporary list of tradesmen and artisans, the next class up, shows that almost all the wives had work, mostly connected with their husbands'. There were exceptions: three women were attorneys, one kept a coffee house in Kensington, some dealt in produce or made clothes, one in Hoxton even ran a manufactory of muslin shawls employing several workwomen. But for the gently reared, such employment relegated them to a class unthinkably inferior. Mary Wollstonecraft was not yet a class rebel. She had no intention, with her touchy pride, of sinking herself lower than her father's financial failure had already dropped her. "Nothing so painfully sharpens sensibility as such a fall in life," she said later.[29] The one thing she had to hang on to was her station; the jobs a lady could take with propriety and still remain a lady seemed bad enough to her, and she equated propriety with work proper to her class. Her choice was further limited by her lack of education; Jane Arden's credentials included Dr. Arden's instruction, which enabled her to become a governess. Mary had to settle for being a paid companion.

There were emotional difficulties as well, for concern for her family held her back for many months. When she first spoke about finding a situation, they talked her out of it. When she later proceeded to find an eligible one and made ready to leave, Elizabeth Wollstonecraft begged, wept, and pleaded with her until Mary unwillingly let the job go by. Her mother wanted and needed Mary, for she had borne enough: her husband's folly and brutality; her favorite son's withdrawal and marriage in London in 1778; and possibly Henry's illness. The younger girls, Eliza and Everina, were at school in Chelsea; only James and Charles were at home. Wollstonecraft also put pressure on Mary, attempting to exercise his parental rights. This was easier for the girl; she could face him down without guilt. "She had her father's spirit of independence, and determined to shake off the galling yoke . . . and try to earn her own subsistence," she wrote later. In the spring of 1778, near her nineteenth birthday, she decided to accept a job as paid companion to a Mrs. Dawson of Bath, a wealthy, imperious widow with a record of wearing out a sizable number of previous employees. Mary Wollstonecraft was ready. She anticipated the challenge with spirits that lifted as she prepared to go. In *A Vindication of the Rights of Men,* she wrote:

> My father may dissipate his property, yet I have no right to complain—but should he attempt to sell me for a slave, or fetter me with laws contrary to reason; nature, in enabling me to discern good from evil, teaches me to break the ignoble chain.

Or more simply, from the same book: "Self-preservation is, literally speaking, the first law of nature."[30]

II

The Bitter Bread of Dependence

Chapter 4

In April or May of 1778, Mary Wollstonecraft packed her best belongings—Bath was the most fashionable of resorts, and even a dependent young gentlewoman would be expected to be suitably outfitted—and took a coach to Bath. She probably left from one of the London stations of the Bath and Bristol routes, from the Swan with Two-Necks Inn at Doctors Commons or the Black or White Bear Inns in Piccadilly. Each passenger was allowed fourteen pounds of luggage, child on lap extra; proprietors were not responsible for jewels, money, writings, and so forth. Guards were provided, and all guaranteed to go smoothly "if God permit." The fast balloon coaches made the trip in sixteen hours, although there were complaints that at such speed passengers could not enjoy the sights enroute. The cheaper, heavier post coaches took two days.[1] Westward across England and down from the hills into the Avon valley, the journey ended in the marketplace at the center of Bath; the splendid, newly completed Guildhall's Adam-style façade at the northeast corner of the marketplace, the great, late-Gothic abbey at the south end, gardens and the river beyond—it was a delightful terminus.

Mary Wollstonecraft was an experienced traveler by now, having followed her father around the country since childhood, but Bath was the most elegant town the "awkward rustic," as she described herself, had ever seen. Bath was a triumph of Georgian city planning, designed for people to enjoy themselves. One could promenade over Poultney Bridge and along streets and sweeping crescents lined with handsome townhouses with porticoes and pilasters, all in pale marmalade Bath stone. Mary's employer, Mrs. Dawson, lived at her son William's house on Milson Street, the center of stylish Bath. Nearby was the octagonal chapel, worldly, elegant, and light, frilled with moldings of dainty garlands. Up the street, two blocks away, were the New Assembly rooms, lofty and spacious without being grand, perfect for the organized socializing for which Bath was noted. When Maria Holroyd's sister Louisa visited her aunt in Bath, she said of being introduced to so many strangers, "I felt like a Learned Pig"; conversation was of "mountains, Henri Quatre, dying a gown, making a pudding, Sully's Memoirs, Vineyards, good singing, chess, cards, or anything else you can possibly think of." There were concerts, card parties, dancing parties, and tea parties. One went to evening parties "at a little after 6 or 7, and [returned] at nine," having been offered tea, wine, bread and butter, milk punch, and cake. Great balls with as many as 700 people ("most stupid," said Louisa, as there were no interesting men there) were held twice if not four times a week in the winter season. It was a movable house party. Everybody met, incessantly, at these events, at each other's homes, at the theater where Mrs. Siddons played to full houses, and at the Pump Room. New visitors were accommodated by a master of ceremonies to whom they were introduced; he found dancing partners for the girls and saw that everyone knew everyone else. As in most resorts social barriers were somewhat relaxed; Jane Austen's Sir Walter Elliot might not expect a welcome from his aristocratic cousin when he was in London, but in Bath he "will always be worth knowing; always acceptable" as a fashionable person "who drinks the water, gets all the new publications, and has a very large acquaintance." *The Bath Chronicle* published delightful tidbits of gossip, such as the historian Catherine Macaulay's shocking marriage (at forty-seven, to a young man of twenty-one) and subsequent ostracism from Bath, and the fight between Mr. Brereton and Mr. Dawson over who would be selected Master of the Ceremonies. Eminent visitors were announced as they arrived: "The Duke of Hamilton . . . Rev. Mr. Burney and Lady, Mr. Boswell . . . General Burgoyne . . . Count and Countess Du-

Barry . . . Mr. & Mrs. Dawson [and, in December of 1778] Rev. Mr. Waterhouse."[2]

The book of the year was Fanny Burney's *Evelina,* the story of a girl's coming out into the world of fashion and her capture of the perfect husband, wealthy and aristocratic—a theme the genius of the genre, Jane Austen, would later perfect. Bath was, like London during the season, a major debut center; to be an eligible girl there was very heaven, for one was surrounded by men and could constantly display oneself in the most alluring finery. To be a paid companion like Mary Wollstonecraft was to be on the sidelines more modestly dressed, watching with mingled envy and contempt the typical debutante she might have been—"a marriageable miss, whose person is taken from one public place to another, richly caparisoned," she later wrote.[3] The beauties and beaux of Bath, whom in Beverley she had expected to join, were now beyond her scope. Her first duty was to accommodate the formidable Mrs. Dawson; to sit quietly or politely pass the tea, to respond demurely if anyone took notice of her, to be cheerful, appreciative, and available in mind and body to her employer. It was the first time she had had to practice unremitting self-control.

Sarah Dawson may have been a difficult woman, but Mary Wollstonecraft was impressed with her comportment and determined to derive whatever benefit she could from the situation. "The family I am with here is a very worthy one: Mrs. Dawson has a very good understanding, and she has seen a great deal of the world; I hope to improve myself by her conversation, and I endeavour to render a circumstance (which was at first disagreeable) useful to me," she wrote.[4] So she kept her eyes and ears open; but still it was a situation that augmented her pride, her sense of being different, her resentment. Depression and physical symptoms plagued her frequently as she struggled to find a measure of contentment and philosophical adjustment.

Two months after her arrival, she discovered that Dr. John Arden and his family were living at Bath, where the doctor was giving lectures as he had in Beverley on "Geography, the Elements of Astronomy, and uses of the Globes and Maps."[5] Elated at the possibility that Jane might be with them, she hurried to call. Jane, however, was still employed in Norfolk with the family of Sir Mordaunt Martin, but Mary at least had the pleasure of old acquaintances close at hand. She wrote Jane immediately—the girls had not been in touch for three years—and Jane replied. Mary then brought Jane up-to-date on her family's misfortunes, the Clares, her love for Fanny, her frame of mind:

> I am happy, my dear girl, to find by your letter that you are so agreeably situated;—your mild and amiable temper will always command the love and esteem of those who have the happiness of being well acquainted with you, and I am glad to hear that the family you are with, are of a kind to set a value on merit, for generally speaking to deserve and gain esteem are two very different things.—I hinted to you in my last that I had not been very happy—indeed, I have been far otherwise:—Pain and disappointment have constantly attended me since I left Beverley. I do not however repine at the dispensations of Providence, for my philosophy, as well as my religion will ever teach me to look on misfortunes as blessings, which like a bitter potion is disagreeable to the palate tho' 'tis grateful to the Stomach—I hope mine have not been thrown away on me, but that I am both the wiser and the better for them.—Tho' I talk so philosophically now, yet I must own, when under the pressure of afflictions, I did not think so rationally; my feelings were then too acute, and it was not 'till the Storm was in some measure blown over, that I could acknowledge the justness of it:—Young people generally set out with romantic and sanguine hopes of happiness, and must receive a great many stings before they are convinced of their mistake, and that they are pursuing a mere phantom; an empty name . . .
>
> It is almost needless to tell you that my father's violent temper and extravagant turn of mind, was the principal cause of my unhappiness and that of the rest of the family.
>
> . . . a pretended scheme of economy induced my father to take us all into Wales. . . . Business or pleasure took him often to London, and at last obliged him once more to fix there.—I will not say much of his ungovernable temper, tho' that has been the source of much [uneasiness]* misery to me;—his passions were seldom directed at me, yet I suffered more than any of them—my spirits were weak—in short, a lingering sickness was the consequence of it, and if my constitution had not been very strong, I must have fallen a sacrifice long before this.—as it is, my health is ruined, my spirits broken, and I have a constant pain in my side that is daily gaining ground on me:—My head aches with holding it down . . . I have only to add that my father's affairs were

* In original, word is crossed out.

so embarrassed by his misconduct that he was obliged to take the fortune that was settled on us children; I very readily gave up my part; I have therefore nothing to expect, and what is worse depend on a stranger.—I must not forget to tell you that I spent some time with a Clergyman and his lady—a very amiable Couple:—they took some pains to cultivate my understanding (which had been too much neglected) . . . I should have lived very happily with them if it had not been for my domestic troubles, and some other painful circumstances, that I wish to bury in oblivion.—

At their house too, I enjoyed the society of a friend, whom I love better than all the world beside, a friend to whom I am bound by every tie of gratitude and inclination: To live with this friend is the height of my ambition, and indeed it is the most rational wish I could make, as her conversation is not more agreeable than [entertaining]* improving.

I could dwell for ever on her praises, and you wo[d] not wonder at it, if you knew the many favors she has conferred on me, and the many valuable qualifications she possesses:—She has a *masculine* understanding, and sound judgment, yet she has every feminine virtue. . . .

—My father has a house near Town, and I hope he will see his error, and act more prudently in future, and then my mother may enjoy some comfort.

—My sisters are at School in Chelsea;—they are both fine girls and Elizabeth in particular is very handsome;—My eldest Brother has been married some time to a very agreeable woman, and is now a father. . . .

. . . Your sisters are I think very much improved: Elizabeth is exceedingly so. . . . As a correspondence will be dull without some swain to talk of, pray tell me when you write, if you have met with an agreeable Norfolk Swain to help render the Country so delightful:—you had I am sure a little spice of romance in your composition and must before this time have had a predilection in favor of some happy man;—tell me all about it, it will be kind in you, as I want something to divert my mind—Joking apart—I should be glad to hear that you had met with a sensible worthy man, tho' they are hard to be found—You never mention your old friend Miss R– Send me some account of her . . . I have written a vast deal, and shall now only assure you that my best wishes will ever attend you, and that I am yours affectionately

Mary Wollstonecraft.[6]

Mrs. Dawson spent the summer of 1778 in Southampton; the change revivified her young companion, whose ill health had caused

* Crossed out.

Mrs. Dawson enough concern to make her send Mary to a physician. His prescription, sea bathing, was "of signal service," Mary said. Louisa Holroyd enjoyed the same pleasure on her trip there; "I have had a nice dip, the machines are very convenient with a curtain all around that nobody can see you . . . one woman gives you her hand and in you jump." Where Louisa complained about Southampton's "nasty little narrow streets," however, Mary found the seaside resort most pleasant:

> The situation is delightful, and the Inhabitants polite and hospitable:—I received so much civility that I left it with regret.—I am apt to get attached to places, and tho' backward & reserved in forming friendships, yet I get sometimes so interested in the happiness of mere acquaintances that it is the source of much pain to me.—

But she wrote Jane Arden that she felt much better; the best medicine undoubtedly had been the kindness and attention she had received. She did not, however, hope to recapture her old vivacity, she told Jane, but was trying for "a cheerful settled frame of mind . . . I would not have you think I repine at what has befallen me. Reason as well as religion convinces me all has happened for the best . . . tell me that you are merry and well, and I then will laugh and sing."[7]

Mrs. Dawson returned to Bath in October. Mary Wollstonecraft found her situation increasingly distasteful. The weather worsened; she was lonely and starved for affection and intimacy instead of the "civility" of the Dawsons and the brilliance of the social life, which she now began to avoid whenever she could. "I am quite a piece of still life," she wrote Jane, "not but that I am a friend to mirth and cheerfulness; but I would move in a small circle;—I am fond of domestic pleasures and have not sufficient spirit to bustle about." Bath's crass affectations, the essential vacuity of a country club existence in which she had no part and no security, reinforced her longing for a quiet and loving home. Above all she wanted that "pleasure, for which I had the most lively taste—I mean the simple pleasures that flow from passion and affection," as she later said.[8] The Reverend Mr. Joshua Waterhouse, who arrived in Bath that winter, presented her with the problem of a worldly relationship that did not fit her requirements.

This clergyman, thirteen years older than Mary, had been considered one of the handsomest and best-dressed men in St. Catherine's College, Cambridge. He moved in high society, frequented Bath and Bristol, and was an inveterate lady's man. His correspondence, discovered when he was found murdered in 1827, consisted almost entirely of love letters. Among these letters were some from Mary Wollstonecraft.[9] The number, contents, and dates are unknown (the letters vanished soon after their discovery); in any case Mary rarely dated her letters by year, but there is good reason to assume that the pair met during Mary's two years with Mrs. Dawson. As a paid companion, Mary had to accompany her employer when required, sit with her when she received visitors, go with her to assemblies and balls that Waterhouse undoubtedly attended. On such occasions, Bath being small and exceedingly convivial, Mary was decently introduced to many people, treated with varying degrees of politeness, and allowed her own friends and relationships, as in Southampton. She was, after all, a gentlewoman, although down on her luck. She was an attractive young woman, not pretty like her sister Eliza, but tallish, with auburn hair and light brown eyes and a good body. Her dress and coiffure did credit to her wealthy employer.

Once interested in someone she could be seductive in her own way. The only woman to describe her, Mary Hays, later wrote of her:

> Her person was above the middle-height, and well proportioned . . . her hair and eyes brown, her features pleasing, her countenance changing and impressive; her voice soft, and tho' without great compass, capable of modulation. When unbending in familiar and confidential conversation, her manners had a charm that subdued the heart.

Godwin spoke of her at her best, in

> all the simplicity and vicacity of a youthful mind. . . . She was playful, full of confidence, kindness and sympathy. . . . Her voice . . . cheerful; her temper overflowing with universal kindness; and that smile of bewitching tenderness . . . illuminated her countenance, which all who knew her well recollect, and which won both heart and soul, the affection of almost everyone that beheld it.[10]

This was Mary Wollstonecraft when she was happy. If Joshua Waterhouse stopped to chat with Mrs. Dawson's young companion, he may well have been intrigued by her and received that charming smile.

Waterhouse was in and out of Bath from 1778 to 1780. It is impossible to know exactly when the attachment was formed or how far it developed on either side, but it must have preceded the writing of

Mary Wollstonecraft's first book in 1786, *Thoughts on the Education of Daughters*. Judging from that book she found men like Waterhouse very interesting, but guarded herself against a decided preference for him:

> Nothing can more tend to destroy peace of mind than platonic arrangements. They are begun in false refinement, and frequently end in sorrow . . . if a woman's heart is disengaged, she should not give way to a pleasing delusion, and imagine she will be satisfied with the friendship of the man she admires, and prefers to the rest of the world. . . .
>
> There are quite as many male coquets as women, and they are far more pernicious pests to society, as their sphere of action is larger, and they are less exposed to the censures of the world. A smothered sigh, a downcast look, and the many other little arts which are played off, may give extreme pain to a sincere, artless woman.[11]

There are traces of her contact with Waterhouse in her novel of 1787, *Mary,* in an unnamed character, a man "of polished manners and dazzling wit. . . . This man had known the mistress of the house in her youth; good nature induced him to visit her; but when he saw Mary he had another inducement. . . . He knew men, as well as books; his conversation was entertaining and improving." In the book this man drew the heroine out, enjoying her "artless flights of genius . . . capacious mind," her spontaneity and naturalness.[12]

The heroine of *Mary* observed her visitor, found him "vain in his abilities, and by no means a useful member of society," and decided to improve him. She found it "very difficult to . . . reconcile him to the weakness, the inconsistency of his understanding; and a still more laborious task for him to conquer his passions." In *Thoughts* Mary Wollstonecraft indicated that she governed her behavior accordingly:

> I am very far from thinking love irresistible and not to be conquered. . . . A resolute endeavour will always overcome difficulties. I knew a woman very early in life warmly attached to an agreeable man, yet, she saw his faults; his principles were unfixed . . . She exerted her influence to improve him, but in vain did she for years try to do it. Convinced of the impossibility, she determined not to marry him, though she was forced to encounter poverty and its attendents.[13]

It is highly unlikely that Waterhouse thought of marrying a portionless puritanical girl who was one of his many flirtations. The evidence would seem to indicate that Mary may have been attractive and attracted to Waterhouse at Bath, that she wished he had been a proper object for her affection, but that she never had any serious disturbance on his account. As far as can be ascertained from her books and letters, she was not involved with a man until after Fanny Blood's death. The episode is significant only in so far as it may illustrate that Mary was preoccupied with virtue and with Fanny Blood, was forever wanting to improve people, and disapproved strongly of Bath's society and those, like Waterhouse, who were its leaders.

Provincial Mary Wollstonecraft's initiation into high society was formative; in her two years with Mrs. Dawson she learned to distrust its values and articulate her own. Mrs. Dawson's sister's daughters, for example, were being educated "in a stile I don't approve of," she told Jane Arden, "that is, she seems to wish rather to make them accomplished and fashionable than good and sensible, in the truest sense of the word." Later, she was more scathing about such education:

> They had various masters to attend them, and a sort of menial governess to watch their footsteps. From their masters they learned how tables, chairs, etc., were called in French and Italian . . . they neither acquired ideas nor sentiments, and passed their time, when not compelled to repeat *words,* in dressing, quarrelling with each other, or conversing with their maids by stealth, till they were brought into company as marriageable.
>
> Their mother, a widow, was busy in the meantime in keeping up her connections, as she termed a numerous acquaintance, lest her girls should want a proper introduction into the great world. And these young ladies, with minds vulgar in every sense of word, and spoiled tempers, entered life puffed up with notions of their own consequence, looking down with contempt on those who could not vie with them in dress and parade.[14]

Although not bashful or falsely innocent—in Beverley she had sent Jane Arden Goldsmith's *Letters from a Chinese Philosopher,* in which several episodes satirize prostitutes and Pompadours in frank terms—Mary was shocked at the sexual teasing practiced by the girls she met. She was a long time outgrowing a sense of shame about sex. At thirty-three she still remembered indignantly "the jokes and hoyden tricks which knots of young women indulged themselves in, when in my youth accident threw me, an awkward rustic, in their way. They were almost on a par with the double meanings which shake the convivial table when the glass has circulated freely." Mary was something of a prude, a consequence, in her case, of overvaluing sex. She was disgusted by "immodest remarks and questions"; of hypocritical girlish innocents she said, "with respect to love, Nature, or their nurses, had taken care to teach them the physical meaning of the word . . . they expressed gross wishes in not very delicate phrases, when they spoke freely." Interestingly, she was even more repelled by shamelessness between women than between men and women. She called for "decent personal reserve" with significant emotion: "women are in general too familiar with each other. . . . Why in the name of decency are sisters, female intimates, or ladies and their waiting women, to be so grossly familiar as to forget the respect which one human creature owes to another?"[15]

Above all she contrasted artificial manners, snobbery, and petty rounds of meaningless activity with the "particular affection" and domestic tranquility she wanted. Having begun her job with some degree of optimism and sense of accomplishment, she was soon discontent, at times bitterly so. She learned to handle her employer "by method, constancy, and firmness." According to the *Memoirs*, "Mrs. Dawson would occasionally confess, that Mary was the only person that had lived with her in that situation, in her treatment of whom she had felt herself under any restraint." The lady could not have been as difficult as Edward John Wollstonecraft or as severe as Elizabeth. But hypersensitive, proud Mary hated the life she led for two years as a paid companion:

> with strangers, who are so intolerably tyrannical, that none of their own relations can bear to live with them. . . . It is impossible to enumerate the many hours of anguish such a person must spend. Above the servants, yet considered by them as a spy, and ever reminded of her inferiority when in conversation with superiors. If she cannot condescend to flattery, she has not a chance of being a favorite; and should any of the visitors take notice of her, and she for a moment forget her subordinate state, she is sure to be reminded of it.
>
> Painfully sensible of unkindness, she is alive to every thing, many sarcasms reach her, which were perhaps directed another way. She is alone, shut out from equality and confidence . . . and the concealed

anxiety impairs her constitution; for she must wear a cheerful face, or be dismissed. The being dependent on the caprice of a fellow-creature, though certainly very necessary in this state of discipline, is yet a very bitter corrective.[16]

There were other young women of Mary Wollstonecraft's class who, even though more fortunate than she, shared her misanthropy. Fanny Burney recorded in her Diary an amazing conversation she had in Bath at an evening party in June of 1780, with a so-called Miss White.

Miss White is young and pleasing in her appearance, not pretty, but agreeable in her face, and soft, gentle, and well-bred in her manners . . . very soon, and I am sure I know not how, we had for topics the follies and vices of mankind, and indeed, she spared not for lashing them. The women she rather excused than defended, laying to the door of the men their faults and imperfections; but the men, she said, were all bad —all in one word, and without exception, sensualists!

I stared much at a severity of speech for which her softness of manner had so ill-prepared me. . . .

. . . she then led to discoursing of happiness and misery: the latter she held to be the invariable lot of us all; and "one word," she added, "we have in our language, and in all others, for which there is never any essential necessity, and that is—*pleasure!*" And her eyes filled with tears as she spoke.

"How you amaze me!" cried I, "I have met with misanthropes before, but never with so complete a one. . . ."

She then, in rather indirect terms, gave me to understand that she was miserable at home, and in very direct terms, that she was wretched abroad; and openly said, that to affliction she was born, and in affliction she must die, for that the world was so vilely formed, as to render happiness impossible. . . ."

. . . I now grew very serious, and frankly told her that I could not think it consistent with either truth or religion to cherish such notions.

"One thing," answered she, "there is, which I believe might make me happy, but for that I have no inclination: it is an amorous disposition. . . . the finding one worthy of exciting a passion which one should dare own to himself. That would, indeed be a moment worth living for! but that can never happen—I am sure, not to me—the men are so low, so vicious, so worthless! . . ."

"If, however," she continued, "I had your talents I could, as bad as this world is, be happy in it . . . Oh, if I could write as you write!"

"Try," cried I, "that is all that is wanting: try. . . ."

"Oh no! I have tried but I cannot succeed. . . ."

". . . if you wait to be happy for a friend resembling yourself, I shall no longer wonder at your despondency."

"Oh!" cried she, raising her eyes in ecstasy, "could I find such a one!—male or female—for sex would be indifferent to me. With such a one I would go to live directly . . . should I lose such a friend, I would not survive. . . ."

"Surely you cannot mean," said I, very gravely indeed, "to put a violent end to your life?"

"I should not," she said, again looking up, "hesitate a moment."

. . . I urged her to tell me by what right she thought herself entitled to rush unlicensed on eternity, she said, "By the right of believing I shall be extinct." I really felt horror'd.

"Where, for Heaven's sake," I cried, "where have you picked up such dreadful reasoning?"

"In Hume," said she; "I have read his *Essays* repeatedly."

A few days later, Fanny Burney renewed her conversation with this young woman. "With her romantic, flighty, and unguarded turn of mind. . . . She is in a very dangerous situation, with idéas so loose of religion, and so enthusiastic of love. What, indeed, is there to restrain an infidel, who has no belief in a future state, from sin and evil of any sort?" Miss Burney recommended books "on the right side" to this girl whose unhappiness had made such an impression on her.[17]

Anger at men, at sensuality, and at worldliness; pessimism; violent and decided emotionality; the prevision of suicide over a love disappointment; the desire for love as a solution to unhappiness; even the wish to write; all of these savor strangely of Mary Wollstonecraft, except for Miss White's irreligion. Mary until 1787 was a faithful churchgoer, urgently devout, convinced that God would redeem her unhappiness and that she would go after death to "a better world . . . abode of peace," as she wrote to Jane Arden. No letter of this period indicates even a temporary suspension of faith. If it were not for that, and the fact that there is no indication she and Fanny Burney ever met, one could imagine the latter saw, on an evening when she was feeling especially rebellious, depressed, and out of control, the young Mary Wollstonecraft.

Mary had the pleasure of Jane Arden's company for part of her term of employment, for in early 1780 Jane took a position with a Lady Ilchester at Redlynch, Somerset, close enough to Bath for the girls to see each other at intervals for a brief period. But Mrs. Dawson had connections in Windsor; her son had a house there, Leonard's Hill, and her sister lived nearby with three growing daughters. After the Bath season ended in 1780, probably in early summer, she gave Mary a vacation and removed to Windsor, where her companion was to join her. Mary took the post coach to London—not to her family now at Enfield in the northern suburbs but to Fanny Blood in Waltham Green. She stayed there for a week of happy intimacy, during which she became all the more convinced that the only personal happiness she could rationally expect was with her friend. Fanny was in better health, and there was no talk of moving to a softer climate. Hugh Skeys was not around. The two young women made plans to live together in the nearest possible future. Two years had gone by; Mary was now twenty-one. She *would* not spend her life attending rich old ladies; yet unless she moved decisively in some direction, more years would pass in the same way. Whatever ambitions or rosy hopes she had had now seemed unreal. Going home was out of the question. Therefore, she and Fanny would somehow earn their own living and make a life together.

She left Fanny, resolved but unhappy, for she had to return to servitude for an indefinite time. She found herself, at Windsor—"this gayest of all places," where George III and his court resided—in a state of depression and withdrawal so paralyzing that she could hardly drag herself around to fulfill her duties. Her mornings were especially difficult, after restless nights. On one such day, before breakfast, she wrote Jane Arden a letter she had owed her for some time, apologizing for her delay, and listing her miseries: "ill-health and lowness of spirits, a kind of indolence growing upon me," melancholy and listlessness, disgust with "genteel life" and "unmeaning civilities." She wanted to retire from the world. Frustration plunged her into lethargy, which frightened her—even false hopes would be better than none, she wrote, and realistic solutions, no matter how difficult, devoutly to be desired. Jane and her sister, whose economic situation was not unlike Mary's, were planning to open a school in Bath. Mary envied their opportunities:

"Let not some small difficulties intimidate you, I beseech you; struggle with any obstacles rather than go into a state of dependence:—I speak feelingly." But she became more resolute when she spoke of Fanny:

> The next time we meet, it will be for a longer continuance, and to that period I look, as to the most important one of my life:—this connexion must give the colour to my future days, for I have now given up every expectation and dependance that would interfere with my determination of spending my time with her.—I know this resolution may appear a little extraordinary, but in forming it I follow the dictates of reason as well as the bent of my inclination; for tho' I am willing to do what good I can in my generation, yet on many accounts I am averse to any matrimonial tie:—If ever you should venture may success attend you;—be not too sanguine in your expectations, and you will have less reason to fear a disappointment;—however it don't much signify what part in life we bear, so as we act with propriety.[18]

Mary had another reason to be unhappy; she was not on good terms with her family, who considered that she had deserted them. She corresponded with her father, but her mother, still resentful, maintained a cold silence Mary found threatening. When seventeen-year-old Eliza felt free to express the family's hostility, she had the power to evoke defensiveness and deep anxiety in her older sister. Mary replied to her:

> I this morning received your letter which was truly welcome to me, as I found by it you still remember me; but I must say, I should like to be remembered in a kinder manner. There is an air of irony through your whole epistle that hurts me exceedingly . . . one affectionate word would give me more pleasure than all the pretty things that come from the head; but have nothing to say to the heart.—Two or three expressions in your last particularly displeased me, you mention my *condescension,* and early *enquiries*—I know not what to make of those words.—I did not answer my Father's letter because my stay at Bath was so uncertain . . . but as soon as I was settled at Windsor I writ to him, and flattered myself I should be favoured with a line or two in return. —As to Everina's illness my Father only mentioned it in a careless manner to me, and I did not imagine it had been so bad, even now I am ignorant of the nature of her complaint tho' I am very anxious about it.
>
> You don't do me justice in supposing I seldom think of you—the

happiness of my family is nearer my heart than you imagine—perhaps, too near for my own health or peace—For my anxiety preys on me, and is of no use to you. You don't say a word of my mother. I take it for granted she is well—tho' of late she has not even desired to be remembered to me. Some time or other, in this world or a better, she may be convinced of my regard—and then may think I deserve not to be thought so harshly of. But enough on this subject. Love me but as I love you, and I'll be contented.

. . . I hope Charles continues to improve, I long to see him. . . . I hear Edward goes on very well, that he is paying off his debts, and that by this time he is again a father.

I have got no table in my room, and I am obliged to sit sideways to a chest . . . on which I endeavour to write. 'Tis drawing near twelve o'clock—and I must be up soon to dress my hair to go to eight o'clock prayers at the royal chapel—I have promised to show a nephew of Mr. Dawson's the way—and I assure you that I am in the truest sense of the word your most affectionate sister.

Mary Wollstonecraft

Pray make my love and duty acceptable to every part of the family—and beg them all to receive me with smiling faces—for I cannot bear frowns —or sneers.[19]

Mary had not shaken off the guilt she felt when she left home, and the fact that she rushed to Fanny rather than home for her holiday did not lessen that guilt, nor did her decision to live with Fanny as soon as possible. That happiness, which seemed to be coming closer, enlivened the summer of 1780. Mary was in a good mood when she wrote her last letter to Jane Arden from Windsor. The "unweeded garden" of life she sometimes spoke of was a pleasant place and its inhabitants—George III, his "splendid stud" of a son, his court—were at best delightful, at worst figures of ridicule. She could accept failings without total rejection and enjoy the scene around her without relinquishing her own standards. She was young, strong, hopeful of her future with Fanny, anticipating a propitiating visit to her family with pleasure, at her most gay and tender. Even Jane's recent failure to write did not disturb her:

Here I am, quite alone.—Mrs. Dawson is gone to pay a visit, and I have the whole house to range in.—I cannot now I have so much time put off answering your last epistle which was truly welcome to me.—I indeed began to wonder at your silence, tho' I hardly deserved a speedy reply, but you used me better than I merited, and I am determined to let you see that I intend to be a regular correspondent.

Windsor is a most delightful place;—the country about it is charming, and I long to live in the forest every time we ride through it.—The only fault I find is that it is too gay;—I should like a more retired situation. I go constantly to the Cathedral:—I am very fond of the Service. —I have beside made some visits. Mrs. Dawson has a sister who lives near here;—she is a most pleasant and entertaining woman and behaves to me in the politest manner. . . . You cannot imagine how amazingly they dress here;—It is the important business that takes up great part of the time of both old and young.—I believe I am thought a very poor creature, but to dress violently neither suits my inclination, nor [power]* purse. . . . The King is quite a domestic [character]* man and it is pleasing to see him surrounded by his children . . . he killed three horses the other day riding in a hurry to pay a visit; this has lost him my warm heart;—I cannot bear an unfeeling mortal:—Indeed I carry my notions on this subject a great way:—I think it murder to put an end to any living thing unless it be necessary for food, or hurtful to us.—If it has pleased the beneficent creator of all to call them into being, we ought to let them enjoy the common blessings of nature . . . I have sometimes saved the life of a fly, and thought myself of consequence:

—I am running on in a romantic way—to change the subject, let me tell you, that the Prince of Wales is the principal beau here;—all the damsels set their caps at him, and you would smile to hear how the poor girls he condescends to take notice of are pulled to pieces:—the withered old maids sagaciously hint their fears, and kindly remark that they always thought them forward things: you would suppose a smile or a look of his had something fatal in it, and that a maid could not look at him, and remain pure:—joking apart—you can have no idea of the commotion he throws the good ladies into; he certainly keeps both envy & vanity alive; —but enough of him.—I beg your pardon for not mentioning my family, and thank you for remembering them;—they are all well, and I intend going to them the latter end of this month, and I shall spend as much time with them as I possibly can:—I don't like to think of parting—it will be a severe trial, but I must submit to it . . . I am your ever affectionate friend

Mary Wollstonecraft

* Crossed out.

I have put so much water in my ink, I am afraid you will not be able to read my faint characters, and besides my candle gives such a dreadful light.—I am just going to sup *solus* on a bunch of grapes, and a bread crust;—I'll drink your health in pure water.—I take up my pen again to tell you I have not for a long time been so well as I am at present.—The roses will bloom when there's peace in the breast, and the prospect of living with my ffanny gladdens my heart:—You know not how I love her.—I can hardly bid you adieu, till I come to the bottom of my paper.

To hear often from you will give me great pleasure.—

God bless you.[20]

It was years before she recaptured this buoyance; Mary Wollstonecraft's girlhood had ended.

Chapter 5

MARY WOLLSTONECRAFT left Mrs. Dawson suddenly, but not to live with Fanny Blood as she had hoped. Her own mother became seriously ill, and Mary "eagerly returned to the parental roof, which she had before resolutely quitted," according to the *Memoirs*. It was the kind of crisis to which she reacted with pity and resolution. She became the responsible nurse required for her mother's lingering and hopeless illness, diagnosed as dropsy. In a way, it was fortunate for Mary that circumstance and duty mandated a lengthy, active reparation for past years of resentment and recent months of separation. If her mother had died suddenly without her attendance, Mary would have had a burden to bear. Elizabeth Wollstonecraft now clung to her daughter's strength and character, which before had been a barrier between them, and the two women reached a degree of intimacy under these circumstances that they had never had before. As the *Memoirs* relate: "Mary was assiduous in her attendance upon her mother . . . nothing would be taken by the unfortunate patient, but from the hands of Mary . . . every attention was received with acknowledgements and gratitude."[1]

Dropsy, or edema as it is now termed, is abnormal fluid retention that can be caused by liver, kidney, or heart malfunction, or by cancer. An eighteenth-century physician described the progress of the malady:

> It begins rather often with a swelling of the feet, especially towards evening. . . . The swelling . . . perceptibly increased around the an-

kles, mounts to the legs and thighs. Afterwards, the abdomen swells to great size. From the onset of the disease, little urine is passed, pallor shows in the face, languor and a heavy sluggishness take possession of the limbs. There is little or no perspiration, shortness of breath is induced . . . and the upper parts of the body begin to wither as the lower parts swell. Finally, there appears a constant low fever, together with loss of appetite and insatiable thirst. Sometimes the umbilicus projects, followed by hæmorrhages, ulcers and gangrene of both internal and external areas. Finally—death.

Nursing dropsical patients was extremely demanding. It was the prevailing medical opinion that the patient's thirst was "a most annoying symptom . . . and one to which they should not easily yield. For, as Horace has beautifully expressed it, this dread dropsy is not dispelled by self-indulgence."[2] Mary had to ration her mother's fluid intake. To dispel swelling, carthartics, emetics, and diuretics were given, and the patient was urged not to sleep for long periods, to move as much as possible, and to keep cheerful.

Mary attended her mother night and day, and as the months dragged on, the patient became more and more difficult and demanding. Mary had not only responsibility for her mother's physical care, but for protecting her from Edward John Wollstonecraft. "During my mother's illness, I was obliged to manage my father's temper, who, from the lingering nature of her malady, began to imagine it was merely fancy." Both in *Maria* and *Mary* the description is the same:

As her mother grew imperceptibly worse and worse, her father . . . imagined his wife was only grown still more whimsical, and that if she could . . . exert herself, her health would soon be re-established. In general he treated her with indifference; but when her illness at all interfered with his pleasures, he expostulated in the most cruel manner, and visibly harassed the invalid.

One of his pleasures may have been an affair he began with Lydia, the housekeeper he later married; in *Maria*, "an artful kind of upper servant attracted my father's attention and the neighbors made many remarks on the finery, not honestly got, exhibited at evening service. But I was too much occupied with my mother to observe any change in her dress or behaviour, or to listen to the whisper of scandal."[3] In fact, Mary Wollstonecraft could not have avoided knowing.

She was also forced to recognize the persistence of her ancient problem, her mother's greater love for indifferent Ned. She wrote in *Maria:*

> The neglect of her darling, my brother . . . had a violent effect on her weakened mind; . . . boys may be reckoned the pillars of the house without doors, girls are often the only comfort within. They but too frequently waste their health and spirits attending a dying parent, who leaves them in comparative poverty . . . the son . . . scarcely thought of discharging, in the decline of his parent's life, the debt contracted in his childhood. . . . Great as was the fatigue I endured, and the affection my unceasing solicitude evinced, of which my mother seemed perfectly sensible, still, when my brother, whom I could hardly persuade to remain a quarter of an hour in her chamber, was with her alone, a short time before her death, she gave him a little hoard, which she had been for some years accumulating.[4]

The reward Mary Wollstonecraft had hoped for from her mother, to be first in her affections, was thus denied her until the end.

As edema advances, the lungs begin to fill with fluid, and the patient, in effect, slowly suffocates or drowns. Mary, exhausted by conflicting emotions and terrible responsibility, nursed her mother from late 1780 to April of 1782. Whatever sorrow she might have felt, whatever love the illness had elicited was exhausted, too. There remained only a degree of respect for her mother's integrity and control. The deathbed scene was reported in both of Mary Wollstonecraft's novels:

> "My child," said the languid mother: the words reached her heart; she had seldom heard them pronounced with accents denoting affection; "My child, I have not always treated you with kindness. God forgive me! Do you?"—Mary's tears . . . fell . . . "I forgive you!" said she, in a tone of astonishment. (*Mary*)
>
> My mother . . . solemnly recommended my sisters to my care, and bid me to be a mother to them. (*Maria*)

Her last words, poignant in their awareness of the burden she had been and in their resignation to death as to all her unhappy life, struck Mary Wollstonecraft to the heart: "A little patience, and all will be over!" There was a note of reproach in the phrase. Patience, a virtue Mary knew she herself possessed little of, was the chief quality she had undervalued in her mother. She was to remember the phrase all her life, to repeat it in times of stress. It echoed in the last note she wrote in her life, to Godwin, when she was in labor before her fatal delivery: "I must have a little patience."[5]

Elizabeth Wollstonecraft was buried in St. Andrew's graveyard in Enfield on April 19, 1782. In the emotion of the moment the Wollstonecrafts briefly drew closer. Edward John Wollstonecraft was overcome. Mary wrote in *Maria:* "My father was violently affected by her death, recollected instances of his unkindness, and wept like a child." But, like a child, his reaction was short-lived, and again the family split apart. "My father's grief and consequent tenderness to his children, quickly abated, and the house grew still more gloomy or riotous." In *Maria,* the housekeeper-mistress began to take the part of a fine lady, with the support of her infatuated master: "She uttered with pomposity her bad English, or affected to be well-bred." The proud and sensitive Wollstonecraft children must have been appalled at the insult to their mother, hardly cold, and to themselves. Wollstonecraft seems to have disintegrated to the point of being incapable of functioning as their father. Financially he was also ruined, a fact that Mary discovered during the months she spent at home. He had kept up appearances only by borrowing. Ned took over his father's affairs and seems to have doled out an allowance at his pleasure. "He allowed my father, whose distress made him submit to anything, a tithe of his own . . . my father was totally regardless of futurity," Mary wrote in *Maria.*[6] Ned took both Eliza and Everina into his home in London—the only arrangement feasible since they could not remain at Enfield with their father's mistress. In fact in this crisis Ned behaved well. With a wife and two children of his own, and debts to be paid, two girls of eighteen and sixteen were not responsibilities he could have welcomed.

At fourteen, James Wollstonecraft was able to fend for himself. He had gone to sea two years before and had decided on the navy as a career. In *Maria* the housekeeper attempts to seduce a younger brother, but this seems only fictional evidence of Mary's angry contempt for the woman. Wollstonecraft married her soon after, and they lived together for the rest of their lives. He took her back to Laugharne in Wales—about as far away as he could go—taking twelve-year-old Charles,

Mary's favorite, with him. The solution was probably a relief to his children, if not to poor Charles. There is no mention of Henry.

Mary took care of herself. As she had decided four years before to be independent of her parents, this final dissolution was less shocking to her than it was to her sisters. There was no question of her living with Ned. It is interesting to speculate on what would have happened if Wollstonecraft had looked to his eldest daughter to manage his household, instead of another wife. His marriage left Mary free to do as she pleased. Her mother's death does not seem to have affected her deeply; her sense of just grievance over Ned's favored status, revived at the end, left her with the same resentment she had always felt. She took it out in contempt for her mother's weakness; Elizabeth Wollstonecraft was a symbol of incompetence and blindness to her, faults she freely and contemptuously ascribed to most women for many years, although at the same time she attributed great power to women, a reflection of the major part her mother had played in her life. Mary rarely mentioned the second Mrs. Wollstonecraft, but she and Eliza seem gradually to have accepted her as a decent, well-meaning victim of their incorrigible, degenerating father. Everina resented the marriage for some years. "Say something civil to him, and Mrs. W.," Mary admonished her in 1786, "if it will not blister your tongue."[7]

For years Mary could not think of her father without love and regret. She wrote in *Maria* of his "former occasional tenderness, in spite of his violence of temper, [which] had been soothing to me." He reminded her of Lear after his fall, ruined and mad. She was the faithful daughter; "the start of Cordelia's, when her father says, 'I think that Lady is my daughter,' has affected me deeply," she wrote. But she knew he was hopeless, and as far as is known she never saw him again after he went to Wales. The only thing she could do for him was to take care of him, at a distance, with even greater sense of responsibility than she assumed for the younger children. "A parent, under distressed circumstances, should be supported, even though it should prevent our having a fortune for a child; nay more, should they both be in distress at the same time, the *prior* obligations should be discharged," she said in 1786. This filial piety later dissolved, exposing underlying resentment, and the change seems to have occurred as she became deeply attached to substitutes for her father. By the time of the *Vindications* she repudiated obligation to unnatural and undeserving fathers, although she continued faithfully to support hers. Eliza said later she trembled to think what would happen if he returned to London where Mary was living.[8]

The terrible thing about death, Proust said, is that it always, in some degree, simplifies existence for the survivors. Mary Wollstonecraft was now free to follow her old dream—to live with Fanny Blood. But it was a far cry from the domestic felicity she had looked forward to. Since she was physically exhausted, depressed, and homeless, the Bloods took her into their home in Waltham Green. Externally, it had attractions. Waltham was then a suburban village west of London, where the Thames loops around Fulham on the north bank. It was part of London's kitchen garden, attractive with nurseries, orchards, and truck farms. Fulham Palace, residence of the bishop of London, stands on the right as one approaches Putney Bridge, at that time an ugly and inconvenient wooden structure.

The Blood family situation was stark and cramped, as Mary Wollstonecraft knew from her former visit. She could not have thought of Waltham Green as a permanent home; only her devotion to Fanny and a need for a haven could have taken her there. Their poverty speaks for their generosity: Mrs. Blood and Fanny strained to support them all, while Mr. Blood, incompetent and self-indulgent, contributed little and wasted much. There were at least two other children, Caroline and George, too young to be of help; Mary became very attached to the boy. Although she had been through financial crises in her life, she had never lived in such straits. She herself had nothing, was trained for nothing, and had neither prospects nor energy. She did what she could to contribute to the household. Mrs. Blood earned money by doing fancy needlework for friends and patrons, an exasperating task for an active young woman of intellect to assist in. Fanny remembered that,

> My mother used to sit at work, in summer, from *four* in the morning till she could not see at night, which with the assistance of one of her daughters did not bring her more than half a guinea a week, and often not quite that; and she was generally, at least one third of the year without work, 'tho her friends in that time were numerous. Mary's *sights* and health are so bad you may recollect that she was almost *blinded* and sick to death after a job we did for Mrs. Bensley.[9]

Mary tolerated the drudgery all that summer of 1782 and into the following year because she did not expect it to go on so long. Several months after her mother's death she wrote Jane Arden from Waltham Green that her stay in England was uncertain, for she expected to go to Lisbon. There was no mention of the quality of her life with the Bloods, no rhapsodies over Fanny. Mary seemed tired and worn—"I have already got the wrinkles of old age"—but roused herself to envy Jane a prospective trip to Ireland, a contrast with her own dull confinement. She loved the Irish. Of them she said, "The women are all handsome, and the men agreeable . . . if I was my own mistress I would spend my life with them . . . the men are dreadful flirts, so take care of your heart, and don't leave it in one of the Bogs."[10]

Mary expected to leave England for Portugal with Fanny because her friend was in need of a warm climate. Fanny's always precarious health had worsened under the strain of working to help support her family. She was making prints as well as drawings. But the journey to Lisbon depended on Hugh Skeys, who lived there, and Skeys continued to procrastinate about marrying Fanny. He told Godwin later that his family could not understand why he was interested in a girl without fortune or particular beauty. When and if he definitely proposed, Mary apparently intended to accompany Fanny. Their intimacy, Godwin says, was "rooted and active."[11]

It was a strange relationship on Mary's side. Not only was she jealous of Skeys but she was critical of Fanny and dissatisfied with her company. Yet Fanny was her beloved, and she wanted to live for and with her however she could. She was worried about Fanny's health and began to study medicine. In the novel *Mary* it is the heroine, not a man, who enables Ann to get to Lisbon, the role of rescuer toward which Mary gravitated. But Fanny's happiness at twenty-six still depended on Skeys, as Mary's mother's had on Ned. Mary was entangled in the old coils. She had only Fanny to love, but in her own ambivalent way. In *Mary* she attributed it in part to her own superiority, but touched on another need:

> Before she enjoyed Ann's society, she imagined it would have made her completely happy; she was disappointed, and yet knew not what to complain of. . . .
>
> She had not yet found the companion she looked for. Ann and she

were not congenial minds, nor did she contribute to her comfort in the degree she expected.

Mary had never had any particular attachment. . . . Her friendship for Ann occupied her heart and resembled a passion. She had had, indeed, several transient likings, but they did not amount to love.[12]

Yet Mary clung to the love she felt for Fanny. She had no alternative. Lacking a male interest she convinced herself that she did not want what she felt she could never have, and the result was bitter disdain for those who got it. In October, 1782, Eliza Wollstonecraft married advantageously. At about the same time Jane Arden's sister also married. Mary's letter of congratulation to Jane was caustic and contemptuous:

I congratulate you, my dear Jane, on account of your Sister's wedding. . . . The joy, and all that . . . is certainly over by this time, and all the raptures have subsided, and the dear hurry of visiting and figuring away as a bride, and all the rest of the delights of matrimony are past and gone and have left no traces behind them, except disgust:—I hope I am mistaken, but this is the fate of most married pairs. . . . I will not marry, for I dont want to be tied to this nasty world, and old maids are of so little consequence—that "let them live or die, nobody will laugh or cry."—It is a happy thing to be a mere blank, and to be able to pursue one's own whims, where they lead, without having a husband and half a hundred children at hand to teaze and controul a poor woman who wishes to be free. . . . My sister however has done well, and married a worthy man, whose situation in life is truly eligible.—You remember Bess; she was a mere child when we were together, and it would have hurt our dignity to have admitted her into our Parties, but she must now take place of us, being of the most honourable order of matrons.[13]

In the same letter Mary Wollstonecraft told Jane Arden unexpected delays had retarded her journey to Lisbon with Fanny, but anticipated they would leave in the spring. However, Hugh Skeys did not summon Fanny in the spring of 1783 or for many seasons after. Mary grew more restless. She was going into her twenty-fourth year. Having decided to be an old maid, she demanded activity, scope, and independence. She tried to break Fanny free from the Blood household as she had broken from her own. But Fanny would not leave. It was an added reason for Mary's disillusionment. In the *Memoirs* Godwin accepted her attitude without question:

> Whatever Mary undertook, she perhaps in all instances accomplished; and, to her lofty spirit, scarcely anything she desired, appeared hard to perform. Fanny, on the contrary, was a woman of a timid and irresolute nature, accustomed to yield to difficulties, and probably priding herself in this morbid softness of her temper. One instance that I have heard Mary relate of this sort, was, that, at a certain time, Fanny, dissatisfied with her domestic situation, expressed an earnest desire to have a home of her own. Mary, who felt nothing more pressing than to relieve the inconveniences of her friend, determined to accomplish this object for her. It cost her infinite exertions; but at length she was able to announce to Fanny that a house was prepared, and that she was on the spot to receive her. The answer which Fanny returned to the letter of her friend, consisted almost wholly of an enumeration of objections to the quitting of her family, which she had not thought of before, but which now appeared to her of considerable weight.[14]

Fanny had a mind of her own, but both Godwin and Mary seemed to equate character with doing what Mary wanted. She did succeed in getting Fanny away for a short time. Somehow—perhaps through the Clares—the two girls spent about three months at Thomas Taylor's house in Walworth, where the Clares lived. Taylor was then a young bank clerk living modestly with his wife. He was an ardent student of Greek philosophy. Plato and the mystical neo-Platonists were Truth for him; he made himself their interpreter to the modern world and was even a polytheist. He later said that at this time he thought Mary

> a very modest, sensible, and agreeable young lady . . . always pleased with his conversation on [Plato]; but [she] confessed herself more inclined to an active than a contemplative life. She frequently complimented him on the tranquility of his manners, and used to call the little room which he made his study, "the abode of peace."[15]

It was a contrast to her own dissatisfaction and unrest. She may have gone to Taylor to learn, for she continued to study and read, but she had no way to utilize her work, and Fanny was not capable of sharing her serious intellectual interests. The young women returned to the Blood home, where they remained until the fall of 1783.

Mary Wollstonecraft during this period was like a ship straining against a sea anchor, tacking through the wind and back, unable to make headway. She was dependent on Fanny Blood for the only love and intimacy she had and was without skills for a career commensurate with her ability or desire for independence. The most ambitious course she proposed was no more sensible than it would have been satisfactory. She wanted Fanny to leave the Bloods with her and earn a living by art and needlework. But even that plan depended on Ned's initial help, which was unlikely; he disliked Fanny. Fanny was sometimes on the verge of agreeing to move out, but Mary's own ambivalence would have marred their life together in any case. Until her mother's death Mary had faith that she was being carried along by a difficult but trustworthy universe to a happiness that she could secure by her own efforts. Now she wrote Everina, "I have no hope, nor do I endeavour to attain anything but composure of mind."[16] It was an attitude disconsonant with her usual feeling of omnipotence, a state of mind forced on her by frustrations and sustained in anger and a sense of futility.

How long would she have clung to Fanny? Abruptly, the storm of Eliza's tragedy forced her into action, driven by energies pent up during her abortive attempt to build a life with the friend who could not content her, but whom she could not leave.

Chapter 6

Mary Wollstonecraft, even with her strong character, found it difficult to lead an independent life, but it never occurred to her younger sisters to want such an existence. Lacking Mary's particular motivation and drive, Eliza and Everina had remained under their parents' care except for some time at a finishing school in Chelsea, a center for such establishments, and they had seen no reason to anticipate anything but the normal life of gently reared, protected girls. After their mother's death and the shock of their father's financial collapse and remarriage in 1782, they went to live with Ned because they had nowhere else to turn. Their position was difficult; as young gentlewomen with only small annuities, they were not good matches; nor were they disposed or able to work, except as pride permitted in their brother's household. In addition Ned's wife, Elizabeth, resented her sisters-in-law. Mary later eloquently described their situation:

> Girls who have been thus weakly educated are often cruelly left by their parents without any provision, and, of course, are dependent on not only the reason, but the bounty of their brothers. Their brothers . . . give as a favour what children of the same parents had an equal right to. . . .
>
> Who can recount the misery which many unfortunate beings, whose minds and bodies are equally weak, suffer in such situations—unable to work, and ashamed to beg? The wife, a cold-hearted narrow-minded

> woman . . . is jealous of the little kindness which her husband shows to his relations. . . .
>
> . . . had they been differently educated, the case . . . would have been very different . . . the sister might have been able to struggle for herself instead of eating the bitter bread of dependence.[1]

Eliza Wollstonecraft's temperament was similar to Mary's, but even more unrestrained—hypersensitive, moody, ambivalent, and highly emotional, without reticence or self-control. When Eliza was unhappy Everina called her "the Raven" because she was given to "croaking." "You know," she once wrote Everina, "when I am in the horrors I seem to take pleasure in making those I love feel exactly the same degree of misery"; when successful in this endeavor she rejoiced that normally optimistic Everina had lost the "philosophy I have *so often* been angry with *you* for *possessing*." Her letters are bitter, agitated, and self-pitying; they are also animated, colorful, and funny. In fact, she would have had a delightful literary talent if she had known how to turn her intelligence to account. But she was quite undisciplined; her handwriting is vivid but terrible, irregular, askew, slashed with great underlinings and exclamation points. She had Mary's critical eye and an irrepressible urge to ridicule: "A storm the other day blew in a goodly figure of a man with Parson Woods; and believe me my hair stood almost on end when I found the man *could talk!*" Her instability equaled that of her father. When with Everina on a holiday both girls had ardently anticipated, Eliza ruined their brief time together with complaints and attacks, begged pardon abjectly, and then repeated the same pattern next vacation. She was even more ambivalent about Mary because more admiring and envious of her. Each had strong ties to the other: Eliza for her authoritative, superior sister, Mary for the lively girl she had helped care for as a child. Eliza, however, was lovable in a way the more stable Everina never was. When Godwin met the two, years later, he wrote a friend, "I love Aunt Bishop [Eliza] as much as I hate . . . Aunt Everina."[2]

In 1782 Eliza was pretty, spoiled, thoughtless, irresponsible, and pleasure loving. After several months in Ned's home in London, when she had just turned nineteen, she became engaged to a man approaching thirty. Meredith Bishop was from a well-to-do London family of shipbuilders; his father, Meredith Bishop, Sr., had become a member of the

London Shipwright's Guild in 1736, after apprenticeship to his father. Bishop, Sr., lived at Mill-Stairs, Rotherhite, on the Surrey side of the Thames embankment, and built lighters for unloading cargo ships. Meredith Bishop, Jr., was admitted to the guild in 1775 and was in business with his father until 1780, when the elder Bishop apparently died and the younger Bishop inherited his fortune. The Bishops were evidently men of substance; they were listed in London directories between 1779 and 1788 as "eminent traders." The match was on the surface an ideal one. Because Eliza was a minor, her father sent official permission for the marriage from Wales, signed in a large, wobbly handwriting. Ned acted *in loco parentis* in London. On October 19, 1782, he swore before church authorities that his father's signature was genuine, and he and the bridegroom posted bond of £200 to guarantee the marriage. Ned's own signature on the documents is sharp and firm. The young couple were married the following day in Ned's parish church, St. Katherine's Near the Tower.[3]

When Mary Wollstonecraft told Jane Arden that Eliza had married an eligible and worthy man, she was sincere. It was only for herself that wedded life was undesirable. For most women, particularly one as giddy as Eliza, Mary believed marriage to be the state in which they could be most useful, and she was rigorous on the subject of being useful. As for Eliza's husband, Mary told Everina any decent man of good sense ought to satisfy a sensible woman, although privately she did not think Eliza sensible and she knew little of Bishop's character. She probably expected he would steady Eliza down. Mary said nothing of love in such matches, except to wax sardonic. Romance irritated her; her rejection of it for many years equaled the force with which she repressed it in herself. As it turned out, Eliza and Bishop's marriage was unfortunate, and Mary Wollstonecraft blamed it on love. Love was an "arbitrary passion"; she later said, which leads men to choose pretty, silly wives and foolish girls to expect eternally fervent lovers. The day of reckoning in such a marriage, she admonished, would surely come.[4]

The Bishops' miserable day of reckoning came after the birth of their child, Elizabeth Mary Frances, born on August 10, 1783, ten months after their marriage.[5] Eliza suffered a postpartum breakdown. The first symptom was hysterical deafness, followed by "raving fits." Fortunately for Eliza, Bishop had her taken care of at home rather than institutionalized. Mary Wollstonecraft's availability and experience as a nurse may have had something to do with it; she herself felt that an asylum was a last resort. Mary was sent for probably after the baby was baptized on September 19, for her letters describe the weather in London as extremely cold, and Eliza was by then considered physically well enough to be taken riding in a coach for diversion (at this period, at least a month after childbirth). Mary took charge of the patient, and between Everina's visits reported on her condition to her youngest sister at Ned's house across the Thames. Mary's letters to Everina—or "Averina," as the girl then preferred—make it plain that Mary came to Eliza's with no preconceived prejudice against Bishop, no assumption that there was serious trouble with the marriage. In fact, when she first heard Eliza's wild accusations that her husband had treated her badly, she assumed they were manifestations of madness. Mary's tone was dispassionate and cautious, reserving judgment on the case and indicating some familiarity with insanity. "Patience," she said to Everina—the maternal watchword, with its intimation of resignation to fatality:

> Saturday afternoon
>
> . . . I cannot yet give any certain account of Bess, or form a rational conjecture with respect to the termination of her disorder. She has not had a violent fit of frenzy since I saw you, but her mind is in a most unsettled state, and attending to the constant fluctuation of it is far more harassing than the watching of those raving fits that had not the least tincture of reason. Her ideas are all disjointed, and a number of wild whims float on her imagination, and fall from her unconnectedly, something like strange dreams when judgment sleeps, and fancy sports at a fine rate. Don't smile at my language, for I am so constantly forced to observe her—lest she run into mischief—that my thoughts continually turn on the unaccountable wanderings of her mind. She seems to think she has been very ill used, and, in short, till I see some more favourable symptoms, I shall only suppose that her malady has assumed a new and more distressing appearance.
>
> . . . persons who recover from madness are generally in this way before they are perfectly restored, but whether Bess's faculties will ever regain their former tone, time only will show. At present I am in suspense. . . .
>
> M. W.
>
> . . . We have been out in a coach, but still Bess is far from being *well*. Patience—Patience.[6]

Mary was playing mother to Everina as well as Eliza. The younger girl complained obliquely of her own problems, and Mary checked her with affectionate firmness; one sister in trouble was enough:

Sunday

Averina

I have nothing to tell you that will give you pleasure—Bess is as usual—She has not slept for any length of time this two nights—

. . . in short we are much the same . . . I am really sorry to observe that you are not well—something I am persuaded preys on your mind besides our poor girl's illness—although you are so secret I leave you to time that sovereign alleviator of all griefs—have a little patience and some remedy will occur or you will cease to want it—I speak from experience—time has blunted the edge of many vexations that I once thought I could never bear—I have no hope nor do I endeavour to attain anything but composure of mind and that I expect to gain in some degree in spite of the storms and cross winds of life—A fair wind and a gentle stream will waft this . . . to you—There's a flourish and a pun.

Eliza gradually improved, probably due to time, Mary's presence, and the fact that Bishop perforce kept at some distance, and as her sister became more rational, Mary began to sort out reality from symptom. Eliza had married a man similar to her father; although he did not physically abuse his wife, he was emotional, childish, domineering, erratic—a lion or a spaniel, as one of his acquaintances told Mary. In addition, he seems to have been irrationally jealous. Eliza, unlike her mother, could not adjust. Although there is no way of knowing how long she had been unhappy, a year after her marriage she was terrified and repelled. Instead of acting with patience and self-restraint, Bishop insisted, as Eliza improved, that she live with him as before. He wanted his wife back; he loved her; their marriage vows and his rights tied them indissolubly at bed and board. Eliza frantically refused. Although Mary had no difficulty telling other people what to do, she apparently had too much conventional respect for Bishop's sex to attempt to advise him. Cooped up in the house day after miserable day, Mary soothed Eliza and held off Bishop. When thwarted he developed a low fever, appealing to his sister-in-law to sympathize and side with him. Mary became certain his behavior was incorrigible, since she identified him with her father, and for the same reason she was moved to the point of confusion by his emotion. He was persuasive. Hugh Skeys, who was in London, came to visit, but instead of consoling Mary he was taken over by Bishop. At Christmas, when the Bloods were going through a financial crisis, Mary preferred to borrow the needed £20 from Bishop instead of from Fanny's sweetheart. "He lent it very properly without any parade," Mary wrote Everina, "yet it made me miserable. I saw I was entangling myself with an *obligation*." At the beginning of the New Year, she could see no solution for the Bishop marriage:

Monday morning
January 6 [1784]

To Averina Wollstonecraft at
Mr. Wollstonecraft's, Katherine Street

I have nothing to tell you my dear girl that will give you pleasure—yesterday was a dismal day—long and dreary—Bishop was very ill *etc etc* He is much better today—but misery haunts this house in one shape or another—How sincerely do I join with you in saying that if a person has common sense they cannot make one completely unhappy. But to attempt to lead or govern a weak mind is impossible it will ever press forward to what it wishes regardless of impediments and with a selfish eagerness believe what it desires practicable tho' the contrary is as clear as the noon day—My spirits are harried with listening to pros and cons and my head is so confused that I sometimes say no when I ought to say yes—my heart is almost broken with listening to B. while he *reasons* the case—I cannot insult him with advice—which he would never have wanted if he was capable of attending to it. . . .

. . . B. has made a confident of Skey and as I can never speak to him in private I suppose his pity may cloud his judgment—if it does I should not either wonder at it or blame him—For I that know—and am fixed in my opinion cannot unswervingly adhere to it—and when I reason am afraid of being unfeeling.

Miracles don't occur now—and only a miracle can alter the minds of some people—they grow old and we can only discover by their countenance that they are so. To the end of the chapter will this misery last. . . .

. . . I expect Fanny next Thursday and she will stay with me but a few days—Bess desires her love—She grows better and of course more sad.

With Fanny due to arrive, Mary Wollstonecraft realized she had to proceed in one way or another. She could not stay with Eliza forever, and the desperate girl threw herself on her sister for salvation. She wanted to get away, even if she had to support herself, as Mary warned might happen. She could not bear to live with her husband. Divorce was completely impossible, separation difficult and shameful, for a wife who was responsible for separation was despised and shunned. The practical problems were crushing. Eliza would not function alone—where could she stay, how could she live?

Mary had thrown herself between father and mother; now she interposed between husband and wife. Convinced by Eliza's "extreme wretchedness," certain she would lose her reason permanently if forced to remain, perhaps to have another child, Mary decided to do what she had not been able to do as a child—to rescue Eliza. The ramifications of such an action were profoundly serious. It was equivalent to breaking a Commandment; a husband's rights over his wife were complete, and an unhappy wife admired to the extent she accepted her fate. Church and state upheld the canon. Mary felt both conviction and fear. She needed approval and turned to her brother Edward, as she called him, in this crisis. He was as close to a father as she had, despite their antagonism, and under his roof Eliza could take refuge with a degree of propriety. As she wrote Everina:

> I don't know what to do—Poor Eliza's situation almost turns my brain —I can't stay and see this continual misery—and to leave her to bear it by herself without any one to comfort her is still more distressing—I would do anything to rescue her from her present situation—My head is quite confused with thinking to so little purpose—I should have come over to you if I could have crossed the water—In this case something desperate must be determined on—do you think Edward would receive her do speak to him—or if you imagine that I should have more influence on [him] I will contrive to see you—but you must caution him against expostulating or even mentioning the affair to Bishop for it would only put him on his guard, and we should have a storm to encounter that I tremble to think of—I am convinced this is the only expedient to save Bess—and she declare she had rather be a teacher than stay here—I must again repeat it you must be secret nothing can be done till she leaves the house . . . I have been sometime deliberating on this—for I can't help pitying B. but misery must be his portion at any rate till he alters himself

> and that would be a miracle—To be at Edward's is not desirable but of the two evils she must chuse the least. . . .
>
> . . . if I did not see it was absolutely necessary I should not have fixed on it—I tell you she will soon be deprived of reason—B. cannot behave properly—and those who would attempt to reason with him must be mad or have very little observation—Those who would save Bess must act and not talk—

Ned refused to take Eliza in; he already had Everina and, by this time, Charles as well. However, he must have had sympathy for his sisters, for he did not betray their intention to Bishop. The responsibility was back to Mary Wollstonecraft. She moved quickly; "if we had stayed a day or two longer, I believe it would never have been effected. For Bess's mind was so harrassed with the fear of being discovered, and the thought of leaving the child, that she could not have stood it long." They could not take the baby, for by law Bishop was undisputed master of Eliza, her property, and her issue, and both women knew it.

On the morning of Saturday, January 18, 1784, two days after Fanny's arrival in London, the two friends secretly packed most of Eliza's clothes, a few of which Fanny took to a brushmaker in the Strand, while the bulk went to Ned's. When Bishop left the house, Mary and Eliza stole down the stairs, out the door, and into a hackney coach. "There was as much good luck as good management in it. As to Bess, she was so terrified, that she lost all presence of mind, and would have done anything . . . to make my trial still more dreadful I was afraid in the coach she was going to have one of her flights for she bit her wedding ring to pieces." They changed to a second coach to throw Bishop off the scent, and drove over the Thames across London to Hackney. Someone had reserved lodgings with a Mrs. Dodds in Church Street for "Miss Johnston." The sisters arrived exhausted, apprehensive, and distraught. Hastily, Mary wrote Everina at Ned's. She was quivering with guilt and fear:

> Here we are Averina, but my trembling hand will scarce let me tell you so—Bess is much more composed than I expected her to be . . . my heart beats time with every carriage that rolls by, and a knocking at the door almost throws me into a *fit*. . . . I hope B. will not discover us, for I could sooner face a Lion—yet the door never opens but I expect to see him panting for breath—Ask Ned how we are to behave if he should

find us out for Bess is determined not to return. Can he force her?—but I'll not suppose it—yet I can think of nothing else. She is sleepy and going to bed—my agitated mind will not permit me—Don't tell Charles or any creature—Oh!—let me entreat you to be careful, for Bess does not dread him now as much as I do. . . . Yours,

Mary

She looks now very wild. Heaven protect us!—I almost wish for a husband for I want somebody to support me.

Enclosed was a letter, "a very few proper lines" from Eliza to her husband. Meredith Bishop went straight to Ned's when he discovered his wife had fled. Mary had imagined that he would be wildly angry, alarming even to her brother: "B. would make a more determined person flinch," she said. Instead, he controlled himself and pleaded for Eliza's return for the child's sake if not his own. Everina sent this news on Sunday. The two fugitives by now were feeling the after effects of their trauma. "We have pains in all our limbs. My legs are swelled and I have got a complaint in my stomach etc. etc. etc." But neither would draw back.

Bess is tolerably well; she cannot help sighing about little Mary, whom she tenderly loved, and on this score I both love and pity her. The poor brat! It had got a little hold on my affections; sometime or other I hope we shall get it. . . . Tell our brother that Bess is fixed in her resolution of never returning; let what will be the consequence—And if a separate maintenance is not to be obtained, she'll try to earn her own bread.

Mary had got hold of herself. Only Bishop's unexpected dignity threw her off base, for it was easier to think of him as a brute than a sorrowful husband:

he will burst out at last, and the calm will end in the usual manner [or] he will tell a plausible tale, and the generality will pity him and blame me, but, however, if we can snatch Bess from extreme wretchedness, what reason shall we have to rejoice . . . the thought of having assisted to bring about so desirable an event, will ever give me pleasure. . . . I depend on you to keep Ned firm.

She was avid for news of what she now felt was a triumphant feat—"write to us an account of everything—you cannot be too particular"—

and began to take stock of practical matters. "Send us a few changes—We have neither chemise, handkerchief, or apron. . . . Bess begs you will lock up all the bundles till we know what to do—and the little trunk need not be opened."

Mary Wollstonecraft had acted in great excitement, with little thought of what the next step would be. Having left Bishop's with only three guineas, she and Eliza hoarded another ten Ned or Skeys provided, while they waited to find out what Bishop would do, and Ned tried to negotiate a separation and an allowance. Fanny Blood was distressed at Eliza's sorrow over her child and sent her young brother George to get news from Skeys, who continued to see Bishop and to be influenced by him. Mary also wrote Skeys, but was careful not to give him their address. The sisters remained holed up in their rooms for fear Bishop would discover them. As if to oblige Mary, he began to be difficult. She wrote Everina:

> What will be the issue of this affair 'tis impossible to say—but I am cheered with the hope that our poor girl will never again be in this man's power . . . my spirits do not sink, supported by conscious rectitude I smile at B's malice and almost thank him for it as it gives me fresh strength . . . Had he been only *unhappy* I should have felt some pain in acting with firmness for I hold the marriage vow sacred—but now I am not much disturbed by compassion—As to Skey I try to suspend my judgment with respect to his rather unkind behaviour—It would really give me pain to alter my opinion of him—The humane manner in which he exerted himself was not—could not be assumed it raised in my mind gratitude and esteem—and till I am convinced of the contrary I must think well of him. Tho' he is very *prudent* and a little stupid to be the dupe of B. . . . In his last letter he [Skeys] ventured to advise a reconciliation "that might be productive of perpetual happiness" . . . tho' a few days before he thought their was not the most distant prospect of comfort—and "that she would soon again fall into despair." . . . He said *poor B.* . . . "hoped he might succeed as he thought he would now endeavour to make Mrs. B. happy" . . . 'tis wonderful he could be so deceived . . . 'spite of the suspense Bess is more composed than I have seen her since her illness—that look of extreme wretchedness . . . when she was obliged to bear with B. is in some measure dissipated—but she complains of a headache which may arise from confinement and want of exercise—for we have never stirred.

Old friends offered assistance. Mr. Blood invited the girls to his home; Mrs. Clare came to see them in the rain as soon as she heard what had happened, offered them money, and sent "a pye and a bottle of wine." But Mary Wollstonecraft's "conscious rectitude" was troubled. "I have caught Bishop's complaint and have a little periodical fever that keeps me warm these cold nights," she told Everina. More serious, Eliza still manifested signs of her illness. At night she was restless, at least once irrational, and her original symptom of deafness returned for a time. Mary was frightened and all the more certain that she had done right. When it became clear that the sisters did not intend to recant, some friends gave them up and others, like Mrs. Clare, weakened. The more external pressure Mary felt, the more righteous she became; she wrote Everina:

> I knew I should be . . . the *shameful incendiary,* in this shocking affair of a woman's leaving her bed-fellow, they thought the strong affection of a sister *might* apologize for my conduct, but that the scheme was by no means a good one.

She was irritated with Everina, who was finding it difficult to bear up under criticism, and preached her a tiresome sermon about the warfare of life, the evils of gratification, and the peace imparted by "humbly" relying on God. The immediate drama culminates in a dismal dissertation sanctifying the heroine. It is Mary Wollstonecraft at her most unattractive, sure that God is on her side, even taking some sadistic pleasure in admonishing Everina that she had no right to expect happiness when people as worthy as her oldest sister were resigned to a gloomy existence.

Mary's predilection for the role of rescuer had its origins in her childhood; she was obviously replaying that drama and was frightened by her sacrilegious success. Eliza's choice of a man so similar to Edward John Wollstonecraft, and Mary's ambivalence toward that man, make the family connection complete. Mary trembled at first at what she had done and then justified herself with exaggerated righteousness, also because she was dutiful to the code of the time including the dominance of men and husbands. In fact, as she told Everina, she believed marriage to be a sacrament of the Anglican faith she devoutly professed and formally observed. Mary was not attacking the system or the tyranny of men in general during the Bishop episode, nor did she for several years. She simply reacted to Eliza's particular emergency. In her first book, written two years after the separation, she wrote that "a sensible delicate woman, who by some strange accident or mistake, is joined to a fool or a brute, must be wretched beyond all names of wretchedness," but advised such unhappy wives to resign themselves and find solace in intellectual pursuits and religion.[7] If Mary had not been acutely aware and frightened of Eliza's frailty and incapacity for resignation, demonstrated so terribly, she would have urged her, as she often did with sturdier Everina, to make the best of a bad situation.

In our terms, the villain of the piece is the social mores and the laws of the time, which made it impossible to remedy serious incompatibility decently. The sisters' hope for custody of Eliza's child and separation with financial support was wishful thinking or ignorance. The law was clear: if a husband ill-treated his wife or forced her to leave him, he could be made to support her:

> but if she runs away from him, and he is willing that she abide in his house, he is not liable to give her any separate maintenance . . . if at any time he offers to be reconciled and to take her home, upon her refusal, he shall not any longer be obliged to pay her.[8]

Eliza's child, by law, belonged to Bishop, as did the small annuity she probably brought to her marriage. She could not even see the child without his consent. If Eliza had been able to prove cruelty, Bishop might possibly have been ordered to support her, but by contemporary standards, which neither Mary nor Eliza questioned at this time, he, not she, was the injured party. The only way to obtain absolute divorce was by act of Parliament; such actions, few and far between, were brought only by wealthy and influential husbands against wives. It is no wonder Bishop wanted his wife back, since without great expense and effort he could not marry again while she was alive. Eliza by now wanted no more marriage to anyone. In fact, she was lucky Bishop did not drag her back by force, which he probably could have done.

This episode is one of the most controversial in Mary Wollstonecraft's career. Godwin omitted it from the *Memoirs* probably to protect Eliza. He mentioned only that Mary attended Eliza's "dangerous lying-in," and he mistook the date for 1782 instead of 1783. Eliza had been married fourteen months by January of 1784, ample time to know what she felt and to take some responsibility for the decision. With all her uninhibited complaints in later years, Eliza never gave any indication in any extant letter that she regretted her separation. She was sarcastic on the subject two years later. "I cannot make myself understood here," she wrote Everina from a girls' school in 1786. "Their only amusement [is praying] not forgetting eating, and marrying and so on—The idea of parting from a *husband* one could never make them comprehend, I'd sooner persuade them that a stove might speak." "Mrs. B. may smile," Mary wrote of a loving couple in 1790, knowing Eliza would sneer, "but still I must tell her that in this House she would find domestic felicity, and see caresses pure."[9]

It is also significant that the only negative reaction Ned expressed was to refuse to take Eliza back into his household. He did not tip off Bishop in advance about the escape, and after did his best to negotiate a settlement for her from Bishop. He did "hold firm" as Mary hoped. There is no evidence that he wanted to make Eliza return to her husband, as Hugh Skeys thought might be best, and if Ned had made such a suggestion Mary would surely have remarked on it to Everina at the time. The one thing Ned seems not to have wanted was to take personal responsibility for Eliza, particularly permanent financial responsibility.

The alternative to separation was for Eliza to remain with Bishop. There is reason to believe she could not have borne her marriage, for she continued to be so fragile that Mary worried about her for years; once freed at least she never broke down again. Mary may have had another fear; if her brother Henry had suffered a permanent breakdown, she had reason to take action to prevent the second manifestation of insanity in her family.

Mary Wollstonecraft's part in the separation therefore can be justified. She acted with cause and in character. "I would have people consult their own heart only, and if conscience does not check them, act with vigor and dignity—as St. Paul would advise, and not be conformed to the world," she wrote later.[10] Bishop returned to his home and child resigned to separation; he seems to have pursued his wife no further. But he had neither intention nor legal obligation to support Eliza as long as she refused to return to him. The fact Eliza got no allowance is proof that she would not put herself in that position. She was free—to starve. For Mary Wollstonecraft, the crisis escalated her insistence on exercising her own judgment in lieu of society's: she had carried through a drastic act after which others would come easily. In another way the affair was even more decisive. Although Eliza was well again by mid-February, she was now dependent for her daily bread on Mary. Inadvertently, and with a new responsibility, Mary Wollstonecraft had opened a door to the self-supporting life she had tried to find with Fanny Blood.

Chapter 7

Since 1780 Mary Wollstonecraft had wanted to make an independent life with Fanny Blood. Now in the early months of 1784 she had no intention of relinquishing the opportunity for independence created by Eliza's separation from Bishop. "Mr. Blood sent us an invitation to come to his house," she wrote Everina from Hackney, "but we did not accept." Substituting Eliza for Fanny in her plans, she even considered taking her sister to Ireland, where the scandal of her flight from Bishop would be remote, although this might have meant leaving Fanny. "My sister Mary was at that time extremely fond of Eliza," Everina said bitterly years later when the sisters were estranged.[1] As a victim she had rescued, Eliza elicited Mary's tenderness and commitment; as a valid dependent and responsibility, Eliza freed Mary to set out on the course Fanny had resisted.

The problem of independent subsistence was less dramatic than the escape from Bishop, but scarcely less difficult. "We have been racking our brains and cannot yet fix on any feasible plan," Mary told Everina, now acutely aware that her funds were dwindling and that Bishop was unlikely to make Eliza an allowance. Genteel women who lacked the proper refuge—attachment to a household headed by a male protector or accommodating patron—were in a most unfortunate situation: if they could find some way to eke out a living they were threatened with loss of caste; if they were unable to maintain themselves they could end in the workhouse—or worse. While Mary was in Bath, local papers carried the story of a young woman of Eliza's background—genteel family, Chelsea boarding school education—who, on her father's death, was forced to become a seamstress, was drugged and seduced, became Lord Sandwich's mistress, and ended murdered by a "suitor."[2]

Mary Wollstonecraft first thought of opening "a school or a little shop." "I wish you would sound Ned," she asked Everina, for he was her only source of capital for any venture. Apparently he gave her little encouragement. After Mary and Eliza had been shut up in their Hackney room for a month, Fanny Blood was so distressed at their plight she revived Mary's old plan that they live together on art and needlework. Mary would have preferred a school like Jane Arden's, but "the *monies* did not answer," and the possibility of a home with Fanny in any decent enterprise was irresistible. In mid-February she wrote Everina, attaching a formal proposal for Ned's consideration:

> My dear girl read the enclosed before you look at this, and in it you will find an account of a plan that Bess' melancholy situation retarded—I have maturely considered of it and determined to attempt it. . . . With economy we can live on a guinea a week, and that we can with ease earn. The lady who gave Fanny five guineas for two drawings will assist us and we shall be independent. . . . If Ned makes us a little present of furniture it will be acceptable, but if he is prudent, we must try to do without it.

Fanny's affection, however, had momentarily overcome her awareness of the impracticality of this pitiful expedient, which Mary, in her overeagerness, thought so mature. Lamenting her "folly and inconsideration," Fanny begged Ned (through Everina, for she was afraid to write him directly) not to desert his sisters because of his persistent antipathy to herself and declared she would withdraw rather than jeopardize their chance for a "refuge from poverty":

> Waltham Green, February 18th, 1784
>
> My Dear Everina—
> The situation of our two poor girls grows ever more and more desperate —My mind is tortured about them because I cannot see any possible resource they have for a maintenance. . . . The letter I last night received from Mary disturbed me so much that I never since closed my eyes. . . . I find she wrote to her brother informing him that it was

our intention to live all together, and earn our bread by painting and needlework, which gives me great uneasiness, as I am convinced that he will be displeased at his sister's being connected with me, and the forfeiting his favor at this time is of the utmost consequence. I believe it was I that first proposed of the plan, and in my eagerness to enjoy the society of two so dear to me, I did not give myself time to consider that it is utterly impracticable. The very utmost I could earn . . . supposing I had uninterrupted health, is half-a-guinea a week, which would just pay for furnished lodgings for *three* people to pig together. . . . As for needlework, it is utterly impossible they could earn more than half-a-guinea a week between them, supposing they had constant employment, which is of all things the most uncertain. . . . I will venture to mention to you one plan Mrs. Clare lately proposed . . . a little shop of haberdashery and perfumery, in the neighborhood of Hoxton, where they may be certain of meeting encouragement. Such a shop may be entirely furnished for 50£, a sum which I should suppose might be raised for them if it was mentioned to your brother. However, lest he should be averse . . . from a notion that I should live with them . . . I wish you would take the earliest opportunity of assuring him from me *that on no account whatever will I ever live with them unless fortune should make me quite independent*, which I never expect. My health is now so much impaired that I should be only a burthen on them. . . .

F. Blood

Mary Wollstonecraft must have realized Fanny's fears were justified, for she reverted to her original preference. Godwin says simply, "The project upon which she now determined was no other than that of a day-school, to be superintended by Fanny Blood, herself, and her two sisters." It was the one possible vocation that offered scope to her intellect and ideals. Three years before, when Jane Arden started a similar school in Bath, Mary had written, "your employment tho' a troublesome one, is very necessary, and you have an opportunity of doing much good, by instilling good principles into the young and ignorant, and at the close of life you'll have the pleasure to think that you have not lived in vain."[3] Poor Eliza. When she had declared she had rather be a teacher than stay with Bishop, she was postulating the most dismal alternative she could conceive of. As for Fanny, she could not back out now, for her artistic skills were an asset to attract pupils, and she had put herself in a position where she could not have refused Mary had she wanted to.

The project required more than determination. Mary Wollstonecraft got active assistance, probably including a loan, from a Mrs. Sarah Burgh and her nephew, Mr. Church, who lived in the attractive suburb of Newington Green at the northern edge of London. How Mary met Mrs. Burgh is not known—possibly it was through the Clares—but the sponsorship of this lady was of crucial importance. Widow of the master of a Dissenting Academy who had been a "moral and political writer" worthy of inclusion in Andrew Kippis' *Biographia Britannica*, Mrs. Burgh was a woman "of excellent sense and character, who zealously concurred with him in promoting all his . . . undertakings." She had been a widow when she married Burgh in 1751 and was evidently competent and vigorous. (Burgh advised husbands who had differences with their wives to remember, "that woman is the Weaker Vessel, and that it is for the most part a sign of superior judgment to yield to the Weaker in Matters of Inferior Consequence."[4] One can imagine that this "Weaker Vessel" had a good deal to say as to which were "Matters of Inferior Consequence.") Without Mrs. Burgh's connections it is unlikely that Mary could have become what she did, no matter what her talents and motivation. Call it luck, that sometime reward for spirit, drive, and readiness, which attracted and attached Mrs. Burgh to Mary Wollstonecraft like a veritable fairy godmother.

On Mrs. Burgh's advice, Mary, Eliza, and Fanny first rented lodgings and solicited pupils in Islington, near Mrs. Burgh's home. However no applicants seem to have appeared. Mrs. Burgh then persuaded Mary to move to Newington Green, where she herself lived, and through her exertions some twenty scholars entered the new school in the space of two or three weeks.

Here Mary Wollstonecraft formed associations that changed her life. When she settled at Newington Green she found herself in an atmosphere of liberalism and intellectual distinction that imparted advanced ideas, attitudes, and aspirations she had scarcely been able to articulate before. The area, which included nearby Hoxton where she had previously lived, was an educational center for Protestant nonconformists around which an enlightened and distinguished community was established. The most eminent citizen of Newington Green was Mrs. Burgh's close friend Dr. Richard Price, a famous philosopher, economist, Presbyterian clergyman, and political progressive who knew and corresponded with leading thinkers of his day, men like Joseph Priestley, Benjamin Franklin, Turgot, and Pitt. Two houses down from Price lived Thomas Rogers, a liberal banker whose sons Burgh had taught; one son, Samuel Rogers, became a poet and art patron and later knew Percy and Mary Shelley.

Richard Price was sixty-two when Mary Wollstonecraft met and became close to him in 1784. He was profoundly religious in the same spirit as Mary, who believed in a God "not less amiable, generous and kind, than great, wise and exalted." Although she was a devout Anglican, Mary sometimes went to hear Price preach at the local Presbyterian congregation, where Samuel Rogers remembered seeing her in the pew next to his family's. She was moved by Price, "this respectable old man, in his pulpit," as she described him, "praying with all the simple energy of unaffected piety." However she retained some distaste for Dissenters as a group; "prim littleness . . . cunning" were attributes she assigned them. She thought their meetinghouses "mean," for she was responsive all her life, even after she gave up its rites, to the beauty of Anglican monuments and ceremonies, which she felt added "wings to devotion."[5]

Price's philosophy and political beliefs had a more important influence on Mary Wollstonecraft. She had lived through the American Revolution, the Gordon Riots, agitation for parliamentary reform, without any recorded indication of interest, and there is reason to believe that at that time she substantially accepted the status quo. But everything in her nature and experience responded to Price's views, the liberal platform of the period. Price's faith in progress and perfectability was as devout as his religion, on which it was based. The year Mary Wollstonecraft arrived at Newington Green he interpreted the successful American Revolution in that light:

> Reason, as well as tradition and revelation, lead us to expect that a more improved and happy state of human affairs will take place before the consummation of all things. The world has hitherto been gradually improving. . . . Such are the natures of things that this progress must continue. During particular intervals it may be interrupted, but it cannot be destroyed. . . . There can scarcely be a more pleasant and encouraging object of reflection than this.

Price was a reformer and a libertarian. In supporting the American Revolution he had issued the British a call to conscience, advocating:

> *Physical Liberty* . . . *Spontaneity,* or *Self-Determination* . . .
>
> *Moral Liberty* . . . the power of following, in all circumstances, our sense of right or wrong.
>
> *Religious Liberty* . . . exercising, without molestation, that mode of religion which we think best. . . .
>
> *Civil Liberty* . . . the power of a . . . State to govern itself by its own discretion.

It was a consistent, immediately impressive philosophy for Mary Wollstonecraft, particularly the emphasis on God-given reason, enabling man to find the right in his own conscience and to govern himself. "I have been the object of censure for actions which I consider as some of the best of my life. . . . But being conscious that I have meant well . . . the censure . . . has made no impression on me."[6] It is Price speaking of the abuse he suffered for his political positions, but it could be Mary Wollstonecraft defending her part in Eliza's flight from her husband. Price's interests were as broad as those of his friend Benjamin Franklin, and he enjoyed instructing young people. Intellectually and emotionally he became for Mary her model, teacher, and protector—a benign and superior successor to men like Arden and Clare.

Mary Wollstonecraft was evidently considered by many to be a young woman of unusual substance and charm, for not long after she came to Newington Green some member of the area's elite took her to meet Dr. Samuel Johnson, and the introduction was not made through Price. The "Grand Old Man" of English letters was a vehement conservative and refused to meet Price, Priestley, Wilkes, and their ilk. Johnson was old and seriously ill at this time, but he had always loved bright young women. He had a long conversation with Mary and asked her to come to see him again, which she was anxious to do. Unfortunately, he died in November of 1784, before the visit could be repeated.

Mary Wollstonecraft could not have settled into a more rewarding situation. Her school was at first a success. She was an ardent educator, unfortunate for some of her personal relationships but fundamental in her character. As early as her Windsor days she had definite ideas about what was wrong with conventional education, and at Newington Green she developed her convictions further. Morals, not manners, were her concern. Godwin says she also "had the talent of being attentive and obliging to the parents without degrading herself." If so, she exerted great self-control. "Parents have mostly some weighty business in hand, which they make a pretext to themselves for neglecting the arduous task of educating their children," she wrote. "They are therefore sent to school, and the allowance for them is so low, that the person who undertakes the charge must have more than she can possibly attend to; of course the mechanical parts of education only can be observed." Music, drawing, geography, English—the routine curriculum—were what she had to deliver. She should have been able to offer French as well, for that language was a prerequisite for a superior school. Parental expectations annoyed her; "A teacher at school is only a kind of upper servant, who has more work than the menial ones," she wrote. She, at least, was headmistress.

The school was set up in style. Everina recalled:

> a relation, a Mrs. Campbell, and her little son came to board with them; this success, and the addition of another lady and her three children, induced Mary to take a larger house, the expense of which, and the disappointment about boarders, involved her in some difficulties. She could not get paid for the board of the three children, and the Green was too small a place to allow the day-school to be any considerable object.[7]

Mary Wollstonecraft's confidence, ambition, and sense of what her class position demanded led her to take the larger house, which obligated her for a burdensome rent and several servants; the housekeeper was a Miss Mason. Mary soon found herself in trouble over money. Not only had she borrowed to open her school, but she had to keep borrowing—from Mrs. Burgh, Church, and others—as well as to stave off tradesmen. In addition to her normal expenses she included so many people in the category of her responsibility that she was constantly short of funds. She sent money regularly to her father in Wales, whom Ned kept on short rations, and she was supporting Eliza, Everina, who had left Ned's to join her sisters, and Fanny Blood. Fanny's family had moved to or near Newington Green, and depended heavily on Mary, who often paid their bills. Like her father Mary thought of money as a means rather than an end, and since she liked to manage people, they leaned on her.

The other side of generosity's coin, like pity's, was a demanding and critical nature. As Godwin wrote:

> Mary had a quickness of temper . . . which led her to look into the minds of her acquaintance, and to approve or be displeased. . . . She was occasionally severe and imperious in her resentments; and, when she strongly disapproved, was apt to express her censure in terms that gave a very humiliating sensation to the person against whom it was directed. Her displeasure . . . assumed its severest form . . . when it was barbed by disappointment.[8]

Godwin spoke from intimate experience. Mary's "disappointment," no matter how much one sympathizes with her problems, is a constant and irritating refrain. She, her sisters, and Fanny were together, as she had so devoutly wished, yet a year or so later Mary wrote, "I have often thought that it might be set down as a maxim, that the greatest disappointment we can meet with is the gratification of our fondest wish."

In early August, 1784, about five months after the school was established, Eliza's baby daughter died in London. This tragedy must have stricken the unfortunate young mother, who after her separation from Bishop probably never again saw anything of her baby but its small coffin. However, Eliza does not seem to have blamed Mary or herself, and in no extant letter thereafter is the child mentioned. But after a year of living together, there was conflict between the women of Mary's household. Eliza was either full of the miseries, loved "a dismal tale," as Fanny Blood said, or was childishly flippant, inattentive, and incompetent. Everina, very young in her late teens to have given up a normal girl's life, was high spirited, restive under routine and responsibility. "Eliza turns up her nose and ridicules," Mary wrote, "and as to Everina I can neither *love* or *hate* her—or to use a softer word, [am] indifferent to her." Eliza and Everina both regretted their former genteel status, and both were understandably jealous of Fanny, who tried to assuage their resentment as if they were children. She once wrote them: "Bess—a jealous baggage!—for saying I would not value her love when she sent it.—As for Everina, she knew me better . . . come, we'll kiss and be friends again—for I know you love me a little bit after all; and you ought to know that I love you too."

In this ménage Mary dominated. Godwin said:

> a disproportionate share of every burthen . . . fell to her lot. On the other hand [Eliza and Everina] could scarcely perhaps be perfectly easy,

in observing the superior degree of deference and courtesy, which her merit extorted from almost every one that knew her.[9]

Fanny must have been the buffer in what Mary feelingly described as "those trivial disputes that slowly corrode domestic peace, and insensibly destroy what great misfortunes could not sweep away." Mary expected her sisters to conform to her wishes in every detail, even at breakfast. She said: "I have often felt hurt, not to say disgusted, when a friend has appeared, whom I parted with full dressed the evening before, with her clothes huddled on, because she chose to indulge herself till the last moment."[10]

The most ominous problem was Fanny Blood's worsening health, "materially injured by her incessant labours for the maintenance of her family," and her frustrated love for Hugh Skeys, according to Godwin. She had developed critically serious tuberculosis, and her doctors advised her to move to a warmer climate, a financial impossibility. Toward the end of 1784, Skeys, who was in business in Lisbon, at last wrote a proposal of marriage to Fanny. "It was not," Godwin says, "a time at which it was most obvious to think of marriage," and Fanny naturally hesitated. But Mary, although she realized her friend might be fatally ill, was determined "that nothing should be omitted, which might alleviate, if it would not cure; and accordingly urged her speedy acceptance of the proposal." Godwin makes no mention of what Fanny's parents advised. "Fanny accordingly made the voyage to Lisbon; and the marriage took place on the twenty-fourth of February, 1785," less than a year after Fanny had joined Mary in what was to have been a permanent home for both.[11]

Deprivation of Fanny Blood was a fixative to Mary Wollstonecraft's sense of grievance and self-pity. Through all her previous troubles since she was sixteen she had had Fanny to love; at twenty-six she perceived herself as a victim of misfortune almost unmitigated since birth, deserving sympathy and redress, and this conviction remained with her almost until the end of her life.

After Fanny Blood's departure, she labored under depression and physical symptoms that persisted with some remissions for two and a half years. "True love is warmest when the object is absent," she wrote George Blood of his sister, and she often referred to her own death as an escape. Without Fanny she lived with grief, loneliness, and futility, tormented by anger that made her even more critical. She found flaws in almost every relationship, and it was always someone else's fault. She was fond of Mrs. Burgh's nephew, "the humane *rational* Church," although she complained that she saw him only in the company of "tattling females," that is to say, her sisters; she had a true friend in John Hewlett, a young Anglican clergyman and scholar, but found his wife haughty, disagreeable, and possessive—"poor tender friendly soul how he is yoked." Mrs. Blood was sweet but limited; for Mr. Blood she had nothing but contempt. She saw the Clares in nearby Hoxton until she quarreled with them over George Blood. This younger brother of Fanny was one of the few on whom Mary had settled her affections with simple acceptance and generosity. Almost all her letters of this period were written to him, for in June of 1785 he had to flee Newington Green for Dublin under a cloud. He was accused of getting a servant girl pregnant, an act which George denied and Mary took in a cavalier way; at this point in her life she was convinced servants were sly and often base. Others took it more seriously. Mary had hidden George in her house, given him money, and secreted him into a coach going west, a story Mary's cousin and boarder, Mrs. Campbell, indignantly spread all over Newington Green. Mary was severely criticized for helping George; Mrs. Campbell claimed she had encouraged his "vices." In fact, Mary Wollstonecraft seems to have responded like a mother who takes some pride in her son's masculine adventures, although she also had absolute trust in his loving and faithful nature. She defended him with hauteur against one of the village ladies. "She would have scolded me in the true vulgar female style—if I had not assumed the Princess," she wrote George, using the nickname he had given her:

> Can you for a moment, believe that I am changed? No, I am not a fair weather friend—on the contrary, I think I love most people best when they are in adversity—for pity is one of my prevailing passions. . . . I am not fond of possessions—yet, once for all, let me assure you that I have a mother's tenderness for you, and that my heart dances when I make any new discovery of *goodness* in you.

She advised, encouraged, and mothered him; he returned her devotion, shared her attitudes, and was the confidant of her sorrows. After George's departure, Mary wrote him frequently:

July 3 [1785]

I have been very ill, and gone through the usual physical operations, *have been bled and blistered*, yet still am not well;—my harrassed mind will in time wear out my body.—I have been so hunted down by cares, and see so many that I must encounter, that my spirits are quite depressed.—I have lost all relish for life, and my almost broken heart is only cheered by the prospect of death.—I may be years a-dying tho', and so ought to be patient, for at this time to wish myself away would be selfish. . . . Nothing pleases me. . . . Adieu to the village delights. I almost hate the Green, for it seems the grave of all my comforts. . . .

July 20

My spirits are fled and I am incapable of joy. I have no creature to be unreserved to. Eliza and Everina are so different that I could as soon fly as open my heart to them. . . . My heart—my affection cannot fix here and without some one to love this world is a desert to me.

She resented Hugh Skeys bitterly:

July 25

Skeys has received congratulatory letters from most of his friends and relations in Ireland, and he now regrets that he did not marry sooner . . . he might have spared Fanny many griefs, the scars of which will never be obliterated.—Nay more, if she had gone a year or two ago, her health might have been *perfectly* restored, which I do not now think will ever be the case.

In Portugal Fanny too was suffering. A month after her marriage she forced herself out of an acute "depression of spirits" to write Eliza and Everina. It was more imaginary than real distress, she said, but she had in fact been very ill, coughing and spitting blood. Her doctor had advised her to move from the country into town, where she improved enough to go into society. Skeys was kind and attentive to his wife, Fanny wrote, and even encouraged her to flirt with his friends.

Although Fanny was obviously too sick to have a child safely, such birth control as there was at the time was unheard of for a decent English couple. Fanny became pregnant shortly after her marriage and wrote Mary of her condition in July. Mary wrote George on the twenty-fifth: "Skeys is quite delighted with the prospect, but Fanny is out of spirits, and tired with contending with sickness and care." In mid-August Mary told George, "I wait in vain for good news—she is still very ill and low spirited, a poor solitary creature—and here I am still tied by the leg and cannot go to her."

However, Mary Wollstonecraft was making plans to get to Lisbon to be with Fanny when her child was born. She was fearful Fanny might die during a childbirth certain to be more dangerous than most. If anything could save her, Mary would; at least she would see her, and George as well, for whom Skeys had found a job. She had no money for an expensive trip. She knew the school was in trouble; the indignant Mrs. Campbell and her children had left, as had the housekeeper, Miss Mason, and although Everina had begun to take hold, the task of managing the school for many weeks with only Eliza's inadequate help was beyond her. Mary felt she had to provide for the Bloods, too. Her friends condemned the project as rash, selfish, and extravagant, but she was determined and somewhat revivified. She wrote George Blood September 4:

> I have many difficulties to overcome—yet I am not intimated, tho' almost worried to death—your father is still unprovided for, but I shall endeavour so to manage matters that they may not feel any distress during my absence—for return I must to this delightful spot—my spirits are very much harried [by] vexations and disappointments. . . . Church tells me I shall never thrive in this world—and I believe he is right—I every day grow more and more proficient in that kind of knowledge which renders the world distasteful to me—Well, well, but we'll meet at Lisbon and talk over our past griefs.

Evidently Mary's love and loyalty for Fanny were so poignant as to be irresistible—"I am grown quite meek and forebearing," she wrote George. Mrs. Burgh finally made the journey possible with a loan Mary always believed actually came from the benevolent Price. Since Fanny's child was due in January, Mary left for Lisbon in early November of 1785. Her first sea voyage was rough, but exciting to her. Going south across the Bay of Biscay, the prevailing north wind builds heavy following seas—a most uncomfortable course. Mary wrote her sisters:

> We had such hard gales of wind, the Capt. was afraid we should be dismasted. . . . We were only thirteen days at sea—The wind was so high and the sea so boisterous, the water came in at the cabin windows, and the ship rolled about in such a manner, it was dangerous to stir. The women were sea-sick the whole time.

In the creaking cabin a poor consumptive, reminding Mary of Fanny, coughed and gasped for breath through the nights. Mary, unlike "the women," spent hours on deck enjoying wind and waves. Having had little contact with the lower classes except for servants, she was fascinated by the raucous but fearless sailors, who impressed her as being a strange, not quite human breed.

Exhilarated by her own forward motion, Mary was hopeful for Fanny; but reality at Lisbon was grim:

> My dear Girls—I am beginning to awake out of a terrifying dream, for in that light do the transactions of these two or three last days appear . . . when I arrived here, Fanny was in labour . . . four hours after she was delivered of a boy—The child is alive and well, and considering the *very very* low state to which Fanny was reduced, she is better than could be expected. I am now watching her and the child . . . I cannot write tonight, or collect my scattered thoughts, my mind is so unsettled —Fanny is so worn out, her recovery would be almost a resurrection, and my reason will scarce allow me to think it possible. I *labour* to be resigned, and by the time I am a little so, some *faint* hope sets my thoughts again afloat, and for a moment I look forward to days that will, alas! I fear, never come.
>
> . . . Was not my arrival providential? I can scarce be persuaded that I am here, and that so many things have happened in so short a time. My head grows light with thinking on it.
>
> Wednesday night
>
> Friday morning:—Fanny has been so exceedingly ill since I wrote the above, I entirely gave her up, and yet I *could not* write and tell you so; it seemed like *signing her death warrant.* Yesterday afternoon some of the most alarming symptoms a little abated, and she had a comfortable night; yet I rejoice with trembling lips, and am afraid to indulge hopes; she is very low. The stomach is so weak it will scarce bear to receive the slightest nourishment. . . . The child, tho' a puny one, is well. I have got a wet-nurse for it. . . . I shall write by every opportunity . . . I am tolerably well—and calmer than I could expect to be. Could I not look for comfort where only 'tis to be found, I should have been mad before this—but I feel that I am supported by that Being—who alone can heal a wounded spirit—May He bless you both.

Fanny Blood Skeys died November 29, 1785, shortly after this letter. Her premature baby died soon after. Mary Wollstonecraft had seen her mother die, yet Fanny's was the death she recalled as the most tragic; "Death in all its terrors, when it attacks a friend," she wrote. Because Catholic Portugal forbade heretical burials, Fanny, an Anglican, was buried "by stealth and in darkness," a macabre coda.[12]

Mary Wollstonecraft stayed in Lisbon several weeks. The shock of Fanny's loss was somewhat dulled by the exotic surroundings of her first foreign visit. William Beckford, who arrived there two years after, described the packs of dogs prowling Lisbon's streets, "gobbling up all that falls from the windows"; the dust, racket, beggars, bugs, dunghills, "rotten shoes, dead cats, and negro beldames . . . reading fortunes." "The Inquisition" he added, "often lays hold of these wretched sybils . . . whose howlings struck me with horror." But he enjoyed Lisbon's magnificent gardens, palaces, and grandees. Mary Wollstonecraft, an excellent tourist in the British tradition, was more interested in the moral condition of Portugal than its baroque. Such contrast between poverty and opulence appalled her, as did Latin sexuality—"the lustful prowler," duennas, seductions, and debauchery; it was a grotesque caricature of the English code. Catholicism fascinated and repelled her; she had the Protestant's uneasy attraction to Roman pageantry, was even ravished to tears by the beauty of Church music. But the Anglican ethic reasserted itself. The convents she found rife with intrigue, a selfish retreat from making the world better, a denial of the example Christ set. "The pattern of all goodness went about *doing* good," says the heroine of *Mary* during her visit to Portugal.[13]

Mary Wollstonecraft was not comfortable with the small British colony of businessmen, invalids, and tourists in Lisbon, and especially not with Hugh Skeys. To her he had all the petty faults of a tradesman, including a tight fist. If it occurred to him that his wife's friend had gone into debt to come to her deathbed, he did not feel he had any obligation to relieve her. "Delicacy made me conceal from him my dismal situation, but he must know how much I am embarrassed," Mary wrote. She did ask Skeys for money for Fanny's parents, but could not bring herself to tell him she herself was partially supporting them. He promised to send them a modest sum, and, somewhat inadequately, a roll of dress material waiting clearance at the custom house to Mary. Neither money nor material ever arrived.

There was nothing to stay for. Both Mary and young George

Blood left Portugal about December 20, he for Dublin, she for the dreariness of work and responsibility in England. Sailing in the teeth of a violent storm, which she described in *Mary,* her voyage

> accorded with the present state of her soul. . . . The squalls rattled amongst the sails, which were quickly taken down; the wind would then die down, and the wild undirected waves rushed on every side with a tremendous roar. In a little vessel in the midst of such a storm she was not dismayed; she felt herself independent. . . . stowed between two casks, and leaning on a sail, she watched.

The novel *Mary* omitted a dramatic scene that Godwin reported in the *Memoirs.* Mary's ship came on a foundering French vessel whose captain begged to be taken aboard, but the English master absolutely refused to strain his own ship and provisions. Mary bearded him, threatened to expose him, forced him to relent, and helped the terrified Frenchmen as they struggled onto a safe deck. Her own life had been in danger; even the sailors "believed the world was going to be at an end." The excitement swept her into a rhapsodic reaffirmation of faith in God's support and the certainty of happiness in afterlife with Fanny. She slept in peace that night, she said in the partial account in *Mary.*[14]

The return passage took a full month. Mary Wollstonecraft landed in the dead of winter, passed through London, which, after the glare of whitewashed Lisbon and the clean cold expanses of the seas, seemed hateful to her, and arrived at Newington Green. She had the bittersweet relief of sharing her grief and adventure with her sisters and Fanny's parents, but no respite from care.

She realized that her school was done for. In every direction she saw failure, futility, and misery. She wrote George Blood February 4:

> Your father and mother are tolerably well . . . I am very unhappy on their account, for tho' I am determined they shall share my last shilling, yet I have every reason to apprehend extreme distress, and of course they must be involved in it—The school dwindles to nothing, and we shall soon lose our last boarder, Mrs. Disney—She and the girls quarrelled while I was away, which contributed to make the house very disagreeable —Her sons are to be whole boarders at Mrs. Cockburn's—Let me turn my eyes on which side I will, I can only anticipate misery—Are such prospects as these likely to heal an almost broken heart—The loss of Fanny was sufficient of itself to have thrown a cloud over my brightest

> days—what effect then must it have, when I am bereft of every other comfort—I have too many debts—I cannot think of remaining any longer in this house, the rent is so enormous, and where to go, without money or friends, who can point out—My eyes are very bad and my memory gone, I am not fit for any situation, and as for Eliza, I don't know what will become of her—My constitution is impaired, I hope I shan't live long, yet, I may be a tedious time dying—
>
> Well, I am too impatient—The will of Heaven be done! . . . I have received a very short, unsatisfactory letter from Lisbon . . . to apologize for not sending the money to your father which he promised.

George Blood replied immediately that he had found work in Dublin through a friend of Fanny's whom Mary knew and liked, Betty Delane. Now in a position to help Mary support his parents, he urged her to leave England and her creditors behind and join him in Dublin. She and the girls could open a school there, make a fresh start. This she refused to do, although she knew she could be jailed for debt if worse came to worst. "My creditors have a right to do what they please with me, should I not be able to satisfy their demands," she told George. She was hanging on at the school, unable to see any way of avoiding a crash, guilty and frightened about what would happen to Eliza and Everina:

> I cannot even guess what the girls will do. My brother, I am sure, will not receive them, and they are not calculated to struggle with the world . . . as to your father and mother . . . I earnestly wished to see them settled before I went to *rest*. Indeed, I am far from being well. I have a pain in my side, and a whole train of nervous complaints. . . . My spirits are very, very low . . . so opprest by continual anxiety 'tis a labour to me to do anything. . . . If something decisive was to happen I should be better, but 'tis this suspense, this dread of I cannot tell what, which harasses me.

While she was in this mood, seemingly hardly able to function, providence manifested itself in the form of John Hewlett and her own latent energy. Her actions always spoke louder than her words; given the opportunity, her natural vitality and drive took over. Hewlett had suggested to her previously that she might make money by writing. He himself was about to publish his sermons through Joseph Johnson, and he urged her again to use her experience to write about education. During March and April of 1786, Mary Wollstonecraft wrote her first book, *Thoughts on the Education of Daughters: with Reflections on Female Conduct, in the More Important Duties of Life.*

Thoughts on the Education of Daughters is distinctively Mary Wollstonecraft, based on her specific experience, interpreting life as she saw it, making palpable her personality and philosophy. It is the seedling from which *A Vindication of the Rights of Woman* grew. She wrote very fast, as she was almost always to do, and mostly in the first person, ranging from tart assurance to emotional, self-revelatory description and extensive moralism and religiosity. Free of the self-conscious literary style she used later when she considered herself an author, the book reads as if Mary were speaking spontaneously to her audience: parents first, but influential people of her class as well.

The general philosophy is that of Locke and the liberals. Mary Wollstonecraft had also read and approved William Buchan, James Burgh, Mrs. Barbauld, Mrs. Chapone, and Richard Price. The latter had recently written, "So much is left by the author of nature to depend on the turn given the mind in early life, that I have often thought there may be a secret remaining to be discovered in education, which will cause future generations to grow up virtuous and happy." Such faith in the redeeming function of education was the consensus of the time, hence the flood of books on and for children of the middle and upper classes that were being published. Of these *Thoughts* is an original. One has only to compare a standard work of the time, John Gregory's *A Father's Legacy to His Daughters,* a lugubrious dissertation on the "peculiar propriety of female manners," which assumed, as did all contemporary texts, that a girl's reason for being is to win men's approval by softness, ignorance and innocence (contrived if necessary), and absolute unthinking submission. "Your whole life is often a life of suffering . . . you must bear your sorrows in silence, unknown and unpitied." As for accomplishments beyond the decorative: "I am at the greatest loss what to advise you in regard to books. . . . If I were sure of your strong principles, I would encourage you [but I may] do you an injury by artificially creating a taste, which if nature never gave it to you, would only serve to embarrass your future conduct. . . . I do not wish you to have sentiments to perplex you." Having made it clear that the only possible role for a woman was marriage, Gregory insisted, "I know nothing that renders a woman more despicable than her thinking it essential to happiness to be married," and went on to describe the terrible fate of the spinster, "sinking into obscurity and insignificance."

Hester Chapone's *Letters On The Improvement of The Mind, Addressed to a Young Lady*, which Mary Wollstonecraft admired, is a substantial improvement. Women, if too soft, are weak and cowardly, she said. Spinsterhood was not a disaster. Although a modest amount of learning is "much more than sufficient to store your mind with as many ideas as you will know how to manage," and its purpose to fill idle time, Mrs. Chapone outlined in two of the nine chapters an admirable course of modern and ancient history and literature equivalent to junior college work, with the rationale that a young woman so instructed would make a worthy companion for her husband.[15] She was writing for families of the gentry and aristocracy.

Mary Wollstonecraft addressed herself in great part to badly married women and the not-to-be-married; it was a new departure. Although she made it clear that the purpose of girls' education was to prepare them to fulfill the duties of wife and mother, she was pessimistic, projecting the fate of women like her mother, Mrs. Blood, her sisters, Fanny, and herself. Because life was so difficult, fortune so precarious, she believed girls should be educated to avoid misery and to live with misfortune. Intellect, religion, and independent character had been her own salvation; only these could make life tolerable for others. It is interesting that she indicated no particular hostility to men, and even noted with approval their distaste for women who squabble or paint themselves beyond recognition. She did not think much of the common run of either sex; "Most women, and men too, have no character at all."

Such books of the period usually started with young womanhood and worked toward marriage and motherhood. Mary Wollstonecraft's first chapter began at the beginning—in the nursery—with a slap at, and admonition to, mothers like her own:

> I am sorry to observe, that reason and duty together have not so powerful an influence over human conduct, as instinct has in the brute creation. Indolence, and a thoughtless disregard of everything, except the present indulgence, make many mothers, who may have momentary starts of tenderness, neglect their children. . . .

> The first thing to be attended to, is laying the foundation of a good constitution. The mother . . . ought to suckle her children. . . .
>
> The suckling of a child also excites the warmest glow of tenderness . . . I have even felt it, when I have seen a mother perform that office; and am of the opinion, that maternal tenderness arises quite as much from habit as instinct.

She stated that babies should be treated with firmness and tenderness:

> affection must be shown, and little proofs of it ought always to be given —let them not appear weaknesses, and they will sink deep into the young mind, and call forth its most amiable propensities. The turbulent passions may be kept down till reason begins to dawn.

"Moral Discipline," the second chapter, recalled also her own childhood, for she states it can be instilled only by rational parents "who have subdued their own passions which is not often the case":

> the children are at first made play-things of, and when their tempers have been spoiled by indiscreet indulgence, they become troublesome, and are mostly left with servants; the first notions they imbibe, therefore, are mean and vulgar. . . .
>
> . . . it is of the utmost consequence to make a child artless, or to speak with more propriety, not to teach them to be otherwise . . . cunning is so nearly allied with falsehood, that it will infallibly lead to it. . . .
>
> . . . Restrain . . . but never correct them without a very sufficient cause. Children should be permitted to enter into conversation . . . find out such subjects as will gradually improve them. . . . The understanding, however, should not be overloaded . . . yet there is no reason why the mind should lie fallow . . . promiscuous seeds will be sown by accident, and they will shoot up. . . .
>
> Whenever a child asks a question, it should always have a reasonable answer given. . . .
>
> The first things, then, that children ought to be encouraged to observe, are a strict adherence to truth; a proper submission to superiors; and a condescension to inferiors. . . .
>
> Above all, try to teach them to combine their ideas . . . I wish them to be taught to think.[16]

This last was almost direct from Price. Mary had no awareness of the value of baby talk, fairy stories, or acting out fears and problems in play; fearful of irrationality, preoccupied by morality, she insisted "infantile" tendencies should be curbed.

Thoughts skips from one subject to the next, with moral observation interspersed helter-skelter, just as the ideas occurred to her. This is true within chapters as well—indeed, it is difficult to make a rational outline of any of her nonfiction. "Exterior Accomplishments": "not to be despised, if the acquiring of them does not satisfy the possessors, and prevent their cultivating the more important ones." "Manners": "Let [them] arise from the mind, and let there be no disguise for the genuine emotion of the heart. . . . Feeling is ridiculous when affected." "Dress": "It may be simple, elegant and becoming . . . money is squandered away, which if saved for charitable purposes, might alleviate distress." "The Fine Arts": "if a young person has a taste for them . . . a great blessing it is [if not] persuade them to be silent, and not feign raptures they do not feel; for nothing can be more ridiculous." "Reading": "the most rational employment. . . . I would have every one try to form an opinion of an author themselves . . . I am sick of hearing of the sublimity of Milton, the elegance and harmony of Pope, and the original untaught genius of Shakespeare . . . by some who know nothing." "Boarding Schools": "the virtues are best learned at home."[17]

With the chapter on "The Temper," the governing of which "is truly the business of our whole lives," she seems to have released memories and painful current material that ran on and on until she caught herself and returned to less poignant matters. Everything is there: her parents' faults; her response, pride, remorse, dependence on religion as a check:

> half the miseries of life arise from peevishness, or a tyrannical domineering temper. . . . She who submits, without conviction, to a parent or husband, will as unreasonably tyrannize. . . . Resentment, indeed, may be felt occasionally by the best of human beings; yet humility will soon conquer it, and convert scorn and contempt to pity, and drive out that hasty pride which is always guarding Self from insult; which takes fire on the most trivial occasions, and which will not admit of a superior, or even an equal. . . .
>
> . . . If the presence of the Deity be inculcated and dwelt on till an habitual reverence is established in the mind, it will check the sallies of anger and sneers of peevishness, which corrode our peace, and render us wretched, without any claim to pity.

Following "Temper," with unconscious accuracy of placement, comes a unique chapter, "Unfortunate Situation of Females, Fashionably Educated, and Left Without a Fortune," and here Mary Wollstonecraft, as passionately as a Jane Eyre, describes the plight of the déclassée, the contempt and rejection she met from former equals, her humiliating years with Mrs. Dawson, the miseries of teachers and governesses, the rigid limits of acceptable work for women, the painful need "to keep up a continual reserve with men she has been formerly familiar with."

Again in logical sequence, the chapter on "Love" follows. "I think there is not a subject that admits so little of reasoning as love," she begins, and proceeds to try to be rational:

> People of sense and reflection are most apt to have violent and constant passions, and to be preyed on by them. . . . Perhaps a delicate mind is not susceptible to a greater degree of misery, putting guilt out of the question, that what must arise from the consciousness of loving a person whom their reason does not approve . . . the passion must either be rooted out, or the continual allowances and excuses that are made will hurt the mind, and lessen the respect for virtue. . . . A woman cannot reasonably be unhappy, if she is attached to a man of sense and goodness, though he may not be all she could wish.
>
> I am very far from thinking love irresistible and not to be conquered. . . . Habit and duty will cooperate, and religion may overcome what reason has in vain combatted with. . . .
>
> The heart is very treacherous, and if we do not guard against its first emotions, we shall not afterwards be able to prevent its fighting for impossibilities. . . . Universal benevolence is the first duty.

In the next chapter, "Matrimony," she states: "Early marriages are, in my opinion, a stop to improvement." She believed women should be mature and stable when they marry, not led by "passions," or frivolity, as Eliza had been. "Men have in some respects very much the advantage . . . being obliged to struggle with the world," while the average woman has only "little arts . . . silly capricious humours, which render her rather insignificant and vicious." A cultivated mind is necessary even in a comfortable marriage; "in a miserable one, it is her only consolation," bolstered by religion. Demonstrated fondness between husband and wife made her uncomfortable; "it has ever occurred to me, that it was sufficient for a woman to receive caresses, and not bestow them."

The next chapter, titled "Desultory Thoughts," begins with women's duties—"every kind of domestic concern"—and in noting the advantages of studying medicine, falls into comment on affliction such as Fanny's recent death:

> He who made us must know what will tend to our ultimate good; yet still all this is grievous, and the heart will throb with anguish when deprived of what it loves. . . . Did our feelings and reason always coincide, our passage through this world could not justly be termed a warfare, and faith would not longer be a virtue. . . .
>
> I have almost run into a sermon—and I shall not make an apology for it.

"The Benefits Which Arise From Disappointments," is a chapter which only Mary Wollstonecraft could write. The benefits seem obscure, but she is quite convincing about the disappointments of those, like herself, "Who delight in observing moral beauty . . . their souls sicken when forced to view crimes and follies. . . . To struggle with ingratitude and selfishness is grating beyond expression . . . when we look for happiness, we meet with vexations."

"Servants" is the next chapter. All through the book Mary Wollstonecraft warns of their ignorance, cunning, and corrupting influence on children, revealing the class prejudice shared by Price and other advanced thinkers until the French Revolution. "The ceremonials of religion, on their account, should be attended to," she writes. It is one of the rare examples of hypocrisy in Mary Wollstonecraft. "We cannot make our servants wise or good, but we may teach them to be decent and orderly." "I never knew much social virtue to reside in a house where the Sabbath was grossly violated," she says in the next chapter, on "Sunday Observance." She goes on to devote the section to a sermon on the path of duty.

"The Misfortune of Fluctuating Principles" is a chapter affirming her religious faith: "how people can live without it, I can scarcely conceive." She states, moreover, that reason does not always suffice, may even lead to deism and doubts destructive of peace of mind.

"Benevolence," "Card Playing," "Theatre," and "Public Places" are predictable chapters: she ends the book:

> the mind should catch improvement on all occasions . . . and every thing concur to prepare us for a state of purity and happiness. There vice and folly will not poison our pleasures; our faculties will expand, and not mistake their objects; and we shall no longer "see as through a glass darkly, but know, even as we are known." Finis.[18]

The conflict between reason and passion is a constant theme throughout, and resolution in favor of reason and resignation in religion the lesson. Passion and talk of passion, anger at parents, pride, temperament, longing for love, childish insistence on perfection, fault finding, pessimism, all are counteracted by self-control, conscience, duty, intellect, reason, religious faith, and irrepressible optimism. "Even the errors of passion may produce useful experience, expand the faculties," she affirmed. *Thoughts* is a literal illustration of the high wire on which Mary Wollstonecraft balanced herself.

In an act of disinterested kindness, John Hewlett in late April, 1786, took the manuscript of *Thoughts* to his London publisher, Joseph Johnson, who promptly accepted it and paid the author ten guineas—to everyone's delight. "You never saw such a creature happier than [Hewlett] was when he returned to tell me the success of his commission—the sensibility and goodness that appeared in his countenance made me love the man!" Mary Wollstonecraft wrote George Blood on May 1. At this point, she was in debt to the tune of some eighty or ninety pounds, which her fee might have reduced. Instead, as she told George Blood, "Mr. Hewlett exerted himself to obtain the money for your father." The destitute Bloods had wanted to go back to Ireland; they actually were enroute there with the ten guineas when Mary wrote George. It does not seem to have occurred to her that other obligations—her creditors, some of whom were her friends, and her sisters—should take precedence over Fanny's parents.

However, Mary Wollstonecraft's school was beyond saving, as she herself realized. She had mixed feelings about it. She had had enough of living with Eliza and Everina. Now that Fanny was dead, she preferred to be on her own, a wish she had underestimated or pushed aside until now. At this point she was still not fully prepared to admit her desire, going only so far as to write to George Blood, "I have no objection to living alone now." The failure of the school left no alternative but that the sisters separate. They all agreed to that necessity, and Mary began to work out a practicable course, which was extremely difficult since she was the only one capable of earning her own living.

Eliza was her major problem. In letter after letter to George Blood and later to Everina, Mary Wollstonecraft made it clear how fragile and incompetent Eliza was ("I am particularly anxious about Eliza. . . . Eliza, I don't know what will become of her. . . . Eliza, in particular, is very helpless. . . . Poor Bess," etc.). Four of Mary's letters of 1785–1787 to George Blood have lines someone apparently censored. In three, the lines crossed out directly follow Eliza's name. It is evident that the censored material referred to Eliza in terms damaging to her, to Mary, or to both. A fourth letter, May 1, 1786, like many others spoke longingly of Fanny Blood. "My poor heart still throbs with *selfish* anguish—it is formed for friendship and confidence—yet how often is it wounded." Sixteen censored lines follow; then: "I am however melancholy rather than unhappy now my hopes of happiness are extinct. . . . I am too apt to be attached . . . and have been *sorely hurt.*" One biographer believes Mary was writing of a then current, unhappy romance with Reverend Joshua Waterhouse, who, he also believes, may be "Neptune," an alias Mary used in three letters of 1786–1787—but, as noted earlier, there is no proof she was seeing Waterhouse at this time or had ever seriously loved him.[19] The unreadable lines probably refer to Eliza's frailty, Everina's inadequacy, and Mary Wollstonecraft's conviction that no one appreciated her own selflessness and capacity for love.

One can assume that Eliza was distraught over the necessity for separation and that she expressed herself piteously, for Ned had agreed that Everina should return to him, but Eliza had nowhere to go. Mary Wollstonecraft wrote George Blood she intended to give up the school and retrench her way of living drastically. As for Eliza, "If I could get her recommended to some eligible situation it would be a great weight off my mind—she could not give up the world or live in the style I intend to." Eliza may have been unable to accept the fact that the now separated, penniless Mrs. Bishop could not live in the style Miss Wollstonecraft or Mrs. Meredith Bishop had enjoyed, but she had absolutely counted on Mary for at least shabby gentility in a permanent home after her sister helped her escape from her marriage. Mary managed to become the disappointed one. Godwin said she was naïve enough to count on undeviating gratitude from her sisters and did not understand that the more she did and the closer she became involved with them, the more she was bound to see their faults—"their untractableness and folly"—and to be severely disappointed. "She was the victim of a desire to promote the benefit of others."[20]

Godwin obscures the basic point. Mary Wollstonecraft extended herself for her sisters and later her younger brothers to meet her own needs as well as theirs. The devotion she displayed toward her dependents was sometimes fervent, sometimes resentful, for it conflicted with her own drive for personal satisfaction. Hence her demand for gratitude, her resentment that her sacrifice was not appreciated, her self-reproach at her anger, and her overcompensation in continued sacrifice. She felt wounded by neglect and was angered at ingratitude. Her "exquisite sense" of defects in others and her demand they be and do as she wanted was always a sign that she was excusing her own ambivalence.

But despite guilt and anxiety Mary Wollstonecraft proceeded to close her school. The final hope of settling her major debts had departed with Mrs. Disney and her three children, the last boarders, who never paid their sizable bill. The week after June 18, Mary let her servants go, sold her furniture and whatever else she could dispense with, and moved with Eliza to small lodgings where she continued to teach eleven day pupils. Everina left for Ned's; friends were reconnoitering to find Eliza the least demanding and most protected position possible in a girl's school suitably refined and distant from Bishop. Since Eliza was hardly competent to teach, Mary would have preferred that she be a parlor boarder, but given the financial realities probably the best solution was for Eliza to board in exchange for minor duties. It is difficult to be more precise, since nine lines of Mary's letter to George Blood describing Eliza's situation are censored. Meanwhile, the sisters lived with "rigid economy." Scrounging for a living in near destitution, Mary wrote George, "would have made me shudder some years ago, and now it does not terrify me . . . a little peace is all I desire." A second and third time George Blood urged her to live with his family until she could start a school in Dublin. She refused, absolutely. Ireland no longer appealed to her, she answered; the Irish, as she had found out through Hugh Skeys, were "particularly attentive to appearance," and would never patronize a modest school. Her previous experience with fallen fortunes had been reinforced at Newington Green: "Poverty will oftener raise contempt than pity I learned here—to gain respect of the vulgar . . . you must dazzle their senses—and even must not appear to want of their assistance if you expect to have it." Another reason was her freedom:

> June 18th
>
> To treat you with sincerity my dear boy—I must be independent and earn my own subsistence, or be very uncomfortable—I could not live with your father, or condescend to practice those arts which are necessary to keep him in temper—as to being *under obligation* to him it would never do. . . . Besides how you could think I could sit all day with the family, when you know we could not find conversation, surprises me . . . the confinement of two little rooms would not be *solitude* on the contrary . . . I should . . . always be involved in insignificant cares—I love your mother but she would not be a companion for me, any more than she was for Fanny. . . . I am sick of the world, tis an unweeded garden—I have a number of nervous complaints—I want a friend.

The few pupils she taught in her small rooms merely kept body and soul together, but did not produce enough to touch her debts or to help Eliza. "With great rudeness" one creditor came to dun her, an insult "my unprotected situation naturally produces," she wrote George. She had some faint hope of money from a lawsuit Ned was pursuing against a man named Roebuck. The details are unknown, but it may have involved a "lapsed legacy" she referred to in 1792.[21] If successful, she told George, the legal proceedings would bring "the children's money," but, she added, "I have little reason to expect that I shall ever get it." Among the few occupations open to her that of governess was most profitable, for she could live on nothing while her salary went to the debts and to Eliza. She had several offers to consider, although she would have preferred teaching, for she had just stated in *Thoughts* that the life of a governess was as disagreeable as that of a paid companion. The worst of it, as she wrote George July 6, was the prospect of loneliness, being shut out from friendship, "surrounded by *unequals*—to live only on terms of civility . . . without any interchange of little acts of kindness and tenderness." For a woman who felt she did not want to live with her sisters, this harkening after affectionate companionship suggests how sharply she was at war with herself. "My heart sometimes overflows with tenderness and at others seems quite exhausted and incapable of being warmly interested about any one," she wrote George August 22.

In August Eliza left Newington Green for a boarding school in Market Harborough, Leicestershire, to which Mrs. Burgh had recommended her, while Mary frantically worked at her French, "absolutely essential in my new situation," she wrote George. The most attractive and remunerative job was that offered her through a Mr. Prior, undermaster at Eton, to become governess to the daughters of Lord Viscount Kingsborough of Ireland, eldest son of the Earl of Kingston. The salary was forty guineas a year. By August 22 she had accepted because she had no choice.

Mary Wollstonecraft's aversion to this position was greatly augmented by knowledge that she had failed with her school and by bitter reluctance suddenly to relinquish the world of intellect in which she had established herself. In the spring of 1786 she had been able to surmount depression over Fanny Blood and the resulting "apathy" she dreaded and write *Thoughts*, to give constructive expression to her feelings and ideas; soon after she found the exercise of new powers validated by Johnson's acceptance of the book for publication. But by the summer, instead of being able to capitalize on this success, she was forced into regressive and constricted employment.

She wanted to keep open a way back to her thwarted career, and she found an ally in her publisher. Before leaving for her position in Ireland with the Kingsborough family, Mary Wollstonecraft went to London to meet Joseph Johnson. The interview at his office at 72 St. Paul's Churchyard was mutually intriguing. Johnson was an astute judge of talent and widely admired for his unusually generous interest in his writers. Mary had immediate confidence in him and discussed her problems fully and frankly, making it plain she was going to Ireland with extreme regret and only for the money she had to have. Johnson was most sympathetic to this attractive and gifted young woman and encouraged her to continue writing for him, giving as an example Mrs. Barbauld, one of his successful authors who was also mistress of a school. Novels, works for children, and translations, books such as Mary saw displayed for sale in his shop, were possible successors to *Thoughts on the Education of Daughters* that she discussed with Johnson. His interest gave Mary Wollstonecraft something she could live on during her servitude as governess. At the very least she could write, even in Ireland, and Johnson might publish; at best, someday, she would have a self-supporting literary career.

She went back to Newington Green to arrange her departure for a position so discordant with her ambitions as to be almost unbearable.

Chapter 8

DURING HER TERM as the Kingsboroughs' governess Mary Wollstonecraft discovered that she had genius. During the same period she also came close to a breaking point.

Her departure from England in the fall of 1786 took place under great pressure. Her debts to friends and tradesmen were still hanging over her. She needed a wardrobe suitable for the governess of fashionable aristocrats, pocket money for her trip to Ireland, funds for her father, and, she hoped, a small sum for Eliza. She reluctantly applied to Ned, but he abruptly refused her and she had to ask George Blood to send her material from Dublin to make herself a dress. "I cannot afford to buy one," she wrote him, bitterly reminding him of the fabric Hugh Skeys had promised but never shipped from Lisbon. However, her friends rallied around. Her former housekeeper, Miss Mason, came back to Newington Green to help her make clothes; Mrs. Cockburn contributed a remarkable blue hat; and, most importantly, Mrs. Burgh made a substantial loan that enabled Mary to pay her most pressing debts and leave with gratitude and some consolation.

"I'm on the wing," she wrote Eliza in late September, keyed up at leaving home and in suspense awaiting a summons to meet the Kingsborough children at Eton, from whence they were to proceed to Ireland:

> Poor Mason has been with me—I don't know what I would have done without her—to help me make a greatcoat or anything which required

> thought. . . . Mrs. Burgh has been as anxious about me as if I had been her daughter. . . . Mrs. Price died the other day and Dr. Price intends soon leaving the Green—he has been uncommonly friendly to me. I have the greatest reason to be thankful. . . . Mr. Hewlett desires me to give his love to poor Mrs. Bishop—he would have said compliments if his wife had been by. . . . You can have no conception of Mrs. Burgh's kindness—we are to dine with her tomorrow—she has enabled me to pay Hincman and the rest of my creditors but I told you so before. . . . This is the last letter I shall write to you from this Island—and indeed I never was in worse humour for writing. . . . Edward behaved very rude to me—and has not assisted me in the smallest degree. . . . Is this the World? Yet though many have disappointed me others have gone beyond my hope or expectation—I wish to remember it for I like to encourage an affection for all mankind.

The Kingsboroughs could not be kept waiting; Mr. and Mrs. Prior called Mary early to Eton, where she waited for three weeks. As reality sank in, her misery at the course life had taken and her guilt and anxiety about her sisters increased. It was one thing to know she had taken the only practical course; it was another to contemplate the fact that her decision forced Everina back to Ned's grudging charity and Eliza, "luckless wretch," as she called herself, to a lonely life at a school, living "at the top of the house . . . a Poet's garret," among incompatible strangers who were shocked that she was separated from her husband. The fact that both girls tried to cheer Mary enroute to exile further unnerved her. Eliza sent a going away present with a loving note, which Mary told her was "a cordial to my wornout spirits . . . indeed, my dear girl, I felt a glow of tenderness which I cannot describe—I could have clasped you to my breast as I did in days of yore, when I was your nurse." An October ninth letter to Everina, to whom she could let herself go without compunction, showed even more poignantly her unhappiness at leaving "*home*—delightful word" and her longing for release:

> how grateful to me was your tender unaffected letter—I wept over it—for I am in a melting mood . . . very unwell. . . . A whole train of nervous disorders have taken possession of me—and, they appear to arise so much from the mind—I have little hopes of being better. . . . A disappointment with respect to your visit made me almost faint—last

> Friday. . . . When shall we meet? Your image haunts me—I could take any poor timid girl to my bosom and shield her . . . save her from the contagion of folly or the inroads of sorrow. My thoughts and wishes tend to that land where the God of love will wipe all tears from our eyes. With what delight do I anticipate the time when neither death nor accidents of any kind will interpose to separate me from those I love. . . . Love—A mind that has once felt the pleasure of loving and being beloved cannot rest satisfied with any inferior gratifications. . . . If you possibly can, try to exert yourself or you will fall a prey to melancholy. You require kindness . . . domestic comforts . . . congenial souls—but those around you are the merest earthworms.

In the same letter Mary indicated that she found Eton distasteful. Just across the Thames she could see Windsor Castle's massive tower, familiar from her Dawson days. For four years she had not even been near the kind of world she now saw in miniature in the faculty families at Eton. She measured herself against its superficiality, contrasted it with the quality of the circle she had been part of at Newington Green, and felt her own identity, values, and enlightenment confirmed. "I have had so many new ideas of life, I can scarcely arrange them—I am lost in a sea of thoughts," she wrote Everina:

> I could not lead the life they lead at Eton; nothing but dress and ridicule going forward . . . affected, the women in their manner and the men in their conversation, for witlings abound and puns fly about like crackers. . . . So much company without any sociability would be to me an insupportable fatigue. . . . Vanity in one shape or another reigns triumphant—and has banished Love in all its modifications—and without it what is society? . . . I am convinced too much refinement negates virtue and abilities . . . affection and humanity.

Eton also confirmed her professional opinion that children should be educated at home "with domestic affections, the foundation of virtue." The objections she formed to the great school and its small society were vigorous. She wrote later:

> At boarding-schools of every description, the relaxation of the junior boys is mischief; and of the senior, vice. Besides, in the great schools, what can be more prejudicial to the moral character than the system of tyranny and abject slavery which is established amongst the boys, to say nothing of the slavery to forms, which makes religion worse than a farce?

> There is not, perhaps, in the kingdom, a more dogmatical or luxurious set of men, than the pedantic tyrants who reside in colleges or preside at public schools.
>
> So far . . . from thinking of the morals of boys, I have heard several masters of schools argue, that they only undertook to teach Latin and Greek; and that they had fulfilled their duty, by sending some good scholar to college.
>
> . . . Public education . . . should be directed to form citizens.[1]

Eton's system and objectives were wrong; Mary, in observing them, knew she could do better. "I long to be off," she wrote Everina; her job with the Kingsboroughs might be a worthwhile experiment, for Mrs. Prior had told her that Lady Kingsborough was "a good sort of woman," unhappy with an extravagant husband, concerned for her children, whose education until then had been "ornamental . . . which she thinks ought ever to be a secondary consideration." But Mary reserved judgment on her employer, "for I cannot venture to depend on the opinion of people who are dazzled by her superior station in life," she said. Her own social standing was as always a very sensitive area. "These situations," she said later of her employment, "are considered in the light of a degradation. . . . Nothing as painfully sharpens sensibility as such a fall in life."[2]

The Kingsboroughs bypassed Eton, and Mary was forced to make the journey to Ireland with substitute escorts, a couple she knew were her inferiors, although she was too aloof to determine until she reached her destination that "he is the Butler, and his wife the housekeeper." Enroute, although she dreaded the end of the journey, she wrote Eliza the weather was brilliant, the scenery and the crossing from Holyhead to Dublin delightful, "and what was of still more consequence, I had an agreeable companion—a young clergyman, who was going to settle in Ireland in the same capacity as myself." The man was Henry Gabell, recently of New College, Oxford, now on his way to the family of the Right Honorable John O'Neill, probably as tutor. Mary was quick to make herself interesting to Gabell by her "*tone* of melancholy you observed on our first acquaintance," of which she later reminded him and to which he evidently responded.[3] "He was intelligent, and had that kind of politeness which arises from sensibility," she wrote Eliza.

After spending a few days in Dublin with George Blood and his parents, and renewing her acquaintance with Fanny's old friend Betty Delane, Mary Wollstonecraft traveled the 170 miles to Lord Kingsborough's castle in Mitchelstown, at the center of his huge family estates, arriving at the end of October. Her reaction from the very first was revulsion and despair. "The very sight of its solemn grandeur froze my very blood. I entered the great gates with the same kind of feeling as I should have if I was going into the Bastille," she wrote Everina October 30:

> I have been so low spirited for some days past I could not write. . . . All the moments I could spend in solitude were lost in sorrow and unavailing tears . . . I am in a land of strangers . . . when [more] composed I will write to poor Bess. . . . I cannot write to Mrs. Burgh tonight she would have no patience with me. . . . I hear a fiddle below, the servants are dancing, and the rest of the family diverting themselves —I only am melancholy and alone. To tell the truth, I hope part of my misery arises from disordered nerves, for I would fain believe my mind is not so very weak.

Mary braced herself to take stock of her surroundings and gauge her position. Her employers were aristocrats of immense wealth and power, far beyond any she had ever known. The Kingsboroughs were just over thirty but had been married fifteen years. As third cousins, they had united the family estates. Mitchelstown Castle, which they had renovated in the Italian style, was magnificent, the style of living lavish, the milieu the most splendid society. Mary was impressed, humiliated, and frightened. "I fear I am unequal to the task I have been persuaded to undertake, and this fear worries me . . . I am sure much more is expected of me than I am equal to," she wrote Everina. Her proficiency in the dreaded French was definitely below standards; "I expect to be, in consequence of it, much mortified . . . I am too worried about fancy work, etc., etc." She was especially touchy about her status in this hierarchial establishment. The Kingsboroughs and their female friends in particular she felt examined her "with the most minute attention." "I am treated like a gentlewoman," she wrote her sisters. "But I cannot easily forget my inferior station—and this something betwixt and between is rather awkward. . . . All . . . labour to be civil to me; but we move in so different a sphere, I feel gratified for their attention, but not amused."

In this situation, a minor piece on the board, the character of her employers was crucial. Lord Kingsborough hardly impinged on her territory, his daughters' education. "With his Lordship I have had little conversation, but his countenance does not promise more than good humour, and a little *fun* not refined." But she took cognizance of him as a great landlord. Ten years before Kingsborough had hired Arthur Young, the agricultural authority, to help transform benighted Mitchelstown into an ideal company town, and his estates into a widely known and applauded example of enlightened ownership. In so doing he had provided a school, library, roads, improved husbandry, and local industry for his tenants.

To the governess the dominant personality in the castle was Lady Kingsborough. The author of *Thoughts* had already censured such women in her book:

> In the fine Lady how few traits do we observe of those affections which dignify human nature. If she has any maternal tenderness, it is of a childish kind. We cannot be too careful not to verge on this character; though she lives many years she is still a child in understanding, and of so little use to society, that her death would scarcely be observed.[4]

Partly out of dependence on the mother of the girls she was to teach, partly out of fascination and antagonism, Mary watched, probed, and judged this beautiful aristocrat, of whom she constantly wrote her sisters: "Lady K. is a shrewd, clever woman, a great talker. . . . Lady K. is a clever woman, and a well-meaning one, but not the order of being that I could love. . . . Lady K. is very civil, nay kind, yet I cannot help fearing her—She has something in her person and manner which puts me in mind of Mrs. Hewlett." (The latter, it may be remembered, was hated by the Wollstonecraft sisters for being domineering and jealous.) Lady Kingsborough was eternally lisping, languishing, primping, and caressing her many pet dogs—to Mary's astonishment and disgust.

The Kingsborough household was large, lively, and attentive. "I found I was to encounter a host of females," Mary wrote with the cheerfulness she tried to sustain in her letters to Eliza, "My Lady, her stepmother, and *Mrses* and *Misses* without number." These sorted out, besides the flow of house guests, to include Mrs. Fitzgerald, the stepmother who became fond of Mary, and her three marriageable daughters, "fine girls, just going to market, as their brother says." Of her pupils, whom she first thought "wild Irish," she immediately chose the oldest, fourteen-year-old Margaret, as her favorite; "by no means handsome, yet a sweet girl. She has wonderful capacity. . . . My sweet little girl is now playing and singing to me—she has a good ear and some taste and feeling," she wrote Eliza. An occasional guest like the poet George Ogle, with his pale face and quick wit, interested her. But three weeks after her arrival, although she had succeeded in impressing everyone with her superior qualities, she was overwrought, longing for real intimacy, desperately sorry for herself:

> Oh! my Everina my heart is almost broken . . . I am grown a poor melancholy wretch . . . I long for my eternal rest—my nerves are so impaired I suffer much more than I supposed I should. I want the tender soothings of friendship—I want—but I will be resigned . . . I am an exile—
>
> Confined to the society of a set of silly females, I have no social converse, and their boisterous spirits and unmeaning laughter exhaust me, not forgetting hourly domestic bickerings. The topics of matrimony and dress take their turn, not in a very sentimental style—alas, poor sentiment! It has no residence here. I almost wish the girls were novel readers and romantic—I declare false refinement is better than none at all, but these girls understand several languages and have read *cartloads* of history. . . . I am almost tormented to death by dogs. But you will perceive I am not under the influence of my darling passion—pity; it is not always so, I make allowances and adapt myself, talk of getting husbands for the *Ladies*—and the *dogs*, and am wonderfully entertaining; and then I retire to my room, form figures in the fire, listen to the wind, or view the Gotties, a fine range of mountains near us, and so does time waste away in apathy or misery. I would not write this to Eliza—she cannot discriminate; but to you I *cannot* be reserved—and I hope the dreadful contagion will not infect you. I am thought to have an angelick temper . . . so low am I, that if any one would attempt to smite one cheeck—I should be apt to turn the other . . . I am drinking asses' milk, but do not find it of any service, I am very ill, and so low-spirited my tears flow in torrents almost insensibly. I struggle with myself, but I hope my Heavenly Father will not be extreme to mark my weakness . . . I almost wish my warfare was over.

She was acutely homesick, begged Everina for details about Newington Green friends, particularly Hewlett. But in her duties she found some outlet. Lady Kingsborough had by her own admission to Mrs. Prior left her children's care to others. At once domineering and neglectful, she intimidated them thoroughly, looking in on occasion to lay down the law with more determination than sense. Her daughters and evidently the Fitzgerald girls as well were forbidden, for instance, to read novels lest they become corrupted, while Lady Kingsborough enjoyed the titillation of romances fictional and real. Meanwhile, the "heap of rubbish, miscalled accomplishments," which she insisted on for Margaret, and the whole value system, was offensive to Mary, who apparently asked for and got a comparatively free hand. "I am very much grieved at being obliged to continue so wrong a system," Mary wrote Eliza. "[Margaret] is very much afraid of her mother—that such a creature should be ruled with a rod of iron when tenderness could lead her anywhere! She is to be always with me . . . my pupils are left entirely to my management—only her Ladyship sometimes condescends to give her opinion." The *Memoirs* relate that Mary "immediately restored the children to their liberty, and undertook to govern them by their affections only." Young Margaret, whose violent temper disturbed Mary, became ardently attached to the first woman she could respect, whose influence was decisive in her own life. She told Godwin in 1801 that Mary Wollstonecraft had treated her with "mildness, kindness and respect," in contrast to Lady Kingsborough's "unkindness and tyranny." She said:

> I am convinced that had it not been my peculiar good fortune to meet with the extraordinary woman to whose superior penetration and affectionate mildness of manner I trace the development of whatever virtues I possess, I should have become, in consequence of the distortion of my best qualities, a most ferocious animal.[5]

It was as much by her character as by patient tenderness that Mary won the Kingsborough children. She could not change Lady Kingsborough's standards or erase the children's past training, but she offered herself as an example of excellence.

What her employer denied her children, Mary Wollstonecraft attempted to supply: nurture, dependability, and love. When they became ill, "her Ladyship visited them in a formal way—and I endeavoured to amuse them, while she lavished awkward fondness on her dogs," she wrote. Two months after her arrival she told Eliza that Margaret, who had been dangerously ill, "can scarcely bear to have me a moment out of her sight." Another poor girl to rescue. The governess was drawn not only to her three charges but to the younger children as well. She wrote Everina:

> I go to the Nursery—something like maternal feeling fills my bosom—The children cluster about me—one catches a kiss, another lisps my long name—while a sweet little boy, who is conscious that he is a favorite, calls himself my Son—at the sight of their mother they tremble and run to me for protection—this renders them dear to me—and I discover the kind of happiness I was formed to enjoy.

But Lady Kingsborough enjoyed it not at all. Not only was her children's preference for their governess galling, she felt Mary's critical eye on her and sensed disapproval was being transmitted to the children. She was right. Although Mary was trying to govern her own behavior, she believed children had to be aware of their parents' faults if they were to develop virtues themselves. Antagonism between these two strong women, each aware of the other's power and determined to win out, began politely and proceeded erratically until it became intolerable to both. Lady Kingsborough had other interests; for Mary the contest was a major preoccupation. She felt superior to this woman, more virtuous, far more intelligent, and she determined to prove it. As this drive conflicted with her obligation to her employer, so did awareness of her superiority with her station. She knew how to make that superiority felt. She was, she said in December, a "GREAT" favorite" at the Castle, recognized as an exceptional woman of charm and talent. Lady Kingsborough was interested enough to offer to find jobs for Eliza and Everina in Dublin, a plan Mary relayed to Eliza with the positive hope that they would soon see each other in Ireland. As at Eton Mary gauged herself against those who were supposed to be her betters and found herself superior in intellect and even in the social intercourse the Kingsboroughs invited her to share. She wrote Everina:

> If my vanity could be flattered, by the respect of people, whose judgment I do not care a fig for—why this place it has sufficient food . . . but I

> hate to talk . . . all myself and only make the ignorant wonder and admire.

But triumphs of the drawing room, which she obviously relished, and her success with the children were respites in a state of profound protest that debilitated her. Near the anniversary of Fanny's death she wrote George Blood of her oppression:

> December 4
> Twelve o'clock night
>
> I am indeed very unwell, a kind of melancholy languor consumes me—all my active spirits are fled—everything is tasteless—and uninteresting—I am grown beyond measure indolent, and neglect the few comforts which are within my reach. I find exercise fatiguing and irksome—In short, my nerves have been so much injured I am afraid I shall never be tolerably well—These disorders are particularly distressing as they seem entirely to arise from the mind—and that an exertion of the reasoning faculties would banish them and bring it to a proper tone—but slackened nerves are not to be braced by arguments—physical and mental causes have contributed to reduce me to my present weak state . . . I frequently sit at night an hour or two in thought—about this time last year I closed my poor Fanny's eyes—I have been reviewing my past life—and the ghost of my former joys, and vanished hopes . . . pity me—and excuse my silence . . . for at this time I require the most friendly treatment. . . . I have no just cause for complaint . . . the whole family gives me great attention . . . some . . . treat me with a degree of tenderness which I have seldom met with from strangers . . . I long for the bosom of a friend . . . bitter recollections wound my poor heart which cannot be filled by mere common placid affections. . . . This warfare will in time be over.

Mary Wollstonecraft had always prided herself both on a vigorous constitution and on extreme sensitivity. She had been aware for years that disappointment and grief affected her physical state, and she fought to exert, exercise, reason, or resign herself into health. She had been treated several times by doctors for her symptoms, and since she advocated home study of medicine, she was probably now reading on the subject of nervous disorders herself, for her diagnosis of "slackened" nerves agreed with current medical opinion that nerves were a physical property, delicate or strong in any given individual. During the months of her job with the Kingsboroughs, however, Mary indicated she feared her worse condition also arose "from my mind." She sensed the essential remedies: someone to love and a channel for her ambition such as *Thoughts* had provided when she mourned Fanny Blood. The first being impossible, she reached out for the second. The day after her miserable midnight letter to George Blood, she looked to her frustrated career. Shortly before she had indicated to Everina that she was, after all, a professional writer. This was couched as a joke about the hat Mrs. Cockburn had given her when she left Newington Green: "Tell Mrs. Cockburn—if I make any conquests in Ireland it will be owing to the blue hat—which is the first phenomenon of its kind, that has made its appearance in this hemisphere—there is a phrase worthy of a new author!" On December 5 she wrote her publisher, Joseph Johnson, on behalf of Lady Kingsborough's stepmother, Mrs. Fitzgerald. This lady had consulted Mary about the education of her only son, preferably in a superior family, where sentiments of religion would be fixed in his mind. Mrs. Barbauld and John Hewlett, Mary knew, were setting up such schools. Instead of writing to her old friend Hewlett, she seized the opportunity to contact Johnson, her immediate excuse the fact that he had already mentioned a prospective school of Mrs. Barbauld's along these lines. Her own book, *Thoughts,* of which she had heard nothing, and Johnson's interest in herself were even stronger reasons:

December 5

Sir

I should be much obliged to you, if you would inform me directly, if Mrs. Barbauld, or Mr. Hewlett, have actually carried their plan into execution—and I should be very glad if you would, as soon as convenient, send me a dozen of Mr. Hewlett's spelling-books, for Lady K., His Sermons, and Charlotte Smith's poems, and a few copies of my little book, if it is published. . . .

As I mentioned to you, previous to my departure, that I entered on my new way of life with extreme regret—I am vain enough to imagine you wish to hear how I like my situation. A state of dependence must ever be irksome to me, and I have *many* vexations to encounter, which some people would term trifling—I have most of the . . . comforts of life—yet when weighed with liberty they are of little value—In a Christian sense I am resigned—and contented; but it is with pleasure that I observe my declining health, and cherish the hope that I am hastening to the Land where all these cares will be forgotten.[6]

She had made sure Johnson would not forget her.

In January of 1787 the Kingsboroughs decamped from Mitchelstown to Dublin for the season. They had intended leaving the governess and children at the castle, a prospect Mary dreaded; it is possible, since she was such a favorite, that she persuaded her employers to take her and the children to the city. Mary was given a short vacation, which she spent with friends, the Baillies, in Tipperary. Everything there reminded her of the past: the town resembled Beverley; the lady of the house, Mrs. Blood; and the daughter, Fanny.

The next five months were spent at the great town house of the Earl of Kingston, Lord Kingsborough's father, #3 Henrietta Street, the most exclusive street in Dublin. Here Mary Wollstonecraft was given accommodations suitable to a lady and an opportunity to enjoy her own social life when her duties did not obtrude. "I have much more convenient apartments here," she wrote Everina February 10. "A fine school room—the use of one of the drawing rooms where the Harpsichord is—and a parlour to receive my *male* visitors in—Here is no medium! The last poor governess—was treated like a servant." In the drawing room or the parlor she received her first visitors, Betty Delane, George Ogle, and his wife; they had been mutually impressed with one another at Mitchelstown. Ogle was well known as a poet, "of great merit," according to Mary; he was also politically active as a reforming liberal at this time. He, his wife, and her sister, Miss Moore, visited and received Mary independent of the Kingsboroughs. Henry Gabell was in town until mid-April and was another of Mary's male visitors. Mrs. Fitzgerald and her daughters invited and visited too constantly for Mary—the "voluables" annoyed her. She saw a good deal of Betty Delane; they often spoke of Fanny. "If she weeps," Mary wrote Everina, "what should I do?" She sometimes saw George Blood and his family. She never mentioned her maternal relatives, the Dicksons, although Everina later saw them when she lived in Dublin.[7] Lady Kingsborough, proud to show off her extraordinary governess, sometimes took Mary to various events of the Dublin season. These were more brilliant than those of Bath, splendid functions attended by the cream of society: gala Handel concerts;* the Rotunda, the assembly room of the elite; the theater and the Green Room of the Playhouse,

* Commemorating the world première of *Messiah* in Dublin, April, 1742.

where the fashionable had entry. Dublin, Mary said later, was the most hospitable city she had ever been in.[8]

By the time she arrived in Dublin she knew *Thoughts* had been published; Mrs. Burgh wrote that she had six copies. Johnson sent several to Mary Wollstonecraft "with a very civil note," and also sent Hewlett's *Sermons* and Cowper's *Poems*, which he had published. ("Little Johnson," Mary said of him somewhat condescendingly to Everina.) She had more time to herself while Lady Kingsborough and the Fitzgeralds were occupied with shopping and socializing. "I am then tranquil—I commune with my own spirit—and am detached from the world," she told Everina. Because of her own poor health and Margaret's slow recovery from recent severe illness, she stayed home during inclement winter days. Probably pondering a subject for her next book as well as "for my own private improvement," she wrote Everina that she was reading "philosophical lectures and metaphysical sermons"; Blair's lectures on genius interested her in particular. George Blood gave her an edition of Shakespeare's plays. She continued to work on French, began Italian, and likewise encouraged Everina not to regret past neglect of her education but to exert herself; "our whole life is but an education for eternity."

Her situation was far more stimulating than at the castle, but her nervous condition worsened. Soon after she came to Dublin, at church one Sunday, she became suddenly "discomposed." Alarmed, Lady Kingsborough took her to Betty Delane's residence nearby, where she had to sit down in a "fit of violent trembling" that frightened everyone. Mary wrote Everina in February that she frequently felt near fainting, had "almost always a rising in my throat which I know to be a nervous affection [*sic*] therefore doubly depressing." Lady Kingsborough insisted that she consult a physician, who said she had "a constant nervous fever." Her moods oscillated. "I [am] very melancholy in the morning . . . but at night my fever gives me false spirits," she told Everina.

Part of the immediate problem was her job. Sensitive, resentful, competitive, both proud of her success and contemptuous of it, Mary Wollstonecraft was excruciatingly vulnerable to Lady Kingsborough's fluctuating shows of friendship, condescension, and authority. After making the rounds on arrival, Lady Kingsborough was home more frequently, furbishing her wardrobe for balls, designing wreaths of roses for a birthday dress, demanding attention: "and the whole house from the kitchen maid to the GOVERNESS are obliged to assist," Mary wrote Everina. "You know I never liked Lady Kingsborough, but I find her still more disagreeable now." They clashed over Margaret's regime. "My anxiety on her account is very much augmented by her mother's improper treatment—as I fear she will hurry her into a consumption." Soon their hostility flared out. Mary wrote Everina March 3:

> Indeed, she behaved so improperly to me, once or twice in the drawing room, I determined never to go into it again—I could not bear to stalk in to be stared at, and her proud condescension added to my embarrassment, I begged to be excused in a civil way—but she would not allow me to absent myself—I had too, another reason, the expense of hair-dressing, and millinary . . . just at this juncture she offered me a present, a poplin gown and petticoat, I refused it and explained myself—she was very angry.

Mrs. Fitzgerald took Mary's side; Lady Kingsborough apologized and conceded for the moment. Both Mary and the Lady were what Mary said of the latter, "very proud and ready to take fire on the slightest occasion," and both seem to have made up the episode with attentions as exaggerated as their friction. Mary reproached herself for her involuntary response to these overtures:

> I too frequently am willing to indulge a delightful tenderness, forget the convictions of reasons, and give way to chimerical hopes. . . . Friendship comes from reason, not *starts* of *tenderness*. . . . When I do sit with her she worries me with prejudices and complaints.

Mary wanted badly to make an elegant appearance, to show the great world what she was capable of:

> The day before yesterday there was a masquerade . . . Lady K. offered me two tickets for myself and Miss Delane to accompany me. I refused them on account of the expense of dressing properly. She then to obviate that objection lent me a black domino. I was out of spirits, and thought of another excuse; but she proposed to take me and Betty Delane to the houses of several people of fashion. . . . We went to a great number, and were a tolerable, nay, a much admired group. Lady K. went in a domino with a smart cockade; Miss Moore dressed in the habit of one of the females of the new discovered islands—Betty Delane as a for-

> saken shepherdess, and your sister Mary in a black domino. As it was taken for granted the stranger who had just arrived could not speak the language, I was to be her interpreter, which afforded me an ample field of satire . . . this night the lights, the novelty of the scene, and all things contributed to make me *more* than half mad—I gave full scope to a *satyrical* vein [italics added].[9]

The slip of the pen in the last line is revealing. In the same letter to Everina Mary repeated her symptoms: "spasms" and outbursts followed by lassitude. After the masquerade Lady Kingsborough left for two weeks in the country, and Mary subsided into depression. She was "on the verge of the grave," she told Everina, listless and melancholy; "these darker tinges occur continually they want *relief*—I am only alive to *attendrisement*—Certainly I must be in love—for I am grown 'thin and lean, pale and wan.'" Was Mary in love—and with whom? She was seeing a great deal of George Ogle, a type she had always found intriguing. "He is between forty and fifty—a genius, and unhappy—such a man you may suppose would catch your sister's eye," she wrote Everina in March. In *Mary*, the book she would write shortly after, she said of the heroine: "The society of men of genius delighted her, and improved her faculties—her first favorites were men past the meridian of life, and of a philosophic turn." Ogle apparently was also intrigued; in *Mary*, "some of her artless flights of genius struck him with surprise; he found she had a capacious mind, and that her reason was as profound as her imagination."[10] Lady Kingsborough was also interested in Ogle, perhaps more so because he obviously admired her governess, who by now she clearly saw as a threat. Ogle was the cause of the next hostile episode, after Lady Kingsborough's return in late March:

> Miss Moore and Mrs. Ogle paid me a visit—and her Ladyship followed —Her father in law had dined with her, and she repeatedly requested me to come down to the drawing-room to see him . . . I at last consented —and could perceive that she had a guard over herself—For to tell you a secret she is afraid of me—why she wishes to keep me I cannot guess —for she cannot bear that anyone should take notice of me—Nay would you believe it she used several arts to get me out of the room before the gentlemen came up—one of them I really wanted to see Mr. Ogle . . . as he has the name of being a man of sense Lady K. has chosen him for her flirt.—don't mistake me—her flirtations are very harmless and she can neither understand nor relish his conversations. But she wishes to be

> taken particular notice of by a man of acknowledged cleverness. As he had not seen me lately he came and seated himself by me—indeed his sensibility has ever led him to pay attention to a poor forlorn stranger—He paid me some *fanciful* compliments—and lent me some very pretty stanzas—melancholy ones you may suppose as he thought they would accord with my feelings. Lord K. came up—and was surprised at seeing me *there*—he bowed respectfully—a concatenation of thoughts made me out blush her Ladyship's rouge. Did I ever tell you she is very *pretty*—and *always* pretty.

In the same letter Mary Wollstonecraft told Everina she had spent the previous evening with the Ogles; "the moments glided away enlivened by wit and rational conversation—at midnight I came home to recline on my sopha and think." Ogle did not sit down with Mary in the Kingsborough drawing room because he had not seen her recently but because he enjoyed seeing her often, and she him; her blush proves it. Although she should have been warned by his seductive confidence that he was unhappy, she continued to see him and to be stimulated by him. But she realized on closer acquaintance that he was unashamedly "sensual," which disturbed and repelled her. Like Lady Kingsborough and others she responded to him even though her "reason" told her he was unworthy, then pulled away, confused and agitated:

> I rail at a fault—sicken at the sight—and find it stirring within me—new sympathies and feelings *start* up—I know not myself—" 'Tis these whims," Mr. Ogle tells me, "render me interesting," and Mrs. Ogle with a placid smile quotes some of my own sentiments—while I cry the [physician] *cannot* heal himself—This man has *great* faults and his wife *little* ones—They vex me—yet he says a witty thing and genius and sensibility lights his eyes—tenderness illumines her's . . . I forget reason—the present pleasing impulse rules the moment and it *flies*.[11]

Mary Wollstonecraft's relationship with another man, Henry Gabell, was calmer on the surface, although it has also been conjectured that she was in love with him. The novel *Mary*, which she wrote in June of the year 1787, relates the heroine's frustrated love for a man whose name is Henry; it is a book in which names specific to Mary Wollstonecraft's experience are utilized. She did become friendly with him in Dublin at least, although their intimacy must have been partial because several months later a letter of hers to him makes it clear he knew only fragmentary details of her life. Perhaps she was initially attracted and drew back when he told her he was engaged to a Miss Ann Gage. At any rate, in the small hours of April 14 she wrote him the kind of note that women rarely send men in whom they are not interested:

> My Dear Sir,
> I thought it would be uncivil to send the promised little book, without a line—yet be it known to thee—I am both sick and sleepy—it being past the *witching time of night*—and I have been thinking "how stale, flat, and unprofitable" this world is grown to me—you'll say—I am always running on in the same strain—and, perhaps, tell me, as a friend once before did, alluding to music, that I mistook a *flat* for a *natural.*
> Good night—or good morning
>
> Yours sincerely
> Mary Wollstonecraft
>
> Friday morning, two O'clock—

The next day when he left Dublin, Mary, signing herself "your affectionate Sister Mary," wrote him a letter concluding a discussion they had had on religion and philosophy.[12] If Gabell disturbed her deeply, she hid it successfully.

There is also the problem of "Neptune," an alias Mary Wollstonecraft used in three 1786 letters, which one biographer believes refers to Waterhouse, placing her romance with him in this period. On July 6, 1786 Mary wrote George Blood from Newington Green: "Give my love to your father and mother—and you may do the same to Neptune. I have done with old resentments—and perhaps I was as much to blame in expecting too much as he in doing too little. I looked for what was not to be found." This reference seems one of several to Skeys, about whom Mary complained frequently to George Blood, and the content seems more appropriate to ungenerous Skeys than to a sweetheart she had given up. From Mitchelstown in early 1787 she asked George, "Is Neptune still in Dublin?" He was, for shortly after her own arrival there she wrote Everina:

> I must not forget to tell you that Neptune enquired after me—yet could not find time to visit me. At the Rotunda, where Lady K. took me one evening, he was coming up to speak to me—I was in the *party* of a Lady [of] *quality*—and he wished to speak to me—but I *would* not see him—and from the corner of my eye he might have caught a look of ineffable

> contempt—if he *could* have felt it. I saw him too last night in the Green-room at the playhouse—but he did not attempt to speak to me. He has never called on Mrs. Blood.[13]

There is no trace of Waterhouse in Dublin at this time, and no reason to be indignant that he did not call on Mrs. Blood if he were there, whereas Skeys had an obligation to call on his former mother-in-law. Skeys was remarried and in Dublin while Mary was there; she became quite friendly with his second wife, but continued her violent resentment toward Skeys for several years.

"Certainly I must be in love," she had written Everina, but if she had been serious, she would not have said it in that fashion. A specific man does not seem responsible for her hysterical outbursts and despair at this time, but love is what she said constantly that she needed, a "particular affection" first and foremost. In the Kingsborough nursery she said she saw "the kind of happiness I was formed to enjoy"; she knew then she needed more than the relationship she had treasured with Fanny or hoped for with her sisters. She was entering her twenty-eighth year, a strongly sexed woman of rigorous morality, placed in a provocative atmosphere: elegant women, vital young people, seductive men like Ogle, sympathetic men like Gabell. No wonder she had to deprecate flirtations, languishing and frank sexuality, at the same time she felt their appeal. Lady Kingsborough's coquetry was perhaps not as innocent as Mary first assumed, and Lord Kingsborough's recreations most certainly were not. Arthur Young had been fired because of intrigues between himself, Lady Kingsborough, her husband and a former governess. The couple separated two years after Mary Wollstonecraft departed. It would have been in character for his Lordship to have had his eye on Mary while she was under his roof.

Mary Wollstonecraft did know her employers' amusements were often carnal. "You cannot conceive, my dear Girl," she wrote Everina in May, "the dissipated lives the women of quality lead. . . . The *Great* . . . look not for a companion and are seldom alone together but in bed—The husband, perhaps drunk and the wife's head full of the *pretty* compliment that some creature, that Nature designed for a Man—paid her."[14] Ogle may have tried to see how far he could go with the Kingsborough's interesting and passionate governess. Shortly after she left Dublin Mary said of him that she was "sorry to hear a man of sensibility and cleverness *talking* of sentiment, sink into sensuality." It sounds as if the poet at least telegraphed advances from which Mary withdrew. In such society Mary both desired and did not deign to compete, although she believed "she was born to shine in the most brilliant society."[15] But both in fantasy and reality—in *Mary*, which she was formulating, in her attraction to Ogle and Gabell, and in her contest with Lady Kingsborough—her female instincts were aroused. In spite of the virulent jibes at spinsters' frustrations prevalent at this time Mary Wollstonecraft seems only vaguely to have connected her "nervous disorders" in this acute stage to her sex drive but rather attributed them specifically to deprivation of love. During these months she once complained of "a nervous affection"—a slip for "affliction." She told Everina, "there is no cure for a broken heart . . . I want a tender nurse." Loneliness and starved affection were her perceived problems. When she sought male relationships, something always went wrong; Gabell was engaged, Ogle was a married sensualist she had to spurn. This repression, added to her other problems, by mid-April of 1787 exacerbated her condition to the point that she wrote Henry Gabell: "My reason has been too far stretched, and tottered on the brink of madness."[16] This is not a thoughtless phrase; she must have been thinking of Eliza's breakdown and, if the hypothesis about her brother Henry is correct, of his illness. On May 11 she wrote Everina:

> "That vivacity which increases with age is not far from madness." Says Rochefoucault, I then am mad . . . I give way to whim—and yet when the most sprightly sallies burst from me the tear frequently trembles in my eye and the long drawn sigh eases my full heart—so my eyes roll in the wild way you have *seen* them . . . and yet so weak am I a sudden thought or any *recollected* emotion of tenderness will occasion the most painful suffusion. You know not my dear Girl of what materials, this strange inconsistency heart of mine is formed and how alive it is to tenderness and misery. . . . I sit up very late. . . . 'Tis the only time I *live*, in the morning I am a poor melancholy wretch—and at night *half*-mad.[17]

Four days later, in the midst of writing Everina about family affairs, she said, "The account you sent about Henry has harried my spirits." The mysteriously vanished brother reappears. If Henry was in an asylum, Everina perhaps would have visited her brother in Mary's absence. The timing, at least, is fascinating. By inheritance and from childhood experience Mary Wollstonecraft was susceptible to emotional disturbance. After the loss of Fanny Blood's love, with the added pressure of dead-end employment and frustrated sexuality, she came close to breaking down.

For some, fear engenders courage and misery, motivating force. Mary Wollstonecraft's particular salvation at this time was her drive and her ability to focus it in intellectual pursuits. When she set herself to study in Dublin she was determining to develop fully this aspect of herself, urgent since girlhood. She had always known she was brighter, more sensitive, and stronger than most. The Kingsborough milieu confirmed her opinion that the socially elite could be vulgar, shallow, and stupid; she measured herself and realized that she had extraordinary capacity, even genius, as she began to think of it, the miraculous ingredient that distinguished her from her sisters, or Ogle from the Kingsboroughs. In Dublin she investigated the subject, first in Blair's lecture on genius, and on March 24, in a letter to Everina: "I am now reading Rousseau's *Emile*, and love his paradoxes. He chuses a common capacity to educate—and gives, as a reason, that a genius will educate itself."

She felt the shock of recognition. It was exactly what she had done with her own life. On March 25 she sent Everina George Ogle's definition of genius:

> Genius, 'tis the ethereal Beam—
> Tis sweet Willy Shakespeare's dream,
> the sense upon the wing
> wild Fancy's magic sing
> the Phrenzy of the Mind
> the eye that ne'er is blind
> the Prophet's holy fire
> tis the music of the lyre
> tis the enthusiast's frantic bliss . . .

Again on May 11: "attractive genius—I bow before thee." This was Ogle's attraction: "genius and sensibility lights his eyes."[18] This was the subject of their conversations—his genius, and his appreciation of hers. It could also have been a comforting explanation for her own "Phrenzy of mind," which according to Ogle was proof of superior gifts.

High intellect was connected to religion for her. On April 17, in a letter to Gabell, she took the affirmative on the question "Whether intellectual acquirements gained here are of any service or pleasure hereafter?" Gabell had taken the negative position for "fat contented ignorance." Eloquently, and with growing certainty, Mary Wollstonecraft asserted her philosophy: intellect and sensibility, although painful, were precious and rewarding.

> [I] cannot entirely coincide with you. . . . An Allwise and good Being created nothing in vain. He cannot be mistaken or cause *needless* pain. . . . Why have we implanted in us an irresistible desire to think—if thinking is not in some measure necessary to make us wise unto salvation. Indeed intellectual and moral improvement seem to me so connected—I cannot, even in thought separate them. . . . St. Paul says, "we *see* through a glass *darkly*"—but he does not assert that we are *blind*. . . . In short the more I reflect, the less apt am I to concur with you—if I did, I should envy *comfortable* folly . . . refinement genius—and those charming talents which my soul instinctively loves, produce misery in this world—abundantly more pain than pleasure. Why then do they at all unfold themselves *here?* if useless, would not . . . the tender Father, have shut them up. . . . Besides sensibility renders the path of duty more intricate—and the warfare *much* more severe—Surely *peculiar* wretchedness has something to balance it![19]

Genius was an active factor in morality. In criticizing Lady Kingsborough's character, Mary Wollstonecraft wrote Everina that it required a "peculiar kind of genius" to be truly moral. "Sensibility," she wrote in *Mary,* "produces flights of virtue," although she added it required the curb of reason.[20]

Genius and Virtue—the subject of her next book began to define itself.

On April 14 Mary Wollstonecraft wrote a second time to Joseph Johnson. She gave no indication that she was considering writing another book; in fact, the letter may have been meant to excuse the fact that she had not been able to work.

Dear sir,
I am still an invalid—and begin to believe that I ought never to expect to enjoy health. . . . How can I be reconciled to life, when it is always a painful warfare, and when I am deprived of all the pleasures I relish? —I allude to rational conversations, and domestic affections. Here, alone, a poor solitary individual in a strange land, tied to one spot, and subject to the caprice of another, can I be contented? I am desirous to convince you that I have *some* cause for sorrow—and am not without reason detached from life.[21]

Illness and the job she detested were not the only reasons for her lack of productivity. She was also harassed by family and money problems. Ned had won the mysterious lawsuit against Roebuck, but was withholding Mary's portion of the money gained, which she expected to use to pay her debt to Mrs. Burgh. Mary was unbelieving at first, then furious. She could not bring herself to write her brother and was ashamed to tell Mrs. Burgh or even to let Everina explain; it was too "humiliating," she wrote. Mrs. Burgh, however, wanted her money and knew Ned had it. Mary turned on her old friend in a letter to Everina:

The other day I received a letter from Mrs. Burgh advising me to write to my brother in a very *humble* style, etc. etc. So the money is still in his hands—I do not intend to follow her advice, and suppose she will be displeased. I know she expected that I should make my fortune here—and to pecuniary considerations she thinks everything ought to give way: but it matters not, yet it is by no means pleasant to be under obligation to a person with whose opinions I can so seldom coincide.

Equally ugly was her attitude toward Mrs. Burgh's nephew, whom she also owed. "I find Church is still the same *prudent* creature. I have mentioned his demand to Skeys," she wrote Everina. "You may tell him so—*that* he will find interesting." Mary Wollstonecraft, who was the most improvidently generous person with money, expected reciprocity. She obviously felt Mrs. Burgh and Church should forgive her debts as she would have forgiven theirs. But this nasty attack on Mrs. Burgh, who had done so much for her, had another source. Mary wanted to leave her job as soon as possible but could not resign until she had money to pay her debts and set out on her own. Ned's refusal to pay, and Mrs. Burgh's to forget, meant everything Mary was grinding away to make was obligated to Newington Green; in short, she was running in place. To make matters worse she was worried about her unhappy sisters. Because she herself wanted to leave Ireland she was having second thoughts about Dublin jobs for them, which Mrs. Fitzgerald was investigating now that Mary and Lady Kingsborough were at sword's points. Mary wrote Everina March 25 to withdraw her original proposal and gave as her reason Eliza's incompetence and whining—"I think I hear her gloomy sing song."

Eliza could do nothing but wait for assistance; Everina was forced into action because Ned had apparently decided to get rid of her. A relative on their mother's side, Lucy Dickson, was expected to join his household, which already included his wife, two children, Everina, and young Charles Wollstonecraft, who was studying law in London. Ned therefore invented some sort of "shameful story" about Everina—"he wishes to get you out of the house before Lucy Dickson arrives," Mary grimly concluded—and Everina was casting about for a place to go. She made a conquest of George Blood, who saw her when he visited London in April. "You have rivalled the princess," Mary wrote. "George talks continually of you, and blushes when he mentions your name." Everina had spunk; fortified by her small annuity, she found herself a job teaching school in Henley and left Ned's house forever. But neither she nor Eliza had enough money even to spend a vacation together until Mary scraped up four guineas for them. This was all she could do for the moment. "Until my debts are paid I cannot take *active* steps to make myself useful to those I am interested *about*," she wrote Everina May 15.

By this time she had something in mind once her second half-year's wages came due in the autumn. "I cannot be more explicit or explain schemes which are only in embryo," she wrote Everina. It may be that she had begun her second book; it is possible, too, she was hoping for another source of money. She made it clear she disliked the Irish intensely and intended to get away from their country with or without the Kingsboroughs. "I scarcely know where we shall spend the summer," she wrote Everina May 11. "I am trying to persuade Lady K. to go to the Continent but am afraid she will not. I wish to take in some *quite* new objects."[22] The Kingsboroughs left Dublin for Bristol with their entourage in June. While here Mary was offered some financial help. On June 27 she wrote Eliza triumphantly:

> I have every reason to think, I shall be able to pay my Debts before I leave the Kingdom. A *friend*, whose name I am not *permitted* to mention has insisted on lending me the money . . . I hope to contrive for you and Everina to spend the winter vacation together, as the only alleviation I can devise to render your confinement tolerable . . . I rejoiced to meet with a fellow creature whom I could admire for doing a disinterested act of kindness—In short, it is a present . . . the lending it was first mentioned to me as a delicate way of reconciling me to it. I intend paying . . . everybody, and as Lady K. is in my debt, I shall be able to afford to visit you and Everina.

The unknown benefactor was not Ogle, whom Mary condemned again for sensuality in the same letter; perhaps it was Mrs. Fitzgerald, although Mary had already borrowed ten guineas from her to give Betty Delane before she left Dublin; perhaps Joseph Johnson; or even Lord Kingsborough. The sex of the donor seems deliberately disguised. Although Mary said that despite this expected windfall her nerves were worse than ever, her tone was firm, and she also told Eliza with satisfaction that she was writing: "I *hope* you have not forgot that I am an author." Mary spent the summer with the Kingsboroughs in Bristol completing a "fiction," *Mary*. She had no time for the pleasant resort town; her only comment to Eliza was that the gentry in residence "are not the sort of beings that afford me amusement." In Bristol, the fashionable companion spa to Bath, where as a green girl she got her first glimpse of high society, she proclaimed through *Mary* her superiority to that world.

This book is a dramatization of Mary Wollstonecraft's life and misfortunes. Its full title is *Mary: A Fiction*, but she told Gabell that in it she had "drawn from nature": almost all the characters are given recognizable if not identical names to their models; most of the story is hyperbolic autobiography.[23] The theme is the self-education and fate of a virtuous genius, a Mary Wollstonecraft, and the concept was sparked by what she had recently read in *Emile*. The title page quotes Rousseau: "*L'exercise des plus sublimes vertus élève et nourrit le génie.*" Yet there is not a glimmer of genius in it, for Mary's lack of objectivity and need to reveal what she believed about herself created a heroine extraordinary only in self-consciousness, sanctimony, and self-pity, one given to Eliza Bishop's "gloomy sing-song," which Mary never seemed to realize was her own tune as well. When one imagines the original book that could have been made of Mary Wollstonecraft's life up to that time—perhaps an early *Jane Eyre*—*Mary* is almost ridiculous, even with the genre of the sentimental novel taken into account. However, as documentation of what Mary saw as important, the work is invaluable. *Thoughts on the Education of Daughters* presented her character and philosophy; *Mary*, her emotional life. As she said in the foreword, she intended to exhibit her soul and to prove that it was possible for females, at least in a fiction, to have great mind and character.

With astonishing self-service and revelation, the novel begins: "Mary, the heroine of this fiction, was the daughter of Edward, who married Eliza, a gentle fashionable girl, with a kind of indolence in her temper." Eliza combines something of her namesake and a great deal of Mary Wollstonecraft's mother and of Lady Kingsborough. Eliza is fashionably and unhappily married to a brutal, very rich boor. She is a "mere nothing," a devourer of romantic novels over which she weeps "in copious showers, down beautiful cheeks, to a discomposure of rouge, etc. etc."; she is also a dog lover, and chaste through convention rather than conviction. She adores her older child, a son, "and when Mary, the little blushing girl appeared, she would fend the awkward thing away." The fictional Mary lives her author's childhood: violent father; unloving, ailing mother; favored brother; passionate, conscientious, sensitive daughter devoted to intellectual development, religion, and benevolence. Mary meets a Fanny Blood—Ann—and conceives an ardent attachment to her. At seventeen Mary becomes a great heiress when her brother dies. (Mary Wollstonecraft complained that novels were always about the upper classes, yet in her own fiction chose that station.) Her parents arrange her marriage to Charles, son of the owners of the adjacent estate and younger than his intended. Although Mary "rolled her eyes about [in] extreme horror at taking—at being forced to take, such a hasty step," she consents because she believes she can better help consumptive Ann: "to snatch her from the very jaws of destruction—she would have encountered a lion." She is married at her mother's deathbed, after which her young husband leaves to study abroad.

Mary and Ann live together, with consequent disillusion on Mary's part. There is no Skeys; Mary takes her friend to Portugal to recover her health. Here Mary meets, among the snobbish tourists, a man who

Joseph Johnson *(left)*, bookseller and publisher. He helped Mary Wollstonecraft launch her career and became her close friend. St. Paul's Churchyard *(below)*. From 1787 to 1792 the center of Mary Wollstonecraft's work and social life was at No. 72, Johnson's place of business and home.

NORTH SIDE OF ST PAUL'S CHURCH YARD, WITH THE END OF CHEAPSIDE.

Indeed, we are very happy!——

Look what a fine morning it is.—Insects, Birds, & Animals, are all enjoying existence

Henry Fuseli. Mary Wollstonecraft began by admiring his genius, then loved him. Haughton's miniature *(above, left)* was said to be a striking likeness, whereas Fuseli's self-portrait *(above, right)* no doubt gives Fuseli's dramatic version of himself. Fuseli's naturally vigorous "Debutante" *(right)* a victim of social convention, is here seen forcibly restrained.

Two of William Blake's illustrations of the protagonists of Mary Wollstonecraft's *Original Stories (opposite, above)*. Her educational aims for girls were in sharp contrast to the norm, here caricatured *(opposite, below)*, in Edward F. Burney's "An Establishment for Young Ladies" in which the goal is obviously a suitable marriage.

Mary Wollstonecraft, the intellectual Amazon at thirty-two. This first portrait, by an unknown artist commissioned by William Roscoe, was painted while she was writing *Vindication of the Rights of Woman.* She told Roscoe her book would be an even better portrait.

Mary Wollstonecraft, softer and more complex, painted by her admirer John Opie, probably within a year of the Roscoe portrait and after she had decided to enhance her appearance for Fuseli's sake.

Mary Wollstonecraft's rivals for Fuseli were his beautiful wife, Sophia, shown here in one of the many portraits he did of her, and his ideal of powerful female allure as in "Satan's First Address to Eve."

William Godwin. A sketch by Sir Thomas Lawrence made in 1795, a year before Godwin and Mary Wollstonecraft became lovers. Mary Wollstonecraft's last portrait painted in 1797 by John Opie.

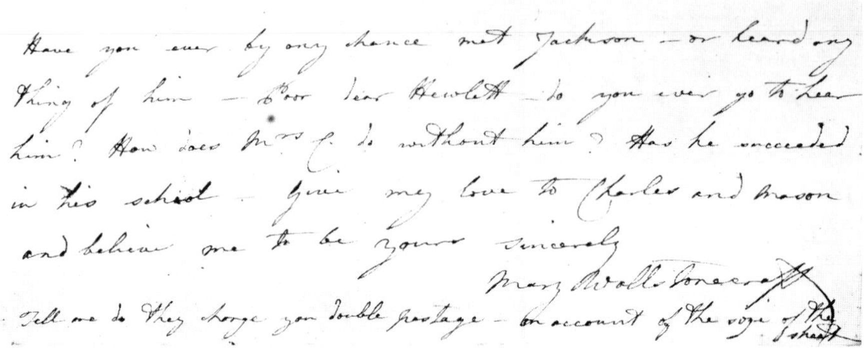
Have you ever by any chance met Jackson — or heard any thing of him — Poor dear Hewlett do you ever go to hear him? How does Mrs C. do without him? Has he succeeded in his school — Give my love to Charles and Mason and believe me to be yours sincerely

Mary Wollstonecraft

Tell me do they charge you double postage — on account of the size of the sheet

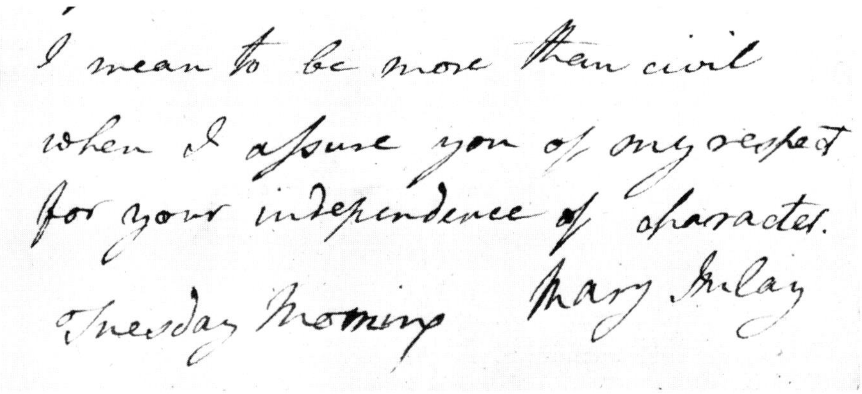
I mean to be more than civil when I assure you of my respect for your independence of character.

Tuesday Morning Mary Imlay

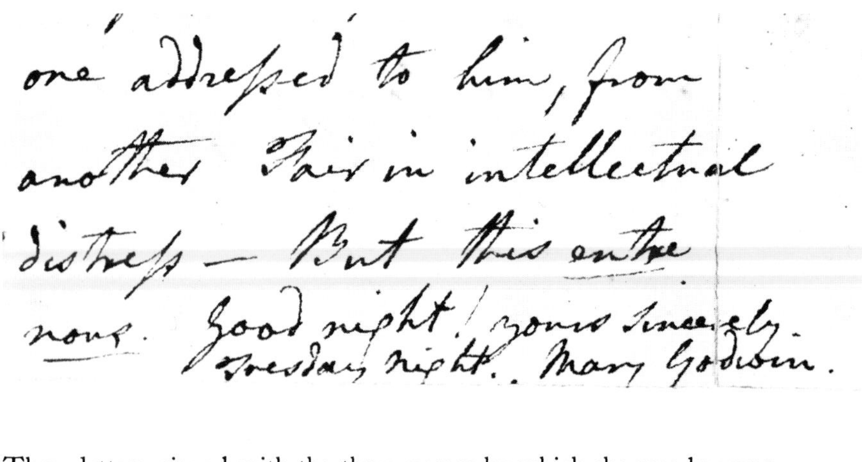
one addressed to him, from another Fair in intellectual distress — But this entre nous. Good night! yours sincerely

Tuesday night. Mary Godwin.

Three letters, signed with the three names by which she was known: Mary Wollstonecraft, Mary Imlay, and Mary Godwin.

is "rather ugly" but with strong lines of genius, with "that kind of awkwardness which is often found in literary men: he seemed a thinker, and delivered his opinions in elegant expressions, and musical tones of voice." Gentle, melancholy, sensitive Henry and Mary are attracted to each other. Abruptly, with the barest mention, Ann dies and Henry takes center stage. His family history resembles that of Henry Wollstonecraft:

> I have myself, said he mournfully, shaken hands with happiness, and am dead to the world. My mother was so attached to my eldest brother, that she took very little pains to fit me for the profession to which I was destined.

Henry's extravagant, ungrateful brother, like Ned, neglected his mother. Henry had been in love with an unworthy lady, but still was "too fond of the elegant arts; and woman—lovely woman!" Look on me as your father, he tells Mary. "If I had had a father, such a father!" she says. That night she dreams she is supporting her dying mother, that Ann is breathing her last and Henry is comforting her. Now Mary realizes she is in love and—as Mary Wollstonecraft herself recently had behaved—"She talked incessantly, she knew not what . . . when she began to laugh she could not stop." Consummated love is impossible because of her marriage, but she vows her sentiments are indelible. "Dear enthusiastic creature," whispers Henry, "how you steal into my soul." Both are wretched but pure. Mary leaves for England, survives a storm at sea, and returns to her family. She announces that she will never live with her husband. "I will work, she cried, do anything rather than be a slave." Easing her aching heart by charity to the poor in the slums of London, she hears nothing from Henry. She meets an older man reminiscent of Waterhouse and distinctly modeled on George Ogle, witty, worldly, sensual, and attractive. But she resists his blandishments and tries to lead him to virtue; she fails, but writes a rhapsody on the sublimity of Christian morality.

Henry returns to England; he is cautious, which Mary resents, but very ill, which makes her tender. Her husband, Charles, announces that he is coming home from the Continent; Mary wonders if it is her duty to live with him. In the meantime she and Henry are caught in a storm while boating on the Thames:

> Mary drew still nearer Henry; she wished to have sought with him a watery grave. . . . Henry saw the workings of her mind—he felt them; threw his arm round her waist—and they enjoyed the luxury of wretchedness. . . . Mary perceived that Henry was wet. . . . What shall I do!—this day will kill thee.

Indeed, the embrace is lethal; he gets worse—"perhaps it was not the cold he caught, that occasioned it." Now that he is dying, they confess their love and weep together. "I am a wretch!" she cries. "I cannot live without loving—and love leads to madness." Henry's mother, blaming herself for her early neglect, asks Mary to help nurse her son. He dies in Mary's arms. Mary and Henry's mother travel to Bath, Bristol, and Southampton. To Mary's disgust, her husband returns. He grants her a year's solitude, after which "she gave him her hand," and lived with him, but when he would "mention anything like love, she would instantly feel a sickness, a faintness at her heart."

In the last chapter, the heroine is in delicate health, not long for this world. Like Lord Kingsborough she has reformed her country estate, "visited the sick, supported the old, and educated the young." Yet benevolence and religion cannot fill her heart. The book ends:

> In moments of solitary sadness, a gleam of joy would dart across her mind—she thought she was hastening to that world *where there is neither marrying,* nor giving in marriage. End.[24]

This then was Mary's reaction to the injustices and struggles of her childhood, to loss of social and financial security. The fictional form allowed her to vent anger on her parents, partially disguised as the Kingsboroughs, although given their true Christian names, as well as on Fanny Blood. It is particularly noteworthy that Ann/Fanny is disposed of peremptorily and a male lover takes over, reinforcing the conclusion already drawn about Mary's interest in men at the time the book was written. This is not the work of a "feminist" but of a woman yearning for a love that fate denies her. Within months of *Mary,* Mary Wollstonecraft was writing *Cave of Fancy,* which continued the same theme: an unhappily married, orphaned girl is in love with a man she cannot marry and that man dies. The close correspondence between the first part of *Mary* and Mary Wollstonecraft's actual life leads one to believe that the last half of the book is at least inspired by real circumstances, however fantasized they may be. As for the lover, neither Waterhouse nor Ogle fits this Henry. Henry Gabell comes closer. There is also Mary's brother Henry, whose mother preferred his older brother and who also may have become ill.

Although these strands cannot be knitted into certain fact, they do show pattern. Whereas in *Thoughts* Mary Wollstonecraft was confident love could be controlled, in *Mary* her heroine has a difficult struggle which fate decides and which breaks her heart. Whatever Mary Wollstonecraft's urges toward a particular man might have been at the time, she was attracted to men who wanted to father her; two types appear in the fiction, the older, worldly man and the younger romantic. Sexual attraction or action results in the death of the lover, and the heroine does penance in good works. Mothers and female friends die. In modern terms this is an ingenuous revelation of an unresolved Oedipal problem, which causes rejection of sex and marriage. The last sentence of *Mary* is emphatic; she even seems to have linked love to madness (her heroine cries, "love leads to madness"). Mary called George Ogle a "half-mad" sensualist. The hysterical outbursts suffered by Mary Wollstonecraft in Ireland are suffered by her frustrated heroine as well. Mary Wollstonecraft was drawn to what she rejected. Her heroine's tragedy is that "my feelings do not accord with the notion of Solitary happiness . . . have I desires planted in me only to make me miserable? will they never be gratified?"[25]

Mary makes manifest Mary Wollstonecraft's situation, that of a passionate, neurotic woman whose puritanism and sense of moral and intellectual superiority block her emotional and physical demands.

Before the Kingsborough family left Bristol in late August of 1787, Mary Wollstonecraft was given time off. During her absence young Margaret was terribly upset. Mary had written Everina that the girl "sees her mother's faults—and sometimes ridicules them—I try to curb her, but fear she will launch out when out of my sight." This was exactly what happened while Mary was away. Margaret and her mother had frequent quarrels, and Lady Kingsborough summarily fired the governess she held responsible. "It disconcerted me at first but I will not dissemble *what* I suffered—though I long expected something of the kind," Mary admitted. She was given the second half of her forty guinea annual salary, but apparently she never took the gift of money she had been offered in late June by someone in the Kingsborough entourage.

Anger and wounded pride aside, Mary Wollstonecraft's only regret was leaving poor Margaret, whom she would have left as soon as opportunity offered in any case. The year was one Mary considered totally wasted. But she had gained more than she realized at the time from the great country estate in Mitchelstown, the elaborate townhouse, and the galas in Dublin, from the variety of worldly and cultivated people she had met. She was undoubtedly a great deal more sophisticated, surer of herself and her capacity, than when she left Newington Green. She had garnered material she would put to good use. She was not yet a radical, but her experience with the Kingsboroughs gave her an understanding of the powerful aristocracy that dominated her society, and further eroded whatever respect she had for its right to rule or its glamour. When she left the Kingsboroughs she had drawn an indelible line between her superior virtue and intellect and the decadence of the nobility; moreover, she had now passed judgment on what she considered to be the contemptible existence of most women. *A Vindication of the Rights of Woman* was generating.

Mary Wollstonecraft had also found a solution for her dangerously overwrought nervous condition. In writing *Mary* she not only rationalized her protests and asserted her personal worth, she discharged emotional pressures that might well have broken her, and with instinctive as well as conscious urgency she moved back on the track of her career.

III

The First of a New Genus

Chapter 9

Like a released prisoner, Mary Wollstonecraft went from the Kingsboroughs directly to what she wanted most from freedom, a writing career under the aegis of Joseph Johnson in London. She appeared suddenly in his office in St. Paul's Churchyard in late August of 1787, a solitary, expectant young woman whose most substantial baggage was the manuscript of her new fiction. She told Johnson she wanted to be a full-time writer and asked for his advice and help. At twenty-eight, without home, roots, job, or mandated future, she knew she now had the opportunity to restructure her life and she was determined to seize it. The prudent course—another income-producing job as teacher or governess, in which shelter she could write as a supplementary vocation—was one she abominated. "Despair and vexations I shrink back from—and *feared* to encounter," she said, for she knew she could not bear the life she had led in the recent past. Yet she knew it was unheard of for a young gentlewoman to live alone and support herself entirely as a professional writer. Apparently she had no funds with which to settle her debts, and she also felt an obligation to help her sisters. She needed reassurance that she could succeed and a base from which to work.

Accustomed as he was to the impulses and intensities of authors, Joseph Johnson reacted to Mary Wollstonecraft's proposal with an imperturbability that at first seemed formal and stiff to her. He was forty-nine years old at this date, a slight man, self-contained, not given to "puffing or parade," as a friend said of him—and justly known for the benevolent humanity Mary quickly discovered in him. In a calm, pragmatic way he assured her she had the talent to support herself if she worked hard. As earnest, he bought *Mary* and discussed other work she could do for him: translations were a sure source of income and she could do original work as well—fiction, children's books. As for her sex, as far as he was concerned it presented no insurmountable problems, and perhaps opportunities, although he was as conscious as she of the break with convention she proposed. The issue was thus settled. Since she had come to London without any preparation, he simply invited her to make his place her home until she was settled, and gave her a room in his quarters above the office, a temporary arrangement the probity of his personal life made respectable.

"I am then going to be the first of a new genus," Mary Wollstonecraft declared. The venture, however, would have been impossible without Johnson's support. Her motivation was parthenogenetic; his was paternalistic and professional. Born of a Dissenting family near Liverpool, Johnson had been publishing and selling books in St. Paul's Churchyard since 1770 and was one of the most astute and famous men of his profession. He had serious chronic asthma, was a confirmed bachelor, and centered his life around his friends—his rooms were a meeting place for intellectuals, particularly liberals—and his work. Johnson was particularly generous with his writers, and was known to buy manuscripts of the needy or promising even if he made no immediate profit from them. *Mary* is a case in point; it never sold, although when Mary Wollstonecraft became famous he tried to revive it. He also had great respect for, and patience with, talent. When Cowper was so discouraged at the poor public reception first given his "The Task" that he decided to write no more, Johnson urged him to continue; and when the work succeeded Johnson gave Cowper £1000 over and above their agreement.

Publishing was a flourishing business; books, newspapers, pamphlets, periodicals streamed from the presses. If Mary Wollstonecraft's contemporaries did not have the genius of Samuel Johnson and his colleagues from the era just ended or that of Wordsworth, Austen, and Coleridge following, they did not lack fecundity. Restless intellectuals and miscellaneous writers were drawn to London publishers, where they were offered a variety of ill-paid jobs but a stimulating life that might bring power and fortune. The same firms printed, published, and sold books, therefore publishers had total responsibility for their works. In this active field Joseph Johnson's authors and imprints were among the best, and their quality and range speaks for his influence: Mrs. Barbauld, Priestley, Erasmus Darwin, Horne Tooke, Maria Edgeworth, young Wordsworth in the early 1790s; fiction, poetry, textbooks, and scientific, medical, and liberal political works. Johnson was also considering launching a progressive monthly magazine.

English women at this time were culturally influential, although less so than in France, and the sort of work Johnson expected at first from Mary Wollstonecraft was aimed at a large and growing market of women readers. The literacy and leisure of middle-class women of Mary's generation far exceeded that of her mother's. "I have heard some ladies," an observer remarked in 1791:

> who neither have nor pretend to have bookish knowledge, use the following words with prompt spontaneity in conversing on common topics, viz. "literature, literary, hilarity, stipulate, excruciating, delusive, juvenile, temerity, contemporary, phenomenon, popular, conservatory," etc. etc. Twenty years ago, scarce one of those words would have been understood, much less used, by the generality of private gentlewomen.

Around ladies of wealth and learning like Mrs. Elizabeth Montagu, queen of the bluestockings, whom Fanny Burney described as "brilliant in diamonds, solid in judgement, and critical in talk," distinguished salons formed. "I never invite idiots to my house," Mrs. Montagu said. She was a friend of General Paoli, a patron of Angelica Kauffman and Hannah More.[1] But most genteel women's lives were still restricted, and the literature they devoured provided vicarious adventures and compensations.

Quantities of books for and about children, sentimental romances spun out in three or more volumes (*Mary* differs only in brevity and pretension), poetry, drama, and some serious literature, were being read and written by women as never before, for women literatae had come into their own on the great wave generated by such men as Fielding, Richardson, and Sterne. Richardson's intimate circle included clever women who published successfully: Charlotte Lennox, Laetitia Pilkington, Hester Chapone, Mrs. Delany, and Mrs. Sheridan, the playwright's mother. Fanny Burney followed her first great triumph of 1778, *Evelina,* with *Cecelia* in 1782; the first edition sold out 2,000 copies in three months.

Women who had to make their living, or part of it, by writing sought, like Hannah More, to have elite sponsors; they were often given pensions by their patrons, and, in general, confined themselves to ladylike subjects. (The only exceptions were women dramatists, by now accepted for a century in England.) To sign with one's own name a commercially published book was just beginning to be acceptable. Fanny Burney published *Evelina* with great trepidation—and anonymously, of course, as a lady should. It became known that she was the author, but her patrons were impeccable and she so poor and charming she did not lose caste. The convention persisted for decades. Many women wrote in secret: Jane Austen's name never appeared on a title page; the Brontë sisters used male pseudonyms. Propriety and upper-class standards favored the author who wrote as an amateur, a man or woman of society who happened to have talent. Even Byron preferred this role.

By the late 1780s it was not uncommon for a woman to appear by name as author, but the more delicate, frivolous, or didactic her work, the more acceptable it was; and it was judged with corresponding condescension: "This work is written by a Lady, consequently not the object of severe criticism," or "many circumstances entitle the softer sex to a more delicate treatment than our own, and therefore it is always with tenderness that we look upon the productions of a female pen."[2] The very few women who ventured outside this circumference were thought to be prodigies, and if like Catherine Macaulay they wrote solid history or discourses on politics, they were considered to have masculine minds of alarming disproportion.

Mary Wollstonecraft thus was originating a new genus when she chose to make her living as a professional writer because she frankly needed and wanted that career. In the same way a man would choose it she used no cloak or excuse; she refused a genteel shelter and lived alone as a man would. What she did need was the emotional and practical help Joseph Johnson gave her when he accepted *Mary* for publication and Mary Wollstonecraft as his protégée. It was a triumph of good instincts on both sides.

Mary Wollstonecraft decided to keep her dismissal from the Kingsboroughs and her plan for a new career secret for the time. Johnson apparently told Godwin she had at first "a vehement aversion to the being regarded, by her ordinary acquaintance, in the character of an author, and to have employed some precautions to prevent its occurrence."[3] Since she had already signed *Thoughts on the Education of Daughters,* it is likely she was more anxious about her ability to succeed as a professional than concerned for her good name; but even more she was determined to avoid the shock, skepticism, and remonstrances she knew would follow an announcement of her intention, and the entangling alternatives her sisters and practical friends (and debtors) like Mrs. Burgh would urge on her. She also had to resist the tug of obligation on her decision for independence, the inevitable corollary of which was that her sisters had to shape their own lives, and this she found difficult to broach directly, face to face. She intended to see Everina and Eliza, both of whom knew she was in England, but during their reunion as far as they knew she was still the Kingsboroughs' governess, and for three months they were none the wiser.

Johnson became Mary Wollstonecraft's man of business as well as her literary godfather in September of 1787. He undertook to find a suitable lodging and servant for her in London while she visited her sisters at their respective schools. She left London the second week in September and went first to the sister whose company she anticipated with the greater pleasure, Everina, at Miss Rowden's school in Henley.

Everina Wollstonecraft at twenty-one or -two was a spirited, sturdy girl, "the thick-legged beauty," someone called her. Mary frequently reproached her for laziness and lack of motivation, but Everina was emotionally stable enough so that Mary could weep on her shoulder, and game enough to have walked out of Ned's house when he and his wife wanted to get rid of her, even if it meant taking a job she hated. Everina missed the vanished pleasures of society, however, and particularly loathed teaching at Miss Rowden's "vulgar" establishment. Since she had to work, she had been hesitantly considering George Blood's suggestion that she and Eliza come to Dublin and open a school, a prospect doubly desirable to the young man because he was seriously devoted to Everina. When Mary arrived at Henley, the sisters discussed the idea. Realistic from sad experience, Mary was convinced Everina and Eliza could not operate a school on their own, and Mary so wrote George Blood on September 11. Not only did they lack capital and that wretched "french," but "Everina's vivacity, would by the injudicious be termed giddiness"; Everina's youth and inexperience, Eliza's "lassitude" (two lines following were censored), all made the scheme impossible, particularly in Ireland where, as Mary's Dublin months had taught her, "everyone's conduct is canvassed, and the least deviation from a ridiculous rule of propriety . . . would endanger their precarious subsistence." Everina did not want to encourage George Blood's affection and had to be prodded to add even a final paragraph to Mary's letter, one of the very few of her communications extant. Always a dilatory correspondent with everyone, she apologized to George for her delay in answering him, and put the quietus on the Dublin project. She was, she wrote: "very disagreeably situated here, and were it not for the comfort I find on reflecting that I am not dependent on Ned and his amiable spouse, I would be quite unhappy . . . till Mary came I don't think I ever discomposed my features with a smile."

To salve her conscience Mary tried a "forlorn hope" two days later through Henry Gabell, asking him to find Everina a position as companion or teacher in Ireland. The passage on her own sorrows reads like an exoneration of the guilt she was feeling:

> My dear Sir:
> I . . . am now with a favorite sister, whose situation is very unpleasant; my anxiety and affection has made me strain every nerve to alter it; but I have continually been disappointed. I dare say you have gathered from my conversation, that I have been in every respect unfortunate . . . relative to those unfortunate females who are left by inconsiderate parents to struggle with the world. . . . I felt what I wrote! . . . The extravagance of a Father, and his second marriage has left my sisters friendless; I would fain be their mother and protector; but I am not formed to obtain the good things of this world. . . . The sister I am at present anxious about, a fine girl, is now a Teacher in a vulgar school . . . she has fine spirits, I grieve to see them broken so soon. . . . She has a small annuity, and I wish to place her in a Gentlemans family 'till fortune smiles on me—or she gains experience . . . I am still on the ramble . . . I suppose *your own Ann*—has informed you that I wrote

to her. I intended visiting her; but it was not convenient. My head is in such a confused state I scarcely know what I am writing—Adieu Mon cher ami

Mary Wollstonecraft

. . . 'Spite of my vexations, I have lately written, a fiction which I intend to give to the world; it is a tale, to illustrate an opinion of mine, that a genius will educate itself.[4]

On the same day Mary wrote Joseph Johnson in London, reasserting her primary concern and assuming the superior tone of author and thinker:

My dear sir
Since I saw you, I have, literally speaking, *enjoyed* solitude. My sister could not accompany me in my rambles; I therefore wandered alone, by the side of the Thames, and in the neighbouring beautiful fields. . . . Were I to give you an account how I have spent my time, you would smile.—I found an old French bible here, and amused myself with comparing it with our English translation; then I would listen to the falling leaves, or observe the various tints the autumn gave to them . . . I was, at the same time perhaps discussing some knotty point, or straying from this *tiny* world to new systems. After these excursions, I returned to the family meals, told the children stories (they think me *vastly* agreeable), and my sister was amused. . . .

. . . Have you yet heard of a habitation for me? I often think of my new plan of life; and, lest my sister should try to prevail on me to alter it, I have avoided mentioning it to her. I am determined!—Your sex generally laugh at female determinations; but let me tell you, I never yet resolved to do, anything of consequence, that I did not adhere resolutely to it, till I had accomplished my purpose, improbable as it might have appeared to a more timid mind . . . I long for a little peace and *independence!* . . . I am not fond of grovelling!

Mary left Everina after a week and returned to London to take the coach to Eliza at Market Harborough in Leicestershire, a visit she did not look forward to. Johnson was thoughtful enough to see her off. She wrote him when she arrived at Eliza's school on September 20 that she did not expect to enjoy the same tranquil pleasures Henley afforded; "I meet with new objects to employ my mind; but many painful emotions are complicated with the reflections they give rise to. I do not intend to enter on the *old* topic." If she refrained from retelling her sorrows, she could not resist impressing him once again with her superiority, social and intellectual:

> You left me with three opulent tradesmen: their conversation was not calculated to beguile the way . . . I listened to the tricks of trade—and shrunk away, without wishing to grow rich; even the novelty of the subjects did not render them pleasing . . . I was not surprised by any glimpse of the sublime, or beautiful—though one of them imagined I should be a useful partner in a good *firm.*[5]

Eliza was even unhappier than Everina, more desperate for relief and less competent to seek a job. Mary spent a week with Eliza, one that tried her patience and resolve, since she had to listen to Eliza's complaints knowing her sister would plead to live with her had she known Mary had been fired and intended to live in London. Meredith Bishop may have died around this time, for his name disappears permanently from London directories after 1787. Mary then returned to London bypassing Newington Green and Mrs. Burgh's keen eye.

At the end of September Mary Wollstonecraft moved into modest rooms Johnson found for her at 49 George (later Dolben) Street on the Surrey side of Blackfriar's Bridge. She was within walking distance of St. Paul's Churchyard, had a servant one of Johnson's relations sent from the country, and scarcely any furniture. Here she set to work on a book for children and tried her hand at "a sort of oriental tale," *Cave of Fancy*. She saw very few people other than Johnson, for she was still anxious to keep her secret. Only on November 7, three months after her great decision, did she tell Everina what she was doing, and even then it took her a quarter of the long letter before she got to the main point. She discussed Gabell's efforts for Everina—they had come to nothing, although she had written again in October; announced that she had sent Mrs. Burgh £20—"I was on every account sorry to part with it, as I am afraid I shall not be able to continue to pay Sowerby [another creditor] and enable Eliza to spend her Holidays in Town"; broke the news that she had been fired by the Kingsboroughs; and finally revealed her secret:

> Before I go on will you pause—and if after deliberating you will promise not to mention to *anyone* what you know of my designs (although you

may think my requesting you to conceal them unreasonable) I will trust to your honor—and proceed. Mr. Johnson . . . assures me that if I exert my talents in writing I may support myself in a comfortable way . . . I tremble at the attempt, yet if I fail I *only* suffer, and should I succeed, my dear Girls will ever in sickness have a home and a refuge where for a few months of the year, they may forget the cares that disturb the rest. I shall strain every nerve to procure a situation for Eliza nearer Town. . . . I would not on any account inform my father or Edward of my designs—you and Eliza are the only part of the family I am interested about—I wish to be a mother to you both. My undertaking would subject me to ridicule—and an inundation of *friendly* advice to which I cannot listen—I must be independent.

. . . freedom, even uncertain freedom, is dear. . . . This project has long floated in my mind—you know I am not born to tread in the beaten track, the peculiar bent of my nature pushes me on.

By omission, Mary thus made it clear she did not intend to have Eliza and Everina live with her.

Everina answered by return post, astounded at this venture, begging for more details. Mary herself was only beginning to believe what she had done was real. She was hard at work on her next book, she replied to Everina, and anticipated finishing before the Christmas holidays, when she expected both sisters to stay with her. Since she had only one bed, Johnson had offered to put them up, but she planned to buy some furniture. When tired of working, she wrote, she went to Johnson's, "and there I meet the kind of company I find most pleasure in"; she had also spent a day with the respectable, established author of children's books, Mrs. Sarah Trimmer. She made it clear, however, that she had sorrows: "an organ under my window has been playing . . . my spectacles are dim—the present sprightly strain seems impertinent—I cannot keep time with it"; and wrote of her career as if it were a charitable enterprise, while more carefully than in the first letter delineating what her sisters could expect from her. A few months cohabitation was reduced to two:

Mr. J. knows that, next to obtaining the means of life, I wish to mitigate [Eliza's] and your fate. I have done with the delusions of fancy, I only live to be useful . . . two months in the year [may be] a little pleasanter than they would otherwise be to you and poor uncomfortable Bess.

Mary asked Everina to continue to conceal her new life from everyone. It is probable Eliza was ignorant of it until the holidays. Seventeen-year-old Charles Wollstonecraft, Mary's favorite brother now articled to and living with Ned in London, heard she was in the city and wrote her, angry that she had not contacted him. All her communications were sent to Johnson's office, and it was here she first met Charles, not at George Street.

As no other woman of her generation had yet done, without supplementary job, income, genteel shelter, or attending family to lend respectability, Mary Wollstonecraft now set out alone to earn a living by her pen. From October 1787 until the spring of 1788 she lived at her writing table in the George Street room, hour after hour, day after day, straining to make good, sometimes apprehensive and depressed, gradually gaining confidence she could make a success. She and Johnson sent each other notes when occasion demanded, and she sometimes walked across Blackfriar's Bridge to St. Paul's Churchyard when she needed solace or when Johnson asked her to dine, but she was not yet on a par with the eminent members of his inner circle. Johnson's introduction of Mary to the limited Mrs. Trimmer shows the level on which Mary Wollstonecraft belonged in his estimation.

If she kept to the schedule she had set for herself, *Original Stories from Real Life; with Conversations, Calculated to Regulate the Affections, and Form the Mind to Truth and Goodness* was completed before the Christmas holidays of 1787. Johnson's reaction to it was generally favorable, but he objected to the preface in which Mary Wollstonecraft, with authoritative bluntness born of recent experience in the Kingsborough milieu, castigated

> the present state of society, which obliges the author to cure those faults by reason, which ought never to have taken root in the infant mind . . . to wish that parents would, themselves, mould the ductile passions, is a chimerical wish, for the present generation have their own passions to combat with and fastidious pleasures to pursue, neglecting those pointed out by nature.

Johnson felt this was a bit strong. Not Mary. She wrote him:

> Though your remarks are generally judicious—I cannot *now* concur with you, I mean with respect to the preface, and have not altered it.

> I hate the usual smooth way of exhibiting proud humility . . . believe me, the few judicious parents who may peruse my book, will not feel themselves hurt—and the weak are too vain to mind what is said in a book intended for children. . . .
>
> If parents attended to their children, I would not have written the stories; for, what are books—compared to conversations which affection inforces![6]

Original Stories was based on her year with the Kingsborough girls—"from real life," as claimed in the title—and incorporates much of her prior experience. In the book the governess becomes a well-to-do lady, Mrs. Mason, "a woman of tenderness and discernment," responsible out of a sense of duty for fourteen-year-old Mary (Mary Wollstonecraft's adolescent alter ego) and twelve-year-old Caroline, both "shamefully ignorant" of moral discipline, which Mrs. Mason, who had subdued her own passions, was determined to give them. Thus every incident becomes an urgent, often severe lesson, as if salvation were at stake, which to Mary Wollstonecraft was almost the case. The utilization of the name Mason is interesting but odd. The Miss Mason who helped at Mary's Newington Green school was reliable, good-hearted, limited, and stolid; after leaving Mary she worked at an unpleasant job, and Mary's letters from Ireland frequently asked for "poor Mason." Mrs. Mason of *Original Stories* seems closer to Mrs. Burgh, a serious and superior woman—and, of course, to Mary Wollstonecraft herself. The character meant a great deal to Margaret, Mary's favorite of the Kingsborough children. Years later when Margaret left her husband, Lord Mount Cashell, she took the name "Mrs. Mason."

In the first chapter Mrs. Mason takes the girls for the daily walk she has decided is necessary to them, and the children happily stomp on insects and worms along the path. Exemplary Mrs. Mason, however, silently and deliberately steps out of the path onto the grass. When questioned, she says she wants to avoid some snails. Why not kill the nasty creatures? asks young Mary. "With great gravity, Mrs. Mason asked how she dared kill anything, unless it were to prevent its hurting her? . . . Then, resuming a smiling face," she tells them God created all to be happy. Young Mary does not think worms important. "Yet," Mrs. Mason says, "God cares for them. . . . You are often troublesome—I am stronger than you—yet I do not kill you." From this bit of sobering logic she goes on to speak of the beauty and balance of nature, using the animals of the fields through which they are walking to illustrate. They see a boy wound a lark and take the mother bird and nest with them to see if they can save the young. Mrs. Mason puts one dying bird out of its pain. "To allow the poor bird to die by inches . . . would be selfishness or weakness. Saying so, she put her foot on the bird's head, turning her own another way."

> Now, said she, we will return to breakfast; give me your hands, my little girls, you have done good this morning, you have acted like rational creatures. Look, what a fine morning it is. Insects, birds, and animals are all enjoying this sweet day. Thank God for permitting you to see it, and for giving you an understanding which teaches you that you ought, by doing good, to imitate Him.
>
> . . . The little girls were very assiduous to gain Mrs. Mason's good opinion. . . .
>
> She was never in a passion, but her quiet steady displeasure made them feel so little in their own eyes, they wished her to smile. . . .
>
> I declare I cannot go to sleep, said Mary, I am afraid of Mrs. Mason's eyes. . . . I wish I were as wise and good as she is.

When the girls squabble, tell petty lies, are greedy, rude, insincere, or selfish, their "tender friend" admonishes and corrects them with examples of unfortunates whom they should pity, the sly, selfish, timid, or bad whom they should eschew, and the strong, kind, and virtuous whom they should emulate.

She takes the children to see poverty and social injustice in the flesh, to develop their social conscience and charitable responsibilities. They visit Crazy Robin, who went mad after his children and wife died during his imprisonment for debt (here Mrs. Mason draws a parallel with the Bastille); Honest Jack, a crippled sailor; an old Welsh harper persecuted and ruined by his landlord; a woman shopkeeper who can scarcely support her jailed son's children because her wealthy clients are dilatory in their payments; a horrible tenement with starving inhabitants. She contrasts grasping, lonely Lady Sly with cultured, sincere, and modest Mrs. Trueman, so like Fanny Blood. She takes them to meet Anna, a school mistress whose extravagant father killed himself, forcing Anna to become the companion of a disagreeable but wealthy woman, until she spurned "the bitter bread" of such dependence and became a self-supporting, useful teacher. She warns them about anger, now "a little despicable vice" rather than the great problem she had judged it in *Thoughts*.

As the children begin to understand and improve, Mrs. Mason becomes more confidential. From her unhappy life the girls learn the value of independence, fortitude, religious faith. She is a widow who has lost her child and found peace, as the heroine of *Mary* attempted to do, in virtue and benevolence. It is she who is the patron or savior of almost all the unfortunates to whom she has introduced her charges. "This is practical prayer," she tells them:

> She laughed with the poor she had made happy, and wept when she recollected her own sorrows; the illusions of youth—the gay expectations . . . I have been very unfortunate, my young friends; but my griefs are now of a placid kind. . . . Early attachments have been broken—the death of friends I loved has so clouded my days; that neither the beams of prosperity, nor even those of benevolence, can dissipate the gloom. . . . I am weaned from the world . . . often wounded by ingratitude . . . and have thrown my eyes round an empty world.

Mrs. Mason tells them of a penniless girl (named Fanny) who married an old rake. "Ah! Why did she marry, said Mary." Snaps Mrs. Mason, "Because she was timid." The girl went mad from grief and was put in an asylum. Mrs. Mason has little patience with weakness and female frailties, even those as minor as taking too long to dress. "Fathers, and men in general, complain of this inattention; they have always to wait for females . . . this . . . weakens esteem. When we frequently make allowance for another in trifling matters, notions of inferiority take root in the mind, and too often produce contempt."[7]

In its emphasis on initiative, independence, and courage, *Original Stories* differed from the common run of such books of the period for girls, and its hovels and miseries were particularly harsh. Mary Wollstonecraft's identification with her subjects and protagonists gave the book bite and character. Although she now seems unduly rigorous, an artist and poet as sensitive as William Blake drew Mrs. Mason as a lovely and loving woman in his illustrations for the book. After its publication in April of 1788, a friendly reviewer praised its judicious subject matter "calculated to convey instruction in the most pleasing form," produced by "a mind that can think and feel."[8] The book is far better organized and disciplined than *Thoughts* or *Mary.* Mary Wollstonecraft had proved she could turn out a professional job of substantial originality. It was a success; there were four editions over a period of thirty-five years.

Eliza and Everina spent the long winter holiday of 1787–1788 at Mary's apartment on George Street, interrupting her momentum and peace. On January 1, 1788, as "the ringing of the bells reminds me that the new year this day begins," Mary wrote George Blood that Eliza was miserable and that Everina had left Miss Rowden's school with no prospective alternative job. "You may suppose that their unsettled state harasses me," she wrote. "In particular I am uneasy about Eliza. I cannot support her, or even recommend her to a more comfortable school. . . . I labour for tranquility of mind and that patient fortitude which will enable me to bear what I cannot ward off."

Eliza dragged herself sorrowfully back to Market Harborough when school reopened the third week of January. Everina remained at George Street several more weeks while Mary arranged to send her to live with a French family in Paris to master the language without which Everina could never get a better job. Since neither *Mary* nor *Original Stories* had as yet been published, and Mary Wollstonecraft's fee for them was insufficient for such an ambitious project, the funds came from an advance Johnson gave Mary. Delighted with his generosity and trust, she gave him the compliment of telling him he transcended his trade:

> My dear sir,
> Remember you are to settle *my account,* as I want to know how much I am in your debt—but do not suppose that I feel any uneasiness on that score. The generality of people in trade would not be much obliged to me for a like civility, *but you were a man* before you were a bookseller —so I am your sincere friend,
>
> Mary[9]

On January 17 Mary Wollstonecraft had told George Blood she was in better health than she had been in years. But after Everina's departure for France in mid-February, she became depressed out of loneliness and lovelessness. She was mourning Fanny Blood afresh, for writing *Mary* had brought the old loss back, and there was no replacement. She corresponded secretly, because of Lady Kingsborough, with young Margaret, who she said might cheer her childless old age. Her only available intimate was young Charles Wollstonecraft, whom she saw often, but her way of loving him was to lecture him constantly in order "to fix some principles in his mind" to counteract Ned's influence. She was mostly alone and at work, took little exercise except for occasional walks across Blackfriar's Bridge to Johnson's, and found it hard to concentrate. March third she wrote George Blood that some of her old nervous complaints had returned—headaches, listlessness, and melancholy. She consulted her Newington Green friend John Hewlett, and went to hear him preach a sermon, written for her, on the certainty of meeting loved ones in heaven. But she forced herself again to study Italian, which she had begun in Dublin, and to improve her French, both needed if she was to translate, as well as to read widely and try to write *Cave of Fancy*. "Many motives impell me on besides sheer love of knowledge," she wrote Everina. "It is the only way to destroy the worm that will gnaw the core, and make that being an isolé, whom nature made too susceptible of affections."

Mary Wollstonecraft never finished *Cave of Fancy*, and it is no loss to literature. However she wrote enough to indicate her state of mind during these months. Like *Mary*, the book is concerned with educating a girl for virtue and wisdom, and with the problem of frustrated love.

Mary apparently drew on Samuel Johnson's *Rasselas* (a melancholy counterpart to *Candide*), the story of a prince of Abyssinia who dwells in an idyllic valley entered only through a fearsome cavern. He is instructed by a sage, and with his sister voyages through the world losing illusions and finally accepting the human condition. *Rasselas* begins: "Ye who listen with credulity to the whispers of fantasy, and pursue with eagerness the phantoms of hope . . . attend to the history of Rasselas." Compare Johnson's words with Mary's at the beginning of *Cave:* "Ye who expect constancy where everything is changing, and peace in the midst of tumult, attend the voice of experience."

Cave consists of one chapter about a sage living in a cavern who adopts a shipwrecked, orphaned little girl, and a second in which a deceased female Spirit materializes to educate the child by narrating the story of her earthly career, which, predictably, had been unhappy from her childhood (like Mary's as well as Fanny Blood's) until her death. The Spirit had passionately but purely loved a young married man, but she married another, older man in order to resist temptation and aid her mother. Subsequently, her true love died, driving the despairing Spirit to rush through wild scenery until she had a mystic illumination; life and death were part of a mighty whole and she would meet her sweetheart in life everlasting. (She also realized that if they had been united on earth, she would not have loved him ardently for very long.) She then turned to charitable works and soon after died lonely but virtuous: "Remorse had not reached me, because I adhered to my principles."

The similarity to *Mary* is striking; Mary Wollstonecraft again imagined an unhappily married heroine and transferred her love for Fanny to a male love who dies. The theme is how to live without love, and the attempt is to channel Mary's own sensibility, which is described at length in the book: "acute senses, finely fashioned nerves, which vibrate at the slightest touch . . . one moment a paradise . . . a cloud arises . . . and the world is an unweeded garden."

On Joseph Johnson's advice or her own judgment, Mary Wollstonecraft stopped work on this book; and after the substantial effort and emotion she put into it, this failure must have contributed to her depression. She liked it well enough, however, to keep it among her papers until she died. The most interesting item in the story is the description of the Spirit's elderly husband, who appears to be Joseph Johnson:

> humanity itself [and] common sense. His friendships, for he had many friends, gave him pleasure unmixed with pain; his religion was coldly reasonable, because he wanted fancy. . . . not having an enthusiastic affection for his fellow creatures, he did them good, without suffering from their follies. He was particularly attached to me, and I felt for him all the affection of a daughter; often, when he had been interesting himself to promote my welfare, have I lamented that he was not my father.[10]

The qualities Mary Wollstonecraft saw as his limitations made Joseph Johnson the ideal mentor for her. She found she could depend on his avuncular affection and consistent rationality in every aspect of her life. Their professional relationship was frank and constructive. Mary felt free occasionally to turn down an assignment she could not handle, and once returned a difficult Italian manuscript saying, "I cannot bear to do anything I cannot do well." She also began to communicate the intimate details of her shifting moods. It was a period of particular instability for her. One Sunday at Johnson's she indiscreetly said something to a guest that got a friend in trouble, and she wrote the publisher that she was so ashamed she would not visit at St. Paul's Churchyard for the balance of the month or even leave her rooms, adding that she had a violent stomachache. Shortly after she took the initiative to write Jacques Necker in Paris via Everina about a translation of his work she planned, and had by then recovered her zest and assurance sufficiently to advise Johnson how other periodicals were reacting to his forthcoming new monthly magazine, for which she was to be a reviewer. Then she reverted, became upset and irritable, and wrote to apologize:

> You are my only friend—the only person I am *intimate* with.—I never had a father, or a brother—you have been both to me, ever since I knew you—I have been thinking of those instances of ill-humour and quickness, and they appeared like crimes.

Johnson's gentle but inflexible realism helped Mary gain an insight into her nature she had never before achieved, expressed in the most perceptive letter she had ever written. Ill and agitated, she nevertheless acknowledged fault not in others but in herself:

> Saturday Night
>
> I am a mere animal, and instinctive emotions too often silence the suggestions of reason. Your note—I can scarcely tell why, hurt me . . . I have been very ill—Heaven knows it was more than fancy—After some sleepless, wearisome nights, towards the morning I have grown delirious. . . . Society was necessary—and might have diverted me . . . but I blushed when I recollected how often I had teazed you with childish complaints, and the reveries of a disordered imagination. I even *imagined* that I intruded on you, because you never called on me—though you perceived that I was not well—I have nourished a sickly kind of delicacy, which gives me many unnecessary pangs . . . I am a strange compound of weakness and resolution! However, if I must suffer, I will endeavour to suffer in silence. There is certainly a great defect in my mind—my wayward heart creates its own misery . . . to weep and dance like a child—long for a toy, and be tired of it as soon as I get it.
>
> We must each of us wear a fool's cap; but mine, alas! has lost its bells and is grown so heavy, I find it intolerably troublesome—Good night! I have been pursuing a number of strange thoughts since I began to write, and have actually both wept and laughed immoderately—Surely I am a fool—

Relieved and more at peace, her vigor soon reasserted itself. She next wrote Johnson:

> Monday morning
>
> I really want a German grammar, as I intend to attempt to learn that language—and I will tell you the reason why—While I live, I am persuaded, I must exert my understanding to procure an independence, and render myself useful. To make the task easier, I ought to store my mind with knowledge—The seed time is passing away . . . I do not complain; on the contrary, I am thankful that I have more than common incentives. . . . You perceive this is not a gloomy day—I feel at this moment particularly grateful to you—without your humane and *delicate* assistance, how many obstacles should I not have had to encounter. . . . Allow me to love you, my dear sir, and call friend a being I respect. Adieu!
>
> Mary W.

Johnson handled her volatility with serene common sense. He accepted the role of Mary's professional and personal supporter as naturally as she, trusting him completely, seems to have expected. Because of debts and family obligations, she was under great financial as well as emotional pressure. He advanced money when needed, and was available to her, busy as he was, almost on demand. He did better than listen sympathetically; he told her she must discipline her self-pity, no matter how realistic her problems. Often she found his stoicism hard to accept. After one evening's conversation she wrote him:

> I thought you *very* unkind, nay, very unfeeling, last night. My cares and vexations . . . do me honour, as they arise from my disinterestedness and *unbending* principles . . . I am not the only character deserving of respect, that has had to struggle with various sorrows . . . Dr. Johnson's cares almost drove him mad—but, I suppose, you would quietly have told him, he was a fool for not being calm, and that wise men striving against the stream, can yet be in a good humour. I have done with insensible human wisdom . . . and turn to the source of perfection—who perhaps never disregarded an almost broken heart. . . . I am ill—I stayed in bed this morning till eleven o'clock, only thinking of getting money to extricate myself out of some of my difficulties.

When she got out of bed that morning, she had a call from one of Johnson's friends, which made matters worse. He carried a proposal of marriage from a well-to-do man she hardly knew, who assumed that her need for security was reason enough for marriage and that, of course, an attractive but penurious young woman would welcome a protector. Many a woman in her situation would have accepted, or at least declined with gratitude; but Mary, although at first confounded, collected herself and wrote Johnson in great and dramatic anger:

> Mr. . . . called on me just now—pray did you know his motive for calling?—I think him impertinently officious—He had left the house before it occurred to me in the strong light it does now, or I should have told him so—My poverty makes me proud—I will not be insulted by a superficial puppy . . . when I meet him at your house, I shall leave the room, since I cannot pull him by the nose . . . God of heaven, save thy child from this living death!

That evening she shot off a brief, proud rejection to her suitor and the next day another that raked him and his messenger over red-hot coals of indignation:

> Wednesday, 3 o'clock
>
> Sir,
>
> It is inexpressibly disagreeable to me to be obliged to enter again on a subject, that has already raised a tumult of *indignant* emotions in my bosom . . . I shall now *condescend* to answer . . . but let me first tell you, that in my *unprotected* situation, I make a point of never forgiving a *deliberate insult*. . . . It is not according to my nature to mince matters—I will tell you in plain terms, what I think . . . as a mere acquaintance, you were rude and *cruel*, to step forward to insult a woman, whose conduct and misfortunes demand respect. If my friend, Mr. Johnson, had made the proposal—I should have been severely hurt—have thought him unkind and unfeeling, but not *impertinent* . . . I am, sir, poor and destitute—Yet I have a spirit that will never bend, or take indirect methods, to obtain the consequence I despise . . . I can bear anything but my own contempt.
>
> In a few words, what I call an insult, is the bare supposition that I could for a moment think of *prostituting* my person for a maintenance; for in that point of view does such a marriage appear to me. . . .
>
> I tell you sir, I am POOR—yet can live without your benevolent exertions.[11]

This furious overreaction, unleavened by the humor of the situation, is the first actual demonstration of Mary Wollstonecraft's attitude toward love and marriage. That she would consider a proposal even from Johnson an unkindness, and one from an ordinary man a positive insult, is baffling given the common practice of the time, unless one perceives that it was not marriage itself she rejected, but a loveless connection—more, that she considered herself above any but the most rarefied love, the most elevated passion, the most superior man. To question this was to deny the superiority she believed set her apart from ordinary women. This valuation of herself was now the keystone of her equilibrium, and she could prove and sustain it for the next several years only by building her career. But spasms of regret for past love, explicitly for Fanny, "that dear friend—whom I shall love while memory holds its seat," and flares of self-pity "for my former cares—and deep seated woes," telegraphed the gravitational pull of persistent need that threatened to bring the structure down on her head.

Meanwhile Mary Wollstonecraft's road to literary success was clear and growing smoother. In April of 1788 *Mary* and *Original Stories* were published. She sent copies to George Blood with professional pride, instructing him to correct minor errors that she had not caught in proof. Unlike *Mary, Original Stories* sold well enough to go into a second edition in 1791, two Irish editions and a German translation thereafter. She next began translating Necker's *De L'Importance des Opinions Réligieuses* for Johnson, a major undertaking requiring several months of work, "and [made] a very advantageous contract for another," probably Campe's *New Robinson Crusoe,* later abandoned. She wrote George Blood May 6:

> I have a variety of other employments, in short, my dear Boy, I succeed beyond my most sanguine hopes, and really believe I shall clear above two hundred pounds this year which will supply amply all *my* wants and enable me to defray the expenses of Everina's journey, and let her remain in Paris longer than I at first intended . . . some difficulties at the outset . . . imperceptibly melt away as I encounter them—and I daily earn more money with less trouble. You would love Mr. Johnson, if you knew how *very* friendly he has been to the princess. . . . I have determined one thing never to have my sisters to live with me, my solitary manner of living would not suit them, nor *could* I pursue my studies if forced to conform. I have taken more exercise lately and sniffed the fragrant gale of spring, and am then excellently well.

Mary Wollstonecraft's rigorous work schedule was particularly satisfying because in exercising her intellect she came to realize its power. In laying *Cave of Fancy* aside she chose sense over sensibility, exploiting another dimension of herself. Her interest in Necker's work is significant, not only because it was demandingly difficult to translate, but because it demonstrates the conservatism of her philosophy and her persisting religious faith in 1788. (At the same time, she advised George Blood not to read Price's *Sermons* because they might disturb his simple faith.) Necker, one of the most famous men in Europe, was considered by the enlightened to be the only man in France who could shore up that tottering system, a belief fully shared by Necker and his daughter, Madame de Staël. He wrote the book in the interval between his dismissal as Louis XVI's director of finance and his recall a year later. In the standard English translation by Mary Wollstonecraft, Necker granted the impact of deism and agnosticism: "What a time have I chosen to entertain the world with morality and religion!" proceeded to praise himself: "Only to conceive it is a great proof of courage," and argued that if the "salutary chain" of religious belief were broken: "you would see every part of the social structure tremble from its foundation, and the hand of government unable to sustain the vast and tottering edifice." Individual morality cannot replace religion because men's passions overcome their reason, according to Necker. Since ignorance and poverty are the fate of the majority of mankind, and since wealth and power of the few are both desirable and inevitable, religion "is precisely adapted to the particular situation of the greatest number of mankind."[12]

At the same time she was translating this Christian *logique*, Mary Wollstonecraft was joining a circle that questioned it—Joseph Johnson's coterie of sophisticated friends, as well as the contributors to his periodical who were her colleagues. In early 1788 Joseph Johnson and Thomas Christie organized *The Analytical Review,* a new magazine of distinctly liberal bent. It was a time of political controversy and crisis, when assumptions of a permanent society based on subordination and religion were under attack. France was in turmoil. Progressive Englishmen were pressing for reforms at home to perfect rather than overturn the system, demanding that it live up to the spirit of the English Constitution and the needs of an enlightened age. This was the tone of *The Analytical*

Review. Johnson's partner, Thomas Christie, a former pupil of Dr. Price, was an unusually learned, enthusiastic, restless young intellectual with great interest in foreign literature and ideas. *The Analytical Review* undertook, "at a time when Literary Journals are more numerous than useful," to be a "History of Literature, Domestic and Foreign on an Enlarged Plan, Containing Scientific Abstracts . . . with Short Characters; Notices; or Reviews of Valuable Foreign Books; Criticisms on New Pieces of Music and Works of Art and the Literary Influence of Europe, etc" written by "some of the most respectable and learned Characters . . . to diffuse knowledge, and to advance the interests of science, of virtue and morality."[13]

Publication began in May of 1788. The scope was indeed as broad and serious as advertised; in its pages the whole spectrum of late eighteenth-century interests and controversies can be traced. For Mary Wollstonecraft it was a forcing bed of ideas, fertile soil in which she could grow as much as she could, from a junior hack to full colleague of major intellectuals who were her fellow reviewers.

Its articles were signed only by initials. Mary Wollstonecraft used "M," "W," and "T."[14] Her assignments at first were reviews of novels, books for and about children and women, subjects of female interest. She was from the beginning assertive, emphatic, and, when displeased, scathing. A novel by an anonymous lady was a: "heterogeneous mass of folly, affectation, and improbability"; Elizabeth Norman's *Child of Woe* had "no marked features to characterize it [and therefore] we can only term it a truly feminine novel," unnatural, affected. Others were: "ridiculous [filled with] childish feminine terms . . . sweet, lovely, dear"; "wretched farrago"; "one of the most stupid novels we have ever impatiently read. Pray Miss, write no more!"

Mary Wollstonecraft could not abide what she considered feminine follies; no one was harder on women. With particular contempt she spurned fantasies of romantic lovers, delusions of eternal happiness. Of Charlotte Smith's *Emmeline:* "the false expectations these wild scenes excite, tend to debauch the mind"; about an anonymous female production: "the lady deserves praise for . . . modesty . . . however it appears strange that the heroine should so often dwell on the beauty of her lover"; of another: "the superlative, the celestial happiness of the marriage state, when congenial souls meet, and the whitest hand in the world receives the most impassioned kisses from the handsomest *male* mouth in the world—a baronet, a lord, or duke—nothing less!"

Mary Wollstonecraft was demanding in the field of education, her specialty. Her praise went to those authors who helped children "*feel* that virtue alone is true greatness" and who made unwearied endeavors to be useful, like Mrs. Trimmer. Mary believed falsely conceived education accounted for women's weaknesses. Her fullest statement on the subject appeared in a review of the third volume of *Sanford and Morton* by Thomas Day, her favorite children's author:

> He wishes to see women educated like rational creatures, and not made mere polished playthings to amuse the leisure of men. . . .
>
> If women are, in general, feeble both in body and mind, it arises less from nature than from education. We encourage a vicious indolence and inactivity, which we falsely call delicacy, instead of hardening their minds by the severer principles of reason and philosophy. . . .
>
> Women, indeed, may be termed . . . overgrown children when educated only for Grace and sensibility. . . . The consequence . . . private misery and public servitude.

Mary took advantage of every opening to increase her status at *The Analytical Review*. In the fourth issue, she reviewed a book on the society and manners of Portugal, and included her own experience of the evil effects of an "absurd religion, and a government the most arbitrary."[15] In England by contrast she thought there was substantial social justice. Shortly after she reviewed a book on physiognomy, a subject of great interest to her, for she believed character showed in the face. Subsequently she took up poetry, biography, drama, moral philosophy, and sermons.

In her reviews and her other writings she took Johnson's criticism when she felt it warranted and learned from his editorial skill: "My dear sir, I send you a chapter which I am pleased with, now I see it in one point of view—and, as I have made free with the author, I hope you will not have often to say—what does this mean?"

The sophistication of her new associations forced her, in the shadow of St. Paul's monumental assurance, to question the forms she had always depended on. But religious content was essential to her. Although influenced by Joseph Johnson's skepticism, she maintained her individuality:

> I send you *all* the books I had to review except Dr. [Samuel Johnson's] Sermons, which I have begun. If you wish me to look over any more trash this month—you must send it directly. I have been so low-spirited since I saw you—I was quite glad, last night, to feel myself affected by some passages in Dr. J–'s sermons on the death of his wife—I seemed (suddenly) to *find* my *soul* again—It has been for some time I cannot tell where. Send me the Speaker—and *Mary*, I want one—and I shall soon want some paper—you may as well send it at the same time—for I am trying to brace my nerves that I may be industrious—I am afraid reason is not a good bracer—for I have been reasoning a long time with my untoward spirits—and yet my hand trembles—I could finish a period very *prettily* now, by saying that it ought to be steady when I add that I am yours sincerely,
>
> Mary
>
> If you do not like the manner in which I reviewed Dr. J–'s [sermon] on his wife, be it known to you—I *will* not do it any other way—I felt some pleasure in paying a just tribute of respect to the memory of a man—who, spite of his faults, I have an affection for—I say *have*, for I believe he is somewhere—*where* my soul has been gadding, perhaps;—but *you* do not live on conjectures.[16]

Dr. Johnson, the deceased, devout high Tory, was not a favorite of liberals, but Mary, probably remembering her interview of years before, treated the sermon on his wife with reverence. However, the book of his other sermons she found in her review "not only gloomy, but narrow . . . the Father of Mercies is sometimes made to appear as a rigid taskmaster." According to the *Memoirs* Mary was a regular churchgoer until 1787, less regular thereafter, and finally gave up public worship altogether.

While reading, reviewing, and learning German, Mary completed her translation of Necker in late 1788, reviewing it herself in *The Analytical Review* in January 1789. "Some liberties are occasionally taken, and we think very properly, by the translator," she wrote of her work, noting Necker's tendency to become verbose and repetitive, a condition she had not been detached enough to correct. But she had mastered the language well enough almost to rewrite a children's book,

Young Grandison, from the French. In the same period she compiled a *Female Reader,* since lost. It was an anthology of *Miscellaneous Pieces in Prose and Verse, Selected from the Best Writers, and Disposed Under Proper Heads; for the Improvement of Young Women,* to which she contributed some pieces, a preface, and original prayers.[17]

These were months of unremitting exertion and remarkable development for Mary Wollstonecraft. She had found the career she wanted and, thanks to Joseph Johnson, had taken full advantage of it. She was propelled by extraordinary drive and found release from loneliness in her accomplishment. In the short period between October of 1787 and January of 1789 she went from gifted, anxious, naïve amateur to disciplined, self-assured, versatile professional in a competitive field, an accomplishment unmatched by any woman at that time. Godwin felt the kind of hack work she did contracted rather than stimulated her talents. But it was indispensable apprenticeship, given her inadequate preparation, during which she enlarged and sharpened her native capacity and made a place for herself, almost *sui generis,* in the world to which she belonged. Mary Wollstonecraft approached her thirtieth year a successfully self-made woman.

Chapter 10

AT THE END OF FEBRUARY, 1789, Mary wrote George Blood:

> Blessed be that Power who gave me an active mind! If it does not smooth, it enables me to jump over the rough places of life. I have had a number of drawbacks on my spirits and purse; but I still cry avaunt dispair—and I push forward. . . .
>
> . . . I am well . . . and enjoy more worldly comfort than ever I did.

Fortified by her professional success, Mary's reactions in her intimate relationships, although perennially difficult, were more manageable. In her letter she referred to Everina and Eliza's "indolence" and other faults in such uncomplimentary terms that nine lines were later censored; but with a sarcastic transition—"what an association of ideas!" —she reverted to the major theme of her own pleasure in work. She continued taking care of her sisters, maintaining Everina for two years in Paris and putting Eliza in a more pleasant situation as a parlor boarder at the school of a Mrs. Bregantz in Putney, a drain on her purse but preferable to having her at George Street. Some of her family obligations were self-imposed, stemming from the conviction that she was the only one capable of managing and from inarticulated determination to replace Ned as head of the family. Her father, still living in Wales with his second wife, depended on Ned for his remittances, but since Ned often held back his father's allowance and misused the estate, Mary persuaded Joseph Johnson to help her contest its control by her brother. This overt declaration of hostilities against Edward Bland agitated Mary, but her victory must have been exhilarating, the more so because her father would have had to indicate he preferred her supervision to Ned's. Once gained, she had the responsibility of handling her father's rents from Primrose Street and other affairs that, as Johnson said later in his understated way, "[were] attended to with no little trouble to both of us."[1] The battle was a running one, however; Ned apparently took over again later, and brother and sister also contested for the allegiance of their youngest brother, Charles. Although there is one mention—in a letter of 1790—of Mary's visit to "Ned's school," which probably refers to Ned's son of the same name, Mary avoided any further contact with Ned and did her best to isolate him from the rest of the family. Her sisters, Charles when she had control of him, and, later, James, stayed with her for holidays or when they were at loose ends.

With her inveterate impulse to love, to improve, and to control, Mary saw her favorite brother Charles as an eighteen-year-old Emile under her maternal hand. As soon as she could she transferred Charles's apprenticeship from Ned to an attorney of her own choosing. She introduced him to promising young men of his own age, such as the aspiring artist, Joshua Cristall, whose older sister Ann was a teacher and poet, later published by Johnson. Mary had great expectations for Charles and paid for her overoptimism with the usual disappointment. Deceptively charming, Charles Wollstonecraft was as erratic, reckless, and willing to throw money around for pleasure as his father had been. He apparently promptly squandered his new opportunity, his reputation, and the trust of his employer, and had to be shipped off to Ireland in April of 1789, leaving Mary to pay for his trip and the damage. "I feel more sorrow than resentment—say that I forgive him—yet think he must be devoid of all feeling if he can forgive himself," she wrote George Blood, begging him to find Charles some kind of job. "I know he will plunge into pleasure while he has a farthing left." When George failed to keep her informed, she became seriously angry with him. "I am not unreasonable," she wrote him. "You might have written to me a few lines . . . you were not shut up in the Bastille . . . I am obliged to recollect that I am writing to Fanny's brother." But some of the pain of

Fanny's loss was dissolving. When Hugh Skeys came to London, Mary wrote George: "I dread—I sicken at the thought, the bare thought of encountering Skeys"; but when she did see him she took it calmly enough and later encouraged George to accept employment through Skeys.

Her worldly comfort, however, was relative, hard won, and precarious, for as soon as she was ahead of one obligation, she found another. In the same letter to George that spoke of her financial security, she delegated him to repay the ten guineas she had borrowed for Bess Delane from Lady Kingsborough's stepmother two-and-a-half years before. "Do not tell your father," she wrote George. "He would call honesty romance." Johnson took the disagreeable business of settling with tradespeople off her hands because she felt she was unsuited to such transactions, which sometimes entailed stalling off payment. She lived with rigidly enforced economy in George Street. Her meals were spartan and rarely included meat. When Thomas Taylor, the Platonist with whom she and Fanny had stayed in Walworth, came to visit, he noticed she used teacups for both tea and wine because glasses were a luxury. Her dress was simple, and she did not permit herself to follow fashion. She was often in debt to Johnson but with a clear conscience, for she had made herself indispensable to him at *The Analytical Review*. Her contributions to the magazine were increasingly abundant, varied, and prominent; by mid-1789 she was responsible for a sizable portion of each issue. Her last letter to Johnson of this period makes clear their mutual respect and affection. "You forgot," she wrote:

> you were to make out my account—I am, of course, over head and ears in debt; but I have not that kind of pride which makes some dislike to be obliged to those they respect.—On the contrary, when I involuntarily lament that I have not a father or brother, I thankfully recollect that I have received unexpected kindness from you and a few others.—So reason allows, what nature impels me to—for I cannot live without loving my fellow-creatures—nor can I love them, without discovering some virtue.[2]

This is her last letter to Johnson that Godwin published, except one from 1792. She probably wrote him rarely, since she now spent many of her afternoons working with him on the magazine and most of her evenings in his rooms. She was also, perhaps, less dependent on Johnson as she established her career and the additional friendships it brought her.

In St. Paul's Churchyard, Mary Wollstonecraft was at an intellectual center of enlightened London. *The Analytical Review* was put together there in Johnson's offices, and in his living quarters above, his authors and friends, eminent acquaintances, and transient celebrities gathered. Johnson's circle was a recognized London institution. It met regularly for three o'clock dinner and stimulating talk, sometimes well into the night; Mrs. Barbauld told her brother after one such evening that she was afraid to admit what time the party broke up. It was a predominantly male group—brilliant, uninhibited, diverse, artists, literary men, political and religious leaders, rising young writers, many at the cutting edge of intellectual London. Johnson, an urbane, dispassionate arbiter, kept his strong-minded friends in some order around his table when the discussion became acrimonious. Mary Wollstonecraft had been invited occasionally to Johnson's when she was a novice. Now one of the publisher's most prolific and promising writers, she took her place in his circle as an equal, no longer a protégée.

The nucleus of the group had standing invitations to three o'clock dinner and attended regularly; Mary Wollstonecraft's days were Tuesday and Sunday. Johnson's intimate circle, many his friends for years, included John Bonnycastle, the famous mathematician with a horse face and spectacular memory, passionately fond of Shakespeare, a great raconteur; Bonnycastle's protégé George Anderson, accountant-general to the board of control and a man of letters; Dr. George Fordyce, Johnson's physician, a great teacher and practitioner who loved society so much he would sit up all night although he had to lecture next day; Alexander Geddes, the radical Catholic scholar; Henry Fuseli, the brilliant literary man and controversial painter. In addition to the regulars, other intellectuals and artists were present at various times: Mary's old friends Dr. Price and John Hewlett; James Hurdis, and Joseph Priestley. William Blake sometimes dined with Johnson, probably introduced there in 1787 by Fuseli, with whom he became close at that time. Johnson employed Blake for several years as an engraver before his genius led him into paths the rationalist Johnson could not follow; it was Blake who illustrated the second edition of Mary Wollstonecraft's *Original Stories,* as well as a children's book she translated from the German.

Conversation at Johnson's was provocative whatever the subject, and this period was one of unprecedented excitement for his circle. The Bastille fell in July, 1789, and the French Revolution was underway in a whirlwind of radical and spectacular occurrences: national elections, the rise of the Third Estate, the sweeping away of ancient laws, confinement of the royal family in Paris. Mary Wollstonecraft was in close association with some of the best minds of her day at a watershed of Western history. She was the only woman considered worthy of habitual inclusion in this intimate intelligentsia, and doubtless she treasured the distinction. As both a woman and an intellectual she formed here one of the momentous relationships of her life.

The painter Henry Fuseli was the phenomenon of Johnson's circle. When Mary Wollstonecraft met him he was exactly the kind of man, as she had said of George Ogle, she was most attracted to, "between forty and fifty—a genius." Fuseli was Hyperion to anyone she had ever known. Eighteen years her senior, he was born Fuëssli in Zurich and educated by his painter-father to be a clergyman, but the boy sketched left-handed under the table while reading religious books with his parent. Zurich was the fountainhead of the Romantic movement then spreading through German-speaking countries, and Fuseli in college was a favorite student of the great Bodner, a leader of the tumultuous, iconoclastic, passionate revolt against old forms. Young Fuseli devoured learning. He was a remarkable linguist, deeply read in Latin, Greek, Italian, and English literature in the original; he also knew Hebrew and some Dutch, was mad about Shakespeare, Milton, Dante, Rousseau. He was ordained in 1761. Excited by French radical thought, he and some fellow students antagonized a powerful local official and had to leave Zurich. Fuseli then traveled through Germany, landed in England at the end of 1763, anglicized his name, lived on translations and articles, kept up his art work, and began haunting Garrick's performances. Drama and melodrama were his forte and his style. Until he was thirty he was not certain if he would specialize in literature or in art, but when Joshua Reynolds saw Fuseli's portfolio and encouraged him to concentrate on painting, he left for Italy for eight years of study. He then returned to Zurich, where he fell passionately in love, proposed, was rejected, and finally settled in London for good in 1778. He had been Johnson's close friend since that time.

When Johnson first introduced Fuseli to Bonnycastle he warned the mathematician: "I will now introduce you to a most ingenuous foreigner, whom I think you will like; but if you wish to enjoy his conversation, you will not attempt to stop the torrent of his words by contradicting him." Fuseli became sulky and withdrawn if he were not center stage. His tempestuous personality was overwhelming. Lavater, his close friend, wrote Johann von Herder:

> He is everything in extremes—always an original, Shakespeare's painter . . . a poet . . . hurricaine and tempest. . . . He despises everything and everybody. . . . His wit is unbounded. . . . His look is lightening, his word a thunderstorm; his jest is death, his revenge hell. At close quarters there is no enduring him. He cannot breath a single common breath.

And Godwin said of him:

> He was the most frankly ingenuous and conceited man I ever knew. He could not bear to be eclipsed or put in the background for a moment. He scorned to be less than the highest. He was an excellent hater; he hated a dull fellow, as men of wit and talents naturally do; and he hated a brilliant man, because he could not bear another near the throne.

Fuseli occasionally wrote reviews of his own books, as he did for a landmark pamphlet on Rousseau in which he said of himself:

> He is evidently a gentleman, a scholar, a philosopher, a genius, and a man of wit . . . while some may question this, others may call him a sceptic and libertine.
>
> . . . He has opinions of his own, so singular, so novel.

Of his paintings Fuseli wrote anonymously in *The Analytical Review:* "This is a sublime scene . . . a happy effort of genius."

Fuseli was capable of passionate devotion to both sexes. His early letters to Lavater address "friend of my soul. . . . Beloved of my soul, how I love you! How I kiss you!"; and a poem he wrote to Lavater reads: "Each tempestuous kiss . . . printed on swooning sweet rosy knolls of desire, secretly ravished—all Freely I'd part with for *your* embrace!" He was sensual and sentimental. He took up with bawds, drew pornography, had torrid affairs, which he talked of freely, painted erotic women and huge-muscled men, and married a beautiful model in 1786, after which he continued to be "always very susceptible of the passion of love." Whenever he spoke of his dead mother, tears came to his eyes. When someone told him no one read Richardson any more, Fuseli said, "Do they not?" "Then by God they ought . . . Clarissa to me is pathetic—is exquisite; I never read it without crying like a child." He was a notorious and colorful curser. "Sophia my love," he is supposed to have said to his wife, "why don't you swear?—you don't know how much it would ease your mind."

Fuseli's paintings call for music by Berlioz. From his immense knowledge he chose lurid subjects that would "interest, astonish, or move; if it did none of these it was worth 'nothing by Gode.' " He specialized in selecting moments of violent drama and emotion: *Satan starting at the touch of Ithurial's lance; Jason appearing before Pelias, to whom the sight of a man with a single sandal had been predicted fatal; Thor in the boat of Hymir, battering the Midgard Serpent, Lady Macbeth sleepwalking, Ajax raging, Chriemhild throwing herself on the dead Siegfried,* and so forth. His first great success was the famous *Nightmare* of 1782; a voluptuous, nightgowned woman flung prone on a divan, a fantastic dwarf squat on her rib cage, a bulging-eyed horse screaming from behind a dark red drapery. (Freud hung a copy of this work in his apartment.) It was reproduced, imitated, used for political caricature for decades, and excited great controversy. "Execrable. . . . Shocking mad, madder than ever, quite mad," Horace Walpole said of Fuseli and his work. When Wordsworth was told Canova thought Fuseli had *fiamma* (flame) and Raphael *fuoco* (fire), the poet rejoined, "He forgot the third, and that is *il fumo* [smoke], of which Fuseli had plenty." But Erasmus Darwin found him "ravishing"; Alderman Boydell chose him to contribute to his Shakespeare Gallery, and he was, if controversial, a substantial success. Blake, himself then ignored by the art world, ranked Fuseli's work with the grandest efforts of imaginative art. Fuseli reciprocated, prophesying that a time would come when Blake would be as much sought after as Michelangelo, Fuseli's hero. The evidences of Blake and Fuseli's influence on each other's art have long been debated.

Although Fuseli was wild about Classical art, it was the art of the sculptor of Laocoön, not the work of Praxiteles; Fuseli once said, "The fear of not being understood, or felt, makes some invigorate expression to grimace," and that is exactly what he seems to have done himself in his art and in his role as a professional character. He had inordinate pride and aggression. He was five foot five, stocky, prematurely white, with a thrusting, aquiline nose, big, penetrating blue eyes, and a wide prominent mouth. He loved to show off and to put down the ignorant with bludgeon wit. His friends claimed he was actually very shy, preferring old and faithful associates who had accepted his value. "I can do without them who can do without me," he said. Under all the bluster and irascibility, however, he was devoted to his close male friends like Johnson, Bonnycastle, and Knowles, and with women, particularly those who admired him, he was gentle and tender.

Since Fuseli came to Johnson's two or three times a week, he and Mary Wollstonecraft met shortly after she settled in London. By 1789 they were growing intimate. She was astounded at his eccentricity and brilliance—as was everybody. His pupil Haydon found him:

> the most grotesque mixture of literature, art, scepticism, indelicacy, profanity and kindness. . . . All of a sudden he would burst out with a quotation from Homer, Tasso, Dante, Ovid, Virgil, or perhaps the *Niebelungen*, and thunder round to me with "paint dat!" Weak minds he destroyed, but he had the art of inspiring young minds with grand and high views. . . . How many delightful hours have I passed with him in one continual stream of quotation, conception, repartee and humour.

In like fashion, "he amused, delighted and instructed" Mary Wollstonecraft, as the *Memoirs* stated. She was fascinated by his German-accented bravura flashing around Johnson's table. One day Fuseli and Bonnycastle, who prided himself on his retentive gifts, competed to see who had the better memory. Johnson proposed each learn by heart the eleventh book of *Paradise Lost.* After three swift perusals, Fuseli was able to recite it perfectly, vanquishing Bonnycastle on ground the mathematician thought he held securely.

Fuseli, who could be brutal, particularly enjoyed baiting Catholic Dr. Geddes, who had a short temper himself.

> One day [Fuseli] indulged himself at Johnson's table, to plague Geddes with uttering a string of truisms: Geddes at length became impatient, and said "I wonder that you, Mr. Fuseli, who have so much ready wit,

> should be uttering dogmas." Fuseli immediately answered, "You, Doctor, to find fault with dogmas—you, who are the son of a dog-ma." The pause between the syllables instantly raised a tumult in the doctor's mind, and he replied, "Son of a b——h I suppose you mean," and . . . left the room to cool himself . . . once or twice around St. Paul's Churchyard.[3]

Fuseli's sadistic side, so apparent in his art, fascinated Mary Wollstonecraft; harshness was allowed to genius. As such, he towered above Johnson, who considered ideas more interesting than urgent. She began to compare the two, and to prefer the genius:

> Those people who follow, with interest and admiration, the flights of genius, or . . . the profound thinker, ought not to be disgusted if they find the former choleric, and the latter morose; because liveliness of fancy and a tenacious comprehension of mind, are scarcely compatible with that pliant urbanity which leads a man . . . to bend to the opinions and prejudices of others, instead of roughly confronting them.

Fuseli was the first painter Mary Wollstonecraft had known, but she developed quickly a passionate interest in art and an appreciation of the sensibility and superiority of artists that was reflected in her writing. Fuseli was delighted to educate her. According to the *Memoirs* he found Mary extraordinarily sensitive and responsive to art and spent hours discussing painting with her. They began to see each other independent of Johnson's dinners. "As a painter, it was impossible she should not wish to see his works, and consequently to frequent his house. She visited him; her visits were returned," Godwin related. They were comparable temperamentally; it is interesting that Godwin used the same appellation for Fuseli that he did for Mary: "an excellent hater." Both despised servitude; she had hated being a governess; he had once been tutor to a young nobleman from whom he parted with blows. "The noble family of Waldegrave took me for a bear-leader, but they found me a bear," he used to boast. Both were fascinated by Rousseau. Mary said of the philosopher that she had always been half in love with him.[4] Fuseli was one of the first to introduce Rousseau to the English public, and had actually met him in Paris when he was a young man. One of Fuseli's favorite propositions was the divinity of genius, that subject of intense interest to Mary Wollstonecraft. Both were enthusiastic about the beginning of the French Revolution. As for religion, Fuseli believed in God, the immortal soul, and an afterlife, although when pressed by John Hewlett on the question of Christ's resurrection would only say it was as well authenticated as any other historical event. His attitude can be correlated with Mary Wollstonecraft's current questioning of her own religious practice.

If Fuseli shook her certitudes and priggishness, he also enjoyed his influence over her ardent, inquiring mind, her responsiveness, and her courage in rebuttal, for they had basic divergences. He believed education was for the chosen few with talent—the privilege of genius. He was an aesthete, a cynic, a hedonist, and, with women, a sensualist. Nearing fifty, he found the presence and enthusiastic admiration of a woman who was even younger than her years nourishing to his insatiable vanity. The salt of sex, spicy and familiar to him, hardly yet tasted by her, was part of their pleasure in one another, but she refused to acknowledge it, and Fuseli, probably realizing this woman, with all her intellectual daring and independence, was virginal, kept their relationship within bounds. "I have," she said, "conversed as man to man [about] the proportions of the human body with artists, yet such modesty did I meet with, that I was never reminded by word or look of my sex . . . of the absurd rules, which make modesty a Pharasaical cloak of weakness."[5] If she preferred the cloak of art appreciation, Fuseli, for whom the body was glorious artistically and sexually, confined his demonstrations to the former aspect. In any case, his taste in women ran to sloe-eyes in heart-shaped faces and to thrusting bosoms like his wife's, Sophia, and the almost brutally voluptuous women he painted.

Later, Fuseli's biographer, Knowles, claimed the painter found Mary Wollstonecraft to be what he most disliked in women, "a philosophical sloven" of coarse dress and lank hair. She was quite poor, of course, having stripped herself for Everina, Eliza, Charles, and her father, but all other evidence, her portraits, the strictures on neatness and cleanliness in her books, and her pride, indicate that she was simply and decently coiffed and dressed—perhaps too decently for Fuseli. In any case, if he found her unattractive he had only to avoid allowing the relationship to develop, which, given his self-centeredness, he could easily have managed. Instead he welcomed, encouraged, and reciprocated her interest. Blake's illustrations of Mrs. Mason in *Original Stories* depict a graceful, soulful, grave, and lissome young woman of character, perhaps inspired by Mary's appearance at this time, for this portrayal is distinctive and quite different from the women pictured in his contemporaneous *Songs of Innocence.* Godwin, who met Mary first in 1792, expected a raw-boned Amazon, but found her "lovely in her person, and in the best and most engaging sense, feminine in her manner." Even Knowles (who never met her) contradicted himself and stated that Fuseli appreciated her "face and person which had some pretensions to beauty and comeliness," as well as her unusual mind. What Johnson thought of the obvious attraction and growing intimacy between his brilliant, eccentric old friend and his vulnerable, ardent younger one is not known, but a contemporary said of Fuseli's behavior: "The coquetting of a married man of fifty with a tender female philosopher of thirty-one can never be an agreeable subject of contemplation."[6]

Mary Wollstonecraft was positive that she was in control of herself. "Virtue is self denial," she said in a letter of this period, and in *Original Stories:* "Nothing, believe me, can long be pleasant, that is not innocent." In an October, 1789 edition of *The Analytical Review,* she scoffed at novels in which romantic was depicted as superior to filial love. She refused to consider that she could be capable of threatening a marriage or betraying her standards of virtue. She believed she was interested only in Fuseli's genius, for, said she, "I always catch something from the rich torrent of his conversation, worth treasuring up in my memory, to exercise my understanding."[7]

Mary Wollstonecraft thus became a friend of the family, going with Fuseli and his wife to theater and other London amusements. And Fuseli became familiar with Mary's family as well. It was all very proper. Everina returned from Paris around the end of 1789 and joined Eliza at Mrs. Bregantz's school in Putney. Both sisters were in London with Mary for holidays, and it is clear from Eliza's letters to Everina that until the spring of 1790, when Eliza left England, they were frequently with Fuseli *en famille.* Eliza spoke of him with mingled hostility and affection. Of his class consciousness she wrote sarcastically: "Even Fuseli was full of these humane distinctions"; she knew all about his youthful love affairs: "Can you help feeling contempt for the man? That could boast of such favors"; more plaintively: "Fuseli . . . said I was fonder of pleasure than any of you"; of a child she loved: "he has a look of tenderness that always puts me in mind of Fuseli."[8]

To some extent, he represented the masculine mentor-friend Mary Wollstonecraft had always been drawn to. This father figure, however, was dangerous. He was closer in temperament to her father than any of her other male friends, a passionate, violent, and eccentric character, with the added glamour of genius so seductive to her. He was hardly nonsexual, as Clare, Price, and Johnson had been. While not unhappily married like Hewlett and Ogle, he was, according to Mary's lights, unworthily married, for she found Sophia Fuseli vacuous if beautiful, and Mary could not conceive or accept that Sophia was exactly what Fuseli wanted. Mary believed sexual attraction should follow the "imagination," and flow from appreciation of the soul and intellect. She had caught herself in time with Henry Gabell, knowing he was engaged. She had managed Waterhouse and Ogle, and perhaps other men, too. As early as 1786, in *Thoughts,* she feelingly spelled out the dangers of platonic friendship between men and women. It makes poignant reading. For with irresistible emotional need, she convinced herself of the purity and rationality of a relationship so inevitably untenable that she doomed herself to punishing defeat.

In the September, 1789 issue of *The Analytical Review,* Mary Wollstonecraft reviewed Gilpin's *Observations of the River Wye,* four months later his *Picturesque Beauty.* She discussed color, harmony, light, and design in a style reflecting Fuseli's influence. She felt Gilpin's drawings showed "want of nerve and boldness"; compared to Fuseli's powerful graphics, Gilpin's work was, as she intimated, lightweight. She did the lead article of February, 1790, on Dr. Burney's *History of Music.* The change of subject matter is clear; other reviewers were initialing some of the entries of female interest although Mary continued with them. But there was also a change of tone, an emphasis on the aesthetic over the moral. "Are the most celebrated poems, in any language, didactic?" she asked. And in the first revelation of her religious uncertainty, she wrote that music, "the food of passion and sensation . . . is the most perfect homage of a being, who gropes in the dark for proofs of its great origin and *definition.*" In a May review she questioned the concept of redemption. By October she seemed to be struggling with the problem of evil, cruelty, and personal unhappiness, no longer sure the Father of Mercies would eventually reward. "It is therefore safest to confess our ignorance and suspend our judgment, or our nature revolts, and we *brand* not nature, but the Supreme Being, with cruelty and oppression or impotence; for no ray of philosophy, has yet visited that benighted land sufficiently luminous to dissipate our doubts." In November, reviewing Catherine Macaulay's *Letters on Education,* she discussed the historian's theories on the origin of evil at length, rather tentatively hoping the existence of evil did not weaken the notion of the irresistible power of God.[9]

At the same time her interest in education, the instiller of virtue, continued. She translated the first volume of a children's book by the noted educational reformer Christian Gotthilf Salzmann, *Moralisches Elementarbuch,* which appeared in October, 1790, as *Elements of Morality* in a deluxe edition with Blake illustrations. She had mastered the German language well enough to be in complete control of her material, compressing and editing with skill and adding points of her own. However, in the second and third volumes, which appeared in January and March of 1790, the translation was more pedestrian; she had lost interest and energy for such routine work by that time. The changes are interesting. The major child characters, Luisa and Ludwig, become Mary and Charles. Salzmann's admiration of aristocratic life is toned down, a religious phrase muted.[10]

The determinative work assignment in this area was her long lead article in the November issue of *The Analytical Review* on Catherine Macaulay's *Letters on Education.* This book was an inspiration in more than the contents, which confirmed and stretched many of Mary's own ideas. Macaulay was the leading intellectual of her sex in England, a woman who commanded universal respect for her historical and philosophical work. Not only had she lived her life as she desired, regardless of convention—in 1778, while Mary was with Mrs. Dawson, Macaulay had married at Bath a man twenty-one years her junior—she thought and worked on a level that challenged Mary to raise her own. Mary's review praised Macaulay's "masculine and vervid" style, her intellectual prowess, and her perception of the way in which education and society debilitated and corrupted women. "The observations of this [last] subject," Mary wrote, "might have been carried much further," something she began to consider doing herself. There was no hint of her reaction to Macaulay's personal life, but in discussing her view of chastity in women Mary Wollstonecraft restated her own concern for virtue; "till the minds of women are more enlarged, we should not weaken the salutary prejudices which serve as substitutes, a weak one we own, for rational principles."[11]

Her own principles were undergoing a test. Even while the professional success she counted on to fill her life was growing, her concomitant need for love became more urgent as it focused on Fuseli. Her former emotional and physical symptoms reappeared. Eliza and Everina were unhappy at Mrs. Bregantz's school; that "and some other things contributed to sink me," she wrote them in an undated letter of the summer of 1790. A friend told her she looked "tolerably well," although she claimed to feel wretchedly ill. "I imagine that I shall not live long—that I am wearing away." Then she caught herself and went on to recommend doses of salts for Everina's eyes and for Eliza's "spots and face." (Mary herself had weak eyes and had to use spectacles and a green shade when working.) Later she did not even try to hide her distress. She was short of money, as she perennially was: "The Painter dunned me every day . . . the man from Primrose Street never brought the rent." When nagging debts were paid she was penniless, forced to get an advance from Johnson. Whereas before she had applied to him readily, she was now reluctant to borrow because she had not been able to work: "I have done so little for him." The reason may also have had to do with her uneasy recognition that he no longer came first for her. She was in the grip of lethargy and depression worse, she wrote her sisters, than any she had ever experienced:

> Heaven grant me patience! I hope it is my body which thus weighs me down, but I know not what to do with myself, or how to shake off the fever which consumes me—as I did not receive immediate benefit from bathing I left it off because it was so expensive—in short, I never was in the State I am at present, for such a length of time—I really do everything which reason suggests—and still have this dreadful complicated, lingering illness. Perhaps when the weather grows cooler I shall be better, it is not of illness I complain I could bear it, but I am very unhappy at being this idle.

Grasping at the efficacy of a change of scene, and in spite of Eliza's annoyance that she was going on holiday, Mary Wollstonecraft accepted the invitation of her old acquaintance from Ireland, Henry Gabell, to visit him and his wife at Warminster, where he was now headmaster of

Winchester School. Gabell had seen the Bastille taken, and Mary anticipated a long, interesting, and pleasant vacation. She was disappointed. She told Everina that Ann Gabell, about whom she herself had been curious, was a large woman who "made me think of a Doric pillar," and had no eyebrows or intellect whatsoever. She reminded Mary of Miss Mason of the Newington Green school; blunt, loud, thick-skinned, dull. Gabell was very demonstrably happy with his coarse wife and their large brood of young children. Mary found it wearing to be the houseguest of comparative strangers, to have to compliment their children, their household, and their felicity, to be charming on call. Although originally interested in Gabell, she did not envy what she found, for she was barely tolerant of ordinary family life; as she wrote George Blood of a prolific acquaintance: "Mrs. S. is sunk into a mere nurse [her] soul is flown—flown." She simply could not see herself in this common domestic scene and its dull neighborhood, so different from the independence and stimulation she relished in London. She arrived at the Gabells' the third week of August; soon she asked Everina to call at George Street: "see if the house still stands—I think of returning in the course of a fortnight." After early morning walks in the countryside, bad weather confined her to the Gabells' domestic joys:

> . . . *Much of a muchness*—you can scarcely imagine *how much* happiness and innocent fondness constantly illumines the eyes of this good couple—so that I am never disgusted by the frequent bodily display of it . . . yet I caught myself wishing this morning for a sight of my little room, and a ramble to St. Paul's Churchyard.

The discrepancy between the headmaster and the genius confirmed the validity of her attraction to Fuseli and the superiority of her standards. By September 4 she had had enough of Gabell's uxoriousness: she felt like an intruder, she wrote, and added that she could never give up intellectual pursuits for domesticity. September 10 she was ready to come home on the pretext of helping Everina decide about a job offer—and said the sacrifice would not be very great for she was bored. She would not again ask Gabell to help Everina, because he and his wife were completely wrapped up in each other, and happiness makes people selfish, Mary decided. Nor would she ask a favor from someone she did not care for. "Will you think me saucy when I say, that you and Eliza appear to me very clever, and *most* agreeable women when compared with the Goddess of this place. Now we are at a distance I long to see you both—though Mrs. B. was on stilts when we parted." Not only did Eliza and Everina look good by comparison with Ann Gabell, Mary Wollstonecraft was more than ever sure she was born for better things than "worthy" happiness. Remembering Milton's description of Adam and Eve in *Paradise Lost,* she wrote Everina:

> I cannot help viewing them, I mean the first pair—as if they were my inferiors—inferiors because they could find happiness in a world like this. A feeling of the same kind frequently intrudes on me here. Tell me, does it arise from mistaken pride or conscious dignity which, whispering to me that my soul is immortal and should have a nobler ambition, leads me to cherish it.

She returned to London, to the little rooms in George Street, to Johnson and her stimulating friends, to Fuseli's fascination—and within a few weeks to a new venture which launched her into fame.

Chapter 11

WHEN MARY WOLLSTONECRAFT RETURNED to London after her holiday in September, 1790, she went back to her Salzmann translation and reviews for *The Analytical Review* with some restlessness. Such work confined her to reacting to the ideas of others, and she had produced no original work of her own for some time. Catherine Macaulay's book on education was a goad to her ambition. Mary found herself reviewing miscellany while massive radical change was transforming France and affecting England, change that stirred her profoundly but to which she had had no professional opportunity to respond.

The French Revolution, as Godwin said, gave a fundamental shock to the human intellect everywhere, and to Mary Wollstonecraft it was a "vehement concussion" that undermined her lingering respect for establishments. She had been rebellious all her life, for in her experience authority had been more tyrannical and unjust than rewarding or sacred. In effect, she had been going through her own revolution for the past three years. The revolution in France spoke not only to her personal revolts, grievances, and anger, it demonstrated their legitimacy, connected them to systemic injustice, and stimulated her to believe that fundamental reform could be built into society. While her political and religious beliefs shifted, her capacity for faith remained constant, based as it was on an intense desire for justice. Although given to talk of pessimism and resignation, she had always acted as if will, intellect, and virtue would prevail. "A desperate disease requires a powerful remedy," she wrote of France, confident the remedy was available.[1] As for the reality of human progress, was she not herself an incontrovertible example?

Idealists, from the elderly liberals who witnessed the second great revolution of their lifetime, to youthful Wordsworth, who rejoiced at being young on a threshold of human history, were convinced that mankind was on the march to inevitable and permanent victory over tyranny through liberty, justice, reason, and humanity. The St. Paul's Churchyard group, which had always been predominantly liberal, was increasingly radicalized after the fall of the Bastille; the world-famous revolutionary activist Tom Paine joined the circle; Blake is said to have worn a liberty cap; even Fuseli was enthusiastic. Although little in Mary Wollstonecraft's current work reflected it, she was excitedly discussing political and social forces in Johnson's rooms, and in the process had buttressed her emotional reaction with philosophical and historical analysis.

Of those who saw utopia approaching, Mary's old friend from Newington Green, Dr. Richard Price, was one of the most zealous true believers. In early November of 1789 Price delivered the annual address before the Society for Commemorating the Glorious Revolution of 1688, and with a simple idealism that even Mary questioned, exulted in the French upheaval:

> THIRTY MILLIONS of people, indignant and resolute, spurning at slavery, and demanding liberty with an irresistible voice; their king led in triumph. And now me thinks I see the ardour for liberty catching and spreading; a general amendment beginning in human affairs.

Strong words in the context of actual circumstances in France. Price went beyond reform and claimed for the English a right based on tradition "to resist power when abused . . . to chuse our governors for ourselves." Edmund Burke, the veteran Whig luminary, was one of the first English political leaders to grasp the implications of the revolution and the changes Price and others like him advocated. While even conservatives like Pitt supported the revolution initially, in the belief that France was at last entering the modern world, Burke took his first public stand to warn against incipient French "excesses of a proscribing, plundering, ferocious, and tyrannical democracy" in an emotional address to the House of Commons in February, 1790.[2]

The Whigs were furious with him. Burke's dramatic warning was all the more impressive because he had supported the American Revolution and was breaking with his party after twenty-six years of partisan loyalty, including the recent regency crisis of 1788–1789, during which time George III was incapacitated by insanity. Burke had helped raise the cry to give the Prince of Wales, a violent Whig supporter, full power.

Actions in England followed words like Price's; progressives agitated with transfused energy for reforms, liberal politicians and activists allied themselves with their counterparts in France, and societies inspired by French models were formed even in the counties. Burke was convinced French contagion endangered England. He began to write a grand attack on the French Revolution and its supporters. For several months, during which political London promised itself a feast, he polished his *Reflections on the Revolution in France, and on the Proceedings of Certain Societies in London Relative to That Event.* It was deliberately published on November 1, 1790, on the anniversary of Price's address.

Mary Wollstonecraft was fresh from her vacation with the Gabells when she, like all London, read *Reflections.* Burke blasted her venerable friend, Price, damned assumptions sacred to advocates of change, and glorified the status quo; hereditary monarchy, aristocracy, and property were the basis of the state, and established religion its bulwark; the lower classes should be kept in their place. The British system, he wrote, guaranteed "our liberties as an *entailed inheritance* from our forefathers," and was sound, just, and fixed, not subject to "general consent" or "natural rights." Playing on emotion with a master hand, Burke appealed to sympathy for the French royal family, particularly for Marie Antoinette, a beautiful princess humiliated by madmen who were tearing down a structure hallowed by time.[3]

Mary Wollstonecraft said she had picked up *Reflections* more for amusement than for information, but she threw it down in righteous indignation. For her own satisfaction, she began to write out a furious rebuttal; Johnson urged her to complete it for publication. As she finished one section, he had it set in type while she went on with the next. "I glow with indignation," she wrote at the beginning, and her slashing polemic quivers with it. "Reverencing the rights of humanity, I shall dare to assert them . . . not intimidated by the laugh you have raised," not daunted by Burke's immense prestige, his age, nor the impropriety of a woman's challenge in the male's field of politics. Badly organized, swift-paced, and intensely subjective, *A Vindication of the Rights of Men* is not only supercharged with her emotion, it is a startling demonstration of the extent to which her personal experience from childhood on had been transformed into radical political conviction. The book is filled with examples from her own life. It is her damnation of Edmund Burke and everything he represented—subordination to authority, establishments, and tradition.

She wrote boldly, in the first person, attacking Burke directly throughout as vain, feverishly eccentric, devoid of principles, antipathetic to reason, power hungry, hypocritical, skulking, and unmanly. Burke appealed to sensibility, a quality she had treasured but now sarcastically labeled "the *manie* of the day." "Even the ladies, Sir, may respect your sprightly sallies. . . . I [am] afraid to derange your nervous system by the bare mention of a metaphysical enquiry." She then proceeded to give the manly response:

> I perceive, from the whole tenor of your *Reflections* that you have a mortal antipathy to reason. . . . The birthright of a man, to give you, Sir, a short definition of this disputed right, is such a degree of liberty, civil and religious, as is compatible with the liberty of every other individual with whom he is united in a social compact.

Where Burke equated tradition and subordination with filial respect, Mary damned them with her own filial hostility and contempt, attacking everything from the English Constitution to tyrannical parents:

> We are to reverence the rust of antiquity . . . if we do discover some errors, our *feelings* should lead us to excuse, with blind love, or unprincipled filial affection, the venerable vestiges of ancient days. . . . This is sound reasoning, I grant, in the mouth of the rich and shortsighted. . . .
>
> . . . There is no end to this implicit submission to authority—somewhere it must stop, or we return to barbarism.

Where Burke praised the traditional aristocratic, political, and economic structures, she exposed their injustices and failures:

> what has stopped . . . progress?—hereditary property—hereditary honours. . . . Property, I do not scruple to aver it, should be fluctuating; which would be the case if it were more equally divided amongst all the children of a family. . . .
>
> [You], an old member of Parliament . . . have been behind the curtain . . . seen the clogged wheels of corruption continually oiled by the sweat of the laborious poor. . . .
>
> You must have known that a man of merit cannot rise in the church, the army, or navy, unless he has some interest in a borough.
>
> Security of property! Behold in a few words, the definition of English liberty. . . . But softly—it is only the property of the rich that is secure; the man who lives by the sweat of his brow has no asylum from oppression. . . . Your contempt for the poor rouses my indignation. . . . They *must* respect that property of which they *cannot* partake! . . . This is contemptible hard-hearted sophistry—It is, Sir, *possible* to render the poor happier in this world. . . . Why cannot large estates be divided into small farms. . . . In this great city, how much misery lurks in pestilential corners . . . how many mechanics lose their employment. . . . Man preys on man; and you mourn for the idle tapestry that decorates a gothic pile.

She wrote of the comfort of true religious devotion for one like herself, who still mourned the friend of her youth, and she accused Burke of being a religious hypocrite: "the rapacity of . . . the priests, secured such vast property to the church . . . when *we*, the people of England, have a son whom we scarcely know what to do with—*we* make a clergyman of him."

Burke's homage to female charm also made her flare up:

> vain inconstant dolls, who ought to be prudent mothers and useful members of society . . . [they] learn to lisp, to totter in their walk . . . systematically neglecting morals to secure beauty . . . being *little, smooth, delicate, fair* creatures. . . . The Queen of France—the great and small vulgar, claim our pity; they have almost supportable obstacles to surmount in the progress toward dignity and character.

On two counts of personal interest she lashed out at Burke; first for the contemptuous levity with which he treated Price in *Reflections;*

second for Burke's flagrant callousness during George III's madness. It is possible it was Henry Wollstonecraft as well as Eliza she was thinking of in the several pages that vividly describe the plight of a victim of insanity and the asylum.

She asserted her faith that the French would create a new, more rational and humane system than England's—"Why rebuild old walls?" —and sanctified her political beliefs: "I reverence the rights of men . . . and I FEAR GOD!" Her fervor led her to fresh extremes: "On what principles, Sir, can you justify the Reformation; which tore up by the roots an Old Establishment . . . had you been a Jew—you would have joined in the cry, crucify him! crucify him![4]

About halfway through this *Vindication* Mary Wollstonecraft suddenly stopped and could not go on. It was more than a political position she was taking in writing out her own bitterness, anger, and past injuries; now doubt and anxiety paralyzed her. She went to Johnson, expecting he would reproach and then encourage her to proceed. Instead, he offered to destroy all he had printed so far if it would relieve her. Her pride was piqued. She went back to George Street and worked without interruption until she had finished. Was it fear of the violent eruption of her feelings, a realization that she had released pent-up hostility—or was she uncertain of her capacity? Whichever, Johnson's response to her block dissipated it. He had treated her like an ordinary fearful woman. She would not tolerate such an assessment. However, she hesitated to appear publicly in the political arena: *A Vindication of the Rights of Men* came out anonymously.

It was fortunate for Mary Wollstonecraft that she was constituted to write with great speed. Burke's *Reflections* was the hottest topic of the day and hers the first rebuttal in print at the very moment authoritative answers were in urgent demand. If her book was intemperate, emotional, and exaggerated, it was precisely the kind of topical, personalized, fiery polemic on which political controversy thrives. It was snatched up by friend and foe, made an extraordinary impact, and sold out at once. There was a good deal of speculation about its authorship. By December 14 Mary had revised the work, and Johnson published a second edition with her name signed to it. If anything, the revision sharpened her personal attack on Burke; but while enlarging passages connected with her family experience, she changed from the first to the third person. She also added a nonpartisan code criticizing hypocritical liberals who talk equality but scrape before the powers that be; she was ready to take on everyone. The revelation that it was a comparatively unknown woman who had produced this bold and comprehensive challenge to the great Burke added to its *éclat*. All the reviewers took note of the fact. Her reply to Burke was followed by innumerable others, some of more substance and lasting value, notably ones by Priestley, Mackintosh, and Mrs. Macaulay, and the most famous, Paine's *Rights of Man*. But Mary had scored first.

"The exercise of our faculties is the great end," Mary Wollstonecraft wrote in *A Vindication of the Rights of Men*, and her success proved how brilliantly she could employ them. Her pride and confidence swelled. It was intoxicating to savor the applause of friends, the confounding of reactionaries, the acclaim and controversy, to be a prodigy among women. She sent the signed edition of her work to Price and he acknowledged it December 17. "He has not been surprised," he wrote, "to find that a composition which he has heard ascribed to some of our ablest writers appears to come from Miss Wolstonecraft [*sic*]. He is particularly happy in having such an advocate." Political lines were hardening. Mary broke at this time—"upon public grounds," according to the *Memoirs*—with an old friend whose religious and political beliefs became more conservative in reaction to the revolution; it may have been John Hewlett, whose views she now criticized in *The Analytical Review* as dogmatic. Her professional success mounted when the second and third volumes of *Elements of Morality* came out in early 1791; the second edition of *Original Stories* with Blake illustrations followed. Johnson promoted her to editorial assistant at the *Review*. She wrote fewer articles as a result, but could choose what she wanted to review and make assignments to others. As for Fuseli, Godwin said the painter's vituperative wit had encouraged her to become even more critical than she normally was.[5] The first *Vindication* seems proof that she had learned from him.

After years of obscurity, defeat, struggle, and scrimping, a world of success and pleasure such as she had never known opened before Mary Wollstonecraft. She was riding the wave of the future, ambitious and certain of greater accomplishment in a time of infinite possibilities, comrade in arms of impressive men like Fuseli, around whom her life centered and whose admiration and affection gratified her personal needs. She was ready to enjoy herself, anticipated settling her debts, expanding her cramped circumstances, and appearing on a grander stage as the renowned Mrs. Wollstonecraft, the courtesy title she was now given. The only hindrance was her perennial obligations—her father, Charles, who now lived with him, her sisters—the drain on her attention and resources. But money was the least of it. She wanted to be free to indulge her own desires without inhibition. Even this problem seemed soluble in the winter of 1790, for Eliza and Everina were evidently on their own in Putney at Mrs. Bregantz's school; when Mary acknowledged their superiority over Ann Gabell in Warminster, her appreciation was in part satisfaction that she had successfully detached them. Rarely, she felt, had the tie compensated for the bind, and having done her duty she looked forward to substantial freedom. It was not that simple. Her sisters, both staunchly pro-French Revolution, were proud of Mary; Eliza reported Mrs. Bregantz's compliments and those of a teacher who "had read the pamphlet and was delighted with it, and . . . wished . . . for half an hour's conversation with Miss W. and the great Pain!" But they were also envious and clinging. It was the latter that Mary could no longer tolerate, and a crisis brought the situation to a head before the Christmas holiday of 1790.

Mary was working hard one day at her desk in George Street, when a creditor appeared. Annoyed and upset, she got him out of the way and went to Johnson to get his advice, the first time she had seen him alone for longer than she had realized. After supper Johnson quietly told her that he was suffering a return of certain grave symptoms in his head and arms and believed he was threatened by a paralytic stroke; he was actually settling his affairs. Mary was overwhelmed, the more so since she knew she had not recently been as attentive to him as formerly. She went home to a restless night, stayed in bed late next morning, and was so agitated she returned to spend the rest of the day with Johnson. At this juncture an emergency call came from Putney, and she rushed to her sisters only to discover the crisis amounted to nothing. There followed a bitter squabble between the sisters, and Mary sped back to Johnson in a rage. She wrote next day to apologize, but since the cat was out of the bag she took the opportunity to bell it, comparing her sisters' incessant demands and complaints with Johnson's generosity and dependability, and demanding "a little peace":

> if I had not cared for my sisters who certainly do not adore me—the last two years of my life might have passed tranquilly not embittered by pecunious cares—and if I had lost my friend, who has been a father and brother to me ever since I knew him! . . . I shall live independent or not at all.

She went on to avow openly her attachment to Fuseli, who was then apparently also ill; if Johnson, who bore tenderly with her faults and exerted himself to help her, should die, "solitary would my life be," she wrote. "The only friend who would exert himself to comfort me is so peculiarly circumstanced he cannot—and he too is sick—yet I know while he lives I shall never want an indulgent warm friend—but his society I cannot enjoy."

The letter was a declaration of intent; there was no clean break, but all three sisters knew there had been a serious fracture. During the next few months Mary took a strange, torturous course that deliberately or unconsciously juggled gratification and guilt, unloading and embracing of obligation, until she felt an acceptable balance had been reached to justify the freedom she wanted. The sisters spent the Christmas holiday together in George Street, in surprising concord with their brother James, from whom they had been estranged for several years. He wanted promotion in his naval career and looked to Mary for the wherewithal. She decided James had improved, a development as irresistible to her as Charles' former illusory progress, and arranged for him to study mathematics with Bonnycastle at Woolwich, for which she, of course, paid. Eliza and Everina were in trouble; Mrs. Bregantz intended to break up her school in the spring. Mary made them agree she could do no more than help find them jobs and expected them thereafter to be more self-sufficient. In spite of her difficulties, Everina turned down a proposal of marriage from George Blood, whom she did not love, and Mary approved the decision, although Everina, and perhaps Eliza as well, would have been taken off her hands permanently. Everina was thus the third Wollstonecraft daughter who rejected marriage.

At the very time Mary announced her determination to free herself as much as possible, she took on a serious, fresh responsibility, partly out of generosity and emotional need, partly perhaps to balance other gratifications she saw as selfish. Ann ——, a seven-year-old orphaned niece of Hugh Skeys' second wife—Fanny Blood's successor—came to live with Mary Wollstonecraft. Everina did not go back to Putney, but took charge of lively young Ann and did French translations for Mary while investigating jobs. By May, Eliza faced reality and reluctantly left England for a position as governess in Wales, visiting her father's farm at Laugharne enroute. Mary had a vivid reminder of unending family burdens. "I really thought I should have sunk into the ground," Eliza wrote of her first glimpse of the former dashing Edward John Wollstonecraft, who had become emaciated, slovenly, snarling, and ill. He was perpetually at Charles, and his well-meaning wife could not control his temper or his debts:

> Still he is able to ride ten miles every day, and eat, and *drink* very hearty . . . when I beg of him to be more careful in money matters, he declares he will go to London, and force Ned; or when I tell him how Mary has been distressed, in order to make him save in trifles, he is in a passion, and exhausts himself. He is mad to be in London.

In early September, Everina also left England for a position as governess in Waterford, Ireland, stopping to see Eliza, who had done nothing but complain to her by mail, as well as to Mary. Soon after Charles returned to London to live with Ned. Mary was angry and hurt, and if only to get him out of Ned's hands again, tried to find Charles a job through a friend of Fuseli's in Liverpool, William Roscoe. Having as usual expected too much, she was disappointed with James, who had thrown her money away trying to get a commission in the navy and finally "condescended to take the command of a trading vessel," sailing off on a voyage of speculation.[6] Once Everina was gone, little Ann, although affectionate and healthy, became troublesome. Mary would not turn her over to servants but, although she learned to manage the child, admitted she was more of a problem than had been anticipated: "she is, as usual, in great spirits—in fact her spirits sometimes oppress me, though I would not for the world damp them." The experiment suffered from having been undertaken with ambivalent motivation and insufficient commitment.

It was no accident that Eliza and Everina ended in Wales and

Ireland, too remote for even occasional holidays in London, nor that Mary betrayed "visible pleasure," which Eliza sensed, when James left for sea; nor that the position Mary wanted to find Charles was in India, and when that failed, in Liverpool. Mary Wollstonecraft was crossing a threshold and in order to pass over it had to be released from the inhibiting, mocking, critical eyes of her family.

Fuseli was the keystone of her new life. He had become essential to her happiness, and she acknowledged the fact with confidence, for she believed that she accepted the limitations of the situation and was in full control of herself. As she had written in *A Vindication of the Rights of Men:* "we must learn to distinguish the *possible,* and not fight against the stream." She saw no reason to hold back from Fuseli, and every reason to concentrate on a relationship in which she was certain she would not overstep the line between fervent admiration and dangerous passion; she even believed, as she made clear in *Vindication,* that she would benefit:

> Sacred be the feelings of the heart! concentrated in a glowing flame, they become the sun of life; and without his invigorating impregnation, reason would probably lie in helpless inactivity, and never bring forth her only legitimate offspring—virtue. . . . In what respect are we superior to brute creation, if intellect is not allowed to be the guide of passion.

She did not see the pertinence of a more crisply realistic statement she had made in the same book: "Instinct moves in a direct line to its ultimate end, and asks not for guide or support."[7]

Everything in and around her urged her on; thirty-two years of repression, absolute conviction that she deserved reparation for her past unhappiness, complete faith in her motivation, confidence in her self-sufficiency at the very time she risked it. Her old assumptions were in flux, inadequate under the pressure of political upheaval, new philosophies, and her dramatic rise. Fuseli's genius gratified her pride, and his connection to her reinforced her superiority. She would have the best of two worlds: a brilliant independent career and a fulfilling if self-limited association with a great man. She was contemptuous of the common run of humanity and common passions. A buried fantasy bordering on the perverse, almost hubristic, was coming to the surface. No "paradisiacal happiness" for her, she wrote. "I have with conscious dignity of satanic pride turned to hell for sublimer objects . . . the grandest of all human sights . . . an outcast of fortune, rising superior to passion and discontent." For this fantasy she chose demonic Luciferian men; "I will make love to the *shade* of Mirabeau . . . I should, in the vanity of my heart, [have] imagined that *I* could have made something of his—it was composed of such materials."[8]

The great Fuseli was her dearest friend, although "peculiarly circumstanced," as she put it. But she refused to admit that his marriage could be an obstacle between geniuses. "She made light of any difficulty," Godwin wrote of her state of mind—and it sounds as if she had been warned. "She scorned to suppose, that she could feel a struggle, in conforming to the laws she should lay down to her conduct." She was quite open about the situation to her friends and to Fuseli. Mary wrote the painter that Sophia had a right to the person of her husband, but she, Mary, "might claim, and for congeniality of sentiments and talents, hold, a place in his heart; for 'she hoped,' she said, 'to unite herself to his mind.' "[9] The genius did not have a fit spouse. Sophia could give him only profane love; Mary would give sacred and sublime.

She now began a platonic honeymoon and flung off old ascetic habits with bridal enthusiasm. Immediately after Everina's departure (so soon that the arrangements must have been made secretly while her sister was still with her in George Street), Mary Wollstonecraft moved to spacious lodgings an artist could visit with pleasure in Store Street on Bedford Square, only a few blocks from Fuseli's. She felt she had been too rigid, frugal, and self-denying, and in a fashion she had never before permitted herself, transformed her appearance, enhanced her femininity, dressed with style and elegance, powdered her hair in the mode of the day. Fuseli's friend William Roscoe, a wealthy literary man and liberal, commissioned a portrait of her by an unknown artist. She wrote Roscoe that she did not think it would be a good likeness, but she was obviously excited about it. Around the same time John Opie, himself a friend and admirer, also painted her.[10] It is interesting to observe variant impressions artists, like biographers, have of their subject. Mary's features are pronounced in both portraits: strong curving eyebrows, almond eyes, definite wide mouth. The first painter saw the intellectual Amazon Roscoe admired, dressed as she must have been before she took pains with herself, keen, challenging, utterly confident. Opie shows a woman of more graceful *tenue* and a deeper, subtler look, with soft cheeks and an almost tender mouth.

She had something more in motion. "Mary was without being a dazzling beauty, yet of a charming grace," Count Gustave Von Schlabrendorf, who was later in love with her, wrote. "Her face, so full of expression, presented a style of beauty beyond that of merely regular features. There was enchantment in her glance, her voice, and her movements." Godwin, who first met her in 1792, also spoke of her charm; he had expected a "sturdy, muscular, raw-boned virago," but found her in spite of initial mutual dislike, quite lovely. Yet it was impossible for her to be as certain of her feminine attraction, which she hardly admitted she wanted to exercise on Fuseli, as of her intellectual bond with him. As she realized and resented, he preferred beauty and good-humored docility in women, and conspicuous allure, which was beneath her dignity and beyond her capability. She wanted to be loved for character, ideals, genius: "A fine woman . . . inspires more sublime emotions by displaying intellectual beauty [but] may be overlooked or observed with indifference, by those men who find their happiness in their gratifications of their appetites." She found herself in a trap; she did not want to be "reproached" for being masculine, or devalued as a woman, but the feminine ideal in her world, no matter how enlightened, excluded and isolated a Mary Wollstonecraft.[11] Fuseli may have told her she was a fine woman. Certainly, like everyone else he told her she had a virile mind; but intellect was considered a male sex characteristic, and a brilliant woman, therefore, logically was masculine, vulnerable to caricature.

She was constantly made aware of her limitations. Fuseli's sexual preferences and love of beauty were evident on his studio walls and worktables when she visited and dined at his home, as she did regularly. He was preparing a painting of a voluptuously naked *Eve before the fall* for the Milton Gallery. Mary was uncomfortable enough about it to joke at the provocation in a rather possessive way to William Roscoe, to whom she wrote:

> Our friend Fuseli is going with more than usual spirit—like Milton he seems quite at home in hell—his Devil will be the hero . . . *entre nous,*

I rather doubt whether he will produce an Eve to please me in any of the situations he has selected, unless it be after the fall.[12]

To please Fuseli's eye and frame her femininity in every way she could allow herself, was expensive. Mary got into debt so deeply she had to turn to George Blood for a loan of £10 shortly after she moved. She was less than honest about the reason, having "lately applied to Mr. Johnson so frequently (to fit Everina out, for her journey, etc., etc.) that I would fain wait a little while before I ask for any more . . . I do not wish Skeys to know anything of this application." She owed only £20, she wrote, "excepting Mr. J." She said nothing to George about her move, and, feeling particularly guilty, never directly told her sisters either; they deduced it only when their letters from Mary arrived "dated *Bedford Square*" with no explanation. But Eliza knew enough to be suspicious. "I conclude from it she is in good spirits and heartily tired of her *daughter* Ann and brimful of her friend, Fuseli," she wrote Everina, October 4, and pressed her sister, to whom she thought Mary might write more confidentially: "What is [she] now absorbed in. Is it *A Love?* or Study, pray let me know."

She was absorbed in both. In early October Mary Wollstonecraft told William Roscoe she was beginning a new book, which he should keep secret. Gaily and confidently she said it was to be a work in which "I myself . . . shall certainly appear, head and heart."[13] It was accurate advance notice of *A Vindication of the Rights of Woman.*

Chapter 12

In the fall of 1791 Mary Wollstonecraft was at a zenith of pride and aspiration, released from austerity, a significant writer from whom further stimulating and virile work was anticipated, and a friend—and in Fuseli's case, particular friend—of prestigious intellectuals. At the beginning of October, shortly after she moved to Bedford Square, she began work on a book that was not only, as she wrote Roscoe, a fusion of heart and head, the accumulated emotion and understanding of her lifetime, but also a revolutionary work by which she proposed to change the world.

Like most progressives, Mary Wollstonecraft believed France was tearing down a rotten system and creating a new and just society, a prototype for the future. The revolutionary constitution, however, promulgated at the time she wrote *A Vindication of the Rights of Men*, left women in their traditional position, without civil or political rights, as the American Constitution had done, and even enlightened leaders assumed this to be obvious verity. Thomas Christie, Johnson's former partner at *The Analytical Review*, judged it: "superior wisdom . . . to honour the sex as not to injure their *real* happiness, or endanger the welfare of society." Talleyrand's new system of national education, proposed to the French Assembly in September of 1791, guaranteed continuation of the sexual status quo by confining state education to boys. Mary Wollstonecraft alone instantly and totally comprehended the significance; rights of men even in the eyes of revolutionaries were to be just that, rights applied by men to men only. In a flash of insight she perceived the female condition as it had never been defined before. Others had argued that law and mores crippled women's potential and forced them into subservience; she was the first to fuse experience, intellect, and emotion, to attack the sexual basis of social and religious tradition, and to bring the issue to life as a philosophically based and practicable reform to be incorporated forthwith in a specific society. It was, in Ruth Benedict's words, "a fight for which the world was not ready, which seemed worth fighting only to one soul then living, to Mary Wollstonecraft herself."[1]

She was one of very few women who had the intellectual capacity to analyze the problem as she did. Only Catherine Macaulay, whom she considered the greatest woman England had ever produced, shared her perceptions; Mary acknowledged the debt owed the recently deceased Macaulay and, in fact, used *Letters on Education* very specifically in her own work. She considered herself a moral philosopher like Macaulay, but *A Vindication of the Rights of Woman* was also a pioneer social study that stripped bare a system and analyzed it in terms of a new insight. Just as revolutions are led by an intelligentsia demanding for others what it has partially achieved for itself, so Mary Wollstonecraft, who had partially liberated herself, fought for sexual revolution from the vantage point of her own achievement, demanding that others be given the freedom and opportunity she exemplified. It was a stroke of genius to associate rights of man with women's subjugation; it took brilliant courage and originality to explode ageless tradition. Macaulay presented the problem; Wollstonecraft made it a cause. In this sense Mary was the only woman who could have written *A Vindication of the Rights of Woman;* it was conceived in her past, generated throughout her life, and born in personal protest. If there are exaggerations and blind spots in the book, they are reactions of a woman whose character was formed under pressure of misery, injustice, and wretched bad luck that she refused to accept. The system had failed her, her mother, and sisters, and she struck at what she well knew to be its heart with the double-edged weapon of anger and hope.

This *Vindication* is as repetitive and badly organized as the first. Johnson knew Mary Wollstonecraft was producing an important work and sent his printer's devil to wait on her doorstep for completed pages; therefore she had little opportunity to correct or reorganize. Under this pressure and in her own excitement, she wrote a kind of rapid stream of consciousness, digressing freely: the book has little form, a good deal of distortion, and enormous drive. The immediate catalyst was Talleyrand's educational program—and the dedication of the work addressed (and reproached) him directly, for she intended nothing less than to inspire him to open educational opportunity to girls—but the problems stemming from her current attachment to Fuseli were an emotional wellspring. The book was written in three months, an accomplishment made possible by certainty, pride, and ardor, to which Godwin was witness. On November 13 he first met Mary when he went to dinner at Johnson's specifically to meet Tom Paine and found Mary holding forth. "I had barely looked into her Answer to Burke, and had been displeased . . . with a few offenses against grammar," he said. "I had therefore little curiosity to see Mrs. Wollstonecraft, and a very great curiosity to see Thomas Paine. Paine is no great talker. . . . I, of consequence, heard her, very frequently when I wished to hear Paine." Mary criticized everything and everyone that afternoon. She was so aggressive and censorious she finally told Godwin that anyone who looked on the bright side as he did, was plain foolish.[2]

Obviously, Mary Wollstonecraft was in a fighting mood. "Consider," she admonished Talleyrand in the dedication of her book:

> whether, when men contend with their freedom, and to be allowed to judge for themselves respecting their own happiness, it be not inconsistent and unjust to subjugate women . . . Who made man the exclusive judge? . . .
>
> In this style argue tyrants of every denomination, from the weak king to the weak father of a family. . . . Do you not act a similar part when you *force* all women, by denying them civil and political rights, to remain immured in their families groping in the dark? . . .
>
> . . . I wish, Sir, to set some investigations of this kind afloat in France; and should they lead to a confirmation of my principles when your Constitution is revised, the Rights of Woman may be respected . . . JUSTICE for one-half of the human race.

As in *Thoughts,* she spoke for middle-class women, "because they appear to be in the most natural state." Aristocrats of both sexes were decadent, she felt, and irrelevant to the future. She began her argument with an attack on tyranny, "the pestiferous purple which render the progress of civilization a curse," and she asserted that God made us capable of enjoying a more godlike portion of happiness. She proceeded to equate political with sexual tyranny; to demonstrate that the tyranny of men over women was based on an assumption that women are born frail morally and intellectually as well as physically, and to point out that this belief was actually motivated by men's desire for convenient, submissive sex objects, accepted by women in return for security, childish dependence, and oblique power, and sustained by the full weight of society's pressure. Since both sexes have immortal souls, for both "the plan of life which enables us to carry some knowledge and virtue into another world, is the one best calculated to ensure content in this." Most women's duties, she admitted, were domestic, but since love cannot survive marriage, women must be intellectual companions to their husbands, and capable of sustaining themselves if disappointed or widowed. Only full educational opportunity and rejection of a double standard, she wrote, could make women "more observant daughters, more affectionate sisters, more faithful wives, more reasonable mothers—in a word—better citizens." Since women educate children, the future of a society even after a revolution had to be founded on women's virtue and dedication. She subjected several typical eminent commentators on women to ruthless dissection: Lord Chesterfield; Dr. Gregory; Fordyce; Mmes. Pozzi, de Staël, de Genlis; even her beloved Rousseau. Of him she said, "I have, probably, had an opportunity of observing more girls in their infancy than J. J. Rousseau."[3]

She put major responsibility for women's situation on men, whose domination of society she accepted in general:

> Let it not be concluded that I wish to invert the order of things . . . men seem designed by Providence to attain a great degree of virtue . . . [but] men have increased that inferiority till women are almost below the standards of rational beings . . . in a state of childhood. . . .
>
> . . . all the causes of female weakness, as well as depravity . . . branch out of one great cause—want of chastity in men. . . .
>
> I know that libertines will also exclaim, that women would be unsexed by acquiring strength of body and mind. . . . I think that, on the contrary, we would see dignified beauty and true grace. . . .

> Let men take their choice. Man and woman were made for each other . . . if they will not improve women they will deprave them.[4]

She also blamed the system as a whole—foolish mothers, disorderly, superficial education, and corrupt society—for making "gentle domestic brutes" or languishing sexual pets of women. Although she did not mention them by name, she constantly illustrated her points with women she had known: her humbly dependent, incompetent, unjust mother; Eliza, too silly to marry sensibly, educated for nothing, clinging "with parasitical tenacity, piteously demanding succor"; Sophia Fuseli, simpering and sexy; Ann Gabell, "a trusty servant"; Lady Kingsborough, a fine lady who took her dogs to bed and let her children grow up crippled, a veritable Messalina "dissolved in luxury . . . irrational monster . . . depraved." She reiterated frequently that women's follies and vices were inevitable given their training and society's expectations, but her descriptions of them were loaded with hostility and contempt:

> artificial weakness produces a propensity to tyrannize, and gives birth to cunning . . . which leads them to play off those contemptible infantine airs that undermine esteem even while they excite desire. . . .
>
> Surely she has not an immortal soul who can loiter life away merely employed in adorning her person. . . .
>
> Pleasure is the business of a woman's life . . . little can be expected from such weak beings . . . when they should reason, their conduct is unstable, and their opinions are wavering. . . .
>
> In the name of reason, and even common sense, what can save such beings from contempt; even though they be soft and fair.[5]

Mary Wollstonecraft's program for women was basically education aimed at virtue and independence. She believed young people should live at home during their schooling, and proposed a national system of state-supported day schools where boys and girls would be educated together in all fields of learning, with separate afternoon trade schools for vocational training. Those of superior ability or fortune would proceed to training suitable for future leaders of society, with part-time, on-the-job experience. She insisted that society's expectations for women should be essentially the same as for men throughout their lives: equal exercise of mind and body; equal maturity, responsibility, and competence; equal intellectual and professional attainments; equal sexual knowledge and restraint. Virtues and values, she said, should have no sex. She foresaw great and beneficial change resulting from such a system, which would make women good citizens and even able to earn an independent living:

> . . . they must have a civil existence in the State, married or single. . . . Women might certainly study the art of healing, and be physicians, as well as nurses. And midwifery, decency seems to allot to them. . . . They might also study politics. . . . Business of various kinds . . . which might save many from common and legal prostitution. . . .
>
> . . . I really think that women ought to have representatives, instead of being arbitrarily governed without having any direct share allowed them in the deliberations of government.[6]

But simultaneously she indicated that most women were indeed innately inferior to men—"the weakest as well as the most oppressed half of the species. . . . I have been led to imagine that the few extraordinary women who have rushed . . . out of the orbit prescribed to their sex, were *male* spirits, confined by mistake in female frames"—and she proudly put herself among "a small number of distinguished women for whom I do not ask a place":

> I declare against all power built on prejudice, however hoary. . . . They may escape, who dare to brave the consequences, without any breach of duty, without sinning against the order of things. . . . They are free—who will be free! . . . There have been many women in the world who, instead of being supported by the reason and virtue of their fathers and brothers, have strengthened their own minds by struggling with their vices and follies; yet have never met with a hero, in the shape of a husband. . . . Thanks to that Being . . . who . . . gave me sufficient strength of mind to dare to assert my own reason, till, becoming dependent only on Him for the support of my virtue, I view, with indignation, the mistaken notions that enslave my sex. . . . I love man as my fellow; but his sceptre, real or usurped, extends not to me, unless the reason of an individual demands my homage.[7]

She saw a power struggle between the sexes—"a state of warfare"—in which women use their sexual allure to dominate men. She nailed male chivalry as proof of the feminine predicament. Even women's love of dress, she said, "is not natural, but arises, like false ambition in men, from a love of power." Women, like despots, had more power than they deserve. She concluded with a succinct statement of her theme:

> Asserting the rights which women in common with men ought to contend for, I have not attempted to extenuate their faults; but to prove them to be the natural consequence of their education and station in society. If so, it is reasonable to suppose that they will change their character, and correct their vices and follies, when they are allowed to be free in a physical, moral and civil sense.[8]

This *Vindication* is remarkably revealing about the Mary Wollstonecraft of 1791. Religion was still for her a source of comfort, though not merely a refuge but a governing principle of conduct. Immortality of the soul was the grand reason to achieve maximum virtue and knowledge. Persistent among the virtues were frankness, fortitude, and rationality; the vices, hypocrisy, dependence, sensuality, and self-indulgence. The impact of her family life was vivid. The chapters on "Parental Affection" and "Duty of Parents" might have been titled "Parental Tyranny and Inadequacy." She attacked primogeniture, female dependency, and aristocrats. The book was permeated with anger and disdain for women. Men were treated ambivalently; she extolled masculine virtues at the same time she attacked men's absolute power and sensuality, and their gullibility as far as women were concerned. Sex was a major villain, and the sexuality of men responsible for corrupt and distorted relations between the sexes. There was a whole chapter on the true modesty of a pure mind, as she saw hers, contrasted with salaciousness and lust. She went so far in rejecting sex as to claim that:

> a master and mistress of a family ought not to continue to love each other with passion. I mean to say, that they ought not to indulge those emotions which disturb the order of society, and engross the thoughts . . . an unhappy marriage is often very advantageous to a family, and . . . a neglected wife is, in general, the best mother.[9]

An interesting conclusion to be drawn from her parents' example, and directly contradicting her simultaneous perception of children's need for domestic peace and stability.

Mary sustained conflicting attitudes toward passionate love. On the one hand, love must be transitory, illusory, or "a plausible excuse to the voluptuary." But she also asserted its merit: "it is far better to be often deceived in love than never to love; to be disappointed in love than never to love." Even more, she glorified it as proof of the immortality of the soul and human grandeur:

> the romantic passion, which is the concomitant of genius. Who can clip its wing? . . . the regulation of the passions is not, always, wisdom. On the contrary, it should seem, that one reason why men have superior judgment, and more fortitude than women, is that they give freer scope to the grand passions, and by more frequently going astray enlarge their minds.[10]

She was contradictory also about the ideal life for a woman such as herself, conceiving the simple existence of a devoted wife and mother as the happiest in the world, while emphasizing the need for women to shun dependency and to transcend common life. She hinted that superior women like herself make their own standards—witness Heloise when she gave up all the world for Abelard. To the chosen few, artists especially, she allowed sensibility and passion: "It is this power of looking into the heart, and responsively vibrating with each emotion, that enables . . . the painter to sketch with a pencil of fire."[11]

Her problem with Fuseli seems clear and poignant. Love of beauty when applied to men's sexual preference became "sensual homage paid to beauty." She asserted the value of the mature intellectual woman, whom the French, she claimed, admired:

> I mean to say that they allow women to be in their most perfect state, when vivacity gives place to reason, and to that majestic seriousness of character, which marks maturity . . . the women who have distinguished themselves have neither been the most beautiful nor the most gentle of their sex. . . . What arts have I not seen silly women use to interrupt by flirtation . . . a rational conversation, which made the men forget that they were pretty women.

And with obvious emotion she wrote that women like herself "were made to be loved, [but] must not aim for respect, lest they be hounded out of society as masculine."[12]

In the contest she was engaged in for Fuseli, his sexuality was a hindrance to the ideal relationship she desired. He was a superior man carried away by his passions. However, Mary intimated that a woman like herself had reserves of passion unknown to ordinary females. "True voluptuousness must proceed from the mind—for what can equal the sensations produced by mutual affection, supported by mutual respect." In addition to its stated purposes, her book was a vindication of Mary Wollstonecraft, the woman of character, strength, and intelligence who could not exist comfortably in a society that repudiated her value. She was willing to fight to assert her worth, although she yearned for simple acceptance in a reasonable society where heroic virtues would be unnecessary. And it was also an address to Fuseli, the man who currently personified masculine rejection of women like herself in favor of conventional femininity. "Women are all rivals," she wrote. If there were any doubt of this motivation, Mary Wollstonecraft herself made it clear in a letter to Imlay a year later: "One reason, in short, why I wish my sex to become wiser, is, that the foolish ones may not, by their pretty folly, rob those whose sensibility keeps down their vanity, of the few roses that afford some solace in the thorny road of life."[13]

Mary Wollstonecraft completed *A Vindication of the Rights of Woman* on January 3, 1792. "I shall give the last sheet to the printer today," she wrote Roscoe. "I am dissatisfied with myself for not having done justice to the subject—do not suspect me of false modesty—I mean to say, that had I allowed myself more time I could have written a better book in every sense of the word."[14] The immediacy and force of the work, however, guaranteed strong public reaction, for it was not a theoretical exploration, as Macaulay's *Letters* had been, but an attack and demand authenticated by intense emotion and specific experience. The book was reviewed widely and favorably at first; by the end of 1792 Johnson had published a second edition and the book appeared in Boston and Philadelphia, in two French translations, and in a German translation by Salzmann. Mary Wollstonecraft had become an international figure, and those who did not actually read her book were nevertheless familiar with its contents.

For many the whole concept was repugnant: Hannah More simply refused to read it ("Metaphysical jargon," she told Walpole); indeed, most women seem to have shrunk from its conclusions. It was parodied, sneered at, and vilified as time went on. Eliza wrote Everina in mid-1793; "the gentry of Pembroke are shocked at M.'s book every one declares it is the most indecent Rhapsody that ever was penned by man or woman. Mr. B. is continually dwelling on the parts that *wound* his modesty most."[15]

Mary Wollstonecraft had hit to the quick of resentment usually so successfully contained by women that only a few people had the insight to discover its existence. Samuel Johnson had once observed: "Women have a perpetual envy of our vices; they are less vicious than we, not from choice, but because we restrict them." When teased about her conquests, Mrs. Pendarves wrote, "Would it were so that I went ravaging and slaying all odious men, for that would go near to clear the world of that sort of animal. . . . They have so despicable an opinion of women, and treat them by their words and actions so ungenerously and inhumanly." One wonders what Fanny Burney's "Miss White" thought of the book. Most interesting are the reactions of some women to whom the book was addressed. One intellectual, Anna Seward, called the book "wonderful. . . . It has, by turns, pleased and displeased, startled and half-convinced me that its author is oftener right than wrong." As conventional a young woman as Maria Holroyd wrote her aunt that she not only had read Mme. Roland's *Vie* without being tarnished, but added, "I should like you also to read Mrs. Wollstonecraft's *Vindication of the Rights of Woman.* There are many sensible and just observations." A thoughtful American girl, Elizabeth Drinker, noted in her diary that she thought Mary Wollstonecraft "a prodigious writer. In many of her sentiments, she . . . *speaks my mind,* in some others I do not altogether coincide with her—I am not for quite so much independence."[16] Aaron Burr heartily agreed with the book, and adapted his daughter's education to its principles. Many progressive intellectuals and writers were deeply interested. George Dyer included Mary Wollstonecraft in an ode to liberty written in 1792.

But as *A Vindication of the Rights of Woman* was a creature of the French Revolution, so it was its victim. As the revolution intensified, all reform, much less radical thought and thinkers, was seen as threatening English security. While Mary Wollstonecraft was writing her book, Paine and his editor, Jordon—Johnson was fearful of publishing Paine—were indicted for the *Rights of Man.* In September, after an evening with Johnson, William Blake advised Paine to flee England immediately, "or you are a dead man!" Paine escaped for France that night, with English government agents hot on his trail. A year after *Vindication*'s publication, just after Louis XVI's execution, Eliza reported that Tom Paine was burnt in effigy at Pembroke, and there was "talk of immortalizing Miss W in the same manner."[17] Except for some liberal intellectuals and an unknown number of dissatisfied women, Mary Wollstonecraft's classic was judged by most a subversive grotesquerie.

Mary Wollstonecraft emerged in January of 1792 from three months absorption in her book "suffering a transient gust of sourish gall," as she told William Roscoe, and "fumes of ill-humour which make me quarrel with myself," which she attributed partially to annoyance at imperfections in her work. She planned to write a second volume of *A Vindication of the Rights of Woman,* and declared she would take her time to perfect it. As was true immediately following her first *Vindication,* of 1790, she did only perfunctory reviews for *The Analytical Review,* seemingly the result of a natural need to refresh herself after intense effort. Although she continued her editorial role as the months went on, she wrote only what was necessary to earn a living and produced no original work at all. Instead of glorying in her renown and zesting to capitalize on it as before, she was restless, dissatisfied, unable to concentrate. "Her pen was palsied," Johnson later told Godwin. "You know the cause."[18]

In the accelerating excitation of the past two years, which climaxed in the passionate exposition of her book, Mary Wollstonecraft had been able to evade imperative personal needs. Now she faced again the sterility of her private life, against which she had formerly protested with such despair. Going on thirty-three, she felt the best years of her life were passing without intimacy and reciprocated love. She refused to resign herself. Fuseli was the man she wanted, and she began to understand that her determination to regulate her love to "strength of feeling unalloyed by passion" was a delusion. She was in love; she saw Fuseli constantly; she was tormented by the limitations of the relationship mandated by his marriage and her principles, and by fantasies of what her life could be if he were free. Unable to forgo the pleasure or resolve the pain, struggling to manage her feelings, she oscillated for months between "that sanguine ardour which it has been the business of my life to depress," as she had written in *A Vindication of the Rights of Woman,* and the depression of its frustration.[19]

Ostensibly she was the established celebrity, sought after, enjoying her success. Her brother Charles was impressed by her transfiguration; "Mrs. Wollstonecraft is grown quite handsome," he wrote Eliza, "being conscious she is on the wrong side of thirty she now endeavours to set off those charms (she once despised) to the best advantage." She made a conquest in February that not only did not infuriate her, as in 1788, but tickled her pride, for feminine success was now important to her. She wrote Everina:

> And be it known to you that my book, etc., etc. has afforded me an opportunity of settling very advantageous in the matrimonial line with a new acquaintance but entre nous a handsome house and a proper man did not tempt me, yet I may as well appear before you with the feather stuck in my cap.

John Opie frequently brought his wife to call—"too much of a flirt to be a proper companion to him," Mary rightly judged; he divorced her three years later, after she eloped with another man. Talleyrand came to London in the spring on a political mission and took tea with the eminent author who had addressed her book to him. The meeting has its comic side: Talleyrand, cold as a serpent, cynical opportunism incarnate, *tête à tête* with Mary Wollstonecraft, ardent, idealistic, and unable to speak much French. (Eliza once said of a Frenchman struggling with English that he understood the language as Mary did French.)[20] The visit must have left both puzzled. And she met Godwin again two or three times in the course of her active social life, but neither liked the other any better.

As for the "standing dish of family cares," as she described it, she compounded them in her usual fashion. Ned was flourishing financially and had resumed control of their father's affairs, but Mary felt she had to supplement the senior Wollstonecraft's inadequate allowance out of her own funds and said she was in continual fear of having him completely dependent on her. She was partially supporting James. Once more she took Charles—again "very much improved"—away from Ned and tried to launch him in a new career. He was delighted, Eliza said, with Mary's kindness and affection, but Mary was short of money because of her obligations and her inability to work, and wrote Everina in February that if she could send £20 it would be very helpful. She was unable to clear her conscience about her sisters. Eliza, in particular, resented *A Vindication of the Rights of Woman,* recognizing herself in many passages as the object of Mary's disdainful pity and Mary as one of the exceptional women praised in the book—"Sappho, Eloisa, Mrs. Macaulay, the Empress of Russia"—leading a glittering life from which she and Everina were brutally excluded. "Beware," Eliza wrote Everina, "and banish Hope . . . I never think of *our sister* but in the light of a friend who had been dead some years . . . perhaps in a better world the Love of Fame cannot corrupt the soul . . . ought not this sudden change in such a character make one feel less indignation and surprise when one meets weak minds, wholly lost in foolish pride." Mary, however, simply withdrew from such complaints; by early July Eliza had not heard from her in over three months.[21]

Mothering her foster child, Ann, supposedly a comfort for her middle age, was equally irksome to Mary, for it was an unnatural substitute for her real desires. Lacking valid feeling for the little girl, she claimed that a person of genius was the most improper person to be employed in education, and blamed the child's character instead of her own inadequacy. She was particularly angry when she discovered Ann had been stealing sugar, the more so because Mary herself was struggling to control certain cravings.

Casting about for satisfaction, Mary apparently now felt the need of a woman friend, although it was impossible for her to return to the devotion she had felt for Fanny Blood. She had met an interesting and attractive couple, recent additions to Johnson's circle. Joel and Ruth Barlow were New Englanders in their late thirties, he a poet whose "Vision of Columbus" was reviewed in *The Analytical Review,* and a former soldier in the American Revolution; she a blacksmith's daughter whose virtues seemed to Mary to be particularly American, praiseworthy, and pertinent to her own quest. Barlow had spent two years in France promoting the Scioto Land Company, which was selling to prospective French settlers lands in western America which it eventually turned out the company did not actually own. This territory was the object of great interest; the French wanted it, the Spaniards were nervous about it, and Americans like Barlow and Gilbert Imlay intrigued to exploit the political and commercial possibilities of the rich prize. (*The Analytical Review* reviewed Imlay's book *A Topographical Description of the Western Territory of North America,* the second book on the subject in its pages during this period.) Barlow came to London in 1791, and was joined later by his wife. Tom Paine sponsored the couple, and Johnson published Barlow's answer to Burke, "Advice to the Privileged Orders," in February of 1792. It was a "sensible political pamphlet" from an intellectual of note, according to Mary Wollstonecraft. Mary thought well enough of her new friends to accept their offer to take her brother Charles with them to America to make his career in farming. He would live there almost as a member of their family, for the Barlows were childless. "Fuseli insisted on making Charles a present of ten pounds," she wrote Everina, "because he liked the scheme." Mary sent Charles to Leatherhead to learn agriculture, at heavy expense but with great hopes.[22]

Mary Wollstonecraft was normally extremely demanding of women, but although she told Everina Ruth Barlow's understanding was only "tolerable," she admired her affectionate, generous nature and, in particular, the quality of her marriage. The Barlows were a rare couple in her experience, equal partners, sharing friends, business and political interests. Ruth had serene self-respect and self-sufficiency, trusting and supporting her husband during his wanderings and speculations. Barlow was enjoying the role of soldier of fortune, with emphasis on the latter to Mary's distaste. When Barlow went back to France in the spring, on a ten day visit that extended for weeks, Ruth often came to breakfast in Mary's study, and the two women talked of family life and their respective national characteristics. Their intimacy was such that Ruth showed Mary one of her husband's letters. The Barlows were married lovers after eleven years together, and Mary could not bear it. She wrote Everina with sour and unwarranted misanthropy:

> Delighted with some of her husband's letters, she has exultingly shown them to me; and, though I took care not to let her see it, I was almost disgusted with the *tender* passages which afforded her so much satisfaction, because they were turned so prettily that they looked more like the cold ingenuity of the head than the warm overflowings of the heart . . . he calls "her arms his heaven."

Ruth Barlow proposed America, the land of equality and opportunity, as a solution for Mary's sisters as well as Charles. Working women, she told Mary, and particularly foreign women, were respected by the best society there, and she offered to take Everina in while Eliza kept house for Charles, an offer Mary unwisely relayed to Everina. However, it became apparent that Barlow was not going to return to America and rural simplicity, but intended to pursue his political and financial schemes in Europe—"fame . . . on this dirty earth," as Mary said. It was her first experience with the American as speculator rather than unspoiled product of a new and more ideal society. At the end of June she decided to go to France herself—in company with Joseph Johnson and Fuseli and his wife—as many English visitors did out of curiosity, whether they favored or opposed the revolution. For her it was particularly exciting. "I shall be introduced to many people," she wrote Everina, "my book has been translated and praised . . . and Mr. Fuseli of course is well known." Barlow made reservations in Paris in her name. She would look out for a situation for Eliza, she said, so she could escape the hard Welsh winter. Eliza, with the perception of a jealous sister, told Everina exactly why "M. & F." were going to Paris:

> when Mrs. W. reaches the Continent she will be but a woman . . . at the very summit of her happiness, for will not ambition fill every chink of her Great Soul? (for such I really think hers) that is not occupied by *Love*. . . . And you actually have the vanity to imagine that in the National Assembly Personages like M. & F. will bestow a thought on two females when nature meant to "suck fools and chronicle small beer."[23]

The foursome set off in early August, got as far as Dover, and stopped. It was no time for political tourism; on August 10 the vanguard of the revolution took the Tuileries, deposed the king, and imprisoned the royal family in the Temple. Mary's party returned to London.

Suddenly bereft of six weeks anticipated close company with Fuseli, Mary Wollstonecraft's frustrated love for the painter broke through the circumference she had drawn for herself. She took a vacation of some kind, returning to London September 12. And then she threw herself against the wall. She still forbade herself sexual union, but by that denial felt that she had earned a right to press Fuseli for more attention and more constant intimacy. When he held off she wrote him of her love, of her despair at his neglect, of the sacrifices and miseries of her wretched past life. It was one of her most self-defeating compulsions, this appeal for the pity that was her own path to love. She acted as if the man she cared for owed her compensatory response and would react as parent to a wounded child, making up for deprivations she had never been able to resign herself to. Fuseli told her what she demanded was dangerous and impossible. "If I thought my passion criminal," she answered, "I would conquer it, or die in the attempt. For immodesty, in my eyes, is ugliness; my soul turns with disgust from pleasure tricked out in charms which shun the light of heaven." Only bits or paraphrases of these letters remain in Knowles' biography of Fuseli; they were afterward destroyed, probably by the Shelley family, proof of their intensity, which must have approached that of her later letters to Imlay. In her few reviews for *The Analytical Review* there are further glimpses of her feelings—an unusual interpretation of Abelard as "the vain and frigid" lover of trusting Heloise; a condemnation of Dr. Samuel Johnson's piety as intellectual cowardice. Some of the "Hints" for *Vindication*'s projected sequel, which Godwin ascribed to this period, are revelatory:

> Indolence is the source of nervous complaints, and a whole host of cares. . . .
>
> . . . when women have an object in view, they pursue it with more steadiness than men, particularly love. This is not a compliment. Passion pursues with more heat than reason, and with most ardour during the absence of reason.
>
> Men are more subject to physical love than women. . . .
>
> I only expect the natural reward of virtue.[24]

When Mary made minor revisions for the second edition of her book, which Johnson issued during 1792 to meet the demand, she removed a phrase in the Introduction that had read: "The male pursues, the female yields." It was no longer an axiom she could accept. Fuseli was squirming and could not find an appropriate way to handle her. Joseph Johnson was watching worriedly over his shoulder. Mary could not, even at the height of her passion, give Fuseli the uncritical admiration he wanted from a woman; "I hate to see that reptile vanity sliming over the noble qualities of your heart," she wrote him. He was sexually attracted to women of uncomplicated passion; woman, he said, was "down from the waist a centaur." This one was not to be made a mistress, however; her moral and physical virginity precluded that possibility, and even if he had wanted it he knew her well enough to be sure she would blow his marriage and his reputation apart. Of all things, he hated, in his vanity, to look foolish, and by the standards of his world nothing was more ridiculous than a man who could neither bed nor dispose of an ardent woman.

By November Mary Wollstonecraft was sufficiently distraught to believe she had found an alternative that would preserve the purity of their relationship and yet permit a not-to-be consummated mutual possession, a strange kind of penultimate intimacy that would not interfere with his marriage. She would live with the Fuselis, guaranteeing not to encroach on Sophia's marital rights. She went to Sophia Fuseli with this proposal. In her desperation and naïveté, Mary must have pictured a scene out of Rousseau in which Sophia and she agreed to share Fuseli, one his body and the other his genius, in a perfectly balanced distribution hallowed by idyllic faith and purity. She herself was sacrificing her need to have first place or none. "Being above deceit," she admitted to Sophia, "I find that I cannot live without the satisfaction of seeing and conversing with him daily."[25]

Sophia Fuseli knew the difference between reading *La Nouvelle Heloise* and acting it out. She probably was not surprised, although she knew gossip had it that Johnson and Mary might marry, and she had the advantage of absolute confidence in Fuseli's basic commitment to herself and thorough knowledge of his character. If she had been sharp, she might have thrown at Mary a line from *A Vindication of the Rights of Woman* on polygamy—"nature never intended that a man should have more than one wife." Apparently, she recoiled in horrified bourgeois indignation and explicitly humiliated this woman, who had so often condescended to her, for presuming that Fuseli had any personal interest in Mary, that he could care about such a masculine woman, that he wanted her disturbing his intimacy with his wife. She ordered Mary Wollstonecraft out of her home.

The blow was terrible. Mary was evicted by a woman who represented everything she disdained in her sex, but who stripped, ridiculed, and defeated her. The intimacy around which she had arranged her life was vaporized and the superiority she claimed for herself invalidated. Like a child she had acted on a deeply desired fantasy and like a child she had been slapped down. It is hard to believe she did not know on some level what would happen, impossible not to speculate about an unconscious need to be checked and punished for her forbidden passion. But two things seem clear. First, Sophia Fuseli brought Mary up short, much as Elizabeth Wollstonecraft had checked her as a child—by reproof and chastisement, "the only thing capable of reconciling her to herself," as Mary often said of her mother's discipline. And second, it was only after this acting out that Mary was able to proceed to a full sex life with a man who was free to be her lover.

Fuseli, hiding meekly (for him) behind Sophia's skirts, acquiesced to Mary's banishment. He could certainly live without her. His wife's initiative was probably the only way out of an impossible situation. His relief is understandable. But his major concern seems to have been his own image; his ego had been wounded, ergo he read Mary out of his life. He later refused to return her letters to her, probably because he wanted to protect himself; but he did not destroy or forbid his biographer to use them, which suggests a need for revenge, and judging from his account of the wretched business after Mary's death, when her memory was generally vilified, he still needed to caricature "one who loved you," as Joseph Johnson wrote him.[26]

Even if her humiliation did not go beyond the Fuselis, Mary Wollstonecraft knew there would be repercussions. The episode was later distorted into a story that William Blake loved Mary and wanted her to live with him and his wife in a *ménage à trois*. It was inevitable close friends would sense something peculiar had happened to separate the erstwhile intimates, and impossible not to meet at the homes of mutual friends. But more importantly, Sophia Fuseli had enabled Mary to face reality. Summoning her self-respect and energy, Mary determined to make a clean break and get away from the circle and associations so inevitably connected with Fuseli. She decided to leave London for Paris, as she had previously intended, for at least six weeks or until "her distempered mind," as Godwin put it, had healed; three months before she had reviewed a novel by Charlotte Smith in which a disappointed lover had done exactly the same thing. In France she could absorb herself in great events that put her personal problems in perspective. She would reconfirm her value by associating with leaders of the revolution who knew her book and reputation. Paris was boiling—war, the September massacres, ascendency of vehement militants, the impending treason trial of Louis XVI. Mary still had faith in the revolution; she wrote William Roscoe November 12 announcing her trip: "Let me beg you not to mix with the shallow herd who throw an odium on immutable principles, because some of the mere instruments of the revolution were too sharp—children of any growth will do mischief when they meddle with edged tools."[27]

Turbulence fit her mood and challenged her courage: "We know M will rather rejoice at encountering what others shudder at," Eliza said, and asked to be taken along, for she had always envied Everina's Parisian experience. Mary refused, but solemnly promised to find Eliza a position abroad, an undertaking that indicates how little she understood revolution and how deeply she felt obligated to her sisters. Charles had left for America without the Barlows; James wrote a "ruinous" letter asking for money, which she neither could nor would send. She busied herself settling her affairs, storing her furniture, preparing to send little Ann back to Ireland, dining in farewell with friends. She wrote Fuseli a simple good-bye, asking pardon for having disturbed "the quiet tenor of his life," but her bitterness was projected elsewhere, and in one instance on an innocent woman. One of Mary's last letters, written in late November before she left London, went to an aspiring and overly humble novice author, Mary Hays, who had asked for advice and help. Mary had mentioned her work to Joseph Johnson, but replied to her:

> trifles of this kind I have always left to him to settle; and, you must be aware, madam, that the *honour* of publishing on which you have laid a stress, is the cant of both trade and sex. . . . This kind of vain humility has ever disgusted me. . . . If you have not a tolerably good opinion of your own production, why intrude it on the public? We have plenty of bad books already . . . when weakness claims indulgency, it seems to justify the despotism of strength.[28]

If female weakness set her teeth on edge, she was herself particularly susceptible, and left for Dover December 8 with conflicting emotions. Johnson, now threatened by poor health and political persecution, was especially dear to her, for he had never failed her, and the only weakness she could permit herself to express focused on him. "On Saturday I actually set out once more for Dover," she wrote Everina, at the port from which she had hoped to embark with Fuseli:

> Yet in going I seem to strive against fate, for had I not taken my place I should have put off the journey again on account of the present posture of affairs at home, which are really rather alarming . . . should any accident happen to my dear and worthy friend Johnson during my absence I should never forgive myself for leaving him—These are vapourish fears—still they fasten on me and press home most feelingly a long comment on the vanity of human wishes.[29]

In the course of one year she had, like Lucifer, been hurled from the heights of active success and confidence to the depths of inertia and secret humiliation, and she felt herself again the outcast of fortune she had admired in *A Vindication of the Rights of Woman,* who would rise superior to passion and discontent. Her last letter to William Roscoe was charged with significant defiance:

> I intend no longer to struggle with a rational desire, so have determined to set out for Paris . . . and I shall not now halt at Dover, I promise you; for as I go alone neck or nothing is the word. During my stay I shall not forget my friends. . . .
>
> . . . I am told the world, to talk big, married me to [Johnson] whilst we were away; but you [illegible] that I am still a Spinster on the wing. At Paris, indeed, I might take a husband for the time being and get divorced when my truant heart longed again to nestle with its old friends; but this speculation has not yet entered into my plan.[30]

It was not speculation but prophecy. The woman had determined to vindicate herself.

IV

Leaning on a Spear

Chapter 13

In mid-December of 1792, in the solstice of season and spirit, Mary Wollstonecraft crossed the English Channel from Dover and went straight to Paris. She had made arrangements to stay with M. and Mme. Fillietaz, she the recently married daughter of the Mrs. Bregantz of Eliza and Everina's former Putney School. Her arrival at the Fillietaz home at 22 Rue Melée was unpleasant; Mary had caught a bad cold enroute, and because her hosts were temporarily out of the city, she entered a large townhouse that was empty except for servants who could understand her halting French as little as she could fathom theirs. "You will imagine how awkwardly I behaved unable to utter a word and almost stunned by the flying sounds," she wrote Everina. Her illness confined her at first to the house, and when she ventured out she found Paris distasteful: filthy streets, extreme contrast between riches and poverty, a turbulent political situation that her language difficulty made even more fearsome and confusing. Solitary and depressed on Christmas Eve, she wrote Everina:

> I apply so closely to the language, and labour so continually to understand what I hear that I never go to bed without a headache, and my spirits are fatigued with endeavouring to form a just opinion of public affairs. The day after tomorrow I expect to see the King at the bar, and the consequences that will follow I am almost afraid to anticipate.[1]

The reality of the revolution struck her full in the face the day after Christmas, when Louis XVI's trial for treason began. "I never had the courage even to look at a person dying on the stage," she once said; whether because of this impressionability, or through fear of mob violence despite precautions taken by the authorities, she did not go to the visitor's gallery of the National Convention as she had expected, but watched in awe and tears from a window in the Fillietaz house as the former king was driven past in a common coach from nearby Temple prison through silent streets on his way to judgment. She felt he, like Lear, was paying a more terrible price than he deserved, and this impending regicide, with all its primitive connotations, stirred frightening fantasies that night, which she tried to calm by writing to Johnson, her touchstone of benign rationality. I wished to wait," she wrote, "till I could tell you that this day was not stained with blood."

> About nine o'clock this morning, the king passed by my window, moving silently along (excepting now and then a few strokes on the drum, which rendered the stillness more awful) through empty streets, surrounded by the national guards. . . . The inhabitants flocked to their windows, but the casements were all shut, not a voice was heard, nor did I see anything like an insulting gesture. For the first time since I entered France, I bowed to the majesty of the people, and respected the propriety of behaviour so perfectly in unison with my own feelings. I can scarcely tell you why, but an association of ideas made the tears flow insensibly from my eyes, when I saw Louis sitting, with more dignity than I expected from his character, in a hackney-coach, going to meet death, where so many of his race have triumphed. My fancy instantly brought Louis XIV before me, entering the capital with all his pomp. . . . I have been alone ever since; and though my mind is calm, I cannot dismiss the lively images that have filled my imagination all the day. —Nay, do not smile, but pity me; for, once or twice, lifting my eyes from the paper, I have seen eyes glare through a glass-door opposite my chair and bloody hands shook at me. Not the distant sound of a footstep can I hear.—My apartments are remote from those of the servants, the only persons who sleep with me in an immense hotel, one folding door opening after another.—I wish I had even kept the cat with me!—I want to see something alive; death, in so many frightful shapes has taken hold of my fancy.—I am going to bed—and, for the first time in my life, I cannot put out the candle.[2]

Unexpectedly terrible and complex as it was, the revolution was what Mary Wollstonecraft had come to observe. She intended to send Johnson articles and even to participate in building the new social order, which she believed to be in process of consolidation. Her credentials were excellent, and her *entrée* into French political circles easily made through the influential English-speaking colony of revolutionary sympathizers in Paris who were allied with the Gironde party, then in control of the government, although threatened by Jacobin "dogs of faction," as Mary called them. "I am almost overwhelmed with civility here, and have even met with more than civility," she wrote. Joel Barlow was in Paris and about to become a French citizen. Her old colleagues Tom Paine and Thomas Christie introduced her to government leaders with whom they associated; Paine was now a citizen of France and elected representative to the National Convention, living in Mme. de Pompadour's former residence; Christie, settled with his sister Jane and new wife, Rebecca, whom Mary liked, was the Paris agent for a London firm supplying flour to France. Mary was welcomed by Helen Maria Williams, an English expatriate writer whom she rather disdained. But Miss Williams was an old Paris hand, an articulate champion of the revolution, a friend of Mme. Roland. Mary welcomed the opportunity to meet the French politicians who frequented Miss Williams' home. Having thus made contact with important Girondists who were, of course, cognizant of her authority, Mary set to work on a plan of education to be presented to the appropriate committee of the convention.

She had hardly gotten established when the political situation worsened. On February 1 France declared war on England, and Mary Wollstonecraft found herself in the precarious position of an English citizen in a city rumbling against foreign and domestic enemies of the state. But she saw no urgent reason to leave France as long as the Gironde remained in power, and she had no prevision of the Terror, unimaginable indeed to anyone at the time. In fact, since her arrival she had actually been looking out for a position for Eliza, and although she told her bitterly disappointed sister that "unsettled conditions" made the search difficult and advised her in mid-February to count on another two months in Wales, at the same time she pledged again that she would not leave Paris until Eliza was settled on the Continent in a situation in which she could become fluent in French. Mary herself did not contemplate a return to England for, as she knew before she left home, England was an unpleasant and possibly dangerous place for pro-revolutionaries like herself. Eliza reported talk of burning "Miss W." in effigy on January 20. After the execution of Louis XVI on the twenty-first, which appalled the English, and the declaration of war, political reaction and repression became equated with patriotism and national security, and increased correspondingly. "I heard a clergyman say," Eliza wrote, "that he was sure there was no more harm in shooting a Frenchman, than . . . a bird . . . the French are *all* atheists, and the most bloody butchers the world ever produced." If forced to leave France because of war or growing inflation, Mary intended to go to Switzerland, but she was able to get funds from Johnson through Christie as late as July, and took advantage of the favorable rate of exchange created by inflation to draw also on money her sisters sent Johnson at her request.[3]

Privately, she had every reason to stay abroad, for she could not face London. Her acquaintances considered her a woman of strong independent character. That façade was never more essential nor more difficult than in these months. Joel Barlow was amazed when he saw the first signs of her susceptibility. "Mrs. Wollstonecraft speaks of you with more affection than you can imagine," he wrote Ruth, who was still in London. "I never knew her praise any one so much . . . it is not to flatter me, for she never flatters anyone. . . . I thought her more of an independent spirit." Mary needed a friend badly; she was "wounded and sick," pervaded by a sense of life "tossed and agitated by the waves of misfortune," as Godwin said. She found little solace in the French, whose frivolity and urbanity grated on her; "those who wish to live for themselves without close friendship, or . . . affection, ought to live in Paris," she wrote Eliza. She was weary, dissatisfied, preoccupied, homesick, yet unwilling to return home when offered the chance. "I should wish rather to talk to you than write," she wrote Ruth Barlow in early February:

> the weather is very bad and I half ruin myself in coach-hire. The streets of Paris are certainly very disagreeable, so that it is impossible to walk for air, and I always want air. . . . I should not be content to speak as so many of the English speak, who talk away with an unblushing face,

and yet I am exceedingly fatigued by my constant attention to words, particularly as I cannot yet get rid of a foolish bashfulness which stops my mouth when I am most desirous to make myself understood, besides when my heart sinks or flies to England to hover round those I love all the fine French phrases, ready cut and dry for use, fly away the Lord knows where. A Gentleman the other day, to whom I frequently replied, oui, oui, when my thoughts were far away, told me I was acquiring in France a bad custom, for that I might chance to say oui, when I did not intend it, *par habitude.*

I am afraid that I have a strange spirit of contradiction in me physically and morally, for though the air is pure I am not well, and the vivacity that should amuse me fatigue me. . . . Yesterday a Gentleman offered me a place in his carriage to return to England and I knew not how to say no, yet I think it would be foolish to return when I have been at so much trouble to master a difficulty, when I am just turning the corner. . . . Still I long to return to my study, where I should be very glad to breakfast with you again—say Amen![4]

Mary Wollstonecraft had concealed the Fuseli denouement from everyone, excepting perhaps Johnson, whose discretion was absolute. Despite her resolution to forget him, she was forcibly reminded of the painter when she met Mme. Madeleine Schweitzer in Paris. Attempting to seem at ease, Mary gave herself away in her account to her sisters of this former flame of Fuseli's from his Zurich days. Eliza, as usual, understood. "Apropos!" she wrote Everina at the end of February:

I am convinced M. has met with some great disappointment . . . she complains of lowness of spirits, etc, etc, talks much in favor of . . . Madame Schweitzer—says she was an old favorite of Fuseli's . . . Mary seems rather *disgusted* with the French in general. Yet I am sure there is a Cause.[5]

Perhaps it was this provocative association that stimulated Mary Wollstonecraft to write Fuseli once more. Although this letter, according to Knowles, concerned French politics, she asked the painter to correspond with her. He did not answer. She did not write again.

In mid-February Mary Wollstonecraft roused herself to write what she planned as the first of a series of articles on the revolution, in the form of letters. She probably sent the piece to England by personal envoy; mails were erratic, even dangerous, and everyone knew letters were opened. If Johnson had printed it—it was only published with her posthumous works—he would have been in danger in England, and she in France, for she said enough to anger both governments. In a "Letter on the Present Character of the French Nation"—a character that she condemned as shallow, pleasure loving, and vain—she looked on the French as a demanding and unrealistic educator would regard children who have been badly conditioned in the past and refuse to be improved by new opportunities: "when I am walking on the *Boulevards,* it occurs to me that they alone understand the full import of the term leisure; and they trifle their time away . . . the most sensual people in the world . . . most polished . . . most superficial . . . cold and artificial."

With her keen nose for wrong, Mary suspected that the revolution had changed nothing in the area of principle—to her the most important of all—much of less human greed and love of power:

> I would I could first inform you that, out of the chaos of vices, follies, prejudices and virtues, rudely jumbled together, I saw the fair form of Liberty slowly rising, and Virtue expanding her wings. . . . But, if the aristocracy of birth is levelled with the ground, only to make room for that of riches, I am afraid that the morals of the people will not be much improved by the change, or the government rendered less venal.
>
> . . . You may think it too soon to form an opinion of the future government, yet it is impossible to avoid hazarding some conjectures, when everything whispers me, that names, not principles, are changed . . . For the same pride of office, the same desire of power are still visible.

One of her remaining illusions, the God-given virtue of the human soul, shriveled:

> I am grieved—sorely grieved—when I think of the blood that has stained the cause of freedom at Paris. . . .
>
> Before I came to France, I . . . anticipated the epoch, when, in the course of improvement, men would labour to become virtuous. . . . But now, the perspective of the golden age . . . almost eludes my sight; and losing thus in part my theory of a more perfect state, start not, my friend, if I bring forward an opinion, which at the first glance seems to be levelled against the existence of God! I am not become an

Atheist, I assure you . . . yet I begin to fear that vice, or if you will, evil, is the grand mobile of action.[6]

It was in this despair of mankind in the aggregate that Mary Wollstonecraft, with her unextinguishable need to believe, found an individual on whom her credence could fasten. She was on the rebound not only from Henry Fuseli but from faith itself.

Gilbert Imlay is a difficult character to bring clearly into focus; much of his connection with Mary Wollstonecraft is obscured by his own misrepresentations, and can only be deduced from her letters (his have disappeared). His activities before and after he met Mary are shadowy. He claimed to have "lived until he was more than five and twenty years old, in the back parts of America," but he was born in Monmouth County, New Jersey in 1754 or 1758, spent his youth there, served briefly as a lieutenant (although he later passed himself off as a captain) in the American Revolution, and only afterward sought his fortune, as did many hungry veterans, in the Western Territory. There, he said, he was a "commissioner for laying out lands in the back settlement," but the records show he was only a deputy surveyor. His trail from 1784 to 1786 winds in and out of various localities and speculations in the Territory; he was several times accused of debt or breach of contract. A former partner in an abortive Kentucky ironworks complained that "deft Imlay" left him holding the bag; he was advertised for contempt and debt until almost the end of the century in the courts of the Territory.

After 1786, his activities are unknown until August, 1792, when his first book was published in London and reviewed favorably in *The Analytical Review*. Imlay was probably in England part of that year, for he knew Thomas Cooper of Manchester well enough to get letters of introduction from him. There is no evidence that he met Mary Wollstonecraft at that time. Imlay may long have been involved in political intrigues for control of Spanish possessions in the Mississippi valley. By early 1793 he showed up in Paris conspiring with Brissot to seize Louisiana, and even hoping to draw the United States into such a conflict. To do him justice, he abominated Spanish tyranny. Because of his book and his representations of himself, Imlay was considered a potential leader for a French expedition to Louisiana. While awaiting a decision on the matter from the Gironde government, he became part of the English-speaking circle in Paris with which Mary Wollstonecraft associated.[7]

Judging from his *A Topographical Description of the Western Territory of North America*, Imlay was not a charlatan, even if he manipulated fact to push his career. His book is an interesting account of the history, terrain, flora, and fauna of the Western Territory, and if he interjected rhapsodic passages, he was indulging his own romantic enthusiasm in the taste of the time in order to contrast the simple manners and rational life of the settlers with the distorted and unnatural habits of the Europeans, which he believed stemmed from aristocratic tradition and bad laws. He had very definite opinions that European liberals shared. He opposed state-established religion: "priestcraft seems to have forged fetters for the human mind." He glorified the American Constitution and progress: "governments will arrive at perfection, and FREEDOM, in golden plumes, and in her triumphal car, must now resume her long lost empire." He denounced the whites' mistreatment of the Indians and spoke passionately for abolition of slavery. He believed the long-run solution to race problems to be intermarriage; color, he wrote, "is of no real importance, when compared to rescuing millions of miserable human beings from odious prejudices."[8]

This is the man who was introduced to Mary Wollstonecraft one evening at the Christie's house in Paris, probably in February or early March of 1793. "I am told," Godwin said in the *Memoirs,* possibly by Mrs. Christie, that Mary disliked and avoided Imlay at first. Mary told Imlay it was his "simplicity of character that first attached [me] to you," an attribute highlighted by the suavity she found in even the most enlightened Frenchmen she met. In her letters, and in the novel *Maria,* she described him as tall, handsome, lean, natural, warm-hearted, cheerful, manly, with a "steady bold step." She saw him as an advanced progressive, "perfectly in unison with [her] mode of thinking," not a genius, but, more important to her now, a virile man of action and genuine feeling. At Christie's, where she went most often, or at Paine's and probably at Helen Maria Williams', whose lover Imlay was rumored to have been, Imlay discreetly but unmistakably courted Mary Wollstonecraft, "contrived, by a hundred little pretexts, to sit near her, to take her hand, or to meet her eyes," as she wrote in *Maria.* She was apparently at her most impressive and appealing, for Gustave Von Schlabrendorf, part of this coterie, was falling in love with her at the same time. External crisis quickened her intimacy with Imlay; under the ominous possibility of a Jacobin coup, which now directly menaced the lives of some and the hopes of all, Mary's circle was meeting almost nightly to share anxieties and to keep up each other's morale. "I used to meet her several times in the week," an eye witness, a young Englishman named Johnson, later told Godwin:

> I have occasionally seen some of the Deputies of the Convention present such as Isnard, Roederer, even Barère. . . . They were well acquainted and visited Miss Wollstonecraft. . . . We used to pass our evenings together very frequently either in conversation or any amusement which might tend to dissipate the gloomy impressions the state of affairs naturally produced.
>
> Miss Wollstonecraft was always particularly anxious for the success of the Revolution and the hideous aspect of the then political horizon hurt her exceedingly. She always thought however it would finally succeed. . . . She likewise visited Made. Rolande whose misfortune she greatly lamented. . . .
>
> . . . Mr. Imlay who had been lately introduced to her . . . appeared to pay her more than common attention.[9]

Some detail may be erroneous—Mary Hays specifically said Mary Wollstonecraft always regretted that she never actually met Mme. Roland, and Godwin never mentioned the acquaintance—but as of April Mary and Imlay were in love. On the fifth, Barlow noted her bitter disappointment that Ruth had not arrived in Paris; on the fifteenth he reported she was depressed; on the nineteenth he wrote his wife:

> Mary is exceedingly distressed . . . to think you are not to come here. She wrote you today, she wrote a long letter before which it seems you have not got. Between you and me—you must not hint it to her nor to J——n nor to anyone else—I believe she has got a sweetheart—and that she will finish by going with him to A——a a wife. He is of Kentucky and a very sensible man. Mum—I will tell you more when I know.

Godwin said Mary had neither adviser nor confidant in this affair, conceiving it "a gross breach of delicacy . . . in a matter of this sacred nature," but her urgent desire to see Ruth Barlow may reflect her need to confide in a woman who understood love and Americans before she committed herself.[10] It is also possible Imlay had told Mary that he was planning to go to America on the Louisiana expedition and wanted her to follow him.

Imlay's novel *The Emigrants* also fits the situation. This book was published sometime before July of 1793, and reads as if it were aimed at convincing Mary Wollstonecraft to accept a lover and go to America with him. This story of a ruined English family—with a selfish, dishonest son—whose daughter finds happiness in the wilds around Pittsburgh, is a vehicle for sexy and melodramatic love scenes. Imlay's personal predilections are clear; the heroine, Caroline, is ravishing to the hero, Captain Arlington, who observes her "half-unzoned . . . to receive the cool breezes which seemed to wanton in her bosom as if enraptured with its sweets." Having rescued her from Indians, the captain guards her sleep at night, at some cost to his peace of mind: "A bosom more transparent than the effulgence of Aurora . . . which was now half-naked. I was obliged to extinguish the light to preserve my reason." A large portion of the book, indeed a major thrust, presented women's educational, social, and legal position in Wollstonecraftian terms, and went beyond *A Vindication of the Rights of Woman* in specific radical proposals for reform of marriage laws, which, the author affirmed, should conform to "the laws of nature" through liberalized divorce or free love. Caroline initially resists her sweetheart's advocacy, but eventually beholds "the fetters that have been so ingeniously contrived to subjugate the human mind" and goes off with the hero to live without ceremony but in permanent bliss in a utopian community on the banks of the Ohio.

It is no wonder that one scholar believes Mary Wollstonecraft helped Imlay write *The Emigrants.* Clearly, she had a hand in sections of the book. A passage on girls' education, for instance, has Mary's intonation in attributing female vices to "unnatural restraints. . . . Everything has been perverted . . . the tyranny of custom has substituted duplicity for candour, the crude sentiments of cunning have destroyed that genuine felicity which flows from the genial current of the human heart."[11] A subplot features the heroine's sister's separation from her husband in England, and the sister's name is Eliza. The book's subtitle recalls *Original Stories:* "Drawn From Real Characters." There is no question Imlay felt strongly on some of the very issues closest to Mary, that he deliberately incorporated aspects of her beliefs and experiences, and that he carried *A Vindication of the Rights of Woman* to the logical conclusion of personal freedom for women.

In the book Imlay argued the naturalness and delight of sexual love with a heroine who at first told him he was using sophistry to excuse his passions, a typical Wollstonecraft remark. But Mary's resistance was dwindling. Five years before she had killed off the first Henry—hero of her novel, *Mary,* and in her personal life, independence had been her defense, religion her support. By the end of her relationship with Fuseli, the defense seemed self-defeating and the support vain. As her letter to Roscoe before she left England indicated, she may have thought only of a vacation romance in France to salve her pride, but her needs were more serious: the urge for sexual love and belonging. Imlay was precisely the sensual man she had formerly condemned, but his confession of past sexual adventures stimulated rather than offended her because she had begun, since Fuseli, to accept like feelings in herself. Her prudery and inhibition had been loosened by French sexual mores and the laxities of a time of revolution. Helen Maria Williams was living with her mother and sister, but John Hurford Stone, her lover who later deserted his wife for her, was in constant attendance, and Mary must have known about the relationship. Her novel *Maria,* which she began after her break with Imlay, is explicitly descriptive of the progress of her feelings. In it, Maria is fascinated by Henry Darnford (again a Henry), who reminds her of Rousseau's St. Preux, but without the latter's delicacy. Darnford tells Maria that powerful emotions have drawn him to her:

> He had the bewitching frankness of nature. . . . He had been a thoughtless, extravagant young man; yet, as he described his faults, they appeared to be the generous luxuriancy of a noble mind. . . .
>
> Accustomed to submit to every impulse of passion . . . every desire became a torrent that bore down all opposition.

Darnford then describes his exploits with "woman, lovely woman!" ranging from his seduction of prudish American girls to his pursuit of European charmers of every class. "In London, my senses were intoxicated. I ran from street to street, from theatre to theatre, and the women of the town . . . appeared to me like angels."[12]

Maria is captivated and attentive: "how often Darnford and Maria were obliged to part in the midst of an interesting conversation." But Mary Wollstonecraft held back out of "my fear of being pierced to the heart by every one on whom I rest my mighty stock of affection," as she once ruefully wrote. In *Maria,* although "she was beloved, and every emotion was rapturous":

> the fear of outrunning his [affection] made her often assume a coldness and indifference foreign to her character; and, even when giving way to the playful emotions of a heart just loosened from the frozen bond of grief, there was a delicacy in her manner of expressing her sensibility, which made him doubt whether it was the effect of love.[13]

As she had with Johnson, Gabell, and Fuseli, with Imlay Mary Wollstonecraft again went through that recitation of her life's sorrows, which was always a harbinger of intimacy with people she needed. "When I first knew you," she wrote Imlay, "I opened my heart to you." Imlay's role, like that of the heroes of *Mary* and *Maria,* was to be father as well as lover. Darnford says his dearest wish is to make amends for the cruelty and injustice Maria has endured, and to replace her unworthy family. "He assured her, calling her his dearest girl, 'that it should henceforth be the business of his life to make her happy.' "

The heroine of *Maria* admits to her lover that in adversity she has brooded over visions of passionate bliss and that she has had to repress her behavior because, as Maria ingenuously confesses, "I found on examining myself, I could not coquet with a man without loving him a little, and I perceived that I should not be able to stay at the line of innocent *freedoms,* did I suffer any."

In the novel Maria further tests her suitor by giving him her memoirs, 161 pages of the story of her life, its injustices and disappointments. He is overwhelmed and kisses her hand as if it were that of a martyred saint: "They met again and again; and Darnford declared, while passion suffused his cheeks, that he never before knew what it was to love . . . represented 'that they might soon be parted,' and wished her to 'put it out of the power of fate to separate them.' "[14]

Imlay, as he made clear in *The Emigrants,* did not mean to avoid parting from Mary by marrying her. He believed formal marriage to be philosophically indefensible and pragmatically unnecessary, a belief which happened to suit his practice—and which Darnford rationalizes in *Maria:*

> matrimony, which till divorces could be more easily obtained, was, he declared, 'the most unsufferable bondage.' Ties of this nature could not bind minds governed by superior principles; and such beings were privileged to act above the dictates of laws they had no voice in framing, if they had sufficient strength of mind to endure the natural consequence.

In mid-April, Mary Wollstonecraft and Gilbert Imlay became lovers. Idealizing him, she believed she could trust him completely, and he apparently justified her faith by his response.

> Maria now, imagining that she had found a being of celestial mould—was happy,—nor was she deceived. He was then plastic in her impassioned hand—and reflected all the sentiments which animated and warmed her.
>
> . . . As her husband she now received him, and he solemnly pledged himself as her protector—and eternal friend.[15]

With this dramatic intensity and exorbitant expectation, dragging her past behind her, Mary Wollstonecraft engaged herself to Gilbert Imlay. In the novel, Maria meets Darnford in a madhouse in which both have been illegally imprisoned. In Paris during the spring of 1793, in the midst of war, violence, and chaos, love must have seemed the only sanity in a world going mad. Mary and her lover saw each other secretly in the city, for she lived with the Fillietazes until the end of May. On May 31 the Gironde government fell, Imlay's sponsor Brissot was thrown into prison, and their friends were captured with him or fled for their lives. Robespierre and Danton ruled France. Foreign moderates were unprotected, suspect. Mary had considered fleeing to Switzerland, but English legislation made it impossible for her to get a passport, and by this time she did not want to leave Imlay. To avoid jeopardizing the Fillietaz family, and to secure privacy as well, she left Paris in early June for the then suburban village of Neuilly. Here, in a small country house surrounded by a garden overlooking fields and a dense wood, Mary and Imlay enjoyed an idyll Rousseau himself could not have staged with greater felicity. In *Maria:* "So much of heaven did they enjoy, that paradise bloomed around them; or they, by a powerful spell, had been transported into Armida's garden."[16]

Even after the protracted, agonized break with Imlay, Mary Wollstonecraft was convinced she had not been deceived in him at first. She told Godwin she believed she "reposed herself upon a person, of whose honour and principles she had the most exalted idea." This Imlay assuredly was not, but there is reason to believe that he was deeply in love and considered himself as committed as she. A lover might well be enchanted at the response in a woman he had so stirred. Godwin, who saw Mary react to happiness with him, knew of what he spoke when he described her reactions as reported to him by one who saw her that spring:

> Her sorrows, the depression of her spirits, were forgotten, and she assumed all the simplicity and vivacity of a youthful mind. She was like a serpent upon a rock, that casts its slough, and appears again with the brilliancy, the sleekness, and the elastic activity of its happiest age. She was playful, full of confidence, kindness and sympathy. Her eyes assumed new lustre, and her cheeks new colour and smoothness. Her voice became cheerful; her temper overflowing with universal kindness; and that smile of bewitching tenderness from day to day illuminated her countenance, which all who knew her will so well recollect, and which won, both heart and soul, the affection of almost everyone that beheld it.[17]

Loving, and feeling totally beloved for the first time in her life, Mary Wollstonecraft relished the delectation of secret romance and uninhibited passion. "Such is the temperature of my soul," she once told Imlay. "For years have I endeavored to calm an impetuous tide—labouring to make my feelings take an orderly course. It was striving against the stream—I must love and admire with warmth, or I sink into sadness." Her confidence, energy, and optimism revived, and with them her zest for work. She brought all her books out to Neuilly from Paris, and began writing a major book, a history of the French Revolution. Her faith had been restored. Sharing intellectual interests with Imlay increased her joy; "The books sent to me are such as we may read together; so I shall not look into them until you return; when you shall read, whilst I mend my stockings." After her work, she walked alone in the forest near her cottage, much to the alarm of the old caretaker of the property, who, like an eccentric genie, brought her the finest grapes to be found in the garden, carped at serving them to anyone else who visited her, and insisted that he should make her bed. She felt lapped in security. Imlay came to dinner with her, or she walked into Paris with a basket of grapes on her arm to meet him at the Neuilly barrier. The honeymoon drifted on with reluctant interruptions, one of which occasioned her first letter to Imlay:

> My dear love, after making my arrangements for our snug dinner today, I have been taken by storm, and obliged to promise to dine, at an early hour, with the Miss –s. . . . I shall however leave the key in the door, and hope to find you at my fireside when I return, about eight o'clock. Will you not wait for poor [Mary]—whom you will find better.[18]

"Trembling back to peace," as Mary told Imlay, she became confident she had found permanent happiness. By June, the lovers were talking of going to America as soon as they had the money to buy a farm, her mother's dream of a cottage in the New World reborn. As *Maria* "found herself more indulgent as she was happier, and discovered virtues in characters she had before disregarded," Mary Wollstonecraft, with remarkable generosity or conscientiousness, expected to share her good fortune with her sisters. One wonders if Imlay knew and approved. On the thirteenth and again on the twenty-fourth of June, without mentioning him, Mary wrote Eliza that brighter days were in prospect:

> I have a plan in my head . . . in which you and Everina are included . . . a mode of bringing us all together again. . . . I am now at the house of an old gardener writing a great book, and in better health, and spirits, than I have ever enjoyed since I came to France . . . do not despair, my dear girl . . . I will render your fate more tolerable, unless *my* hopes deceive me.

This metamorphosis from low spirits to high, from aloofness to warmth, Eliza passed on to Everina with some cynicism. She was hard to deceive. "What say you, Everina, now to the *Continental air*," she wrote July 14. "Or is it love? Ambition or Pity? that has wrought the miracle."[19]

Mary was transported but not transformed; Imlay could not have realized how difficult it would be to make her happiness the business of his life. Reading her August letters to him one sees, with a kind of helpless anxiety, radiant and mature passion coexisting with childlike dependency, crippling susceptibility, and a sense of past grievance:

> Past Twelve o'clock, Monday night.
>
> I obey an emotion of my heart, which made me think of wishing thee, my love, good-night! before I go to rest. . . . You can scarcely imagine with what happiness I anticipate the day, when we are to begin almost to live together; and you would smile to hear how many plans I have in my head, now that I am confident my heart has found peace in your bosom.—Cherish me with that dignified tenderness, which I have found only in you; and your own dear girl will try to keep under a quickness of feeling, that has sometimes given you pain—Yes, I will be *good*, that I may deserve to be happy; and whilst you love me, I cannot again fall into the miserable state, which rendered life a burthen almost too heavy to be borne.
>
> But, good-night!—God bless you! Sterne says, that is equal to a kiss—yet I would rather give you the kiss into the bargain, glowing with gratitude to Heaven, and affection to you. I like the word affection, because it signifies something habitual. . . . I will be at the barrier a little after ten o'clock tomorrow.—Yours—[20]

Their relations were secret for some four months except to the Barlows. Ruth, whom Mary now addressed as "my dear friend," joined her husband in June and spent the summer at Meudon. On Mary's infrequent trips to Paris the two women met "*quite alone,*" at breakfast, as they had in London. Like a honeymooner, Mary preferred to remain almost *incognito:* "I do not wish to spend a whole day in Paris," she wrote Ruth, because she would have to call on Mme. Schweitzer—and perhaps answer questions.[21]

Love and study in the evenings, friendship in the morning, and the blood of revolutionary victims at noon. In July opposition to Jacobin government flared into civil war in the Vendée and the south; the Revolutionary Tribunal went to work with exacerbated savagery. The guillotine was the instrument and the message, a huge death machine dispatching dozens of victims without human assistance but under the eyes of thousands of brutalized, excited, or frightened human beings. The Terror could never have flourished without it; it was efficient and impressive where rows of hangmen or headsmen would have been simply nauseating. Coming into the city one day from Neuilly, Mary Wollstonecraft passed the Place de la Revolution, where pools of blood from the guillotine were still fresh on the pavement. She could not contain her revulsion and spoke out on the spot, to the alarm of passers-by, for public protest was usually fatal in those fearsome days.

In mid-September the authorities began to round up and imprison English citizens; there was a rush on the American embassy for asylum. As the wife of an American citizen, Mary Wollstonecraft would be safe, and such Imlay declared her, obtaining a certificate to that effect from the American ambassador's office in Paris. A ceremony "clogging my soul," as she said, "by promising obedience etc., etc.," meant nothing to her philosophically or emotionally, since she felt her relationship with him was "founded on the natural principles of morality," tying both to absolute fidelity for the duration of their love, which she saw either as eternal or, at worst, subsiding mutually. She never concealed the non-legalized nature of her connection—not that her Paris acquaintances would be concerned. The Christies had left for London; Helen Maria Williams, Von Schlabrendorf, and even Paine, were in imminent danger of arrest and the guillotine.

After she took his name, there was every reason for Mary and Imlay to live publicly together in the domesticity she always craved. As she had said in *A Vindication of the Rights of Woman,* "love always clings round the idea of home." Almost immediately, however, that felicity was interrupted. Imlay and Barlow were going into business, importing goods from a Baltic source through the English blockade via Le Havre, and in September, shortly after Mary's settling in Paris, Imlay went to the port to launch this enterprise. As far as she knew, the project was to establish them modestly on a farm in America; he saw an opportunity to make a killing. Money was in fact necessary, for since mid-July she had been unable to draw on Johnson for funds; but it was with some bitterness and anxiety that she accepted any diversion from their love. She wrote him shortly after his departure:

> I have been following you all along the road this comfortless weather; for when I am absent from those I love, my imagination is as lively, as if my senses had never been gratified by their presence—I was going to say caresses—and why should I not? I have found out that I have more mind than you, in one respect; because I can . . . find food for love

> in the same object, much longer than you can—The way to my senses is through my heart; but, forgive me! I think there is sometimes a shorter cut to yours.
>
> [are] these continual separations . . . necessary to warm your affection.—Of late, we are always separating.—Crack!—crack!—and away you go . . . though I began to write cheerfully, some melancholy tears have found their way . . . whilst a glow of tenderness at my heart whispers that you are one of the best creatures in the world.—Pardon then the vagaries of a mind that has been almost 'crazed by care,' as well as 'crossed in hapless love,' bear with me a *little* longer![22]

Imlay was evidently back and forth until mid-December, managing his complicated speculation with partners Mary Wollstonecraft did not particularly like—Blackden, Leavenworth, Codman, and Clough were the names mentioned in her letters. The credentials of the group, including Barlow's, survived their Girondist affiliation and sufficed to keep them in business even when the Terror mounted. Helen Maria Williams, who advised Mary to destroy the book on the revolution she was writing, was dragged from her bed one night in October and thrown into prison; Von Schlabrendorf was arrested next month. (Mary was courageous enough to visit him in jail.) October 14 Marie Antoinette was guillotined, followed by Phillipe Egalité, Mme. Roland, and hundreds of other victims, famous and obscure. The most horrifying day to Mary Wollstonecraft was October 31; she fell into a dead faint when she heard Brissot and twenty familiar Girondist deputies had been executed in one batch.

By this time she must have suspected she was pregnant; she had conceived the "barrier child" (referring to her early meetings with Imlay at the Neuilly gate to Paris) in mid-August, but she was not certain until she felt life, sometime before Christmas. Imlay was again at Havre when she wrote him the news on a Sunday night. Except for a perhaps exaggerated fear of miscarrying, she seemed happy:

> Ever since you last saw me inclined to faint, I have felt some gentle twitches, which make me begin to think, that I am nourishing a creature who will soon be sensible of my care.—This thought has not only produced an overflowing of tenderness to you, but made me very attentive to calm my mind and take exercise, lest I should destroy an object in whom we are to have a mutual interest, you know. Yesterday—do not

smile!—finding that I had hurt myself by lifting precipitately a large log of wood, I sat down in an agony till I felt those said twitches again.

. . . God bless you! . . .

I am going to rest very happy, and you have made me so.

But there were signs of trouble between the couple. "I do not know why," she wrote Imlay shortly after, "but I have more confidence in your affection, when absent, than present." When he was present, his interest in business, "thy money-getting face," as she said, annoyed and alarmed her, although she added that she respected his exertion. She needed constant reassurance and immediate reciprocity: "Tell me over and over again, that your happiness . . . is closely connected with mine, and I will try to dissipate, as they arise, the fumes of former discontent that have too often clouded the sunshine, which you have endeavoured to diffuse through my mind. God bless you!"

She was passionately in love, "more than I supposed possible," and expected this love to excuse her moods:

Friday morning [Dec. 27]

I have thy honest countenance before me—Pop—relaxed by tenderness; a little—little wounded by my whims; and thy eyes glistening with sympathy—Thy lips then feel softer than soft—and I rest my cheek on thine, forgetting all the world . . . the hue of love . . . has spread over my own cheeks . . . I feel them burning, whilst a delicious tear trembles in my eye. . . . I believe I deserve your tenderness, because I am true, and have a degree of sensibility that you can see and relish.

Two days later she wrote about business she was handling for him in Paris and was able to joke about his absence—she was even fond of his shabby slippers hanging on their bedroom door, she said, but she began to press for some definite news of his return:

Sunday morning [Dec. 29]

You seem to have taken up your abode at Havre. Pray sir! when do you think of coming home! or, to write very considerately, when will business permit you? I shall expect (as the country people say in England) that you will make a *power* of money to indemnify me for your absence. . . .

Am I to see you this week? or this month?—I do not know what you are about . . . as you did not tell me.[23]

By this time Imlay knew for certain, if he had not known before, that he would have to remain at Le Havre at least three more months. He did not tell Mary Wollstonecraft. He hoped unpleasant truth would either be accepted by imperceptible degrees or somehow disappear if ignored; it was his way. Business was part of prized masculine independence—"your struggles to be manly," as Mary rather irritatingly put it—and he probably thought the author of *A Vindication of the Rights of Woman,* no matter how excitable and attached, should tolerate a few weeks of self-sufficiency. It was thoughtless and weak of him at best, in view of her first pregnancy, which would be only two months short of term at the date he thought he would return, of the unpredictable political situation, and of the simple practical fact that she now depended on him for funds. At worst, it was a deceitful preliminary step toward desertion. The first is more likely. Although none of Imlay's letters to Mary are extant, from hers it is clear that he was writing regularly, very often, and with "much considerate tenderness," as she said. When her letters to him were delayed, he was as quickly resentful as she; "I am glad," she wrote him on one such occasion, "that other people can be unreasonable as well as myself." But Imlay's refusal to be specific about returning made her uneasy. Monday the thirtieth she wrote Imlay of a long, affectionate, but depressing letter she had received from Johnson with a parcel of books, of a melancholy letter from Eliza, and of a gay one from Charles. On the thirty-first she wrote again via Imlay's business associate, who was leaving for Havre, "because trifles of this sort" gave her pleasure; and she wrote still again on New Year's Day, this time with explicit resentment. She had not heard from Imlay for two days; her pregnancy was showing; Paine had been arrested at three that morning:

> Wednesday night [Jan. 1]
>
> I hate commerce. . . . The fact of things, public and private, vexes me. . . .
>
> If you do not return soon—or, which is no such mighty matter, talk of it—I will throw your slippers at the window, and be off—nobody knows where.
>
> Finding that I was observed, I told the good women . . . simply that I was with child: and let them stare! and ———, and ———, nay, all the world, may know it for aught I care! . . .

> You may now tell me, that, if it were not for me, you would be laughing away with some honest fellows in London. . . . I should not think such a heartless life worth preserving.

Next morning she added a remorseful note:

> Thursday morning [Jan. 2]
>
> I was very low-spirited last night . . . with your cheerful temper, which makes absence so easy to you.—And . . . I was offended at your not even mentioning it.—I do not want to be loved like a goddess; but I wish to be necessary to you. God bless you![24]

The evening of this postscript one of Imlay's partners inadvertently disclosed to her that Imlay knew he had to be in Havre three more months. Infuriated at this deception and terrified at its possible significance, Mary Wollstonecraft became violently ill and deranged to the point of wanting to abort and die. For five days she was in an agony of despair, alarming those around her, and she sent off letters to Imlay so furiously bitter she later persuaded him to destroy them. On the night of January 6, his first response, quickly followed by others, reached her; it was a tender reassurance of love and a reproach for her lack of faith and her disregard for the business problems that mandated his stay at Le Havre. She wrote immediately and for the next few days in ecstatic relief and remorseful, anxious submission:

> Monday night [Jan. 6]
>
> I have just received your kind and rational letter, and would fain hide my face, glowing with shame for my folly.—I would hide it in your bosom, if you would again open it to me, and nestle closely till you bade my fluttering heart be still, by saying that you forgave me. With eyes overflowing with tears, and in the humblest attitude, I intreat you.—Do not turn from me, for indeed I love you fondly, and have been very wretched, since the night I was so cruelly hurt by thinking that you had no confidence in me.
>
> . . . If you think I deserve a scolding . . . wait till you come back—and then, if you are angry one day, I shall be sure of seeing you the next.

Fear that she might lose their child—"Do you think the creature goes regularly to sleep?"—drove her to weigh the intervals and vigor of its movements, which she was sure had grown fainter during her paroxysms. She was afraid her "caprices of sensibility" might have harmed or even killed the baby, and she told Imlay that she was so agitated her bowels were dreadfully disordered, everything she ate or drank upset her stomach.[25]

Imlay did his best to soothe her. Mary said she would never forget that he answered her furious letters with loving ones and "did not wait to be mollified by my penitence." He had not anticipated her violent reaction nor understood how needful she was; indeed it was only now she began to understand it herself. If she had always insisted on grateful devotion in other relationships, it was a matter of life and death with a lover. Imlay admitted he would have to remain for several months at Le Havre and urged her to join him. He also spoke of the many other children they would have together as among his motives for wanting funds. "What a picture you have sketched of our fire-side!" Mary answered, "I did not absolutely determine that there should be six—if you have not set your heart on this round number." Eager as she was to be with him, she was in no condition to travel for several days, for she was still not certain she would not miscarry. Her letter of January 9 was the first she signed "Mary Imlay":

> Thursday Night [Jan. 9]
>
> your tender epistle of Tuesday gave such exquisite pleasure to your poor sick girl. . . .
>
> I . . . would not, now I am recovering, take a journey because I have been . . . dreading continually the fatal consequences of my folly—But, should you think it right to remain at Havre, I shall find some opportunity, in the course of a fortnight, or less perhaps, to come to you, and before then I shall be strong again.—Yet do not be uneasy! I am really better, and never took such care of myself, as I have done since you restored my peace of mind. . . .
>
> Morning [Jan. 10]
>
> . . . I wish you were here to walk with me this fine morning! . . . when I was so dreadfully out of spirits, I was careless of everything.
>
> I will now sally forth (you will go with me in my heart) and try whether this fine bracing air will not give vigour to the poor babe. . .

She wrote again on the eleventh, assuring Imlay that he should stay at Havre as long as necessary. On the twelfth, she had still not recovered her strength, but was exercising compulsively to make up for past neglect:

> I cannot boast of being quite recovered, yet I am (I must use my Yorkshire phrase; for, when my heart is warm, pop comes the expressions of childhood into my head) so *lightsome,* that I think it will not *go badly with me* . . . I am urged on, not only by an enlivened affection for you, but by a new-born tenderness. . .
>
> I was therefore, in defiance of cold and dirt, out in the air the greater part of yesterday; and, if I get over this evening without a return of the fever . . . I shall talk no more of illness. I have promised the little creature, that its mother, who ought to cherish it, will not again plague it, and begged it to pardon me; and since I could not hug either it or you to my breast, I have to my heart—I am afraid to read over this prattle—but it is only for your eye.

Tuesday the fourteenth she received travel permits. Having been left for so long without adequate funds, she had to borrow £10 from Ruth Barlow for the journey. Without mentioning that necessity, she wrote Imlay she would be with him Friday the seventeenth "in my new apartment—where I am to meet you and love."

> You have, by your tenderness and worth, twisted yourself more artfully round my heart, than I supposed possible . . . I have thrown out some tendrils to cling to the elm by which I wish to be supported—This is talking a new language for me! But, knowing that I am not a parasite-plant, I am willing to receive the proofs of affection, that every pulse replies to, when I think of being once more in the same house with you—God bless you!

Next morning she could not resist sending a note that would arrive only a few hours before her coach:

> Farewell for a moment!—Do not forget that I am driving towards you in person! . . .
>
> . . . I follow the lead of my heart.[26]

Chapter 14

Mary Wollstonecraft joined Gilbert Imlay at Le Havre in mid-January of 1794. Shortly after—"Febry 3d—I believe"—she wrote Ruth Barlow that they were comfortably settled in a pleasant apartment, had hired a maid to do the drudgery and the cooking, which Mary disliked, and were happy and industrious. She signed herself "Mary Imlay." The next four months with Imlay were the most secure and contented she had ever known. She relished their domesticity: walking before breakfast because of her pregnancy, no matter what the weather; dining *tête à tête* before the crackling wood fires she loved, with Imlay carving the roast; supplying his linen shirts; arranging to get "dimity, white calico, or a light-coloured printed calico, for a morning gown." (She must have felt she would never get her waistline back, for she advised Ruth Barlow not to send a "stinted" pattern for the morning gown.) Her household arrangements were successful "if the high price of all the necessaries of life do not ruin US," she wrote Ruth, obviously delighting to use what she called the "matrimonial" pronoun. She was hard at work on her history of the revolution, readying as much as she could, the major portion, to send to Joseph Johnson via a business connection of Imlay's who was going to England. She expected the baby around the beginning of May and was determined to finish the first volume of the book before she gave birth, to her a task completely compatible with domesticity, but complicated by Havre's isolation from the center of political life and the absence of her precious books. "I never see a paper," she wrote Ruth Barlow, asking Joel to send her the *Journal des Débats et des Décrets* of the National Convention. "Tell him that I am now more seriously at work than I have ever been yet, and that I daily feel the want of my POOR BOOKS—Mr. Imlay laughs at my still retaining any hopes of getting them; . . . I am quite out of the world . . . write to me."[1]

If Mary and Imlay had their differences, at this time they were perceived as mutually beneficial. She later described the relationship in *Maria:*

> With Darnford she did not taste uninterrupted felicity; there was a volatility in his manner which often distressed her; but love gladdened the scene; besides, he was the most tender, sympathizing creature in the world . . . ever willing to avail himself of her taste and acquirements, while she endeavoured to profit by his decision of character, and to eradicate some of the romantic notions, which had taken root in her mind.[2]

Imlay's business occupied more of his attention than suited her "romantic notions"; he was importing ammunition, ore, pitch, alum, and other essential goods through Scandinavian connections, and struggling with problems of embargoes, delays, and hostile naval forces. But Mary Wollstonecraft had decided he was performing his share of their respective duties and made up her mind to be helpful and interested, since Imlay's stated objective was funds adequate to purchase a farm in America for them. "Teasing hindrances continually occur to us," she wrote Ruth Barlow that spring, "still we do not despair—Let but the first ground be secured—and in the course of the summer, we may, perhaps, celebrate our good luck, not forgetting good management, together." She was all the more adaptable because her sexual relationship with Imlay was intensely gratifying. He took a short trip on business to Paris in March; she wrote him on the twelfth:

> We are much creatures of habit, my love, that, though I cannot say I was sorry, childishly, for your going, when I knew that you were to stay such a short time, and I had a plan of employment; yet I could not sleep—I turned to your side of the bed, and tried to make the most of the comfort of the pillow, which you used to tell me I was churlish about; but all would not do . . . and here I am . . . seeing you peep over my

> shoulder, as I write, with one of your kindest looks—when your eyes glisten and a suffusion creeps over your relaxing features. . . . So God bless you!

But in her distaste for his commercial enterprises she forgot to enclose a paper he needed. "This comes of being in love at the fag-end of a business letter," she wrote when she forwarded the paper, and mischievously turned his admonition to her service. "You know, you say, they will not chime together—I had got you by the fire-side, with the *gigot* smoking on the board, to lard your poor bare ribs—and behold, I closed my letter without taking the paper up."[3]

Thanks to Imlay's shipping connections, Mary Wollstonecraft was at last able safely and successfully to contact England. The English newspapers had reported in the fall of 1793 that she had been imprisoned in France with her compatriots. Although Joseph Johnson reassured the family on faith that she must be safe, they were extremely worried; none of her letters had reached them since the previous summer. On March 10 Mary wrote Everina a lengthy letter. She mentioned her connection to Imlay with ambiguity—and only three-quarters of the way through:

> If any of the many letters I have written have come to your hands or Eliza's, you know that I am safe, through the protection of an American, a most worthy man, who joins to uncommon tenderness of heart and quickness of feeling, a soundness of understanding and reasonableness of temper rarely to be met with. Having also been brought up in the interior part of America, he is a most natural, unaffected creature. . . . Where is poor Eliza? . . . Will you write to tell her that I . . . still have in mind some places for her future comfort.[4]

Imlay's courier, a Mr. Codman, took this letter directly to England along with the greater part of Mary Wollstonecraft's book, which would have been worth her life had it been seen by the French authorities. By the end of April she had completed the balance of the volume and sent it off to Johnson, with great satisfaction that she had met her deadline. She seems to have equated her book with her pregnancy; "it has grown under my hand," she wrote in the introduction. It was important to her to be able to reassert her faith in humanity and its future as an intellectual corollary to the emotional and physical promise of Imlay and her child, and she made this act of faith in the bloodiest months of the revolution. France was possessed by the Terror, and even as she was completing her book in March, Robespierre sent Hébert and Desmoulins to the guillotine because they opposed the slaughter.

In *An Historical and Moral View of the Origins and Progress of the French Revolution; and the Effect It Has Produced in Europe,* Mary Wollstonecraft came to terms with revolution not by denying its hideous excesses and the evil actions of individuals, which she emphasized repeatedly, but by faith that the masses whose gradual awareness had produced the revolution, would eventually, as their capacities enlarged, progress to create a great and humane social order.

Believing in inevitable if gradual progress, she declared, as Imlay had in his *Topographical Description,* that violent revolution resulted in as much evil as good. However, under conditions of oppression such as the French had suffered, revolution was a necessary last resort. To the degree that they had been "depraved by the inveterate despotism of ages . . . burnt up by the scorching flame of revenge," the masses now reacted with violence. But eventually, the best society the world had ever known would evolve in France.

Mary Wollstonecraft believed that despite transitional or cyclical manifestations of violence, war, and human passion, mankind's capacity to learn and create, to perfect social order, was almost unlimited: "What . . . is to hinder man, at each epoch of civilization, from making a stand, and new modeling the materials . . . I hail the glorious day."[5]

She recounted in detail the key events of the French Revolution from June 1789 to the end of that year, including no new imformation and filling in with long quotations. She judged Necker, whom she had formerly admired and translated, as inadequate, and she praised Mirabeau. The book never comes to life, partly because she had little primary source material at hand (she was criticized by a reviewer for using the *Annual Register* almost verbatim in some sections), partly because she was not personally familiar with what she was reporting (the best literary passage is that describing deserted Versailles, which she had obviously visited), and for the rest because she was concerned with making moral and social judgments. The book influenced Shelley, however, and it had some shrewd political, nonutopian perceptions. She predicted Europe would be in a state of disorder for years to come; she observed that the framers of the French constitution would have been well advised to balance popular power with some representation for the nobles; she was skeptical about heroes and interested more in trends; she realized conventional charity was ineffectual in the modern world and declared that reduction of economic inequality and general improvement of the citizenry were major responsibilities of government; she warned that industrialization was causing men to be "turned into machines."

There were two passages reflecting her current personal situation. One was a statement directed at her differences with Imlay over the importance of commerce:

> . . . how can a man respect himself . . . when he is practicing the daily shifts, which do not come under the cognizance of the law, in order to obtain a respectable situation in life? It seems, in fact, to be the business of a civilized man, to harden his heart . . . the head is clear, because the heart is cold.

The other justified her relations with Imlay: "What is often called virtue, is only want of courage to throw off prejudice, and follow the inclinations which fear not the eye of heaven . . . founded on the natural principles of morality."[6]

On April 27, Mary Wollstonecraft wrote Ruth Barlow, "I am still very well; but imagine it cannot be very long before this lively animal pops on us—and now that the history is finished and everything arranged, I do not care how soon." On May 14, at two in the afternoon, she gave birth to a daughter and named the child after Fanny Blood. That same day the child's birth was registered with Le Havre authorities by Imlay, accompanied by his English landlord, John Wheatcroft, Jr., a soap manufacturer, and Wheatcroft's wife. The infant was described as the issue of the legitimate marriage of Imlay, "negotiant ameriquain," and "Citoyenne Marie Wolstonecraft, son Epouse."[7] Obviously, the couple passed as man and wife. The mother was delighted with her own performance; the experimenter was supremely confident of her methods. Mary was convinced women in labor suffered in some proportion to their fears and expectations and that current lying-in procedures and care of newborn infants were ridiculous; all the hovering was nonsense that interfered with nature. Her local nurse was appalled at the patient's insane insistence that she and her child not be coddled and swaddled. Conventional postpartum care stipulated a long slow recovery commensurate with female fragility: four or five days in bed, a month reclining on a couch to which the mother was carefully carried, later a coach outing and a bit of secluded, cautious walking. Mary spent one day in bed "through persuasion," was up walking the second, outdoors on the eighth. Despite dire warnings, her milk developed easily and profusely. She was a scandal to the women of Le Havre, who called her the "raven mother" because she kept her baby in loose light clothing, with plenty of fresh air. Eight days after Fanny's birth, Mary wrote Ruth Barlow triumphantly, "Here I am, my Dear Friend":

> and so well, that were it not for the inundation of milk, which for the moment incommodes me, I could forget the pain I endured six days ago —Yet nothing could be more natural or easy than my labour—still it is not smooth work . . . this struggle of nature is rendered much more cruel by the ignorance and affectation of women. My nurse has been twenty years in this employment, and she tells me, she never knew a woman so well—adding, Frenchwoman like, that I ought to make children for the Republic, since I treat it so slightly—It is true, at first, she was convinced that I should kill myself and my child; but since we are alive and so astonishingly well, she begins to think that the Bon Dieu takes care of those who take no care of themselves. . . . I have got a vigourous little Girl, and you were so far out of calculation respecting the quantity of brains she was to have, and the skull it would require to contain them, that you make almost all the caps so small I cannot use them; but it is of little consequence, for she will soon have hair enough to do without any—I feel great pleasure at being a mother—and the constant tenderness of my most affectionate companion makes me regard a fresh tie as a blessing. . . .
>
> 23rd . . . I add a line to say that I am now, the 10th day, as well as I ever was in my life—In defiance of the dangers of the ninth day, I know not what they are, ENTRE NOUS, I took a little walk out on the eighth—and intend to lengthen it today—
>
> My little Girl begins to suck so MANFULLY that her father reckons saucily on her writing the second part of the R——ts of Woman.
>
> once more yours—

With Fanny's birth, however, Mary Wollstonecraft's happiness with Imlay began to slip away. Even as she announced her successful delivery to Ruth Barlow, she mentioned Imlay's ill humor at the way his business was going:

> Mr. Imlay has been rendered almost impatient by the continual hindrances, which [come from] circumstances and mismanagement of some of the people intrusted with the concerns of the party—not to talk of the constant embarrassments occasioned by those whipping embargoes, that slip off and on, before you know where you are.[8]

The problem was more serious than she indicated. Adventurous, philandering, and restless as he was, Imlay had always changed his women and his locales when others seemed more attractive. Domesticity was a new experience for him, and after the intensity of his attraction to Mary and the novel excitement of living with her began to subside, his "old propensities," as she called them, beckoned seductively. Mary, on the other hand, had just achieved a way of life she had been drawn to for years and had projected as ideal not long before in *A Vindication of the Rights of Woman:*

> I have . . . viewed with pleasure a [wife] nursing her children, and discharging the duties of her station with perhaps merely a servant maid to take off her hands the servile part of household business. . . .
>
> I have thought that a couple of this description, equally necessary and independent of each other, because each fulfilled the respective duties . . . possessed all that life could give. Raised sufficiently above abject poverty not to be obliged to weigh the consequence of every farthing they spend. . . . I declare, so vulgar are my conceptions, that I know not what is wanted to render this the happiest . . . situation in the world, but a taste for literature, to throw a little variety and interest into social converse, and some superfluous money to give it to the needy and to buy books.[9]

This was not Imlay's view of the good life, although it is not surprising that Mary—and he himself—sometimes thought it was, for Imlay had praised frontier simplicity in *The Emigrants* and undoubtedly was pleased to personify American idealism for her admiration. In fact, he had always wanted to make a fortune. At this time he had absolutely no property of his own, but a great opportunity to become rich, and several avid partners who were spurring him on. If somehow he now found himself with a de facto wife and a child, he still wanted money for maximum personal freedom and pleasure. He concealed his motive from Mary and simply told her that making money was perfectly manly and proper. He repeatedly explained that he only wanted security for her and their future together. In early July he actually bought a home in Havre. But the couple took with them to it their incompatibility. On the eighth, Mary wrote Ruth Barlow that she was well, that the baby was thriving on her "good, that is natural manner of nursing," but added:

> Mr. Imlay has not been well for some weeks past, and during the last few days he has [been] seriously feverish. . . . Ships do not return, and the government is perpetually throwing impediments in the way of business. I cannot help sharing his disquietude, because the fulfilling of engagements appears to me of more importance than the making of a fortune.[10]

Mary Wollstonecraft was unable to soothe Imlay's agitation, much less share it, because she did not approve of its source. If Imlay had been pursuing artistic or intellectual ends, she probably would have been sincerely sympathetic. But her contempt for commerce and materialism, originally a class prejudice, had become part of her philosophy and personal way of life, hence her early perception that the revolution was merely replacing aristocratic with bourgeois plutocracy. Remembering that her father's speculations had destroyed her security and her family, she was profoundly uneasy to see Imlay possessed by the same ambition. "I do not think a *little* money inconvenient," she wrote him, "but should your plans fail, we will struggle cheerfully together—drawn closer by the pinching blasts of poverty." Nothing could have irritated him more. He told her she was childishly romantic. Sensing that his preoccupation encompassed more than financial freedom, Mary tried to deny that fact by treating the problem at face value, and to keep the peace, forced on herself a self-control she felt was unnatural, a hypocrisy that did violence to the spontaneous honesty she prized in herself and her relationships. "Aiming at tranquility," she later wrote Imlay, "I have almost destroyed the energy of my soul—almost rooted out what renders it estimable. Yes, I have damped that enthusiasm of character. . . . Despair, since the birth of my child, has rendered me stupid."

But Mary Wollstonecraft was as constitutionally incapable of disguise as she was convinced of the superiority of her principles. Imlay knew perfectly well what this woman of high tone and low tolerance felt. He kept his own counsels to avoid conflict—"a little reserve of temper, of which," Mary said, "I have sometimes complained!" and which she assumed was the result of his past experience with unworthy women:

> You have been used to a cunning woman, and you almost look for cunning—Nay, in *managing* my happiness, you now and then wounded my sensibility. . . . You have frankness of heart, but not often exactly that overflowing (*épanchement de coeur*), which becoming almost childish, appears a weakness only to the weak.[11]

Imlay was also finding it increasingly tiresome to play the passionate lover with a partner to whom he had become accustomed and from whom he sometimes wished to be free. After the usual six-week postpartum abstinence, Mary Wollstonecraft realized that their sexual relations were less exciting to him. It was impossible for her to be unaware of the change and equally impossible to accept what it meant. The gift of herself seemed so remarkable to her it was inconceivable he would not treasure it. She often wrote of his "suffusion" in making love, the flush of his body and face, which to an inexperienced, self-deluded woman must have seemed proof of his great passion for her unique self. Her self-respect now depended on his demonstrated love, as did the justification, by her own principles and his, for their continued union.

Imlay had begun by desiring a famous, independent, and passionate woman who agreed their liaison would endure only as long as they loved. He now found himself tied to a desperately needful woman who weighed every nuance of his behavior for devotion, rectitude, and compensation for her past unhappiness, a woman who demanded the ultimate commitment of his body and soul and who had herself made that commitment to him. Magnetized by her fervor, he found himself responding often enough to encourage her, for she was exciting, persuasive, and uncompromising. When she pursued she influenced him momentarily. But he could not and would not maintain this intensity. Absent from her or weary of the effort, he reverted to the character he had always been. Tenacious reformer that she was, she could not relinquish hope she could domesticate him, solidifying his better nature as she saw it. Rather than confront the problem or confess, Imlay acted behind her back. The longer this maneuvering went on, the harder it was for him to disentangle himself from the reassurances, hopes, and downright lies her passion extorted from him. "When your coolness has hurt me, with what tenderness have you endeavoured to remove the impression," she wrote him. She was an irresistible force; he a movable object. Taking him literally, as she expected to be taken, she assumed every positive response meant he loved and agreed with her. He was acting in reflex, as he thought a gallant, amiable man should, sometimes meaning what he said, at other times impersonating her ideal of him.

In mid-August, when Imlay went to Paris for a few days on business, their conflict had reached the point where, although her letters included items of business necessary to him, she was explicitly sarcastic on the subject of commerce, and critical of his *nouveaux riches* friends and of him:

> Sunday, August 17.
>
> The H–s are very ugly . . . and the house smelt of commerce from top to toe—so that his abortive attempt to display taste, only proved it to be one of the things not to be bought with gold . . . my attention was attracted by the *pendule*—a nymph was offering up her vows before a . . . fat-bottomed Cupid (saving your preference), who was kicking his heels in the air—Ah! kick on, thought I; for the demon of traffic will ever fright away the loves and graces. . . .
>
> . . . when I began [this letter], I merely thought of business; and, as this is the idea that most naturally associates with your image, I wonder I stumbled on any other.
>
> . . . [I hope still to see] the suffusion I admire . . . if you have not determined to eat and drink, and be stupidly useful to the stupid.

Several days later she acknowledged that his sexual desire for her—his "suffusion"—had diminished. She was searching for comfort in the child who resembled him.

> Havre, August 19, Tuesday
>
> I want you to promote my felicity, by seeking your own . . . unless the attachment appears to me clearly mutual, I shall labour only to esteem your character, instead of cherishing a tenderness for your person.
>
> . . . the little one . . . begins to call for me . . . she has got into my heart and imagination, and when I walk out without her, her little figure is ever dancing before me. . . .

> You too have somehow clung round my heart—I found I could not eat my dinner in the great room—and, when I took up the large knife to carve for myself, tears rushed into my eyes.[12]

After Imlay's return to Havre in August, the baby caught small-pox. Mary Wollstonecraft, convinced the French did not know how to treat the dreaded illness, "determined to follow the suggestions of my own reason," as she later told Everina, "and saved her much pain, probably her life . . . by putting her twice a-day into a warm bath."[13] If the emergency brought the parents closer together, it was temporary. About this time Imlay seems to have decided to dissolve his quasi-marriage, or at least to get away from it for a time. In September he announced he had to go to London on business. He told Mary he expected to secure the funds for their American farm and return to France in two months. Whether he had resolved to desert Mary and found this a convenient way to begin, or whether he simply welcomed the opportunity for an extended absence, his technique was exactly what it had been the previous year when he left Mary in Paris and went to Havre. Now he urged her to move back to Paris to wait for him. The city was safer since Robespierre's downfall and execution in July, and Mary had friends there. If he intended to leave her permanently, he was considerate enough to place her where she had connections—and at a distance from the Channel port.

Mary gave Imlay letters for her sisters, saw him off, and took the coach to Paris. Although she was apprehensive about his leaving, she made no fuss about accompanying him; she hated the very idea of going home. The political climate there was worse than when she had left. In the autumn of 1793, radical activists in Scotland had been tried, convicted, and transported for treason, and in early 1794 another such major trial, in which Joseph Johnson had to give testimony, had taken place in London, although the defendants were found innocent. In addition, in France Mary's relationship with Imlay, and particularly Fanny's status, were accepted as they could not be in England. There were rumors about her, but they were, as Johnson had heard and as Charles Wollstonecraft had written that summer from Philadelphia, that she had "married a Captain Imlay of this country," and had a child. "Yet Mary cannot be MARRIED!!" Eliza wrote Everina; she had been wondering all along about the term "protector" Mary had employed in writing about Imlay. In her letters home Mary now did not mention wedlock, but introduced Imlay "as a brother you would love and respect," and made it clear he was the father of her child. She suggested Everina visit Paris in the spring if peace should come, but made no offer this time to get Eliza a position in France. She signed herself "Mary Imlay," and left the obvious conclusion to be drawn for the moment.[14]

On her arrival in Paris about September 20, Mary Wollstonecraft found the political situation somewhat better; she wrote Imlay September 23: "They write now with great freedom and truth, and this liberty of the press will overthrow the Jacobins," although she added two weeks later that she feared "the last slap of the tail of the beast." Her daily life was satisfactory except for "little plagues" she mentioned infrequently. More seriously there were "some people here who have ruffled my temper," a reference to Imlay's American business associates in Paris, Blackden, a sot, and the ominous "——," whom she loathed. The nurse she brought from Havre was pregnant and almost useless. Fanny was a joy, "all life and motion." Mary wrote Imlay week after week of the child's development:

> Her eyes are not the eyes of a fool—I will swear. . . . My little darling grows every day more dear to me . . . begins to show her teeth and use her legs. . . . I am fatigued with dancing her, and yet she is not satisfied . . . our darling is become a most intelligent little creature, and as gay as a lark, and that in the morning too, which I do not find quite so convenient. . . . I am sorry you are not here, to see her little mind unfold.

She believed a child should enjoy a multitude of stimuli and frequently took Fanny out with her. "Besides looking at me there are three things which delight her," she wrote Imlay, "to ride in a coach, to look at a scarlet waistcoat, and hear loud music." In October she hired another nurse, Marguerite, with "more vivacity, which is better for the child." No longer completely tied down, she wrote Imlay that she began to be "employed and amused":

> making a progress in the language amongst other things. I have also made some new acquaintance. I have almost *charmed* a judge of the tribunal, R–. . . . If you do not haste back, I shall be half in love with the author of the Marseillaise, who is a handsome man, a little too broad-faced or so, and plays sweetly on the violin.[15]

She met Babeuf, a precursor of socialism, and believed him, as few then did, to be the most extraordinary political thinker she had ever known. She renewed her association with Madeleine Schweitzer, who had read a German translation of Imlay's *Topographical Description* and asked Mary to send the author her love "on account of what you say about the negroes." But Mary's superior attitude toward women offended Mme. Schweitzer, who later took revenge by writing of Mary at this period:

> I was very fond of Mary Wollstonecraft . . . and should have liked to regard her with constant affection, but she was so intolerant that she repulsed those women who were not inclined to be subservient to her; whilst to her servants, her inferiors, and to the wretched in general, she was gentle as an angel. Were it not for her excessive sensibility, which too often gains the upper hand, her personality would be exquisite. I passed one evening with her in the country. . . . Mary was sitting with the Baron de W beneath a tree gilded by the rays of the setting sun. . . . I said . . . "Come Mary—come, nature lover,—and enjoy this wonderful spectacle." . . . But, to my great surprise, Mary was so indifferent that she never turned her eye from him by whom she was at the moment captivated. I must confess that this erotic absorption made such a disagreeable impression on me, that all my pleasure vanished.

Mary Wollstonecraft had certainly changed her attitude toward sex. Von Schlabrendorf later told of her riposte to a smug and frigid Frenchwoman—*"Tant pis pour vous, Madame, c'est un défaut de la nature."*[16] But if Mary preferred men to sunsets, she was certainly not romantically interested in anyone but Imlay, despite Mme. Schweitzer. A male witness, Alexander Hamilton Rowan, saw Mary in a different light, as a devoted wife. Rowan was a wealthy Irish liberal who had escaped to Paris from a Dublin jail after conviction for sedition. He met the famous author at one of the Republican fetes then popular:

> Mr. Bingham who was with me, joined a lady who spoke English, and who was followed by her maid with an infant in her arms, which I found belonged to the lady. Her manners were interesting and her conversation spirited, yet not out of her sex. Bingham whispered to me that she was the author of the *Rights of Woman.* I started! "What!" said I within myself, "this is Miss Mary Wollstonecraft, parading about with a child at her heels, with as little ceremony as if it were a watch she had just bought

at the jeweler's. So much for the rights of women," thought I. But upon further inquiry, I found that she had, very fortunately for her, married an American gentleman a short time before the passing of that decree which indiscriminately incarcerated all the British subjects who were at that moment in this country. My society, which before that time, was wholly male, was now most agreeably increased, and I got a dish of tea, and an hour's rational conversation whenever I called on her.

The relative duties of man and wife was frequently the topic of our conversation. . . . Her account of Mr. Imlay made me wish for his acquaintance. . . . Mr. Imlay was expected over here; but his affairs keep him in England.

Rowan twice wrote his wife of Mary Wollstonecraft's insistence "that no motive on earth ought to make a man and wife live together a moment after mutual love and regard are gone." Mary added "that when a person whom we have loved was absent, all the faults he might have were diminished, and his virtues augmented in proportion."[17] These were the horns of her dilemma; the impalement was gradual, as excerpts from her letters to Imlay in England illustrate:

September 22

shall I talk about alum or soap? There is nothing picturesque in your present pursuits. . . .

Believe me, sage sir, you have not sufficient respect for the imagination—I could prove to you in a trice that it is the mother of sentiment, the great distinction of our nature, the only purifier of the passions. . . .

If you call these observations romantic . . . I shall be apt to retort, that you are embruted by trade, and the vulgar enjoyments of life—Bring me then back your barrier-face. . . .

Evening, Sept. 23

. . . there [is] something in the assertion of man and wife being one . . .

I have got a habit of restlessness at night . . . when I am alone, that is, not near one to whom I can open my heart, I sink into reveries and trains of thinking, which agitate and fatigue me.

This is my third letter; when am I to hear from you?

Paris, Sept. 28

I cannot help being anxious to hear from you; but I shall not harass you with accounts of inquietudes. . . . Adieu, my love! Take care of yourself, if you wish to be the protector of your child, and the comfort of her mother.

October 1

It is a heartless task to write letters, without knowing whether they will ever reach you. . . . I just now stumbled on one of the kind letters, which you wrote during your last absence. You are then a dear affectionate creature, and I will not plague you. After your return I hope indeed, that you will not be so immersed in business, as during the last three or four months past . . . a thousand tender recollections efface the melancholy. . . . I feel that I love you; and, if I cannot be happy with you, I will seek it no where else. . . . I long to hear from you.

October 26

My dear love, I began to wish so earnestly to hear from you, that the sight of your letters occasioned such pleasurable emotion, I was obliged to throw them aside till the little girl and I were alone together;

. . . Will you not then be a good boy, and come back quickly to play with your girls? but I shall not allow you to love the newcomer best. . . .

. . . yet do not imagine that I childishly wish you to come back, before you have arranged things. . . .

P.S. You would oblige me by delivering the inclosed to Mr. Johnson. . . . It is for a person uncomfortably situated.[18]

Imlay received Mary's gift of money and forwarded it to Eliza, who was still in Wales and more wretched than ever. When she knew Mary was safe in France, Eliza had given her employer several months notice and was agonizing over what she would do—join Mary, go to Everina in Dublin, or wait for help from her brothers. She had borrowed money from Johnson until even that generous man drew back. Some of what she got went to her father, whom Ned kept in short supply; in addition she was taking expensive French lessons from a refugee priest in case she went to France. Imlay's presence in England without Mary, and his failure to communicate with her sisters, gave Eliza, as she wrote Everina, "a dreadful complaint in my b——s . . . every hope for ourselves . . . Blasted. . . . Could he not have written us?" She now wrote Imlay in London in care of Johnson, pressing him for information about Mary's possible arrival in England. Imlay's reply, his only extant letter of the period, was uncomfortable, hypocritical, and tortuous:

> My Dear Madam—Mr. Johnson gave me your acceptable favor inclosing one to Mrs. Imlay, saying it was for her, which leaving me ignorant of being included, I could not return an immediate answer since which time I have been out of Town. I hope this circumstance will appear to you a sufficient apology for my silence, and that you will be pleased to consider it a good reason for preventing a forfeit of that claim to humanity or at least respect and esteem for a person so affectionately loved by my dear Mary as yourself, which you say had already been impressed on your mind.—
>
> As to your sister's visiting England, I do not think she will previous to a peace, and perhaps not immediately after such an event—However, be that as it may, we shall both of us continue to cherish feelings of tenderness for you, and a recollection of your unpleasant situation, and we shall also endeavour to alleviate its distress by all the means in our power. The present state of our fortune is rather [*blank*] However, you must know your sister too well, and I am sure you judge of that knowledge too favourably to suppose that whenever she has it in her power she will not apply some specific aid to promote your happiness. I shall always be most happy to receive your letters, but as I shall most likely leave England the beginning of next week, I will thank you to let me hear from you as soon as convenient, and tell me ingenuously in what way I can serve you in any manner or respect. I am in but indifferent spirits occasioned by my long absence from Mrs. Imlay, and our little Girl, while I am deprived of a chance of hearing from them.—
>
> Adieu, yours truly,
>
> G. Imlay[19]

In fact, Imlay was enjoying the fleshpots of London, hoping Mary would fade out of his life, and playing a despicable farce abetted by his partner "——" in Paris. While his straight man led off with their agreed excuses to Mary—a fresh development in their business, a new opportunity—Imlay delivered his lines—affection, unfortunate delay, reassurances. The two month absence stretched into three. Imlay wrote Mary that he would leave for France not "next week," as he had told Eliza to be done with her, but in time for Christmas. By this time Mary was weary, depressed, and anxious—but credulous enough to expect him day by day. Instead, at Christmas, she received a letter from him, ostensibly from the English port of Ramsgate, telling her he had to go back to London. At first she accepted with melancholy resignation:

Dec. 26

return to me when you have arranged . . . matters, which —— has been crowding on you. I want to be sure you are safe . . . For, feeling that I am happier than I ever was, do you wonder at my sometimes dreading that fate has not done persecuting me? Come to me, my dearest friend, husband, father of my child! . . . With you an independence is desirable; and it is always within our reach, if affluence escapes us—without you the world again appears empty to me. But I am recurring to some of the melancholy thoughts that have flitted across my mind for some days past.

Two days later she was still making an effort to be reasonable, but the significance of his latest excuses—both a possible voyage to Scandinavia and the need to remain longer in England—had begun to sink in, touching a heretofore unspoken apprehension that he might be through with her. She included a half-joking warning that she would not sit still if he traveled on:

December 28

——, I know, urges you to stay, and is continually branching out into new projects, because he has the idle desire to amass a large fortune, rather an immense one. . . . But we who are governed by other motives, ought not to be led on by him. When we meet we will discuss this subject. . . . It appears to me absurd to waste life in preparing to live.

Stay, my friend, whilst it is *absolutely* necessary—I will give you no tenderer name, though it glows at my heart. . . . *I do not consent* to your taking any other journey—or the little woman and I will be off, the Lord knows where. . . . I will not importune you . . . I long to see you—and, being at peace with you, I shall be hurt, rather than made angry, by delays—Having suffered so much in life, do not be surprised if I sometimes, when left to myself, grow gloomy, and suppose that it was all a dream, and that my happiness is not to last.

The next day she burst out:

December 29

How I hate this crooked business! . . . Why cannot you be content with the object you had first in view, when you entered into this wearisome labyrinth?—I know very well that you have imperceptibly been drawn on. . . . Is it not sufficient to avoid poverty?—I am contented to do my part. . . . And, let me tell you, I have my project also—and, if you do not soon return, the little girl and I will take care of ourselves; we will not accept any of your cold kindness—your distant civilities—no; not we.

This is but half jesting, for I am really tormented by the desire which —— manifests to have you remain where you are.—Yet why do I talk to you?—If he can persuade you—let him! . . . if our affection be mutual . . . you will act accordingly.

. . . I grow sad very often when I am playing with [Fanny]. . . . These appear to me to be true pleasures—and still you suffer them to escape you. . . . It is your own maxim to "live in the present moment"—*If you do*—stay, for God's sake; but tell me the truth—if not, tell me when I may expect to see you.

The day after, following an argument with "——", she was more definite and more desperate, for "——" had taunted her, and not for the first time, with Imlay's love affairs in London:

December 30

—— talks till he makes me angry, of the necessity of your staying two or three months longer. . . . I am determined to earn some money here myself, in order to convince you that, if you chuse to run about the world to get a fortune, it is for yourself—for the little girl and I will live without your assistance, unless you are with us. . . .

The common run of men have such an ignoble way of thinking, that, if they debauch their hearts, and prostitute their persons . . . they suppose the wife, slave rather, whom they maintain, has no right to complain, and ought to receive the sultan, whenever he deigns to return, with open arms, though his has been polluted by half a hundred promiscuous amours during his absence.

I consider fidelity and constancy as two distinct things; yet the former is necessary . . . if a wandering of the heart, or even a caprice of the imagination detains you—there is an end of all my hopes of happiness—I could not forgive it, if I would.

. . . When I am thus sad, I lament that my little darling . . . is a girl . . . I have ever declared, that two people, who mean to live together, ought not to be long separated—If certain things are more necessary to you than me . . . Say but one word, and you shall never hear of me more—If not—for God's sake, let us struggle with poverty. . . .

This is the first letter in this strain that I have determined to forward to you; the rest lie by.

During January of 1795, now actually in financial as well as emotional distress, and physically ill from a terrible cold that persisted and worsened over the next two months, Mary received just enough communication from Imlay to confuse and immobilize her. On the ninth she got a hasty note telling her he doubted he could return in February. "My God," she replied. "Anything but these continual anxieties." Although she could hardly bear to think of again having to live without love, she admitted she had sometimes worried about his affection even before he left for England. She now planned to wean Fanny in the spring in order to be able to earn a living. Her pride was temporarily predominant: "I do not chuse to be a secondary object." However on the fifteenth her tone changed when she received two affectionate letters from him: "It is pleasant to forgive those we love . . . my anger died away." On the thirtieth she had had no answers to several letters and wrote bitterly and briefly to give him some business news.

At the beginning of February Imlay wrote a curt letter asking Mary to join him in England if she wished, but at the same time indicating he might soon return to France. By this time he had a particular mistress, a young actress, and must have hoped to avoid Mary altogether. She replied in despair:

February 9

The melancholy presentiment has for some time hung on my spirits, that we were parted forever. . . . my head turns giddy, when I think that all the confidence I have had in the affection of another is come to this.

I did not expect this blow from you . . . but for [Fanny], I would cease to care about a life, which is now stripped of every charm. . . .

Perhaps this is the last letter you will ever receive from me.

Feb. 10

Yesterday —— very unmanlily exulted over me, on account of your determination to stay. I had provoked it, it is true, by some asperities against commerce. . . .

. . . For a year, or two, you may procure yourself what you call pleasure; eating, drinking, and women; but . . . I shall be remembered with regret—I was going to say remorse. . . .

> You will think me mad: I would I were so, that I could forget my misery. . . .[20]

She was now so ill she thought she might die of consumption and begged Imlay to honor her request that Fanny be brought up by a German friend in Paris. She had cut her expenses sharply, but she was writhing over her dependence on —— for money—"I have gone half a dozen times to the house to ask for it, and come away without speaking." She was also caught between her desire to join Imlay and her fear to return to and perhaps be deserted in England, a country she now felt she detested. She was particularly worried about Fanny's bastardy: "brought up here [in France], my girl would be freer."

Imlay must have realized that he was in a perilous situation, for Mary was getting desperate. "Your reputation will not suffer," she had written him. "I shall never have a confidant." But obscure decline for one so famous—and so articulate—was unlikely. Cornered, and perhaps even moved, he repeated his invitation with more loving assurances. Months later he claimed his conduct had always been consistent and "unequivocal." "It was not," Mary Wollstonecraft said, and with justification:

> before I returned to England, you took great pains to convince me, that all my uneasiness was occasioned by the effect of a worn-out constitution—and you concluded your letter with these words, "Business alone has kept me from you—Come to any port, and I will fly down to my two dear girls with a heart all their own."[21]

Unable to fathom the extent of his deception, she believed what she wanted to believe. She did, she told him, "think you had a struggle with old propensities; but still I thought that you had a magnanimity of character, which would enable you to conquer yourself." Clinging to that hope, although shaken and exhausted, she finally agreed to come to England. At the end of February Imlay told James Wollstonecraft, who had showed up in London, that he expected Mary in April, and in March he even dispatched a servant to help her leave Paris for Havre, put their house there up for rent, and embark. At Havre in early April Mary gave up nursing Fanny—"my only pleasure"—which she had refused to do earlier in Paris when so advised by her doctor. She wanted to be free for Imlay. She was ready to leave on April 7, but was miserably uncertain of her reception in England. "I sit, lost in thought, looking at the sea," she wrote Imlay, "and tears rush into my eyes, when I find that I am cherishing fond expectations . . . lie still, foolish heart!" Even her departure on or about April 9 was ominous; the ship ran aground in harbor, and she had to return briefly to an empty house. She wrote her friend Rowan, "I seem to hear the ticking of a clock; and there is no clock here."[22]

However, she made the Channel crossing with resuscitated expectation. "Here we are, my love," she wrote Imlay April 11 from Brighton. "What does your heart say?" She set out for London with Fanny and the nurse, Marguerite, next morning, hoping Imlay would be at his hotel to welcome her and that all would be restored between them. She found him formal and constrained. By April 16 he was living in the same house with her, one he had taken for the purpose on Charlotte Street in Rathbone Place; but he was perfunctory in his attentions, avoiding any definite declaration of intent, and he continued secretly to see his mistress.[23]

Mary Wollstonecraft hoped time and propinquity were working for her and determined to put the best face on her situation. In fact, she said later that her health and spirits improved in London. She saw Joseph Johnson, who told a friend he had never seen her so well and happy, and she paid a call on Fuseli. Her brother James was still in London; she gave him £10 to send their father in James' name, fearing Wollstonecraft might come to London if he knew she were there. After some two weeks she decided how to deal with the problem of her sisters, Eliza, in particular, who, she learned through Johnson, was to leave her job in early May and was in a fever of excitement and worry. Eliza had heard in March from James that Imlay was a "fine, handsome fellow," but had heard nothing more from Imlay himself, who she believed to be rolling in money. After Mary's arrival Eliza anticipated being called to London and taken care of. The last thing Mary could have wanted was Eliza in her household permanently or even temporarily; she was too proud to acknowledge her anomalous position, afraid of Eliza's penetrating eye and Imlay's impatience, and above all intent on restoring his love. But she wanted to make some provision for Eliza. Although, as she told Imlay, she felt she had to restrain her natural generosity, "because I felt your property was in jeopardy," she either believed he was on the verge of achieving his fortune or was willing to utilize that possibility to fend off Eliza. At the end of April, she composed and sent a careful but firm letter with a gift of money to poor Bess:

> I arrived in town near a fortnight ago, my dear girl, but having previously weaned my child on account of a cough, I found myself extremely weak. I have intended writing to you every day. . . . When Mr. Imlay and I united our fate together, he was without *fortune;* since that, there is a prospect of obtaining a considerable one. . . . He is the most generous creature in the world, and if he succeed . . . he will . . . enable me to be useful to you and Everina—I wish you and her would adopt any plan in which five or six hundred pounds would be of use. As for myself, I cannot yet say where I shall live. . . . It would give me the sincerest pleasure to be situated near you—I know you will think me unkind—and it was this reflection which has prevented my writing to you sooner, not to invite you to come and live with me.—But Eliza, it is my opinion, not a readily formed one, that the presence of a third person interrupts or destroys domestic happiness—Excepting this sacrifice, there is nothing I would not do to promote your comfort. I am hurt at being obliged to be thus explicit, and do indeed feel for the disappointments which you have met in life. . . . Do, pray, write to me immediately, and do justice to my heart. I do not wish to endanger my own peace without a certainty of securing yours—Yet I am still your most sincere and affectionate Friend.

Conceiving Mary to be lolling in a luxurious bower of bliss, Eliza exploded hysterically. "This I have just received," she wrote Everina in Dublin, copying the traumatic letter in full:

> Good God! what a letter! How have I merited such pointed cruelty—I may say insolence—When did I wish to live with her? at what time wish for a moment to interrupt their *Domestic* happiness? . . . Are your eyes opened at last, Everina! . . . Instantly get me a situation in Ireland, I care not where . . . tell me you can procure bread, with what Hogs I eat it, I care not . . . She shall never hear from *poor Bess again*. . . . Alas, poor Bess!

Eliza then scrawled a single furious sentence on Mary's letter and sent it back "to the author of the 'Rights of Woman.'" Mary replied; Eliza answered; but after that exchange the sisters corresponded no more, for events were developing badly in London. James told Eliza May 8 that Mary was "less composed and happy than formerly."[24] She was, in fact, in terrible conflict and misery. She was living in the same house with a man who no longer behaved as a lover, but was a constant stimulation and humiliation to her. He would say nothing explicit, however, and she could not face reality. "I will be *good*, that I may deserve to be happy," Mary had written Imlay at the beginning. In that spirit she decided to demonstrate her willingness to sacrifice and cooperate, putting Imlay under further obligation and at the same time relieving the discomfort she had felt in taking money from him. He had intricate commercial dealings in Scandinavia that required attention, and she offered to make the trip in his stead. On May 19 he executed a document for that purpose, naming "Mary Imlay, my best friend and wife" his agent. "Thus confiding in the talent, zeal, and earnestness of my dearly beloved friend and companion, I submit the management of these affairs entirely and explicitly to her discretion."[25] He had been maneuvered into gratitude, or he was overjoyed to get her away.

At about the same time Mary Wollstonecraft decided to broach head-on the paramount problem of their relationship. "Discussions ('explanations' they were called) followed," according to Godwin, during which Imlay first attributed his constraint to business problems, then admitted he had changed and had been unfaithful, while she shed pride and principle to retrieve him, violating her own strictures on infidelity and loveless union. He said he was torn between "zest for life," freedom, and pleasure, and affection for her and their child. Until he chose, they agreed he should move out. "It seems to me," she wrote him May 22, after he left Rathbone Place, "that I have not only lost the hope, but the power of being happy. . . . My friend—my dear friend—examine yourself well . . . discover what you wish to do . . . tell me frankly, I conjure you!"[26]

Imlay found a way to make himself clear. Mary Wollstonecraft either did not know about his mistress or thought he had given her up. A few days after he moved, she discovered he was still seeing the actress, and she refused to live with that truth. To exist without Imlay's love was terrible; to be rejected for an identified vulgar rival was intolerable. In an agony of wounded pride, anger, vengefulness, and self-hatred, she decided to kill herself. Preserving her superiority to the end, she prepared a letter, possibly for Johnson, "warmly in your favor," as she told Imlay later, exculpating him from the blame she felt, "to prevent odium from being thrown on you." She then sent Imlay a letter of despairing, bitter farewell and set about her suicide. The method she chose or how near she came to succeeding even Godwin never knew, but Mary's account of the heroine's suicide in *Maria* was perhaps close to what actually happened.

> She swallowed the laudanum; her soul was calm . . . nothing remained but an eager longing to forget herself—to fly from the anguish she endured . . . from this hell of disappointment.
>
> "What have I not suffered!—May I find a father where I am going" . . . a stupor ensued, a faintness—"Have a little patience," said Maria, holding her swimming head (she thought of her mother), "this cannot last long."[27]

In the unfinished book, Mary Wollstonecraft outlined a version of Maria's death and wrote out another one in which she is revived by a nurse. On this occasion Imlay saved Mary, as she surely desired. He got her suicide letter in time to rush to her in distraction and horror, and prevented her death. "I will live for my child," Mary had the heroine of her novel decide. But in her own life it was her fantasy—her "involuntary hopes" that Imlay's pity would bring him back to her—that was restored to life. She had demonstrated the lengths to which she would go and the depth of her need for Imlay. He was remorseful about the first and less discouraging about the second. He had been excited from his aloofness if not to passion, at least to an emotional declaration of affection. He was also frightened, for he worried about her suicide letter to him, which did not speak of him "with respect." He was even more apprehensive about what she had said in the public letter, which she had destroyed.

Having punished Imlay and herself, Mary Wollstonecraft was able to leave him on June 6, about a week after her intended suicide, for her trip to Scandinavia. She believed she had reformulated her relationship with Imlay in the most advantageous way possible for the time being: They had agreed in the emotion of the past week that it was to be based on honorable, indelible, lifelong devotion and complete candor. During her absence Imlay was to examine himself carefully to decide once and for all if he could live with Mary "in something like a settled stile," or better still "in the exquisite pleasure which arises from a unison of affection and desire," as she wanted. If not, they would at least be loving friends. "A true friend is a treasure," she told him. Above all, "do not deceive me!" she begged. Imlay agreed to meet her in three months in Switzerland or Germany to bring her his final decision. He even promised to send Mary's family money while she was gone, and he appeared to be pained at parting with her, which led her "to indulge the hope that you will feel me necessary to you—or why should we meet again?"[28]

Mary Wollstonecraft believed she had secured the first stage of the real journey she intended to make—that back to Gilbert Imlay.

Chapter 15

Mary Wollstonecraft's port of embarkation for Scandinavia was Hull, thirty miles from her childhood home in Beverley. She took the coach from London with her maid, Marguerite, and year-old Fanny, traveled through the night of June 9, during which the child would not rest quietly with anyone but her mother, and arrived worn out in Hull at one in the afternoon of June 10, having retraced the trip she had made with her family from Barking to Yorkshire when she was nine. Hull itself was familiar from those days. This proximity to her girlhood, peaceful and stable in retrospect, nourished her conviction that her subsequent life had been a series of dislocations, disappointments, and tragedies. Before she even looked for an inn, she wrote Imlay a short, emotional letter from the post house: Fanny was playing near her, imitating the sound of the mail horn:

> Imlay,—dear Imlay,—am I always to be tossed about thus?—shall I never find an asylum to rest *contented* in? How can you love to fly about continually—dropping down, as it were, in a new world—cold and strange!—every other day? Why do you not attach those tender emotions around the idea of home, which even now dim my eyes?—This alone is affection.

Imlay had sent Mary Wollstonecraft off with only vague instructions about getting a ship for her passage, but a London friend had insisted she take a letter of introduction to a local physician. This man found a cargo ship loading for Elsinor, Denmark, whose captain agreed to land Mary's party in Arendal or Gothenburg, Sweden. While awaiting departure she lived with the doctor and his family; he was a man of intellect, his wife, an attractive woman. "I can admire, you know, a pretty woman," Mary wrote Imlay bitterly, "when I am alone," and gave another turn to the screw, saying "poor Fanny was never so happy in her life, as amongst their young brood." Delayed for eleven days in Hull by a persistent, chilling northeast wind, "bowed down . . . forced into resignation by despair," she wrote terrible and pathetic letters to Imlay every day but one, until the day of sailing. She received three from him assuring her he wanted to promote her happiness and that their "fortune was inseparable." Her letters to him ran the gamut of possible appeals:

Friday, June 12

> You have a heart, my friend, yet, hurried away by the impetuosity of inferior feelings, you have sought in vulgar excesses, for that gratification which only the heart can bestow. . . .
>
> . . . I cannot help thinking that it is possible for you, having great strength of mind, to return to nature . . . which would open your heart to me—I would fain rest there!
>
> . . . I have looked at the sea, and at my child, hardly daring to own to myself the secret wish, that it might become our tomb. . . . I cannot, indeed, without agony, think of your bosom's being continually contaminated.

Saturday Morning. [June 13]

> I am harassed by your embarrassments, and shall certainly use all my efforts to make the business terminate to your satisfaction . . . my little darling is calling papa, and adding . . . Come, Come! . . . I am convinced that my exertions will draw us more closely together.

Sunday, June 14

> I wake in the morning, in violent fits of trembling . . . despair damps my rising spirits, aggravated by the emotions of tenderness.

Tuesday Morning [June 16]

> I seem to be fading away—perishing.

Thursday [June 18]

> I will not, my dear Imlay, torment you by dwelling on my sufferings.

Saturday [June 20]

> I have lost the little appetite I had; and I lie awake, till thinking almost drives me to the brink of madness. . . . I never forget . . . the misery.[1]

It may be sufficient to observe that Mary Wollstonecraft was passionately in love, desperately fighting to keep a man whose waverings continually revived her hope and determination, and that she was unable to give up the fulfillment of life-long needs once they had been gratified by Imlay. Even so, such irrational tenacity—which was to continue for almost another year—requires examination. While she was waiting in Hull, Mary's hosts took her to revisit Beverley. She wrote Imlay:

> I ran over my favorite walks, with a vivacity that would have astonished you—The town did not please me quite so well as formerly—It appeared so diminutive; and, when I found that many of the inhabitants had lived in the same houses ever since I left it, I could not help wondering how they could thus have vegetated, whilst I was running over a world of sorrow, snatching at pleasure, and throwing off prejudices.[2]

But there was less distance between Mary Wollstonecraft's former and present selves than she believed. Over and over again in the face of his proven duplicity, she wrote Imlay that she did not believe he was the man he seemed to be. She was never completely disabused of that illusion. It is obvious from the passage in *Maria,* so ingenuous and prototypical as to be almost quaint, in which Mary described her heroine's suicide attempt, that Mary was unconsciously replaying and failing to reorder a primitive and inexorably fixed drama. ("May I find a father where I am going—'have a little patience' . . . she thought of her mother.") On this level Imlay reenacted her divided father—adventurous, emotional, and loving; unscrupulous, self-indulgent, and untrustworthy—while she at one and the same time played the role of her mother, even to her degradation and submission, as well as the child in revolt at being rejected in her favor. Her reactions to defeat are also familiar: self-pity, playing on the pity of others, longing for death.

She had made herself into a valuable and famous woman through pride and ambition, but that achievement only exacerbated her present situation. "Accuse me not of pride," she wrote Imlay from Hull, "but sometimes I have wondered that you did not set a higher value on my heart." She referred to her "strong and original mind," her powerful emotions, as "the distinctive characteristics of genius." To maintain this sense of her superiority she had to hold on to Imlay, even if she risked ridicule and shame by flouting the rules that forbade a decent woman to make advances to a man and dictated that she fade away if he did not want her. Or, if forced to part with Imlay, she had somehow to make a victory of it. Previously, she had prized independence, but that solution had proven untenable and was now irretrievable. "What a long time it requires to know ourselves," she wrote at this time, "and yet, almost every one has more of this knowledge than he is willing to own, even to himself." She wrote Imlay: "I may perhaps be, some time or other, independent in every sense of the word—Ah! there is but one sense of it of consequence. I will break or bend this weak heart."[3] The fact that she was making a trip away from Imlay was a move in that direction, and in the course of it she began for the first time in over a year to work on a book, a financial, professional, and emotional alternative to dependence on him. But after believing she had secured "particular affection," intimacy, and erotic satisfaction, she had a mortal dread of being forced back to self-sufficiency, because she associated it with unbearable loneliness, isolation, and failure. If it were not for her child, she wrote Imlay several times, she would rather be dead.

Mary Wollstonecraft's struggle to keep Imlay has been thought strange and humiliating. Given the profound and ramiform significance losing him had for her, the wonder is that she survived the disengagement.

After a week in Hull she was told to board ship. "The quitting England seems to be a fresh parting," she wrote Imlay. "Surely you will not forget me—a thousand weak forebodings assault my soul." From June 16 to 20 the wind stayed in the northeast and her ship pitched at anchor part way down the two-mile-wide Humber Estuary, in weather so stormy Mary was forced to keep to her cabin, comforting Marguerite, who was violently seasick, nursing fractious, teething Fanny, and fighting off nausea in herself from the incessant movement and frightful stench of the vessel. On the eighteenth, the pilot brought her an affectionate letter from Imlay, which "afforded me some comfort—and I will try to revive hope." On the nineteenth she took Fanny ashore "to seek for milk, etc. at a little village, and to take a walk." Next day the captain sailed back to dock to post her last letter and looked vainly for a final one from Imlay. "You might have known, had you thought," she wrote him, "that the wind would not permit me to depart." The wind at last turned fair on the twenty-first, and Mary Wollstonecraft's ship stood out to sea.[4]

Scandinavia was not a region for tourism in the eighteenth century. Traders dealing in cotton or china, importers of iron, timber, or naval stores, occasionally traveled there, but for most English, it was a remote, ruggedly exotic area. Mary Wollstonecraft's ship was fitted for cargo, not passengers, and her eleven days aboard were extremely rough and uncomfortable. The landfall overshot Gothenburg Bay, and the ship floated many miles from shore in a dead calm. Mary had to insist—and finally pay well—before the captain allowed his men to row her, Fanny, and protesting Marguerite to a lighthouse on the desolate mountainous coast, where a startled local pilot found the odd trio and took them to his home. Excited out of her exhaustion, Mary found the scene thrilling: rocks, sea, silence, the luminous northern summer night. She climbed up to get a better view, found a "good omen," heartsease, growing at her feet, and put it in a letter to Imlay with tears in her eyes. That night she made arrangements for transportation to Gothenburg the next day, closely questioned her host, enjoyed his fish and cheese, rejected his brandy, "the bane of this country," and decided to record her travels for a future book.[5]

This was the pattern of her three month excursion. She wrote extensive notes on her trip which she later made into a book, published as *Letters Written during a Short Residence in Sweden, Norway, and Denmark.* It is a work of particular fascination because it is explicitly her daily account rewritten in the form of letters from herself to the unnamed American father of her child, a man from whom she has been reluctantly separated. In this format she was able freely to recapture as they occurred the interacting trains of thought, mood, and experience so typical of her. She was also dealing capably with Imlay's business, like the responsible partner of a firm, which had been predicted of her. She was an indomitable and perceptive tourist. As an intellectual she looked for ways to understand nature, society, and human development, and to settle troubling conflicts within her own philosophy. Always obsessed with Imlay, she alternately felt hope and reason for life or pessimism and need for resignation—or reason for death. Together with the letters she was actually sending Imlay, the published book illustrates this voyage at its many levels.

At the outset she was a physical and nervous wreck from the strain of the previous six months. The morning she was to leave the coast she suddenly blacked out, fell on the rocks, and cut her head. She proceeded to travel the twenty miles to Gothenburg in a rude cart over precipitous, rutted roads. The city inns were "mere stables," and that night, June 29, when she wrote Imlay, she was cold and hungry. "For God's sake, let me hear from you immediately, my friend! I am not well and yet you see I cannot die." For almost two weeks she worked as Imlay's agent from the Gothenburg home of Elias Bachman, his negotiant, who had gone to law on Imlay's behalf with one Peter Ellyson. She was empowered to ascertain the amount of damages owed Imlay, receive money recovered, and direct all concerns as she deemed best. She was lionized by the best society the city offered, although she wrote Imlay that everything fatigued her: "I cannot bear these continual struggles . . . this is a life that cannot last long"; and she urged him again to decide whether they would live together or part.[6]

Meanwhile, she made a quick assessment of backward Swedish culture. War-enriched Gothenburg society, she concluded in her book, was a ludicrous imitation of highly developed French civilization, which she now appreciated as never before.

> The more I see of the world, the more I am convinced that civilization is a blessing not sufficiently estimated . . . it not only refines our enjoyments, but produces a variety which enables us to retain the primitive delicacy of our sensations. Without the aid of the imagination, all the pleasures of the senses must sink into grossness.

Gothenburg society was vulgar: smörgasbord followed by huge meals twice a day, during which "the bottle must be pushed about"; idleness, gossip; tastelessness in art, gardens, fashion, and ideas. Swedish women, she wrote to her unnamed correspondent, were fat as featherbeds, "a comfortable idea, you will say, in a cold climate," and she teased him because he had once said American girls were sexually freer than English due to the warmer American climate. Swedish women, she noted, were quite promiscuous—and stupid. They insisted on loading their children with heavy clothes in summer, refused to bathe them, and fed them salt fish and brandy, "prejudices" they adhered to in spite of the author's attempts to enlighten them. She admired the simplicity of the lower classes, but was indignant at their oppression, particularly the plight of lower-class women, who, she observed, had the worst jobs, even walking barefoot in winter to wash linen through holes broken in the ice.[7]

After several days in Gothenburg Mary felt stronger. She often climbed and explored in the adjacent countryside, and slept every night in the country to enjoy the marvelously pure air. She wrote Imlay on July 3 in answer to a gloomy letter she received from him:

> Love is a want of my heart. . . . I have examined myself lately with more care than formerly. . . .
>
> I have the sincerest esteem and affection for you—but the desire of regaining peace, (do you understand me?) has made me forget the respect due to my own emotions. . . .
>
> . . . When we meet again, I will not torment you, I promise you. I blush when I recollect my former conduct. . . .

But next day, she wrote him: "I cannot tear my affections from you. . . . Do not tell me that you are happier without us—Will you not come to us in Switzerland? . . . my imagination is perpetually shading your defects, and lending you charms."

Three days later, when the mail arrived with no letters from him, "wounded to the soul," she wrote, "believe me, there is such a thing as a broken heart!" Anxious about her employer's state of mind, Marguerite offered to go with her on a necessary side trip to Norway, but Mary decided to leave Fanny behind with her maid because of the rigors of such travel, and delaying for one more post that still brought no letters, she left Gothenburg and coached north with two German travelers through Stromstad toward the narrows of the Skagerak. July 14, at the Norwegian frontier, she wrote Imlay, comparing her sorrows to Lear's "pangs of disappointed affection," and recalling Imlay's earlier pledge to make her happy. She ended defiantly: "Act as you please—there is nothing I fear or care for! When I see whether I can, or cannot obtain the money I am come about, I will not trouble you with letters to which you do not reply."[8]

She was traveling through magnificent but increasingly rugged country—peaceful landscapes, redolent of herring manure on closer approach; great forests of pine and fir such as she had never seen; wild rocky country, "the bones of the world"; mountain streams; exquisite summer nights when both sun and moon were visible. The fascination of such adventure delighted her and set her speculating in her book on a variety of ideas, about possible climatic influence on differing national characteristics, which, she concluded, modern communication would someday diminish, about botany, natural history, the origins of man—"I think the first dwelling of man happened to be in a spot like this which led him to adore a sun so seldom seen." Then, "[a] dish of coffee, and fresh linen . . . wrapping my great coat about me, I lay down on some sails at the bottom of the boat." She crossed the border to Lauvrik in Norway, where the locals were amazed at the rare sight of a foreign woman and touched by her weary delicacy. Her thoughts turned to herself and her child: "I dread to unfold her mind, lest it should render her unfit for the world she is to inhabit—Hapless woman! What a fate is thine. . . . With trembling hand I shall cultivate sensibility, and cherish delicacy of feeling. . . . I sharpen the thorns that will wound the breast I would fain guard."[9]

When she reached Tonsberg, her destination, on July 16, she had no letters awaiting her from Imlay. On the eighteenth she wrote him briefly:

> I hope [to] discharge all my obligations of a pecuniary kind.—I am lowered in my own eyes, on account of my not having done it sooner.
>
> I shall make no further comments on your silence. God bless you![10]

She had business in Tonsberg with the mayor, but his absence forced her to halt some three weeks in the ancient town between sea and forest. It was an inadvertent rest cure. Floating in reveries, always out in the open air, even sleeping in the fields, wandering by day on foot or horseback, dozing to the "prattling of the sea amongst the pebbles," her physical health returned, and she lost a morning fever that had dogged her since London. She was lapped in delicious silence, punctuated by occasional cow bells and the sound of water. She learned to row, trailing her hand to catch a jellyfish, finding lonely coves in which to bathe.

She felt nature to be restorative, eternal, a great mystical and physical design of which she was part, and in her book she linked it to love, devotion for her dead friend, Fanny Blood, and sexual pleasure with Imlay. Her responsiveness to nature was:

> but the unfolding of that love which embraces all that is great and beautiful. . . . I recollect views I have seen . . . looks I have felt in every nerve. . . . The grave has closed over a dear friend, the friend of my youth; still she is present with me . . . another, the fire of whose eyes still warms my heart . . . the rosy tint of morning reminds me of a suffusion, which will never more charm my senses . . . my bosom still glows . . . I blush at recollecting past enjoyment.

But she balanced that revelation with concern for human beings in society. Pristine nature, she wrote, could not suffice man; his full development was tied to civilization. Despite her romantic predilection for the simplicity and frankness of peasants, "I begin to think that I should not like to live continually in the country, with people whose minds have such a narrow range." Aware of persistent human problems, she brooded over a young village woman deserted by her husband, "this most painful state of widowhood," which in her book she hinted reminded her of her own. Yet she preferred Norway to Sweden for its spirit of equality and justice (no primogeniture, she discovered), humane laws, free press, decent prison and education systems, gay Sundays so unlike the gloomy English ones, liberal citizens who eagerly questioned her about the French Revolution. She welcomed signs of cultural progress, harbingers to her of moral improvement, and in one passage of her book even judged commercial enterprise such as Imlay's a socially constructive development. "I never, my friend, thought so deeply of the advantage gained by human industry. . . . The world requires, I see, the hand of man to perfect it."[11]

After two weeks in Tonsberg Mary Wollstonecraft got two letters from Imlay. He said he still had not made up his mind about their future, but repeated that he would honor his promise to meet her in Germany or Switzerland in September. She replied with revived hope and a fresh reason for their union—Fanny. "I wish for us to live together, because I want you to acquire a habitual tenderness for my poor girl." In that event, she promised she would not expect passionate love from him. But soon after she wrote:

> on examining my heart, I find that it is so constituted, I cannot live without some particular affection—I am afraid without a passion. . . .
>
> This state of suspense, my friend, is intolerable; we must determine on something—and soon;—we must meet shortly, or part forever. I am

> sensible that I acted foolishly—but I was wretched. . . . Expecting too much, I let the pleasure I might have caught, slip from me. I cannot live with you—I ought not—if you form another attachment . . . I will be dead to you. I cannot express to you what pain it gives me to write about an external separation—You must determine—examine yourself—but, for God's sake! spare me the anxiety of uncertainty! . . .
>
> I ought to beg your pardon for having sometimes written peevishly.

August 9, five unsatisfactory letters from Imlay reached her. She replied stiffly:

> One, dated the 14th of July, was written in a style which I may have merited, but did not expect from you . . . you shall not be tormented by any more complaints. I am disgusted with myself for having so long importuned you with my affection.—
>
> My child is very well. We shall soon meet, to part not more, I hope —I mean, I and my girl.[12]

She did not write Imlay again for two weeks, and in renewed resentment and restlessness went on a tour of the offshore islands. Describing this bleak coast in her book, she wondered what would happen when even intense cultivation could not support the earth's population—"Universal famine?" The book recorded her conflict between her new recognition of the benefits of commerce and industry, and her aversion to the primitive entrepreneurs she was meeting—"depraved by a sordid love of money which repells me"—men who reeked of "smoking, drinking brandy, and driving bargains. . . . Yet I perceive even here the first steps of the improvement which I am persuaded will make a very obvious progress in the course of half a century." Ambivalent about what constituted the good life, she decided, "I should like to divide my time between town and country; in a lone house, with the business of farming and planting, where my mind would gain strength by solitary musing; and in a metropolis to rub off the rust of thought, and polish the taste." She returned to Tonsberg and to longing for Imlay: "I reasoned and reasoned; but my heart was too full to remain in the house, and I walked till I was wearied out."

Her task was completed at Tonsberg, and Mary Wollstonecraft went on in black melancholy through Moss to Christiania, now Oslo. She welcomed the more sophisticated and intellectual society, but regretted the factors she felt produced it: ecological scars caused by development, "human industry in the shape of destruction," and strong government, here the "cloven foot of despotism." Hearing of romantic country and simple noble inhabitants in the far north, she wondered if Rousseau's fables of primitive utopia could be true and was tempted to see for herself. Although she knew men everywhere had to be "the same compound of wisdom and folly, who must occasionally excite love and disgust, admiration and contempt," she added wistfully that this description of idyllic reality "was given me by a man of sound understanding." Unable to resolve conflicting ideals, she settled for a warning: "England and America owe their liberty to commerce, which created a new species of power to undermine the feudal system. But let them beware of the consequences: the tyranny of wealth is still more galling and debasing than that of rank."[13]

Impatient to get back to Fanny and, in spite of herself, to the mails, she left for Gothenburg in a bad mood, savoring morbidity when she passed a great forest denuded by fire: "I cannot tell why—but death under every form, appears to me something like getting free—to expand in I know not what element." She reached Gothenburg on August 25, and was so gratified by her reunion with Fanny that she wrote Imlay resolutely:

> August 26
>
> I have promised her that I will fulfill my duty to her; and nothing in future shall make me forget it. . . . Vigour, and even vivacity of mind have returned. . . . As for peace, we will not talk about it. I was not made, perhaps, to enjoy the calm contentment so termed.

And she went on to answer his three letters just received:

> You tell me that my letters torture you; I will not describe the effect yours have on me. . . .
>
> Certainly you are right; our minds are not congenial. I have lived in an ideal world, and fostered sentiments that you do not comprehend—or you would not treat me thus. I am not, I will not be, merely an object of compassion. . . . Something emphatical whispers me to put an end to these struggles. Be free—I will not torment, when I cannot please. I can take care of my child; you need not continually tell me that our fortune is inseparable, *that you will try to cherish tenderness* for me. Do no violence to yourself! . . . support I need not, whilst my faculties are undisturbed. I had a dislike to living in England; but . . . I may

> not be able to acquire the sum necessary to maintain my child and self elsewhere . . . be not alarmed; I shall not force myself on you any more.

Believing for the moment she wanted only to finish the business and meet Imlay on the Continent for a final, even terminal resolution, she proceeded with Fanny and Marguerite to Copenhagen, where she was to dispose of goods held by Myburg and Company. Copenhagen had recently been devastated by a great fire, which the Danes accused Pitt, Mary's political enemy, of having planned; "poetical justice," she wrote in her book, "that while this minister is crushing at home plots of his own conjuring up, he should, with as little foundation, be accused of wanting to set the world on fire." She saw there a festive crowd leaving a public execution and came to a modern analysis of crime and punishment: "The fear of ignominious death, I believe, never deterred anyone from the commission of a crime. . . . It is a game at hazard, at which all expect the turn of the die in their own favour . . . the same energy of character which renders a man a daring villain, would have rendered him useful to society had that society been well organized."[14]

She disliked Denmark; the men were money-grubbing, self-satisfied sots, the women social climbers, the children unruly, the political leaders, such as the prime minister to whom she was introduced, reactionary. She lamented the fate of the Danish princess Matilda, who had been imprisoned for infidelity to her mentally retarded husband, a story also featured in *The Emigrants*. She was sick of sightseeing and increasingly agitated about her approaching decisive rendezvous with Imlay. In Copenhagen she got another letter from him that was indefinite about their meeting and decidedly cool in tone. She replied angrily on September 6:

> Gracious God! It is impossible for me to stifle something like resentment, when I receive fresh proofs of your indifference. What I have suffered this last year, is not to be forgotten! . . .
>
> I do not understand you. It is necessary for you to write more explicitly . . . I cannot endure this suspense—Decide. . . . I shall not write to you again, till I receive an answer to this. I must compose my tortured soul.

In her book she proceeded to give Imlay a public dig. Breach of faith in engagements, she wrote, was considered by Danes to be more disgraceful than adultery, and she added that men were tyrants: "Still harping on the same subject, you will exclaim—How can I avoid it, when most of the struggles of an eventful life have been occasioned by the oppressed state of my sex." Leaving Copenhagen for Hamburg, where Imlay was supposed to write her of their meeting, she traveled through Holstein, brooding about the futility of human egotism when she saw a battle regiment of soldiers. "It is the preservation of the species, not of individuals, which appears to be the design of the Deity throughout the whole of nature," she wrote in her book. God had become an impersonal force, indifferent to suffering. She hated Hamburg, thought the Germans vulgar materialists, and went to stay at nearby Altoona, a center for French refugee aristocrats, whose noble grace under pressure of poverty and exile appealed to her in spite of her political views. Post after post she waited in Altoona for word from Imlay. "I am sad," she wrote toward the end of her book, making her actual situation quite clear to the public. "Innocent and credulous as a child. . . . Ah! shall I whisper to you—that you yourself are strangely altered since you have entered deeply into commerce." "I am labouring to write calmly," she wrote Imlay September 25, demanding to receive word from him.[15]

Her letter crossed his, which she got on the twenty-seventh. Imlay indicated any meeting with Mary was useless and put the responsibility on her recent letters. He hinted that he had another mistress. Mary's questions, he wrote with unusual roughness, were "extraordinary and unnecessary"; he saw no reason for any further discussion, but left that to her to decide. She replied immediately:

September 27

> I had decided . . . the negative was to come from you.—You had perpetually referred to your promise of meeting me in the autumn—Was it extraordinary that I should demand a yes, or no? I see only a desire to heave a load off your shoulders . . . I am strangely deficient in sagacity.—Uniting myself to you, your tenderness seemed to make me amends for all my former misfortunes.—On this tenderness and affection with what confidence did I rest!—but I leaned on a spear, that has pierced me to the heart. . . . I shall take no step, till I see or hear from you.

She spoke of returning to England, of going to France, of securing independence for Fanny. But suddenly, contradicting her intention to do nothing until hearing from Imlay, she took the first ship for England. She stopped at Dover October 4 instead of going on to London because "I have no place to go to," she wrote Imlay, and she was afraid to surprise him. She insisted on seeing him "once more, and immediately," and she reverted to the wish she had never relinquished, that Imlay would return to her. She ended her letter on a mordant, threatening note: "I am unable to tear up by the roots the propensity to affection which has been the torment of my life—but life will have an end!"[16]

About October 7 she had an answer from Imlay and on the shaky strength of it went to London. He put her in lodgings, assured her over and over that he did not have a new love, and was sufficiently elusive for Mary to cling to hope. Then he went off, for he actually had been established in a house with a mistress for some time, and left Mary to find out the truth for herself. In a few days she was reduced to cross-examining her cook, who finally told her where and with whom Imlay was living. Mary went straight to Imlay's house, saw for herself, and confronted him in a terrible scene that she never gave any detail of, even to Godwin. Mary was undoubtedly wildly furious and recriminatory, and Imlay probably retaliated as a weak and guilty man might, with some brutality. Loathing him and herself, she returned to her apartment and again prepared to die; revenge on Imlay and surcease for herself. The prospect made her calm and clear-headed. She wrote a line across the first section of some lessons she had begun to write for Fanny: "The first book of a series which I intended to have written for my unfortunate girl"—a strange relic for the child. She then wrote Imlay:

> I write you now on my knees; imploring you to send my child and the maid . . . to Paris, to be consigned to the care of Madame–. . . .
>
> Let the maid have all my clothes, without distinction.
>
> Pray pay the cook her wages, and do not mention the confession which I forced from her—a little sooner or later is of no consequence. Nothing but my extreme stupidity could have rendered me blind for so long. Yet, whilst you assured me that you had no attachment, I thought we might still have lived together.
>
> I shall make no comments on your conduct; or any appeal to the world. Let my wrongs sleep with me! Soon, very soon shall I be at peace. When you receive this, my burning head will be cold.
>
> I would encounter a thousand deaths, rather than a night like the

> last. Your treatment has thrown my mind into a state of chaos; yet I am serene. I go to find comfort, and my only fear is, that my poor body will be insulted by an endeavour to recall my hated existence. But I shall plunge into the Thames where there is the least chance of my being snatched from the death I seek.
>
> God bless you! May you never know by experience what you have made me endure. Should your sensibility ever awake, remorse will find its way to your heart; and, in the midst of business and sensual pleasure, I shall appear before you, the victim of your deviation from rectitude.[17]

Mary Wollstonecraft walked out of her apartment and went down to the Thames. It was evening. She hired a small riverboat and told the boatman to take her to Battersea Bridge. When she asked him if the bridge was deserted at that hour, he told her there would surely be people around. She told him to row further upriver to Putney, landed there, and went out onto the ugly wooden bridge she had known since the time she lived in Fulham with Fanny Blood. The river there runs strong, eddying, and murky. It was now quite dark and pouring rain. She decided to weight her clothes in the rain so she would sink more easily, and walked up and down the bridge quite alone for half an hour, until she was satisfied her skirts were thoroughly drenched. She jumped from the highest point, hit the water, pressed her skirts close to her body when she did not sink immediately, went under, rose twice in spite of her resolution, swallowed water deliberately, and went under again, finally losing consciousness. Her fall was seen by some boatmen who dragged her floating body out about 200 yards downriver and carried her, still insensible, to a tavern called the Duke's Head. They found a physician who was able to revive her. It was not known until much later who she was, but somehow she was taken back to her lodging.[18]

Imlay sent a doctor to her and had Mrs. Christie, Mary's friend from Paris, take Mary into her home on Finsbury Square to recover. The drama continued where it had left off; to blight the rest of Imlay's life, Mary had been willing to die, and she used her survival to stave off the blight of her own. As Godwin said naïvely in the *Memoirs,* "The present situation of Mary, of necessity produced some further intercourse between her and Mr. Imlay." Imlay did not visit her, as he said, out of "delicacy," but wrote offering support money and saying he "knew not how to extricate ourselves out of the wretchedness into which we have been plunged." Mary wrote back, "You are extricated long since"; and went on to appeal to his guilt, pity, and fear:

> I have only to lament, that . . . I was inhumanly brought back to life and misery. But a fixed determination is not to be baffled by disappointment; nor will I allow that to be a frantic attempt, which was one of the calmest acts of reason. In this respect, I am only accountable to myself. . . .
>
> . . . I am unable to discover what sentiment of delicacy would have been violated, by your visiting a wretched friend—if indeed you have any friendship for me.—But since your new attachment is the only thing sacred in your eyes, I am silent—Be happy! . . . perhaps I am mistaken in supposing that even my death could, for more than a moment . . . damp your enjoyment.
>
> When I am dead, respect for yourself will make you take care of the child. . . .
>
> God bless you!

Spurning his offer to make her financially comfortable, she wrote again, "You are now perfectly free.—God bless you." But Imlay was not free. He continued to press money on her, to write with affection, and even went to see her "to oblige other people," Mary said resentfully and possibly accurately, for she was on home ground in London. But even more, he began to intimate that his present love affair was far from sacred, purely sexual, and perhaps short-lived; he only knew he could not leave his mistress quite yet. Mary had an answer; she offered to move in with them for Fanny's sake and, as she later told Godwin, "even . . . to improve" Imlay's mistress. Dumbfounded into acquiescence, Imlay actually took Mary to see the house he was about to rent, but his mistress, like Sophia Fuseli, must have protested, for the lovers moved alone—"an open avowal that you abandon me," Mary wrote him. However, Imlay could not or would not tell her their relationship was at an absolute end, and this she insisted on. "Let me see," she wrote him, "written by yourself—for I will not have it through any other medium—that the affair is finished." Apparently, he was not ready to write that statement.

Mary Wollstonecraft's presence at the Christies was awkward because Thomas Christie was in his in-laws' carpet business, and Imlay had dealings with him. Mary therefore moved, but only a few doors away, to 16 Finsbury Square. She saw almost no one but Mrs. Christie for weeks, "buried alive," she wrote Imlay, "in this tomb." Toward the end of November Imlay went off to Paris with his mistress for three months, returning Mary's letters and leaving a letter assuring her that she would look back some day on this "decided conduct" and realize that it was not "unfeeling" but for their mutual good. His principles of freedom and hedonism, he said, were "the most refined . . . exalted." She replied November 27 that his actions had "almost overturned my reason":

> is it not possible that *passion* clouds your reason, as much as it does mine? . . . to have no principle of action, but that of following your inclination, trampling on the affection you have fostered, and the expectations you have excited?
>
> My affection for you is rooted in my heart.—I know you are not what you now seem—nor will you always act, or feel, as you now do. . . . Even at Paris, my image will haunt you . . . my head is confused—Right or wrong I am miserable! . . . You would render mothers unnatural—and there would be no such thing as a father!—If your theory of morals is the most "exalted," it is certainly the most easy . . . to please ourselves for the moment, let others suffer what they will!
>
> . . . my heart thirsts for justice from you.

The returned letters were "a register of sorrow," she said. There were seventy-five; Imlay had kept them all. What happened eventually to his is unknown. Shortly after, December 8, she wrote him in Paris:

> Resentment, and even anger, are momentary emotions with me—and I wished to tell you so, that if you ever think of me, it may not be in the light of an enemy.
>
> . . . I began even now to write calmly, and I cannot restrain my tears.
>
> I am stunned!—Your late conduct still appears to me a frightful dream.—Ah! ask yourself if you have not condescended to employ a little address, I could almost say cunning, unworthy of you? . . .
>
> . . . it seems to me, when I am more sad than usual, that I shall never see you more.—Yet you will not always forget me. . . . I know that your mind, your heart, and your principles of action, are all superior to your present conduct. You do, you must, respect me—and you will be sorry to forfeit my esteem.

> You know best whether I am still preserving the remembrance of an imaginary being. . . . Still I have an affection for you.—God bless you.[19]

Mary Wollstonecraft's uncontainable, gravitational persistence, surging on regardless of reality, comes close to the pathological. One strikingly irrational and key component was her fantasy that Imlay was someone other than the man he actually was, a delusion that perhaps made Mary more bearable to herself. Her letter has an astounding ending: "I once thought I knew you thoroughly—but now I am obliged to have some doubts."

Ironically, Imlay's characteristic self-indulgence and dishonesty forced Mary to take a decisive therapeutic step out of the revolving cage of her compulsions. While Imlay was in Paris she found herself accountable for debts he had contracted. To pay them, in her eyes a question of her own honor, as well as to sustain herself and Fanny without recourse to him, Mary decided she had to go back to writing. Joseph Johnson agreed to publish the book based on her travels, and she began to work again. The task was bitter because she combined what she had written about Scandinavia with her concurrent longing for Imlay, and she had her letters to him before her. But it was productive because she decided "to let my remarks and reflections flow unrestrained" in epistolary form, which suited her emotional needs and subjective intent perfectly.

The book was a godsend to Mary Wollstonecraft. Apparently no one but Imlay, the Christies, and possibly the discreet Johnson knew about her situation until this time. A friend of Fuseli's, Joseph Farington, reported her suicide attempt in his diary a year later, but the full story was not publicly known until after her death. Although she assured Imlay she would never "publically complain," something he feared, writing and publishing *Letters Written . . . in Sweden* gave Mary a way of relieving her feelings and a legitimate excuse to reveal with delicacy just enough of her tragedy to get the general sympathy she needed without directly accusing Imlay. It was also a vehicle through which she could display all her charm, personality, and intellect to convince the public of her distinction and value. She said as much in the introduction; "A person has a right . . . to talk of himself when he can win our attention by acquiring our affection."

Mary Wollstonecraft thus succeeded in assuaging her thirst for justice from Imlay in sublimated form, without the bitterness so apparent in her private letters to him. In fact, Godwin said she never thereafter spoke of him harshly or allowed anyone to criticize him in her presence. At the same time she was communicating with Imlay, for the book is full of private references and jokes only he could interpret, and further, showing him what he was missing. She was winning her own kind of victory over him, and the book is strangely serene and affirmative for all its emotion, free of the tense belligerence and arrogance of her former works. In an artless and doubtless sincere passage, she told her readers (three months after her second suicide attempt) that she could not bear to think of being annihilated, "the only thing of which I have ever felt a dread."[20] She was able to integrate new political and social experience with her basic trust in progress; despite the temporary outrages of war, revolution, and human passions, she affirmed at the book's end that beneficial change was transforming Scandinavia and all European society.

Johnson published *Letters Written . . . in Sweden* in early January, 1796; it was widely read and translated into several languages. Mary Wollstonecraft remained controversial. In the Library Company of Philadelphia there is a first edition of her book bound in boards decorated with large hearts and annotated sympathetically by one reader, but another reader has written indignant comments in the margins ("this *sans-culotte* Voltaire," etc.) and fiercely inked out a sentence in which Mary questioned the reality of a Day of Judgment. Most reviewers were favorable, however, and a sizable public reacted as Mary Wollstonecraft desired to what is a lovable book. Interestingly enough, two men used that term. "Have you met with Mary Wollstonecraft's Letters from Sweden and Norway," Southey asked a friend. "It has made me in love with a cold climate, and frost and snow, with a northern light." (There is no snow in the book.) "If ever there was a book calculated to make a man in love with its author, this appears to me to be the book," Godwin said, putting his finger on her motivation:

> She speaks of her sorrows, in a way that fills us with melancholy, and dissolves us in tenderness, at the same time she displays a genius which commands all our admiration. Affliction has tempered her heart to a softness almost more than human; and the gentleness of her spirit seems precisely to accord with all the romance of unbounded attachment.

If there were any doubt about the response she sought, Mary Wollstonecraft received—and kept—a long love letter from an unknown former acquaintance, who proposed that she and he "dissolve in bliss" together:

> I think I discover the very being for whom my soul has for years been languishing. One who, the woman of reason all day, the philosopher that traces compares and combines facts . . . in the evening becomes the playful and passionate child of love; one who would realize all the fond raptures of my fanciful and ardent youth and by the very remembrance of whom I perceive myself restored as it were to all my boyish simplicity: One in whose arms I should encounter all that playful luxuriance, those warm balmy kisses, and that soft yet eager and ecstatic assaulting and yielding known only to beings that seem purely etherial.[21]

By January Mary Wollstonecraft had also finished the sketch of a play based on her recent experience, which Godwin described as a comedy, probably meaning it had a happy ending. It was refused for the stage and destroyed by Godwin after her death because he considered it crude and imperfect. Work was a question of life as well as living for her. She was still desolate, and when she spoke of herself she often broke down. In late January she wrote her friend Rowan, then operating a calico mill in Wilmington, Delaware, with her brother Charles:

> what can I say to you—I am unhappy—I have been treated with unkindness—and even cruelty, by the person from whom I had every reason to expect affection—I write to you with an agitated hand—I cannot be more explicit . . . I looked for something like happiness—happiness! . . . and the heart on which I leaned has pierced mine to the quick. . . . When I am more composed I will write to you again . . . tell me something of Charles—I avoid writing to him because I hate to explain myself—I still think of settling in France, because I wish to leave my little Girl there—I have been very ill—Have taken some desperate steps—But now I write for independence . . . do not mistake me—Mr. Imlay would be glad to supply all my pecuniary wants; but, unless he returns to me himself I would perish first.
>
> Mary Imlay

Although she signed "Wollstonecraft" to *Letters Written . . . in Sweden,* privately she was using Imlay's name. "It was not," Godwin reported she said, "for the world that she did so—not in the least—but she was unwilling to cut the Gordian knot, or tear herself away in appearance, when she could not in reality." Counting as she always did on the magnetism of pity, she expected her close friends to come to her as if on condolence calls, for she was in mourning limbo, bereft, although not accepting a final loss. To her disappointment, Fuseli did not appear. She wrote him, therefore, with resentment and asked him to return her letters as if to tidy up her past life:

> When I returned to France, I visited you, Sir, but finding myself after my late journey in a very different situation, I vainly imagined you would have called upon me. I simply tell you what I thought, yet I write not, at present, to comment on your conduct or expostulate. I have long ceased to expect kindness or affection from any human creature, and would fain tear from my heart its treacherous sympathies. I am alone. The injustice . . . hopes blasted in the bud, which I have endured, wounding my bosom, have set my thought adrift into an ocean of painful conjectures. I ask impatiently what—and where is truth? I have been treated brutally; but I labour to remember that I still have the duty of a mother to fulfill.
>
> I have written more than I intended—for I only meant to request you to return my letters: I wish to have them, and it must be the same to you. Adieu![22]
>
> Mary

Fuseli refused to return the letters, possibly fearing he would find himself and their former relationship in Mary's next book. However, Mary Hays, the neophyte author Mary Wollstonecraft had once snubbed, did visit her. Miss Hays was by now a disciple of William Godwin, having gotten to know him in 1793 when he responded to her fan letter praising his *Political Justice.* She was an intensely serious woman, rather a climber, and in some ways a less attractive and gifted Mary Wollstonecraft, even having recently been through an unfortunate love affair. She decided to bring her eminent acquaintances together. Although Mary Wollstonecraft had taken a dislike to Godwin when they met in 1792, she must have been interested to see him now, for *Political Justice* catapulted him to instant geniushood in 1793, and his novel *Caleb Williams* was a great artistic and popular success in 1794. As she knew, during the treason trials of 1794 he had risked everything to support his accused friends. Godwin was too thin-skinned not to remember Mary Wollstonecraft's sharp and hostile tongue, but reason, his god, forbade holding grudges, and he wrote to accept Mary Hays' invitation to take tea January 8 with her and "Mrs. Wolstonecraft":

> of whom I know not that I ever said a word of harm, & has frequently amused herself with deprecating me. But I trust you acknowledge in me the reality of a habit upon which I pique myself, that I speak of the qualities of others uninfluenced by personal considerations, & am as prompt to do justice to an enemy as to a friend.[23]

Mary Wollstonecraft's unhappiness was evident on this occasion; Godwin says he felt "sympathy in her anguish," and at the end of the month he was reading *Letters Written . . . in Sweden,* which enchanted him. She left no record of her initial reaction to him, but doubtless was gratified by the concern of a man of his stature. This relationship and any other activity of hers, however, were shoved into the background in February, when Gilbert Imlay returned from Paris.

In his absence Mary had found excuses for his behavior and clung to his earlier disavowal of permanent interest in his mistress. She wrote asking to see him again, reminding him of his former assurances, recalling to him her ideal of his "magnanimity of character":

> As the parting from you forever is the most serious event of my life, I will once expostulate with you . . . I know the soundness of your understanding. . . . You tell me "that I torment you."—Why do I?—Because you cannot estrange your heart entirely from me—and you feel that justice is on my side. . . . When your coolness has hurt me, with what tenderness have you endeavoured to remove the impression. . . .
>
> Imlay, Imlay, believe me, it is not romance, you have acknowledged to me feelings of this kind.—You could restore me to life and hope. . . .
>
> I would owe everything to your generosity—but, for God's sake, keep me no longer in suspence!—Let me see you once more![24]

"With unjustified passion," according to Godwin, Imlay refused to see her, and with passion justified or not, her thirst for justice returned full force. When two weeks had elapsed without a sign of him, she created a scene of melodramatic confrontation that sounds more designed than fortuitous. She went with toddling Fanny to the Christies' one evening when the company included Imlay. When Mrs. Christie heard Mary's voice in the hall, she rushed out of the parlor and begged her not to enter. As Godwin described the episode:

> Mary, however, was not to be controlled. She thought, as she afterwards told me, that it was not consistent with conscious rectitude, that she should shrink, as if abashed, from the presence of one by whom she deemed herself injured. . . . She entered; and in a firm manner, immediately led the child, now near two years of age, to the knees of its father. . . . Mr. Imlay retired with Mary into another apartment, and promised to dine with her at her lodging, I believe, the next day.[25]

Imlay showed up at Mary's the following day. Always susceptible to her and doubtless rueing the embarrassing exposure of the previous night, he was soothing and affectionate, and offered again to support Fanny since Mary would take no money from him for herself. This she was willing to accept. He made a particular point of urging Mary to keep his name. She had a flash of hope. But she was only going through the motions, as was he. She left London the next day to spend the month of March near Sonning, Berkshire, with an old and intimate friend of whom little is known, a Mrs. Cotton. Here, at last, three years after the beginning, she was able to make an end of Imlay. She said later of the heroine of *Maria* that although "stunned by an unexpected blow; yet life, however joyless, was not to be indolently resigned, or misery endured without exertion, and proudly termed patience." Perhaps she was now able to see that she had been her mother's daughter in a way she could not tolerate, and she had come to some sense of the significance of her own life, first articulated in *Letters Written . . . in Sweden:*

> All the world is a stage, thought I, and few are there in it who do not play the part they have learnt by rote; and those who do not, seem marks set up to be pelted at by fortune; or rather as signposts, which point out the road to others, whilst forced to stand still themselves amidst the mud and dust.[26]

The spring season in the countryside and the sympathetic, respectful attentions of Mrs. Cotton and her gentry neighbors were salutary. She had another letter from Imlay, sarcastic on the subject of her ideals and accusing her of sophistry compared with his consistency and forbearance. It seems to have annoyed rather than distressed her, and reinforced her definitive if still oddly incredulous recognition of Imlay's moral and emotional incompatibility. She replied in her last letter to him:

> You must do as you please with respect to the child.—I could wish that it might be done soon, that my name may be no more mentioned to you. It is now finished.—Convinced that you have neither regard nor friendship, I disdain to utter a reproach, though I have reason to think, that the "forbearance" talked of, has not been very delicate.—It is however of no consequence.—I am glad you are satisfied with your own conduct.
>
> I now solemnly assure you, that this is an eternal farewel.—Yet I do not flinch from the duties which tie me to life.
>
> That there is "sophistry" on one side or another, is certain; but now it matters not on which. On my part it has not been a question of words. Yet your understanding or mine must be strangely warped—for what you term "delicacy," appears to me to be exactly the contrary. I have no criterion for morality, and have thought in vain, if the sensations which lead you to follow an ancle[*sic*] or step, be the sacred foundation of principle and affection. Mine has been of a very different nature, or it would not have stood the brunt of your sarcasms.
>
> The sentiment in me is still sacred. If there be any part of me that will survive the sense of my misfortunes, it is the purity of my affections. The impetuosity of your senses, may have led you to term mere animal desire, the source of principle; and it may give zest to some years to come.—Whether you will always think so, I shall never know.
>
> It is strange that, in spite of all you do, something like conviction forces me to believe, that you are not what you appear to be.
>
> I part with you in peace.[27]

And so it ended, as such divorcements are apt to, not on a great chord but with a last irresistible and useless exchange of justification.

V

Home, to Depart No More

Chapter 16

When Mary Wollstonecraft returned to London from Berkshire at the beginning of April, 1796, she was entering her thirty-seventh year, and in some respects it was as if she were starting all over again.

Having disburdened herself of Gilbert Imlay, she was strangely rootless. She was out of touch in every sense with her family: a father in Wales she had not seen in years; Ned, from whom she had completely broken; Everina and Eliza, both governesses in Ireland; James at sea; Charles in America; Henry vanished. Her old social and intellectual circle based on Fuseli and Joseph Johnson had nearly dissolved: the former was estranged from her, the latter unhappily forced by the political climate to curtail his liberal policy and guard his contacts. "Mr. Johnson's house and spirits were so altered," she told Godwin later, "that my visiting him depressed instead of exhilarating my mind."[1]

The current of social progress Mary Wollstonecraft believed ordained was running in reverse. Her compatriots saw progressives as Jacobins, and manifestations of discontent as "the beginning of a General Revolution." As one quite sophisticated and reasonable conservative declared, "it makes one wish for a Military Government, or even Despotism, in preference to such liberty." Religious observance, some hypocritical, some enthusiastic, was much in vogue. These were "prejudices" Mary Wollstonecraft had thought on their way to extinction. "The state of public affairs here [is] not in a posture to assuage private sorrow," she wrote Rowan. "The English seem to have lost the common sense which used to distinguish them."[2]

She felt drained, wasted, futile, and alien. "I wish to leave England forever, yet have not determined where," she wrote Von Schlabrendorf. "What place can please when we are tired of ourselves. . . . Philosophy cannot fill an affectionate human heart."[3] Mary Hays told Godwin Mary seemed in poor health, and that her heart was broken. But Mary Wollstonecraft was detached even from Imlay. Not long after her return she met him riding out on the New Road from London, as she was walking into the city. He got down from his horse and walked with her for a while, and she reported later that she felt little emotion. As far as is known she never saw him again.

Although she still spoke privately as if her life were in ruins, she acted with resolution. Sensibly, her first step, immediately after she got back to London, was to move away from Finsbury Square with its terrible echoes, and to relocate with Fanny and Marguerite in furnished rooms in Pentonville, a suburb at the northern edge of London. She left her furniture in storage, where it had been since late 1792, because she intended to make enough money to settle permanently out of England, preferably on the Continent, where she felt Fanny would be best off. Simultaneously, she took up her London professional life where she had left it almost three and a half years before; she went back to work for Johnson at *The Analytical Review* as reviewer and editorial assistant, producing her first article in the May issue. She also began to work on a substantial new novel.

Because she was famous and since *Letters Written . . . in Sweden*, an interestingly tragic and romantic figure, people sought her out and she began to accept invitations beyond the small group of friends whom she had seen during her mourning period. She and the portrait painter John Opie found much in common; he had been deserted by his wife and was divorcing her. But she also wanted fresh social stimulation. "I like to see new faces, as a study," she said, and became a regular dinner guest at the Francis Twiss's "every third Sunday, nay oftener," she told Godwin, "for they sent for me when they had any extraordinary company."[4] Twiss was a scholar who had formerly loved Mrs. Siddons and married her sister; through him and his wife Mary became friendly with the great actress, the "Tragic Muse," who had been captivated by her book. Mary was back in circulation.

She continued to be known as, and even to sign her personal letters, "Imlay," although Mary Hays urged her to return to "Wollstonecraft," and the general public believed she was married to a man who either had deserted her or hidden a previous marriage from her. Godwin's explanation in the *Memoirs* was that it would have been awkward to change abruptly the title she had used for three years; surely, she was also concerned for Fanny's status. It was an odd situation. She was quite open about her unmarried state with good friends such as Opie, and, although she did not flaunt it for the delectation of the prurient, she deliberately informed at least one person who she knew would spread the truth. Probably she felt she had been Imlay's wife morally, which was all that mattered. At any rate her conventional friends such as the Twisses and their circle pretended they had not heard rather than forgo the pleasure of her company.

As the Imlay trauma lost its power to hurt her, Mary Wollstonecraft was able to build on it. If in modern eyes the Fuseli-Imlay period can be seen as a delayed and protracted identity crisis for Mary, a breaking down of internal and external repressions to a full comprehension of herself, Mary Wollstonecraft then proceeded, as exceptional spirits must, and within the limitations of her insight, to act on this discovery with integrity, initiative, and certainty. This development is quite clear in *Maria,* the novel she was working on at the time. Interpreting the heroine's mistaken confidence in her deceitful lover, Darnford, Mary wrote:

> There are mistakes of conduct which at five-and-twenty prove the strength of the mind, that, ten or fifteen years after, would demonstrate its weakness, its incapacity to acquire a sane judgment. The youths who are satisfied with the ordinary pleasures of life, and do not sigh after ideal phantoms of love and friendships, will never arrive at great maturity of understanding; but if these reveries are cherished, as is too frequently the case with women, when experience should have taught them in what human happiness consists, they become as useless as they are wretched. Besides, their pains and pleasures are so dependent on outward circumstances, on the objects of their affections, that they seldom act from the impulse of a nerved mind, able to choose its own pursuit.[5]

The passage is particularly interesting because Mary Wollstonecraft, in her mid-thirties, is accusing herself of weakness and bad judgment at the same time she identifies herself with twenty-five-year-old Maria, whose naïveté at that age is praiseworthy. In another passage she says that Maria was too inexperienced to realize that Darnford was predominantly interested in varied sexual gratification; in having women rather than a woman. Mary had not acted her age with Imlay and she blamed part of her immaturity on current mores, which limited women's experience, retarded their development, distorted their judgment, and left them unnaturally, sometimes painfully vulnerable. Jane Austen's *Sense and Sensibility*, conceived about this time although not published until later, illustrates through Elinor and Marianne Dashwood alternative reactions of sensitive young gentlewomen to the vulnerability Mary Wollstonecraft described. Elinor protects herself by caution, repression, self-control; Marianne, of "that open, affectionate, and lively manner which it was no merit to possess" (according to the author), rushes into attachment with an attractive, unscrupulous man who leaves her for a wealthy marriage. Overcome by the kind of grief and shame Mary felt over Imlay, Marianne parallels her reaction; she almost dies of a putrid fever and declares that it would have been "self-destruction" had she succumbed. Elinor, momentarily acknowledging the power of passion, and Marianne, who has been punished enough for acting on it, settle down to the safety of sensible marriages. Decent restraint, submission to power, is the lesson.

Mary Wollstonecraft did not retreat from vulnerability into caution, recantation, or misanthropy; she went on to pursue "life and happiness" on realistic but strongly individual terms. As Godwin said rather delicately, "She set a great value on a mutual affection between persons of an opposite sex. She regarded it as the principal solace of human life." In *Maria* Mary was quite frank about the imperative of physical attraction and added the right of sexual love with a chosen man to the other rights of women. It must be noted that Imlay's influence in this respect was crucial and valuable.

> Those who support a system of what I term false refinement, and will not allow great part of love in the female, as well as male breast, to spring in some respects involuntarily, may not admit that charms are . . . necessary to feed the passion. . . . To such observers I have nothing to

> say. When novelists or moralists praise as a virtue, a woman's coldness of constitution, and want of passion, and make her yield to the ardour of her lover out of sheer compassion, or to promote a frigid plan of future comfort, I am disgusted . . . let us not blush for nature!

Her most poignant regret was not the loss of Imlay, but of all the lonely years before him. Maria's advice to young women was to live and love:

> I would then . . . lead you very early in life to form your grand principles of action, to save you from the vain regret of having, through irresolution, let the spring-tide of existence pass away . . . unenjoyed.—Gain experience—ah, gain it—while experience is worth having, and acquire fortitude to pursue your own happiness. . . . What is wisdom too often, but the owl of the goddess who sits moping in a desolated heart. . . . Had I not wasted years in deliberating, after I ceased to doubt, how I ought to have acted—I might now be useful and happy . . . let not [my] example, or the frigid caution of cold-blooded moralists, make you endeavour to stifle hopes . . . to fly from pleasure is not to avoid pain![6]

This was Mary Wollstonecraft's reaction to her own experience with Imlay. She knew she wanted sexual and emotional fulfillment as well as political justice and intellectual freedom, and she intended to lead her future life accordingly. In this integration, she was able to handle old problems—anger, egotism, self-pity—with new grace and more valid compassion for others, and even with that most marvelous of human adaptations, a sense of humor.

William Godwin regulated his days meticulously: serious reading before breakfast, writing from nine to twelve, visits paid or received until dinner. He lived in Somers Town, near Pentonville, in philosophical simplicity and parsimony, with a daily charwoman to clean his lodgings and leave him a mutton chop in a dutch oven. As a bachelor and celebrity he also ate out frequently. His faithful friend, "janitor, or jailor" James Marshal, took care of other practical details. Godwin unfailingly recorded the gist of each day's important events in his journal. On April 14, 1796, he wrote "Wolstonecraft calls." Mary, who had just moved to Pentonville, had walked in on her new neighbor. Spontaneity was not on Godwin's schedule, and he was evidently startled, if pleased, for in the *Memoirs* he defended this "deviation from etiquette" by praising Mary's good instincts and independence; "she had through life trampled on those rules which are built on the imbecility of her sex."[7]

A week later, for the afternoon of April 22, he noted "Imlay calls," believing that to be Mary's due title. Later that same day Mary came to dinner at his "little deserted mansion," as he called it, for a rare party he had been teased into giving by his friends, "a party of twelve persons," he recalled, "the most of whom good-humouredly invited themselves to dine with me, and for whom I ordered provisions from a neighbouring coffee-house."[8] It was a memorable occasion for Mary Wollstonecraft as well as for Godwin, for she saw the philosopher at his best, among some of the most stimulating and impressive of his circle.

The other female celebrity present besides Mary Wollstonecraft was Mrs. Elizabeth Inchbald, a beautiful actress turned playwright and novelist, of whom it was said that when she sat down in the middle of a room "as was her wont," the men deserted all other women and flocked around her. Godwin was taken with her; she knew it and was quite possessive of him. The eminent Dr. Samuel Parr also dined with Godwin that night. He was known as the "Whig Johnson"; a reformer and intellectual churchman, he had hung his portrait of Burke upside down to protest Burke's *Reflections,* the book that Mary Wollstonecraft had answered in *A Vindication of the Rights of Men.* Parr's brilliant protégé, James Mackintosh, was another guest; he, too, had published an answer to Burke, one more thoughtful and solid than Mary's. Thomas Holcroft, Godwin's closest friend, was present, a self-educated, versatile literary man who once memorized Beaumarchais' *Marriage of Figaro* by sitting through four Paris performances, and then translated it and played the barber on the English stage. They were all noted conversationalists: Mrs. Inchbald was "a piquante mixture between a lady and a milkmaid," Parr was magisterial, Mackintosh glittering, Holcroft forceful and literal (Coleridge was once asked "if he was struck *with* him, and he said, he thought himself more in danger of being struck *by* him . . . he would not let me get on at all, for he required a definition of even the commonest word, exclaiming, 'what do you mean by a *sensation,* Sir? What do you mean by an idea?' ").[9]

Godwin himself was at the height of his powers and success, the preeminent radical intellectual of England, and he spoke in his rather thin voice with more authority, confidence, and expansiveness than when Mary Wollstonecraft had first met him as a comparatively obscure man. Standing, he was not impressive; his head was too large for his body, his dress sober. Seated, he had more character: strong hairline, forehead, and chin; large deep-set eyes; an attentive, benign expression. If Southey complained about the length of Godwin's nose, Southey himself had good reason to be sensitive on that point. Northcote painted Godwin in profile, and it is the portrait of a distinguished, masculine intellectual who knows his own worth. In any case, few people bothered about Godwin's appearance at this age; it was sufficient that he was a genius.

Godwin was born in 1754, three years before Mary Wollstonecraft, in Wisbech, the seventh of thirteen children, "the perfect flower," as his biographer, Brown, said, "of a stock devoted for many generations to non-conformity and to moral inculcation." He was sent out to nurse for his first two years, and said he "was brought up in great tenderness. . . . While my mother lived, I always felt to a certain degree as if I had somebody who was my superior, and who exercised a mysterious protection over me. I belonged to something. . . . I hung to something." Godwin felt he was never his father's favorite, a coolness the son returned. Craving distinction almost from the cradle, the child evidently resented his minister-father's scrupulous but modest religious career as much as his "ill-humour and asperity." Literally from his high chair, small William "preached sermons in the kitchen, every Sunday afternoon, and at other times, indifferent to the muster of persons present at these exhibitions, and undisturbed at their coming and going." He was possessed by an ambition to be the great minister and scholar his father was not, to fathom religious truth, to win souls to his own ardent excellence; he stole the key to his father's meetinghouse to preach and pray over less sanctified schoolmates. His precocity developed under exceptional masters. Of himself at eleven he said:

> It was scarcely possible for any preceptor to have a pupil more penetrated with curiosity and a thirst after knowledge. . . . All my amusements were sedentary; I had scarcely any pleasure but in reading; by my own consent, I should sometimes not so much have gone into the streets for

> weeks together. . . . My vocation to literature was decisive. . . . Add to this principle of curiosity a trembling sensibility and an insatiable ambition . . . indescribable anxiety . . . for approbation . . . a nice and delicate feeling, that found no gratification in coarse applause . . . proudly enveloped . . . in the consciousness of his worth.

During his rigorous and profound education, Godwin consumed learning, world literature, theology, and metaphysics with inexorable determination—"indefatigable in my search after truth," famous at Hoxton College "for calm and impassionate discussion . . . for the intrepidity of my opinions and the tranquil fearlessness of my temper."[10] From twenty-two to twenty-seven he oscillated between the ministry and literature; under radical modern influence his severe Calvinism and Tory adherence turned to Unitarianism and Whig advocacy. His religious deconversion disturbed him deeply, but he pursued it with stubborn integrity. By 1787 he was an avowed atheist.

At twenty-seven Godwin decided to gain his fame as a writer while continuing his lifelong schedule of study. He settled in London, producing translations, articles, novels, and biography. He was poor but refused Sheridan's offer to pay him to write for the Whig party; he would be no one's man but his own. While making a place for himself in intellectual London, he chose to confine his private life to a small circle of equally serious-minded colleagues, men like Holcroft, George Dyson, and Marshal, with whom he worked out many of his ideas. The major condition of their association was "Perfect Sincerity" and candor in order better to find "Immutable Truth" and optimum usefulness to mankind. This led to frequent passionate confrontations, raging disputes, and wounded feelings, for Godwin was thin-skinned. "*Démêlé*," his shorthand for such episodes, appears often in his journal. But in the stringent process all were to grow toward disinterested perfection. There is something at once admirable, delightful, and asinine about Godwin's assumption that he could reach absolute dispassionate integrity; he even rejected individual in favor of universal ties of affection.

Godwin's most spontaneous emotion was anger—in all sincerity, of course. He had for several years, when he could hardly support himself, charge of a young cousin, Thomas Cooper. In pursuit of the boy's education Godwin gave himself minute and conscientious instructions on patience and sympathy, qualities which he did not possess. Once young Cooper left out for his mentor to see a memorandum of just grievances:-

He called me	*a foolish wretch*	In my presence
He said	*I had a wicked heart*	ditto . . .
I am called	*a Brute*	in my absence
I am compared to	*a Viper*	ditto . . . etc.

Godwin replied by handing the young man a letter:

> My dear Boy—I am more pleased than displeased with the paper I have just seen. It discovers a degree of sensibility that may be of the greatest use to you, though I will endeavour to convince you that it is wrongly applied . . . I love confidence. . . .
>
> . . . The love of independency and dislike of unjust treatment is the source of a thousand virtues. If while you are necessarily dependent on me I treat you with heaviness and unkindness, it is natural you should have a painful feeling of it.
>
> But harshness and unkindness are relative. . . . In fact, can my conduct to you spring from any but an ardent desire to be of service to you. . . . My time is of the utmost value to me, yet I bestow a large portion of it on your improvement.
>
> . . . I care nothing about myself in this business. If I can make you virtuous and respectable hereafter, I do not care whether I then possess your friendship, I am contented you should hate me. I desire no gratitude, and no return of favors, I only wish to do you good.

In the summer of 1791, "the main crisis of my life," Godwin determined to write a great book that would "place the principles of politics on an immovable basis . . . to tell all that I apprehended to be truth, and all that seemed to be truth, confident that from such a proceeding the best results were to be expected."[11] In early 1793 his *Political Justice* appeared, rocketing him to the preeminence that he had always believed would be his. Beginning with a magnificent indictment of English society as presently constituted—"God himself has not the right to be a tyrant," he had said as a young minister—he demonstrated that economic inequality and exploitation were at the root of social ills. He believed in the tradition of Helvétius and Price that man through reason could approach perfection, equality, and peace. Society corrupts and restricts; Godwin proposed simply to abolish institutions, organizations, contracts, marriage, all coercion. Thus man would be able to be truly and freely moral; morality is reason, vice only error, duty "moral arithmetic." He proceeded with simplistic logic to the edge of unreality. For example, if one were forced to choose between saving the life of one's mother or that of a great and valuable man, one saves the latter. Deifying individuality, and perhaps because of his own phlegmatic integrity, Godwin believed mankind was capable of emulating his own dedication, prudence, rationality, selflessness, and self-control. *Political Justice* was not proscribed during this time of reaction only because, as Pitt is supposed to have observed, radicalism in expensive, heavy volumes could hardly infect the masses.

Illustriously controversial, Godwin was pointed out in the streets, acclaimed, denounced, discipled; with inimitable complacency he asserted fame did not corrupt him, although he admitted with his dense veracity that "the frame of mind in which I found myself exalted my spirits, and rendered me more of a talker than I was before or have been since, and than is agreeable to my natural character." Late in 1794 he produced *Caleb Williams*, a dramatic and powerful novel that further astounded his public. It is a gripping story of psychological conflict, of interchangeable good and evil, of murder, and of nightmare pursuit. Godwin wrote it very fast and in a high state of excitement, propelled for what seems to have been the only time in his life by direct contact with nonconscious sources. It was the implacable pursuer in this book with whom Byron threatened his bride on their honeymoon: "he bade me remember *Caleb Williams* and threatened me I should be miserable for life, and the victim of another Faulkland," poor Annabella testified.[12] The book was also an inspiration for *Frankenstein*.

The following year Godwin was stirred from "fearless tranquility" and distaste for cooperative activity into public defense of Holcroft, Horne Tooke, and other dissidents tried for high treason. It was Godwin whose magnificent appeal helped exculpate the accused; Godwin who, knowing himself a marked man, attended the long trials every day; and Godwin to whose bench Holcroft walked from the dock the moment he was freed. When Horne Tooke discovered who had written the great appeal that he felt had saved his life, the cynical Tooke publicly kissed Godwin's hand in gratitude.

Liberals, the young in particular, were tremendously excited by

Godwin, as they were by the revolution. Coleridge wrote a sonnet to him; Wordsworth enjoined a friend to throw away all his books and read "Godwin on necessity"; Southey said his philosophical principles "form the basis of my character."[13] But Godwin's triumph came at the close of the rationalist-idealist tradition, and his philosophy had little practical relevance for the nineteenth century. He had peaked too late for his time and too early for his own good. Conservatives denounced him, and he would not make common cause with dissident activists who were attempting to organize the working class. He even rebuked them for stirring passions instead of allowing reason to do their work. Having incurred animosity from the left as well as the right, his logic caught between upheaval and reaction, Godwin's subsequent career amounted to reiteration, revision, and living off his reputation—although it was years before this was apparent.

But from the beginning there was something terribly sad about Godwin; he structured his life with methodical industry and rationalized candor in lieu of trusting himself. "One of the leading passions of my mind has been an anxious desire not to be deceived," he said. "This has led me to view the topics of my reflection on all sides; and to examine and re-examine without end, the questions that interest me." He moved slowly, chewing over problems until he could digest them, fueling himself for ponderous progression, which rolled on in the names of reason and truth. "Ductility is a leading feature of my mind," he said. This basic uncertainty drove him to behavior almost compulsively systematic, following logic on a plank so straight and narrow he could walk it over the brink of common sense without hesitation. Southey later said, "Godwin is always exposing himself in a posture which says 'come kick me!' "[14]

With all his sobriety Godwin adored the stimulus of London and intellectual society, but his instinctual life was almost atrophied. For forty years he believed, as he read in Jonathan Edwards and discussed with his friend Fawcet, that affection and love were irrelevant and passion mankind's passing phase. He was like a large body of water that imagines itself a broad and majestic river, but whose waters in reality are dammed, tepid, stagnant, and shallow. He did not want to be touched; when he was a boy, his tutor's flogging of his "sacred person" appalled him; as a philosopher he could not abide the thought of coercion or community. He was less an anarchist than an emotional stylite. At such distance he could follow another beat only when he saw someone to lead him; it is no wonder he found Mary Wollstonecraft attractive. Success had relaxed his guard to the point of permitting him to admire women and enjoy their admiration in return and to become receptive to the concept that feeling had value. It is interesting that *Letters Written . . . in Sweden* captivated him. "Anything which excites emotions, has charms for me,"[15] Mary Wollstonecraft had written, the antithesis of Godwin's rationality, but a view he pondered as a new truth to be taken into consideration. In his youth he had begun a play about Iphigenia; Mary, another noble victim, had living charm, splendid courage, and intuitive insight that amazed him. She offered her own certainty without threatening his, and showed him the possibility of verities long denied.

On her side, Mary Wollstonecraft admired Godwin's persistent truth seeking, courageous integrity, and the artless sincerity that enabled him to qualify and modify his concepts no matter how laboriously constructed. His moral and political values were entirely compatible with hers. And he was a genius. Mackintosh, even when he recanted liberalism, asserted that Godwin "deserved the respect of all those . . . who still wish that some men in England may think for themselves, even at the risk of thinking wrong; but more especially of the friends of liberty, to whose cause he has courageously adhered." Holcroft said simply: "He is beyond his age."[16]

Moreover, Godwin was at this time admired by several unusual women: Mrs. Inchbald, Maria Reveley, the beautiful Mary "Perdita" Robinson, and charming Amelia Alderson, who "found him indeed eloquent, entertaining and luminous in argument . . . every day passed with him has endeared him to me more strongly." He had the attraction for Mary Wollstonecraft of being, as Southey saw him, "a good creature—brimful of benevolence—as kind-hearted as a child could wish," a man of benign dependability, a quality that she now chose over the excitement of her father and Imlay and the selfishness of Fuseli. She also realized Godwin was interested in exploring the charms of aesthetic and personal expression, even of love, and she was ready to help him. She wanted an honorable successor to Imlay. "If still these appetites continue strong, / Thou mayest consider, I am yet but young: / Consider too, that having been a wife, / I must have tasted of a better life. . . . I pleased myself, I shunn'd Incontinence, / And, urg'd by Strong Desires, indulg'd my sense."[17] These are lines from Dryden's *Guiscard and Sigismunda,* to which Mary had the unhappily married heroine of *Maria* turn when attracted by another man. Mary did not want to live celibate.

Mary Wollstonecraft and Godwin saw each other frequently from the date of Godwin's dinner party through early summer of 1796. From April 29 on he referred to her in his journal as "Wolstencraft." She had set him straight on Imlay, and Godwin, who had denounced marriage in *Political Justice* as "an affair of property, and the worst of all properties," must have found her even more interesting in consequence. On May 13 Mary wrote Von Schlabrendorf a letter about Imlay's desertion in the old self-pitying tone, but probably it was only to bring him up to date, since he had not received, or replied to, a similar letter she had sent him several months before. During this period Godwin was courting Amelia Alderson by mail in Norfolk; he was apparently on the verge of a serious attachment to a woman. However, the only information about his developing relationship with Mary is general and comes from the *Memoirs:*

> It grew with equal advances in the mind of both. It would have been impossible for the most minute observer to have said who was before, and who was after. One sex did not take the priority which long-established custom has awarded it, nor the other overstep that delicacy which is so severely imposed. I am not conscious that either party can assume to have been the agent or the patient, the toil-spreader or the prey. . . . When, in the course of things, the disclosure came, there was nothing, in a manner, for either party to disclose to the other.[18]

Mary Wollstonecraft, with her gift for intimacy, was aware that Godwin found it difficult to trust and articulate his feelings. She seems to have been tactful, receptive, and helpful because she was truly fond of him. In late June, he sent her a somewhat laborious poem of admiration—a good try, but hardly the production of a Rousseau (that "true Prometheus of sentiment," who, Mary wrote in *Maria,* "possessed the fire of genius necessary to portray the passion, the truth of which goes directly to the heart"). She replied July 1 with perception, encouragement, and gaiety, which covered a concern for emotional veracity, and sent with her letter a volume of Rousseau's glorification of passion as an example:

> I send you the last volume of "Héloise" . . . you may chance to wish for it. You may perceive by this remark that I do not give you credit for as much philosophy as our friend, and I want besides to remind you, when you write to me in *verse*, not to choose the easiest task, my perfections, but to dwell on your own feelings—that is to say, give me a bird's eye view of your heart. Do not make me a desk "to write upon," I humbly pray—unless you honestly acknowledge yourself *bewitched*. . . . I think I observe that you compliment without rhyme or reason, when you are almost at the loss what to say.

Godwin left London at the beginning of July for a three-week visit to his mother in Norfolk, during which he also spent time with Amelia Alderson. In his absence Mary Wollstonecraft retrieved her stored furniture and moved closer to his home, to 16 Judd Place in Somers Town itself, "probably without exactly knowing why," Godwin said in the *Memoirs*—but one wonders. On July 13 Godwin wrote her from Norfolk; it was a reply to her letter of July 1, and it was one of incipient commitment. What it lacked of Rousseau's poetry, it made up for in self-consciously humorous but unmistakable intent to meet her standards of feeling, facetiously calling to witness all the gods in whom he did not believe:

> that your company infinitely delights me, that I love your imagination, your delicate epicurism, the malicious leer of your eye, in short every thing that constitutes the bewitching tout ensemble of the celebrated Mary. . . .
>
> . . . Shall I write a love letter? May Lucifer fly away with me, if I do! No, when I make love, it shall be with the eloquent tones of my voice, with dying accents, with speaking glances (through the glass of my spectacles) with all the witching of that irresistible, universal passion. . . . When I make love, it shall be in a storm, as Jupiter made love to Semele, & turned her at once to a cinder. Do not these menaces terrify you?
>
> . . . Shall I send you an eulogium of your beauty, your talents & your virtues? Ah! that is an old subject; beside, if I were to begin, instead of a sheet of paper, I should want a ream.

Shall I write to citizeness Wolstonecraft a congratulatory epistle upon the victories of Buonaparti? . . .

Cause Margaret [Marguerite] to drop a line into my letter box, signifying to the janitor, or jailor, Mr. Marshal, that I expect to arrive on this day sevenight at seven o'clock in the morning, to depart no more. . . .

Your admirer,
W Godwin

Oddly enough, three days before this letter was written, Godwin proposed to Amelia Alderson; she was an irresistible coquette, "a bitch," Godwin once told her, and apparently he was swept off his feet on this occasion. Amelia Alderson was not, however; she refused Godwin, but with enough affection and respect to sustain their mutual regard. Godwin returned to Somers Town about July 20, and Mary Wollstonecraft made it clear she had expected him to call on her immediately:

Had you called . . . yesterday I should have thanked you for your letter —and—perhaps, have told you that the sentence I *liked* best was the concluding one, where you tell me, that you were coming home, to depart *no more*—But now I am out of humour I mean to bottle up my kindness, unless something in your countenance, when I do see you, should make the cork fly out—whether I will or not.—

Mary—[19]

Absence had clarified the feelings of both. "We met again with new pleasure," he said, "with a more decisive preference for each other . . . each felt half-assured, yet each felt a certain trembling anxiety to have assurance complete. . . . It was friendship melting into love." Godwin now read her *Mary;* "the feelings are of the truest and most exquisite class," he said. She considered it a crude production, but doubtless, as with all her loves, encouraged his interest in her youthful miseries. Her early August notes to him, gay and provocative, indicate the degree of their intimacy and her confidence, even when Mrs. Inchbald or the visiting Amelia Alderson interposed.

I suppose you mean to drink tea with me, *one* of these days. How can you find in your heart to let me pass so many evenings alone—you may saucily ask, why I do not send for Mr. Twiss—but I shall reply with dignity in silence—so mum.

> . . . you have been dining, I suppose, with Mrs. Perfection [Inchbald], and comparisons are odious.
>
> I spent the evening with Mademoiselle Alderson—you, I'm told, were ready to devour her—in your little parlour. . . .
>
> Miss Alderson was wondering, this morning whether you *ever* kissed a maiden fair—As you do not like to solve problems *on paper*, TELL her. . . .
>
> I supped in company with Mrs. Siddons, last night. When shall I tell you what I think of her?
>
> Won'tee, as Fannikin would say, come and see me today? and I will go home with you to hear your essays. . . . I called on you yesterday, in my way to dinner, not for Mary—but *to bring* Mary—
>
> Is it necessary to tell your sapient Philosophership that I mean MYSELF.

On Saturday August 13, Godwin and Mary exchanged a declaration of love and probably their first passionate embraces; "you set my imagination on fire," he wrote her. "For six & thirty hours I could think of nothing else. I longed inexpressibly to have you in my arms." But he was too unsure of himself to follow through immediately. "Why did I not come to you?" he wrote. "I feared still that I might be deceiving myself as to your feelings & that I was feeding my mind with groundless presumptions. I determined to suffer the point to arrive at its own denouement."

Monday evening "chez moi" according to his journal, they had an unsatisfactory meeting during which Godwin did not consummate the affair. "The fervour of my imagination was exhausting itself," he wrote her. "Yet this, I believe, is no uncommon case." Tuesday morning she sent him one of her usual brief notes with the newspaper, via Fanny and her nurse; "*Entre nous*, did you feel very lonely last night?" She was too pert. Godwin sent back a reply significant for their future, completely candid and with a legitimate demand for consideration.

> I have been very unwell all night. You did not consider me enough in that way yesterday, & therefore unintentionally impressed upon me a mortifying sensation. When you see me next; will you condescend to take me for better for worse, that is, be prepared to find me, as it shall happen, full of gaiety & life, or a puny valetudinarian?

That night Godwin decisively but briefly took her to bed, probably at his house, but after that "furtive pleasure," as he described it, Mary Wollstonecraft was confused and frightened. In the morning she wrote him:

> I have not lately passed so painful a night as the last. I feel that I cannot speak clearly on the subject to you, let me then briefly explain myself now I am alone. Yet, struggling as I have been a long time to attain peace of mind (or apathy) I am afraid to trace emotions to their source, which borders on agony. . . . Mortified and humbled, I scarcely know why—still, despising false delicacy I almost fear that I have lost sight of the true. Could a wish have transported me to France or Italy, last night, I should have caught up my Fanny and been off in a twinkle, though convinced that it is my mind, not the place, which requires changing. My imagination is for ever betraying me into fresh misery, and I perceive that I shall be a child to the end of the chapter. . . .
>
> I would not be unjust for the world—I can only say that you appear to me to have acted injudiciously; and that full of your own feelings, little as I comprehend them, you forgot mine—or do not understand my character. It is my turn to have a fever today—I am not well —I am hurt—But I mean not to hurt you. Consider what has passed as a fever of your imagination . . . and I—will become again a *Solitary Walker*. Adieu! I was going to add God bless you!—

At one that afternoon Godwin left at her house a reply perfect in its artless devotion and reassurance:

> I had rather at this moment talk to you on paper. . . . I should feel ashamed in seeing you.
>
> You do not know how honest I am. I swear to you that I told you nothing but the strict & literal truth. . . .
>
> . . . nothing that I have seen in you would in the slightest degree authorize the opinion that, *in despising the false delicacy, you have lost sight of the true.* I see nothing in you but what I respect & adore.
>
> I know the acuteness of your feelings, & there is perhaps nothing upon earth that would give me so pungent a remorse, as to add to your unhappiness.
>
> Do not hate me. Indeed I do not deserve it. Do not cast me off. Do not become again a *solitary walker*. . . .
>
> . . . I find in you one fault, & but one. You have the feelings of

> nature, & you have the honesty to avow them. In all this you do well. I am sure you do. But do not let them tyrannize over you. . . .
>
> Suffer me to see you. Let us leave every thing else to its own course. . . .
>
> Be happy. Resolve to be happy. You deserve to be so. Every thing that interferes with it, is weakness & wandering; & a woman, like you can, must, shall, shake it off. . . .
>
> . . . Do you not see, while I exhort you to be a philosopher, how painfully acute are my own feelings? I need some soothing, though I cannot ask it from you.

They were feeling each other out with awkwardness understandable in new lovers, Mary remembering the adroit Imlay, Godwin clumsy in his inexperience and self-doubt. At two that afternoon Mary composed a letter assuring him he had "calmed my mind . . . haunted by old sorrows," and routed her fears, and asked him to come to four-thirty dinner *à deux*, for she had arranged to have Fanny out of the house, and "you ought to come and give me an appetite for my dinner, as you deprived me of one for my breakfast." She took the letter to him at three o'clock. Godwin was so overwhelmed to see her happy and loving that he did not immediately understand her "plan for staying, which it was morally impossible should not have given life to the dead," as he wrote hastily just after she left him. He then came to her house, but they could not make love because Mary Hays arrived, having been previously invited to spend the evening with Mary.

Next day, Thursday the eighteenth, Godwin came to Mary's again, but the presence of Marguerite in the next room upset and inhibited him. However, Mary told him later that she had taken her maid into her confidence, and that night he noted in his journal that he had stayed "chez elle." Mary felt the need to test Godwin again Friday and sent him a fable comparing herself to a sycamore whose early buds were shriveled by frost. Godwin was annoyed and hurt at the manipulation and again demanded attention for his own needs; "I need soothing, & you threaten me," he replied in a stiff note. Three days later she was still apologizing to him for her involuntary reaction: "I am sometimes painfully humble—Write me, but a line, just to assure me, that you have been thinking of me with affection, now and then—Since we parted."

Godwin was beginning to understand as well; he immediately

replied: "Humble! for heaven's sake, be proud, be arrogant! You are—but I cannot tell what you are. I cannot yet find the circumstance about you that allies you to the frailty of our nature. I will hunt it out."[20]

From this time on the lovers settled into a relationship that satisfied both. Neither wanted wedlock, he out of philosophical aversion, "she felt she had been too much, and too rudely spoken of" over Imlay, whose name she still used. In addition, both had financial problems. Godwin made just enough to live on. He was working on *The Enquirer*, a book of essays, a dramatization of *Caleb Williams*, and his usual course of study. Mary was struggling to sustain herself and Marguerite and Mary, the two servants necessary to her professional life, as well as Fanny, for whom Imlay never provided the support he had offered; in fact Mary was still paying off his debts. Johnson regularly advanced her funds. Having made contact with her family, she was sending her father money, trying to make Charles contribute from America, and worrying about her sisters' positions. She had resumed correspondence with Everina, but not with Eliza, who was still offended. "I must reckon on doing some good, and getting the money I want by my writings," Mary told Godwin. "I shall not be content merely to keep body and soul together."[21] She had no desire to draw Godwin into her obligations.

Two such divergent personalities inevitably had their differences. Mary insisted on the value of imagination, immediacy, and her particular form of religious devotion; Godwin on organization, self-control, and reason. At times he seems to have been afraid of her intensity. Both found criticism, which in perfect sincerity they were bound to offer, hard to accept, but after some reassurance she agreed to take his instruction in grammar and structure, and he—"this boy-pupil," as he said—to take lessons in emotion. Always susceptible, sometimes irritable and depressed, she could express herself freely, fortified by his dependability; he was often obtuse, but so completely sure of his feelings and ideals that he refused to coddle her. This honesty, so different from Imlay's pliancy, she could meet with her own. Their relationship combined passion, companionship, domestic pleasure, and mutual respect. Living in close proximity, although not in the same house, they shared books, papers, and tasks; dropped in at odd times; and sent frequent notes:

Mary: Should the weather continue uncertain *suppose* you were to bring your tragedy here—and we shall be so snug—yet, you are such a kind creature, that I am afraid to express a preference, lest you should think of pleasing me rather than yourself—and is it not the same thing?

Godwin: Your proposal meets with the wish of my heart: I called at half after two yesterday to obtain this point from you.

Mary: As you are to dine with Mrs. Perfection today, it would be dangerous, not to remind you of my existence . . . take care not to look over your left shoulder—I shall be there. . . .

Godwin: I will report my fealty this evening. . . .

Mary: Give Fanny a biscuit—I want you to love each other. . . .

I send you a family present [her Bible?], given me, when I was let loose in the world . . . return it—I do not intend to let you extend your skepticism to me—or you will fright away a poor weary bird who, taking refuge in your bosom, hoped to nestle there—to the end of the chapter.

Mary: I seem to want encouragement—I therefore send you my MS [*Maria*].

Mary: Labouring all the morning, in vain, to overcome an oppression of spirits, which some things you uttered yesterday, produced . . . you remarked, relative to my manner of writing—that there was a radical defect in it. . . . I must either disregard your opinion, think it unjust, or throw down my pen in despair; and that would be tantamount to resigning existence; for at fifteen I resolved never to marry for interested motives, or to endure a life of dependence . . . I have even now plans at heart, which depend on my exertions. . . . By what I have already written Johnson, I am sure, has been a gainer. . . . I am compelled to think that there is something in my writings more valuable, than in the productions of some people on whom you bestow warm eulogiums—I mean more mind—denominate it as you will—more of the observations of my own senses, more of the combining of my own imagination—the effusions of my own feelings and passions than the cold workings of the brain. . . .

I am more out of patience with myself than you can form any idea of . . . have scarcely written a line to please myself . . . since you saw my MS.

Mary: I would leave you a God bless you—did you care for it; but, alas!

you do not, though Sterne says that it is equivalent to a—kiss. [Mary was here repeating the very phrase as well as the benediction she used with Imlay.]

Mary: . . . You are to give me a lesson this evening. . . . I shall not be very angry if you sweeten grammatical disquisitions. . . .

Mary: Fanny was so importunate with her "go this way Mama, me wants to see Man." . . .

I wanted to tell you that I felt as if I had not done justice to your essay. . . . You are a tender considerate creature; but, entre nous, do not make too many philosophical experiments. . . . I shall come to you tonight, probably before nine. . . .

Godwin: . . . as you once said, I shall cork up my heart; to see whether it will fly out ce soir at sight of you.

Mary: . . . after finishing your essays . . . sensations . . . have been clustering round my heart . . . reminding myself, every now and then, that the writer *loved* me. . . . Voluptuous is often expressive of a meaning I do not now intend. . . . I would describe one of those moments, when the senses are exactly tuned by the rising tenderness of the heart, and according reason entices you to live in the present moment. . . . It is not rapture.—It is a sublime tranquility. I have felt it in your arms. . . .

Mary: . . . Looking over some of your essays, this morning, reminds me that the one I most earnestly wished you to alter . . . was that on Public and private Education—I wanted you to recommend, *Day* Schools. [Godwin added a last paragraph in response.]

Mary: You tell me, William, that you augur nothing good, when the paper has not a note, or, at least, Fanny to wish you a good morning—

Now by these presents let me assure you that you are not only in my heart, but my veins, this morning. I turn from you half-abashed . . . some look, word or touch thrills through my whole frame. . . . When the heart and reason accord there is no flying from voluptuous sensations, I find, do what a woman can—Can a philosopher do more?

Godwin: I have been a prisoner all this morning—If I do not hear from you, I shall expect you to tea. Dyson . . . would probably stay with me alone till midnight. . . .

Mary: Poor Fannikin has the chicken-pox—which I am glad of—as I know what is the matter with her. Business takes me to Mr. Johnson's today. . . .

Mary: . . . Why could you not say *how de ye do* this morning? It is I who want nursing first, you perceive.

Mary: . . . Though I am not quite satisfied with myself, for acting such a mere Girl, yesterday—yet I am better—What did you do to me? . . .

Godwin: Will you do me the favor to send Caleb Williams to Mr. Stoddart. . . .

Adorable maîtresse! J'espère que vous êtes plus gaie ce matin!

Mary: . . . I am glad to discover great powers of mind in you, even at my own expense. . . .

You do not know how much I admired your self-government last night. . . . I am glad that you force me to love you more and more, in spite of my fear of being pierced to the heart by every one on whom I rest my mighty stock of affection.

Mary: I was vext, last night, to hear the rain patter. . . . Did he get wet? poor fellow. . . .

Will you give Mary the coat you mentioned, for her boy . . . and the corn plaster, for me. . . .

Godwin: . . . The rain fell, but did not wet me; I wore a charmed skin. . . .

Mary: . . . you damped my spirits last night. . . .

Can you solve this problem? I was endeavouring to discover last night, in bed, what it is in me, of which you are afraid. I was hurt at perceiving that you were . . . mine is a sick heart; and in a life, like this, the fortitude of patience is the most difficult to acquire.

Godwin: Mr. Allen has been with me; Mr. Carlisle is coming. . . . I wish you did not dine at Mr. Johnson's. . . .

Mary: Mrs. Cotton comes tomorrow. . . . She talks of a *few* days. Mon Dieu! Heaven and Earth.

Mary: I send you your household linen—I am not sure that I did not feel a sensation of pleasure at thus acting the part of a wife, though you have so little respect for the character. There is such magic in affection.

Mary: . . . should you . . . *think* of inquiring for the fourth act of Mrs. Inc's comedy—why it would be a pretty mark of attention.—And—entre nous, *little* marks of attention are incumbent on you at present. . . .

Godwin: . . . I am glad to hear how enchanting and divine you will appear this evening.—You spoil little attentions by anticipating them.

Mary: I wish you would always take my ye for a ye; and my nay for a nay . . . that you could distinguish between jest and earnest . . . when I am really hurt or angry I am dreadfully serious. Still allow me a little more tether. . . . Let me, I pray thee! have a sort of *comparative* freedom, as you are a profound Grammarian, to run round, as good, better, best;—cheerful, gay, playful; nay even frolicksome, once a year—or so. . . . Send me a *bill of rights*—to this purport. . . .

. . . I hate to disguise any feeling, when writing or conversing, with you, cher ami.

Godwin: I can send you a bill of rights. . . . But . . . how can I distinguish always between your jest & earnest. . . . But I will try. . . .

Mary: . . . Our *sober* evening was very delicious—I do believe you love me better than you imagined you should—as for me—judge for yourself.[22]

Beloved, secure, relaxed, Mary Wollstonecraft was at her most delightful. Her liaison with Godwin was their secret, but she joined his circle of friends: the Fenwicks; Dyson, brilliant and violent, with whom she argued about *Maria;* dull Marshal, who fell asleep one night when Coleridge recited; Holcroft, who invited her to dinner; Carlisle, the eminent physician and medical reformer (who had a plan "for knocking up the rascally exorbitance of physicians, surgeons, and apothecaries by combining with a physician of known skill to receive small fees, and a druggist to administer prescriptions, pure and at a just price"); Basil Montagu, with whom she and Godwin took an excursion to her childhood home, Barking ("You, Mrs. Imlay, and Basil Montagu in the same post chaise!" the irrepressible Amelia Alderson wrote Godwin, "How I envy the horses . . . two Antonys and a Cleopatra"). Mary also continued her own life in society as Mrs. Imlay, and was much in demand. She was engagingly animated, expressive, and responsive while projecting her normal sense of superiority, as Southey saw:

> Of all the [countenances of] lions or *literati* that I have seen here . . . Mary Imlay's is the best, infinitely the best; the only fault in it is an expression . . . indicating superiority; not haughtiness, not sarcasm in Mary Imlay, but still it is unpleasant. Her eyes are light brown, and, though the lid of one of them is affected by a little paralysis, they are the most meaning I ever saw.

She intrigued Hazlitt, who told of a dinner given her, Curran, Sheridan, and Mrs. Inchbald by John Kemble, "when the discourse almost wholly turned on Love. . . . What a subject! What Speakers, and what would I not give to have been there." Opie visited and took her around frequently enough to stir rumor that they might marry. "But you are the man," she told Godwin.[23] Opie later married Amelia Alderson.

For the first time in her adult life, Mary enjoyed women friends as equals. In 1789 she had reviewed one of Mrs. Inchbald's plays with asperity ("insipid dialogue . . . uninteresting charicatures . . . childish tricks"); now she could say of her rival in Godwin's admiration: "we had less wit and more cordiality—and if I do not admire her more I love her better—She is a charming woman!" Mary Hays, lugubrious and clinging after her unfortunate love affair, mocked by Amelia Alderson as old, ugly, and ill-bred, was treated by Mary with sympathy and tact, for Mary realized Godwin's frustrated "Aide de Camp" envied her: "She has owned to me," Mary wrote Godwin, "that she cannot see others enjoy mutual affection from which she is disbarred—I will write her a kind note to day to ease my conscience, for when I am happy myself, I am made of milk and honey, I would fain make everybody else so." Amelia Alderson, who had imagined Mary awesome, found her "so capable of feeling affection that you cannot fail to excite it," and felt free to write her of compliments Mary Wollstonecraft would have scorned in former days: "Warren Browne . . . talked in a very warm manner of you. . . . 'She is a very voluptuous looking woman.' I stared! not that I disputed the propriety of that epithet as applied to you. . . . I can see you blush at this distance n'importe—a blush is very becoming."[24] Another woman Godwin loved, Maria Reveley, became Mary's friend. Perdita Robinson was another; formerly notorious as the mistress of the

Prince of Wales, of Fox, and of Tarleton, she was now partially paralyzed, deserted with hardly a penny, and supporting herself and a fatherless daughter by her pen. She was a fervent liberal who shared Mary's interest in women's emancipation.

Mary Wollstonecraft had apparently decided not to write a second volume of *A Vindication of the Rights of Woman,* but she was pursuing the subject in another form. From sometime in the spring of 1796 until her death, she worked on a major book, *The Wrongs of Woman: Or, Maria,* a novel intended to dramatize the effects of social mores and legal restrictions on her sex. Her decision to use fiction probably came from her need to incorporate her experience with Imlay. His influence is evident throughout.

The book opens with a young wife, Maria Venables, imprisoned in an insane asylum by her evil husband. Maria gains the sympathy of her hard-hearted warder, Jemima, and through her makes contact with another prisoner, Henry Darnford, who, although the *déjà connu* is never fully developed, has rescued her once before. They fall in love and meet secretly. Jemima then tells the story of her life. Born the bastard child of working-class parents, she had been brought up in torment, and as girl and woman had been seduced, exploited, and brutalized.

Maria gives Darnford a memoir of her own life, which she is writing for her baby daughter. The basic family situation of *Mary* is repeated in Maria's girlhood, but there are significant changes. The paternal figure is split between a father who is as much a victim of his own weakness as he is a tyrant and a benign uncle. The favored older brother remains a rapacious, dishonest ingrate.

In *A Vindication of the Rights of Woman* Mary Wollstonecraft had addressed women's condition with anger for the victims and compensatory but contemptuous sympathy; in *Maria* she achieved empathy and compassion. Maria's feeling for her mother, although critical of her "indolence" and favoritism, is distinctly more loving and sympathetic. At her mother's death, Maria's "tears of affection . . . bedewed my mother's grave." As has been noted, Maria specifically identifies with her mother when she later attempts suicide. Maria has two sisters whose predicament is recognized as well as the heroine's own. Their wicked brother has usurped the settlement made on them by their mother, leaving them penniless. The younger, like Everina, has sufficient abilities for any profession, "had there been any profession for women, though she shrank at the name of milliner or mantua-maker as degrading to a gentlewoman." This is "false pride," Maria believes, for independence outweighs caste. She finds her sisters jobs as governesses. The younger dies.

In the novel Mary Wollstonecraft made some reparation to her own sister, for she put Maria in Eliza's position, much exaggerated, that of a dreadfully unhappy wife married very young to a repulsive man, a repository of all male villainies. Maria has submitted dutifully to Venables' petty and grand tyrannies, including his adulteries, which have not prevented his enjoying "the smiles of the world." She has remained faithful to him although tempted by other men. Told she will inherit her uncle's estate, she finds her husband suddenly more attentive, for Venables is a swindler in danger of exposure and needs his wife's money. She becomes pregnant by him. Venables tries to sell Maria to a wealthy friend in order to get cash, as did the husband of Imlay's character Eliza in *The Emigrants.* Maria then revolts and announces that she is leaving him forever and will provide for herself and her unborn child. Venables locks her in her room. She escapes and hides, like Eliza Bishop. She bears a daughter, who, according to her uncle's will, has been left the greater portion of his money to keep it out of Venables' hands. Venables kidnaps the baby and puts Maria into the insane asylum —where the book opens.

After Darnford's sympathetic reaction to this memoir, he and Maria become lovers, escape from the asylum with Jemima's assistance, and live together. Venables pursues them and sues Darnford for seduction and adultery. (Mary was quite familiar with the process of such trials through John Opie's experience; he sued his wife's lover in the spring of 1796.) Darnford has to leave England on business, and Maria goes into court to argue her right to get a divorce and live as she pleases: "born a woman,—and born to suffer, in endeavouring to repress emotions . . . she only felt in earnest to insist on the privilege of her nature. The sarcasms of society, and the condemnation of a mistaken world, were nothing to her, compared with acting contrary to these feelings which were the foundation of her principles."[25] The judge rejects her argument and upholds her husband's right to her body, child, and property.

Maria's story is told in two volumes, of which only the first was completed. Mary Wollstonecraft left notes for a third volume in which Darnford deceives Maria and leaves her; she attempts suicide and either dies or is saved by Jemima, who brings in Maria's child lisping " 'Mama!' " There is no indication that Mary would have taken Maria on to the kind of happiness she herself was finding with Godwin. Her design, as Godwin pointed out, was to make her story subordinate to a great moral purpose that both he and Mary were convinced the work would impress on the world. However, Godwin's friend Dyson read the book in manuscript and told Mary her heroine's husband was not despicable enough to excuse Maria's behavior, criticism Mary was upset over; and when the book was published posthumously, it had little impact except as another reason to condemn Mary Wollstonecraft. The reactionary *Anti-Jacobin Review* damned the work and its author as subversive of morality.

To the modern reader *Maria* is melodramatic, wildly improbable, and, despite all the lurid episodes, downright dull. There is a curious and fundamental illogicality about it. As Imlay had, Mary Wollstonecraft ardently espoused woman's right to love and her right to divorce. But she and her heroine were seen as cruelly martyred victims of men who claimed equivalent freedom of action. However, *Maria* has its interesting features. Jemima represents the first serious treatment of a proletarian woman of the time, and there are other secondary female characters, working women, almost all victims of men and society, whose misfortunes complement the heroine's. Mary Wollstonecraft attempted to take her old sense of injustice beyond parental failings, to cross class lines and expose the real evils of the double standards in economic power, legal rights, personal development, and sexual freedom imposed on all women. It was a grand and worthy effort made in the wrong form. Fiction was not Mary's *métier*, but she required its use so as to include another case she wanted to make, the rationale for her relationship with Imlay and with Godwin. Godwin's presence and advice may have drained from the work its drive and spontaneity, Mary's primary assets; it was the only book she ever struggled over, rewrote, and tried to structure. In fact, it might be argued that *Maria*'s artificiality is due partly to the fact that Mary was forcing her issues, pushing herself to express vehement indignation during the very time she was enjoying substantial private happiness with Godwin.

There was one serious threat to Mary Wollstonecraft's contentment in her liaison with Godwin—pregnancy. Married women could and did pass off illegitimate children on complacent or unknowing husbands; unmarried women risked complete and shameful ostracism. Godwin and Mary must have worried about this possibility and perhaps even attempted within the limits of their insufficient knowledge to prevent conception. But some four months after they became lovers, Mary's notes to Godwin indicate that she feared she might be pregnant. On December 6, 1796 she wrote Godwin she felt "extreme lowness of spirits . . . torpor of mind and senses." On the seventh she castigated him for obtaining wretched theater seats for her while he and Mrs. Inchbald enjoyed the best. "I am determined to return to my former habits, and go by myself and shift for myself," she wrote him. "I was a fool not to ask Opie to go with me." On the twelfth she told Godwin her cold and cough were worse: "The dress of women seems to be invented to render them dependent, in more senses than one." Next day she was annoyed because he had left her for supper at Mrs. Reveley's: "that looks so much like indifference, I do not like it." "I do not intend to *peck* you," she concluded. Godwin was not helpful: "I feared Cupid had taken his final farewell," he replied facetiously. Mary was hiding her need behind pride: "If you intend to call say when, because I do not wish you to come, at the moment of dinner, when you do not dine with me," she wrote him on December 18.

Counting from a September 29 note to Godwin hinting at her menstruation, Mary Wollstonecraft had missed her late November period. Her fear of a second illegitimate child, of social disgrace and isolation, was heightened by Godwin's reluctance and denseness. Just before Christmas he seemed to accept the possibility of a child, which might open "your heart, to a new-born affection. . . . There are other pleasures in the world, you perceive, beside those known to your philosophy." But on December 28, when she must have been almost certain of her condition, she wrote him, "I dare say you are out of patience with me."[26] By December 31 there was no question about her pregnancy, yet no answer that easily met it. Marriage was the logical course, but Mary hated the idea of forcing Godwin to abandon his public position and private convictions against it, particularly since she knew how important intellectual consistency was to him. Godwin wanted to behave well, but was too honest to make an unconstrained offer of marriage and too limited and unworldly to understand what Mary faced. In the *Memoirs* he wrote that Mary "was unwilling, and perhaps with reason," to be an outcast. As for her, she believed marriage "as presently constituted" unjust toward women; "with proper restrictions, however, I revere the institution which fraternizes the world." She had had enough of the "odium of society" and feared its effect on her children. She wanted security and permanence, and when, at the New Year of 1797, Godwin still held back only out of principle, she retreated into coldness:

Godwin: You treated me last night with extreme unkindness . . . You wished we had never met; you wished you could cancel all that had passed between us. Is this . . . not the language of frigid, unalterable indifference? . . .

Mary: This does not appear to me just the moment to have written me such a note. . . . I am, however, prepared for anything. I can abide by the consequence of my own conduct, and do not wish to involve anyone in my difficulties.

. . . You do not, I think make sufficient allowance for the peculiarity of my situation. But women are born to suffer. . . . You must have patience with me, for I am sick at heart. . . .[27]

The difficulty Mary Wollstonecraft most hated to involve Godwin in was her perennial lack of money. "All the tradesmen send in their bills," she wrote Everina. "Then I gave young Cristall* all the money I had. I am continually getting myself in scrapes of this kind. . . . I was obliged to let my father have all my money." She was having trouble getting money from Johnson, who she said was "either half ruined by the present public circumstances or grown strangely mean," and she knew he would cease his aid if she should marry. On New Year's Day Godwin offered to ask his friend Thomas Wedgwood for a loan. "I cannot bear that you should do violence to your feelings," Mary wrote Godwin. "No, you shall not write—I will think of some way of

* Joshua Cristall, then a student at the Royal Academy.

extricating myself." She need not have been so disturbed; following his own doctrine of universal benevolence, Godwin later developed into a notoriously complacent borrower. On this occasion he reluctantly wrote for and received £50, under the guise of needing it for himself.

January was an uncomfortable month. Mary was working strenuously, was sometimes depressed, was often nauseous, "the inelegant complaint," she wrote Godwin, "which no novelist has yet ventured to mention as one of the consequences of sentimental distress . . . it is very distressing to be thus, neither sick nor well, especially as you scarcely imagine me indisposed." At the beginning of February her spirits improved. Apparently, Godwin had accepted the fact that they should marry when her pregnancy became obvious. On the third she went to Dr. George Fordyce, probably for a routine examination. In the middle of the month Everina Wollstonecraft arrived for a visit, which, in interrupting the couple's intimacy, restored it completely. Everina was enroute to Josiah Wedgwood II as governess, a position Godwin and Mary doubtless got her. For three weeks she stayed with Mary, projecting dour disapproval. "The evenings with her silent, I find very wearisome and embarrassing," Mary wrote Godwin. Everina disliked Godwin personally and philosophically, blaming him for Mary's predicament; "her union with Godwin was woeful and most afflictive," she said later. Everina departed March 6, in the evening. "Those to come," Mary wrote Godwin in relief, "are our own."[28] By the middle of March her notes to Godwin were positively gay, and his normally affectionate. On March 29, when Mary was in her fourth month, they went quietly to St. Pancras Church and were married, with Marshal and the parish clerk to witness. "Panc" was Godwin's journal note of the event.

Both husband and wife were embarrassed when it came to announcing their marriage. For Mary it meant broadcasting that she had never been Mrs. Imlay, a situation she handled badly. In a pompous letter to Amelia Alderson, which she signed "Mary Wollstonecraft, femme Godwin," she wrote:

> The wound my unsuspecting heart formerly received is not healed. I found my evenings solitary [*sic!*], and I wished, while fulfilling the duty of a mother, to have some person with similar pursuits, bound to me by affection; and beside, I earnestly desired to resign a name which seemed to disgrace me.[29]

"Pray don't set me any more tasks," she wrote Godwin. "I am the awkwardest creature in the world at manufacturing a letter." She made Godwin tell Johnson: "I have just thought that it would be very pretty in you to call on Johnson to-day—It would spare me some awkwardness, and please him." Godwin informed Thomas Wedgwood in an inimitable letter throwing the burden on Mary and concluding by touching him for another £50:

> Some persons have found an inconsistency between my practice in this instance and my doctrines. But I cannot see it . . . an attachment between two persons of opposite sexes is right, but . . . marriage, as practiced in European countries is wrong. I still adhere to that opinion. Nothing but a regard for the happiness of the individual, which I have no right to injure, could have induced me to submit to an institution which I wish to see abolished. . . . Now that we have entered into a new mode of living, which will probably be permanent, I find a further supply of fifty pounds will be necessary to start us fair.

Godwin's pious mother sent affectionate, evangelical, and practical greetings: "Your broken resolution in regard to mattrimony incourages me to hope that you will ere long embrace the Gospel. . . . Could send you a small fether bed." Godwin wrote Holcroft only that he was married, but not to whom. Holcroft's enthusiastic congratulations must have helped assure Godwin that philosophical consistency was not the ultimate virtue: "I think you the most extraordinary pair in existence."

Naturally, the world enjoyed the situation. "Numberless are the squibs that are thrown out at Mr. Godwin on the occasion, and he winces not a little on receiving them," wrote Mrs. Barbauld. Fuseli wrote Roscoe: "The assertrix of female rights has given her hand to the *balancier* of political justice." Both partners expected Mrs. Godwin to be on surer footing than the fictional Mrs. Imlay. However, the marriage scandalized their conventional friends, who, oddly enough, now refused to be contaminated by a woman whose marriage forced them to admit what they had suspected or known all along, that she had been an unmarried mother. The Twisses and Mrs. Siddons dropped her. Mrs. Inchbald's pique was more personal and more vicious. She wrote Godwin:

> I most sincerely wish you and Mrs. Godwin joy. But, assured that your joyfulness would obliterate from your memory every trifling engage-

ment, I have entreated another person to supply your place, and perform your office in securing a box on Reynold's night. If I have done wrong, when you next marry, I will act differently.[30]

Mrs. Inchbald was persuaded to renew the theater engagement and included the Godwins with several other guests on April 19 but she behaved to Mary that evening in front of the others in a way Godwin never forgot—"base, cruel, and insulting." Mary Wollstonecraft was humiliated, and flared out at Godwin when they returned home that night. Next morning he sent her a note from his study:

I am pained by the recollection of our conversation last night. The sole principle of conduct of which I am conscious in my behaviour to you, has been in every thing to study your happiness. I found a wounded heart, &, as that heart cast itself upon me, it was my ambition to heal it. Do not let me be wholly disappointed.

By that afternoon Mary had calmed down. She replied:

Fanny is delighted with the thought of dining with you—but I wish you to eat your meat first, and let her come up with the pudding. I shall probably knock at your door in my way to Opie's; but, should I not find you, let me now request you not to be too late this evening. Do not give Fanny butter with her pudding.

The Godwins had decided on their own style of marriage, which continued the life they had been living before. Godwin told Wedgwood, "we do not entirely cohabit." Originally Godwin's idea, it suited both perfectly. On April 6 they had moved to rooms at 29 Polygon in Somers Town, a detached block of houses facing outward, with courts or gardens running into the center. Godwin at the same time took an apartment some twenty doors away, to which he went every morning and remained sometimes for meals, more often returning to Polygon for dinner. Mary's study was her own, as were her ideas. "I mean still to be independent," she wrote Amelia Alderson, "even to the cultivating sentiments in my children's minds, (should I have more) which he disavows."

It was a time of adjustment for both. In her lofty way Mary did not expect to cope with the practicalities she had always shoved onto others and which Godwin expected to shift from the charwoman and Marshal to Mary. She wrote him several days after their marriage:

> I am not well today my spirits have been harassed. Mary will tell you about the state of the sink & do you know you plague me (a little) by not speaking more determinately to the Landlord of whom I have a mean opinion. . . .
>
> . . . I wish you would desire Mr. Marshall to call on me. Mr. Johnson, or somebody, has always taken the disagreeable business of settling with trades-people off my hands—I am, perhaps as unfit as yourself to do it—and my time appears to me, as valuable as that of any other persons accustomed to employ themselves. . . . I am tormented by the want of money—and feel, to say the truth, as if I was not treated with respect, owing to your desire not to be disturbed.

Mary Wollstonecraft's professional life went on as before on her book and at *The Analytical Review,* but she also wrote an article "On Artificial Taste," which appeared in the April, 1797 issue of the new, liberal *Monthly Magazine* published by a colleague of Johnson's in St. Paul's Churchyard. As she maintained in her exchanges with Godwin, Mary insisted in this essay that poetry had to be created out of direct response to stimuli, nature, and emotion, unadulterated by academic formulation, tradition, or sophistication—although this very essay was exceptionally labored. She also made it clear she believed, unlike Godwin, in a pervasive God.

Mary and Godwin continued separate social lives and agreed not to presume on each other's old friendships. But Mary was apparently more generous in this respect than Godwin. "I want you to visit [Johnson] often of a Tuesday," she wrote him. "This is quite disinterested, as I shall never be of the party." Holcroft wanted Mary to come to dinner on Sundays, but Godwin objected, and therefore Mary declined, although, she wrote Godwin, "I think you right in the principle; but a little wrong in the present application." She was used to enjoying social Sundays at the Twisses, and having been rejected by them, "thrown out of my track," as she said, "[I] have not traced another."[31]

The couple entertained a varied and interesting circle at home. Many young intellectuals who had gravitated first to Godwin found Mary more rewarding. Southey, according to Byron, positively fell in love with her. Although Southey and Godwin did not like each other, Mary, "by her invitation," had Southey to dinner and he paid her several morning calls. Everything she said, he claimed, was "wise and true." Both were still fascinated by the French Revolution and radical approaches to social and economic equality. "Babouef," they agreed, "was a great man." Southey recalled:

> Mary Wollstonecraft told me he was the most extraordinary one she had ever seen—and in the orgasm of the Revolution the system of total equalization would have been wise. It would have rendered any return to common systems impossible and excited insurrections all over Europe.

Mary may even have told Southey about her suicide attempt, for later he wrote that "a person who had attempted suicide by drowning and was restored relates that the sufferings were long and painful. The mind had been in the highest possible state of stimulation."[32]

Hazlitt, son of friends of Godwin's family, also saw a good deal of the couple and told Coleridge he admired "the playful easy air" with which Mary turned off some objection of Godwin's. Coleridge replied "this was only one instance of the ascendancy which people of imagination exercized over those of mere intellect." Although Coleridge thought little of her "talent for bookmaking, he had a great idea of Mrs. Wollstonecraft's powers of conversation." Hazlitt may have been present at an interesting dinner party at the Godwin's, which included Fuseli, on whom Godwin had called in February, Horne Tooke, Curran, and Grattan. Tooke, according to Hazlitt, was "the best intellectual fencer of his day. He made strange havoc of Fuseli's fantastic hieroglyphics, violent humours, and oddity of dialect. Curran . . . was lively and animated . . . but . . . had the worst taste I ever knew. His favorite critical topics were to abuse Milton's *Paradise Lost* and *Romeo and Juliet.*" On this particular evening, whether infuriated by denigration of his favorite poets or the fact that he was not the center of attention, Fuseli "suddenly retired from their company, and joining Mrs. Godwin in the drawing room, petulantly said to her 'I wonder you invited me to meet such wretched company.' "[33] By this time Mary Wollstonecraft must have smiled at the "reptile of vanity" she once told the painter disfigured his genius.

Godwin wrote in the *Memoirs* that Mary had gained considerable tranquility before her marriage, and after it "the improvement in this respect was extremely obvious. She was a worshiper of domestic life."

> the serenity of her countenance, the increasing sweetness of her manners . . . were matters of general observation to all her acquaintance. She

> had always possessed . . . the art of communicating happiness, and she was now in the constant and unlimited exercise of it. She seemed to have attained that situation, which her disposition and character imperiously demanded, but which she had never before attained.

Godwin benefited equally, turning universal benevolence into palpable human contact. In his benignity it never occurred to Godwin he might withhold love from Fanny. "Mary loved to observe the growth of affection between me and her daughter," he wrote. Mary's rearing of the child was a revelation to him; "the mirror of patience," he thought her, "little troubled with skepticism and uncertainty," as he had been with his ward, Thomas Cooper.

Mary's pregnancy became another reason for deep mutual satisfaction, "the source of a thousand endearments," Godwin wrote. The couple's household arrangements reflected their partnership as independent and loving equals:

Mary: I am well and tranquil, excepting the disturbance produced by Master William's joy, who took it into his head to frisk a little at being informed of your remembrance. I begin to love this little creature, and to anticipate his birth as a fresh twist to a knot, which I do not wish to untie. . . .

. . . I am not fatigued with solitude—yet I have not relished my solitary dinner. A husband is a convenient part of the furniture of a house. . . . I wish you, from my soul, to be riveted in my heart; but I do not desire to have you always at my elbow—though at this moment I did not care if you were.[34]

The marriage had its difficult moments; Godwin naturally tended to idealize it in the *Memoirs*, but he later acknowledged that "the partner of my life was too quick in conceiving resentments," which was accurate, and added "but these were dignified and restrained," which was not. Particularly in situations that threatened her, the young Mary Wollstonecraft, who told Jane Arden she must have first place or none, could be heard again. One morning in late May, the couple had an altercation apparently over Mrs. Inchbald; Godwin, having denounced the lady for her brutality to Mary, could see no reason why he should not continue to see and to admire her for her residual virtues. Mary attacked Mrs. Inchbald's "criminal compliance with the prejudice of society," while Godwin told Mary she was harboring *"savage resentment, and the worst of vices."* Mary reacted momentarily as if Godwin had utterly failed her. It was a defect of her mind, as she said, that led her to expect tenderness in those she loved and to be disappointed at their incalculable selfishness.

Likewise, Mary was disturbed in early June when Godwin and Basil Montagu left for a two-week excursion to Etruria. Mary made Godwin fix the precise day she could expect him back, "not to torment me by leaving the day of your return undecided." She felt ill the day after he left, although by the sixth she had recovered and was content as long as Godwin kept to his schedule. Every two or three days he wrote her long letters about his adventures and the flattering receptions he was meeting, with loving remembrances to her, to Fanny, whom he had promised a Wedgwood mug, and to "William." His humor, however, could be incredibly gross. "Take care of yourself, my love, and take care of William," he wrote. "Do you not be drowned, wherever I am." But when Godwin delayed his return a day or two, writing Mary "delays are not necessarily tragical," she was dramatically bitter. She wrote him that his tenderness had "evaporated," that he preferred "the homage of vulgar minds," and she accused him of "icy Philosophy."

The most serious conflict of their brief marriage resulted from Godwin's interest in a Miss Pinkerton, who was flattering and pursuing him. Mary was suspicious in June; "She has more in her than comes out of her mouth," she told Godwin. On July 4, finding herself in Sophia Fuseli's shoes, Mary reacted with a despair that was both ironic and poignant, denouncing Godwin as if he were Imlay or, if she had thought of him, Edward John Wollstonecraft.

Mary: I am absurd to look for the affection which I have found only in my own tormented heart; and how can you blame me for taken refuge in the idea of a God, when I despair of finding sincerity on earth? . . . My old wounds bleed afresh—What did not blind confidence, and unsuspecting truth, lead me to—my very soul trembles sooner than endure the hundred part of what I have suffered, I could wish my poor Fanny and self asleep at the bottom of the sea. . . .

Godwin: I thought you expressed yourself unkindly . . . last night. . . . Today you have called on me, & said two or three grating things. Let me intreat you, not to give me pain of this sort, without a determined purpose, & not to suppose that I am philosopher enough not to feel it. . . .

Mary: I do not quite understand your note—I shall make no comments on the *kindness* of it, because I ought not to expect it according to my ideal—You say "WITHOUT a determined purpose." Do you wish me to have one?

After another month of pressure Mary got her way; on August 9 Godwin agreed that she should send Miss Pinkerton a note he amended slightly, asking her to cease her visits. The young lady withdrew, "sensible of the impropriety of my conduct," as she tearfully acknowledged to the Godwins.[35]

Mary Wollstonecraft's maturity was rooted in the "original defect" of her early life, and she never outgrew her fierce and fearful reaction to suspected rejection by those who loved her but would not prefer and protect her as she demanded. "*Strong indignation* in youth at injustice . . . appears to me the constant attendant of superiority of understanding," she wrote, forever young in that respect. She wanted to feel, and through feeling to understand and to live. It was more important to her than tranquility. At the beginning of her sexual relations with Godwin it is obvious she was trying to find another Imlay in him, as she had tried to find dependability and integrity in Imlay. Such polarity of needs makes for a very painful equilibrium, and Mary Wollstonecraft paid a price for it. At the end of her essay on poetry, which stressed the value of "quickness of senses," she warned against allowing physical responsiveness to become a preference for "the sensual tumult of love." She had been overwhelmed by erotic gratification and had been injured because of it by Imlay. Now, instead, she chose "the calm pleasures of affectionate friendship," declaring that "content, not happiness, is the reward of virtue in this world." It is a startling admission of the discrepancy she felt in spite of her better judgment, between her passion for Imlay—"happiness"—and her life with Godwin—"content." One of the last books she read was a collection of letters she criticized because, as she told Godwin, they "have no voluptuousness for me."[36]

Godwin understood much of what drove Mary, and his refusal to play up to her romantic overexpectations, her spasms of anger and self-pity, helped her to the greatest measure of happiness she had ever known. He not only loved her, he marveled at her mind, her taste, the assurance that welled up out of the currents of her conflicts, and he recognized she had reached a compelling amalgamation of heart and head he could neither match nor resist. "In a robust and unwavering judgment of this sort, there is a kind of witchcraft," he wrote. "When it decides justly, it produces a kind of responsive vibration." Mary's capacity for tenderness, previously more spoken of than sustained, increased with Godwin, as did her humor, for she could make fun of her own egotism and Godwin's pedantry.

Mary: I must tell you that I love you better than I supposed I did, when I promised to love you forever—and I will add what will gratify your benevolence, if not your heart, that on the whole I may be termed happy. You are a tender, affectionate creature; and I feel it thrilling through my frame giving and promising pleasure.

Godwin: You cannot imagine how happy your letter made me. No creature expresses, because no creature feels, the tender affections so perfectly as you do: &, after all one's philosophy, it must be confessed that the knowledge, that there is some one that takes an interest in our happiness something like that which each man feels in his own, is extremely gratifying.[37]

As Joseph Johnson observed, Mary Wollstonecraft was never one to conceal what she felt. Her last portrait, painted by Opie during her pregnancy, differs from the first by more than a chronological six years. Her former combativeness and expectancy are subdued. She is more self-contained, reflective, and ripe, and she has managed to transform self-pity into a sense of tragedy. Perhaps she was beginning to pose a little for posterity, realizing she would be judged for her life as well as for her *Vindication*. From one of her last letters it is clear she was secure and ready:

> Those who are bold enough to advance before the age they live in, and to throw off, by the force of their minds, the prejudices which the maturing reason of the world will in time disavow, must learn to brave censure. We ought not to be too anxious respecting the opinions of others —I am not too fond of vindications.—Those who know me will suppose that I acted from principle. Nay, as we in general give others credit for worth, in proportion as we possess it—I am easy with regard to the opinions of the *best* part of mankind.—I *rest* on my own.[38]

Chapter 17

DURING THE SUMMER of 1797, Mary Wollstonecraft made preparations for the birth of her second child with complete confidence. She was working on a book of lessons, begun for Fanny some two years before. The lessons progressed from single words to simple phrases to episodes, all drawn from a child's experience. Some are designed to encourage independence, consideration, and family unity, many were meant to ease Fanny's adjustment to a rival baby brother, as if to give the child what Mary felt she herself had missed. The strictures are occasionally grating to modern ears, but the tone and phrasing are tender and empathetic compared with *Thoughts on the Education of Daughters* or *Original Stories*. Mary even looked back on her own mother with nostalgia:

> My mamma took care of me, when I was a little girl like you. . . . When you were a baby, with no more sense than William, you put everything into your mouth. . . . See how much taller you are than William. In four years you have learned to eat, to walk, to talk. . . .
>
> . . . You think, that you shall soon be able to dress yourself entirely? I am glad of it. . . .
>
> . . . papa . . . fell asleep on the sopha. . . . So you came to me, and said to me very softly . . . Whisper—whisper.[1]

Mary Wollstonecraft had always been ahead of her time in weighing the importance of infancy. She was planning a book in the form of letters on pregnancy and infant care, combining her own experimental regime with the professional advice of Dr. Anthony Carlisle. The project may have been inspired by a letter Amelia Alderson wrote asking Mary to give a pregnant friend "in detail, your method of nursing Fanny." Now three and a half, Fanny had always been dressed as lightly as the climate would allow and encouraged to play outdoors. She was apparently particularly sturdy and rosy-cheeked. In the uncompleted introduction for this book, Mary Wollstonecraft spoke up forcefully for the guidance of matrons and professionals, who, she observed tartly, were in need of it: "I must suppose, while a third part of the human species, according to the most accurate calculation, die during their infancy, just at the threshold of life, that there is some error in the modes adopted by mothers and nurses."[2]

Mary's second pregnancy was apparently not as comfortable as her first. She had suffered from morning sickness at the beginning, and although she worked and exercised regularly, and even visited intimate friends through July, her eighth month, she mentioned on occasion to Godwin that she was "not quite well," "fatigued," "a little the worse for my yesterday walk," had a "pain," or needed "a few minutes rest." She was thirty-eight years old.

Since February she had been checked medically by an old friend from Johnson's circle, Dr. George Fordyce, and by Dr. Carlisle, Godwin's friend. But for the birth she engaged a Mrs. Blenkinsop, midwife at the Westminster Lying-in Hospital, an institution devoted to care of working-class women. Mary felt it immodest for a man to attend a woman in such an intimate situation, and for years she had insisted midwifery was a profession in which women should be predominant and more respected, a cause supported by Dr. Fordyce as well. Mary believed childbirth to be a perfectly natural process, and having delivered Fanny with comparative ease she scorned fashionable physicians and the usual malaise. She would be downstairs for dinner the day after William was born, she told Godwin, and no nonsense about reclining for weeks.

On Monday, August 28, Godwin called on Fuseli and Mrs. Inchbald, and went to see *The Merchant of Venice.* Tuesday he and Mary Wollstonecraft went walking. That evening they read *Werther* together—Werther, of whom she reminded him. At 5 A.M. Wednesday the thirtieth Mary felt the first signs of labor. After breakfast Godwin went as usual to his rooms nearby to work; shortly after Mary sent him a note:

> I have no doubt of seeing the animal today; but must wait for Mrs. Blenkinsop to guess the hour—I have sent for her—Pray send me the news paper—I wish I had a novel, or some book of sheer amusement, to excite curiosity, and while away the time—Have you anything of the kind?

Mrs. Blenkinsop arrived by nine. Godwin was rereading *Mary* in his study. In a few hours Mary Wollstonecraft sent him a second note:

> Mrs. Blenkinsop tells me that Every thing is in a fair way, and that there is no fear of the event being put off till another day—still, *at present,* she thinks, I shall not immediately be freed from my load—I am very well—Call before dinner time, unless you receive another message from me.

Godwin stopped on his way to afternoon dinner at the Reveleys'. The pains, which had begun slowly, were increasing; by two o'clock Mary went upstairs to her room. She told Godwin she did not want to see him there until she could present him with his newborn son. At three she wrote her last note: "Mrs. Blenkinsop tells me that I am in the most natural state, and can promise me a safe delivery—But that I must have a little patience"[3]

This final word, left without closing punctuation, this word spoken by her mother on her deathbed and thereafter by Mary when trying to accept forces greater than herself, is poignant and ominous.

Godwin had an early supper with Eliza and John Fenwick, saw Mrs. Blenkinsop, and went back to his study from seven until ten that night. At 11:30 Mary Wollstonecraft gave birth to a girl. Obedient to her instructions, Godwin waited downstairs in the parlor for her summons, but it was almost three hours before Mrs. Blenkinsop descended in great anxiety to tell him that the placenta had not been expelled, that she dared not proceed and needed a doctor. Godwin, thinking Mary might be dying, rushed to Westminster and brought back Dr. Louis Poignard of that hospital, who, as was the usual practice, simply thrust his hand or a spoonlike instrument through the distended cervix and pulled out the placenta "in pieces, till he was satisfied that the whole was removed," as he told Godwin. During the operation Mary hemorrhaged and several times fainted from agony such as she said she had never known. When Godwin came to her bedside she smiled and told him she would have died except that she was determined not to leave him.

She then asked to see Dr. Fordyce, and despite Poignard's objections, her friend arrived for consultation at three o'clock Thursday afternoon. Finding no particular cause for alarm and pleased that a female midwife had successfully delivered the patient, Fordyce departed. Godwin was so frightened he stayed in Mary's room most of Thursday, but he began to be reassured, and Friday Mary was so cheering that he went out on business, but he stopped to see Dr. Carlisle, his own physician. Joseph Johnson called at the Polygon that day, and by evening Godwin was sure Mary was recovering normally.

Saturday, Dr. Carlisle stopped in and several friends called. By evening Mary's condition had grown worse. Maria Reveley took Fanny home with her, and Mrs. Fenwick arrived to nurse Mary and care for the baby, also named Mary.

Sunday, still confident this was a temporary setback, Godwin breakfasted at home with Montagu and went out with him in the afternoon to visit Opie among others, two of whom were physicians. While he was gone Mary showed the first signs of serious infection, high fever followed by "a sort of shivering fit." Godwin's sister had been invited to dinner, but Mary asked that she not come and directed Godwin's own meal be served in the parlor rather than the dining room just under her bedroom, for her chills were so severe that her bed shook the floor. Anguished that he had not been there when she asked for him earlier, and after witnessing her second violent chill that evening, Godwin heard Mary say this was "a struggle between life and death," but could not believe it. Poignard now dropped out in mortification, and Fordyce was put in charge. Mrs. Blenkinsop returned.

Monday Fordyce decided the patient should not nurse the baby and ordered puppies to draw off Mary's milk, a grotesque and unnecessary substitute for palpation, but one which gave Mary excuse to joke and try to cheer poor Godwin. "I intreated her to recover," he said. Johnson and Mary Hays called. Eliza Fenwick moved in for the night, and Marshal also spent the night at the Polygon in case a courier was needed. The baby was sent to Maria Reveley's.

Tuesday Fordyce made his regular call in the morning and in the afternoon brought Dr. John Clarke, a well-known specialist on problems of childbirth. Clarke could act only on available contemporary medical knowledge; in his book on diseases of lying-in he had admitted that the cause of puerperal fever was "disputed" and that "more than half of those who had been seized with it have fallen sacrifice to its severity." Physicians were, in effect, reduced to treating symptoms with emetics, blisters, wine, bark, and opium. Fordyce thought Mary might need another operation to remove remaining bits of the placenta. Whether some tissue was left or whether Poignard had inadvertently pierced the thin, distended uterus, Mary's infection was far advanced and Clarke knew he could not operate without killing her. He prescribed opium for her pain. Basil Montagu, who, with Marshal, Dyson, and Fenwick, was constantly on hand for errands, was sent to Fordyce's to get the drug, ran back with it to the Polygon, and helped raise Mary in bed to administer it. He related that when the opium gave her relief, Mary turned her head to Godwin, who was holding her hand, and said, "Oh, Godwin, I am in heaven," whereupon he, always precise, replied, "You mean, my dear, that your physical symptoms are somewhat easier." Mary Hays now took turns with Eliza Fenwick to nurse. Mary asked for Mrs. Cotton, but it was too late to send for her.

Wednesday, September 6, a week after her delivery, Clarke, Carlisle and Fordyce decided the only chance of strengthening the patient was to give her ample doses of red wine, a task that fell to Godwin, now desperate, who began to spoon it out to her at four in the afternoon, knowing "neither what was too much, nor what was too little," until seven o'clock, when a servant told him she thought Mary "was going as fast as possible." Frantic, he sent Basil Montagu across London to fetch Carlisle from a dinner party four miles the other side of the city; they got back to the Polygon within three-quarters of an hour, to Godwin's ineffable relief. Carlisle stayed at the house until the end, and Godwin said he himself was scarcely ever out of Mary's room. But that night he got some sleep while Carlisle watched by Mary's bedside. She had the most devoted care and told her nurse Godwin was "the kindest, best man in the world." Like many who react badly to emotional pressure, she bore physical pain well; "nothing," Godwin wrote, "could exceed the patience and affectionateness of the poor sufferer."

Thursday morning Carlisle told Godwin Mary was surprisingly

better, but Godwin would not allow himself to hope again. He was wise. Thursday night Carlisle told him Mary might die at any moment. "She did not appear to me to be in that state of exhaustion," he said in the *Memoirs,* but in his journal that night he wrote: "dying in the evening."

Friday, Mary was feeble, straying, complained once of being annoyed by her nurse. "Pray, pray, do not let her reason with me," she told Godwin, and for the first time she spoke as if she expected to die. "Idea of death; solemn communication," Godwin wrote in his journal. However, he did not reveal what that special communication was. Opie called that day, and Godwin's sister came to stay at the Polygon. Godwin noticed on Friday night that when urged to sleep Mary closed her eyes and tried to breathe as if she were sleeping. Her chills had stopped. Carlisle was amazed that she was still alive.

Saturday morning Godwin knew Mary would die soon and felt he must talk to her about the two children. Carlisle warned him not to hint at death. Pretending, therefore, to ask how she wanted Fanny and Mary handled during her illness, Godwin tried to elicit some direction for their rearing. "I know what you are thinking of," she said, but could add little else.

Saturday night, a stormy wet night, Godwin went to bed after midnight, telling Carlisle to wake him at any sign.

Sunday morning September 10 at six o'clock, dawn of a clear and beautiful day, he was called. An hour and forty minutes later Mary Wollstonecraft died. "This light was lent to me for a very short period," he wrote in the *Memoirs,* "and now it is extinguished forever." In his Journal that morning he found it impossible to write the words; he could only trace her death:

> Sept. 10. Su. 20 minutes before 8. ——————————[4]

Godwin wrote two letters Sunday afternoon announcing Mary's death, one to Mrs. Inchbald, the other to Holcroft; "look at me, and talk to me, but do not . . . exhort me, or console me." That night Montagu, Marshal, Godwin's sister, and the child Fanny had dinner with him. During the next three days close friends called, notices were sent of the funeral to those for whom Godwin felt Mary Wollstonecraft had "particular esteem," and letters dispatched with the news. Mary Hays wrote Hugh Skeys and Mrs. Cotton. Godwin could not bring himself to write Everina, or Eliza with whom Mary had had no known communication for two years. Mrs. Fenwick was delegated to write Everina. "I am a stranger to you, Miss Wollstonecraft," she began, and after describing what had happened went on to say:

> No woman was ever more happy in marriage . . . how happy she had lately been and how much she was admired and almost idolized by some of the most eminent and best of human beings. . . . Mr. Godwin requests you will make Mrs. Bishop acquainted with the particulars. . . . He tells me that Mrs. Godwin entertained a sincere and earnest affection for Mrs. Bishop.

There is no record of the sisters' reaction.

Joseph Johnson wrote Fuseli the day of the death: "One who loved you, and whom I respected, is no more—Mrs. Godwin died this morning." And to Godwin: "I have had daily notices of what I dreaded to hear, and nothing but Mrs. G's strength of constitution left me the faint hope of her recovery. . . . I knew her too well not to admire and love her."

Johnson went to see Godwin on the twelfth, and was shown a list of those invited to the funeral. That afternoon Johnson suggested a significant addition:

> In the list you shew'd this morning, I did not observe the name of Fuseli, it is true that of late he was not intimate with Mrs. Godwin, but from circumstances that I am acquainted with, I think he was not to be blamed for it; before this they were so intimate and spent so many happy hours together in my house that I think I may say that he was the first of her friends; indeed, next to ourselves I believe no one has a juster sense of her worth or more laments her loss.[5]

Johnson was a perceptive man who knew Fuseli thoroughly, and Knowles said the painter felt the kind of grief that "does not give utterance to words" and simply postscripted a letter to Roscoe with, "Poor Mary!" Opie wrote that he would attend the funeral; John Hewlett regretted because of a "particular engagement in the way of my profession." Godwin's friend Tuthil explained he would not assist at religious ceremonies. Godwin himself was too overwhelmed to go to the burial at St. Pancras. That day, Friday the fifteenth, he stayed at Marshal's house. About ten o'clock in the morning, as Mary Wollstonecraft was being buried, Godwin wrote Carlisle;

> I am here, sitting alone in Mr. Marshall's lodgings during my wife's funeral. My mind is extremely sunk and languid. But I husband my thoughts, and shall do very well. I have been but once since you saw me, in a train of thought that gave me alarm. One of my wife's books now lies near me, but I avoid opening it. I took up a book on the education of children, but that impressed me too forcibly with my forlorn and disabled state with respect to the two poor animals left under my protection, and I threw it aside. . . . It is pleasing to be loved by those we feel ourselves impelled to love. . . . If you have any of that kind of consolation in store for me, be at the pains to bestow it. But, above all, be severely sincere. I ought to be acquainted with my own defects.[6]

Poor Godwin had nothing for which to reproach himself, although like most survivors he needed reassurance. Carlisle, Montagu, Johnson, Holcroft, Opie, Dyson, the Fenwicks, and other close friends were with him during the next few days. Fanny came home on the sixteenth, and Godwin that day finished rereading *Mary*. On the seventeenth the baby Mary came home under Eliza Fenwick's care, and Godwin began to read *Maria*.

Ten days after Mary Wollstonecraft's death Godwin gave up his separate rooms nearby and moved into her study, hanging her last portrait over the desk, reading through her unpublished papers and private letters. By September 24 he had decided to edit and publish them and immediately to write her memoirs; he noted in his journal for that day: "Life of Wt., p. 2." He had a great deal of information about her life, having, as he said, "repeatedly led the conversation of Mary to topics of this sort; and, once or twice, made notes in her presence." He also had whatever letters from Imlay, Fanny Blood, the Wollstonecraft family, and others, which Mary had kept, all of which have since disappeared. He began to gather information from her friends, wanting especially to fill in the years before he met her. Johnson sent him notes, but Everina would not answer his request. When Godwin got a condolence letter from Hugh Skeys in Dublin, he took the opportunity to ask Skeys' aid in getting facts out of Mary's sisters. Skeys did so, and on November 24 Everina wrote Godwin with tense hostility:

> Sir.
>
> I have delayed writing to you a long time; and my principal reason was the extreme loathness I felt to fix my attention on a disagreeable subject without the certainty of answering a good end: but as . . . you are in a hurry, I think it wrong to be any longer silent.
>
> When Eliza and I first learn't your intention of publishing immediately my sister Mary's life, we concluded that you only meant a sketch to prevent your design concerning her memoirs from being anticipated. I thought your application to us rather premature, and had no intention of satisfying your demand till we found that Skeys had proffered our assistance without our knowledge—he then requested us to answer his questions, and give him dates, which we complyed with, though reluctantly. At a future day we would willingly have given whatever information was necessary; and even now we would not have shrunk . . . did we suppose it possible to accomplish the work you have undertaken in the time you specify. . . . I am sorry to perceive you are inclined to be minute, when I think it is impossible for you to be even tolerably accurate.

Everina proceeded to give Godwin such terse grudging answers to his specific questions, that he had to get other information and advice from Skeys, who thanked Godwin "for the alterations you have made at my request," probably the omission of Eliza's breakdown and separation. (Godwin was careful not to keep the letter requesting changes.) Skeys wanted to impress Godwin; "I do not so materially differ from you as you seemed to think—you are a Philosopher, and I am merchant," he wrote, and, "I married twice without getting one penny fortune . . . my own family, cannot comprehend my motives," plus a great deal more in the same vein.[7] Mary Wollstonecraft's assessment of him had been perfectly accurate.

Some four months after Mary's death, Johnson published Godwin's four-volume edition of the *Posthumous Works of the Author of a Vindication of the Rights of Woman,* which included her letters to Imlay and the unfinished *Maria,* and at the same time his *Memoirs of the Author of a Vindication of the Rights of Woman.* Trusting as he did in the benefits of truth, Godwin believed he would do justice to his wife, encourage others to follow what he felt was her splendid example, and lay to rest "malignant calumny, or thoughtless misrepresentation." Instead, his candid revelations of her intimacy with Fuseli, Imlay, and himself brought down on his head and her reputation a storm of violent, outraged, righteous condemnation that persisted for years. Even some of Godwin's friends broke with him, including Dr. Parr, who wrote him that he had "been shocked, in common with all wise and good men." Roscoe wrote a poem on the flyleaf of his copy of the *Memoirs:*

> Hard was thy fate in all the scenes of life,
> As daughter, sister, mother, friend, and wife,
> But harder still thy fate in death we own,
> Thus mourn'd by Godwin with a heart of stone.[8]

In his naïveté Godwin also misjudged the conservative temper of the time. Mary Wollstonecraft's obituaries had been generally respectful, even those written by enemies of her liberal political views. But when *Posthumous Works* and the *Memoirs* exposed scandalous details about her personal life, conservatives seized on them as proof of the inevitable, abominable results of liberalism and free thinking, and rabid reactionaries began to use "lascivious" Mary Wollstonecraft and "shameless" Godwin to attack the perceived enemy of the English status quo, Jacobinism, which in fact the couple had hated. To make matters worse, it had become public knowledge that the third daughter of Mary Wollstonecraft's former employers the Kingsboroughs, had been seduced by a cousin, and it was widely said that years before the girl's governess had morally corrupted her. There was even a story going around that there had been an improper relationship between Mary and Lord Kingsborough. Mary Wollstonecraft had her supporters in the opposite minority political camp, as well as vocal friends, particularly Mary Hays, but they were forced to the defensive by Godwin's disclosures and the sheer weight of the dominant view.

In the popular mind Mary Wollstonecraft became such a notorious figure of depravity that her family suffered severely. Her sisters' employers and friends in Ireland were horrified. Everina wrote Eliza that she had suffered "a paroxysm of despair," and the sisters considered going to America to escape "the present storm . . . and the prejudices." Mary's nephew Ned was brought up to dread the mention of his aunt's name.[9]

Some months after Mary Wollstonecraft's death, Godwin published a novel, *St. Leon,* whose heroine embodied his tender memories of Mary. He also recanted his previous theories of love and marriage. However, the book showed signs of his continuing bad judgment and premature decline. Southey told Coleridge he thought it "at times powerfully written—but it is dilated or diluted. St. Leon always acts so like a fool. . . . The passage about voluptuousness, which recommends a course of brothel studies . . . Godwin ought to have recollected what allusion his enemies would immediately make. I was quite pained and irritated at the man's folly."[10] That year in the index of the first issue of the *Anti-Jacobin Review,* under the heading "Prostitution," the editors advised "See Mary Wollstonecraft."

Although Mary Wollstonecraft's attitudes were at times reflected by her contemporaries—for example, in an occasional sarcastic drawing of Fuseli's or, more profoundly, in Blake's poetry, and by some liberal intellectuals, eighteenth-century concepts of proper femininity developed into Victorianism almost as if Mary Wollstonecraft had never lived. It was not that her ideas and example were not taken seriously, they were—as a serious threat.

The year of her death Thomas Gisbourne published *An Enquiry into the Duties of the Female Sex,* which specifically noted "some . . . bold assertors . . . stigmatizing, in terms of indignant complaint, the monopolizing injustice of the other [sex]; laying claim to coordinate authority"; Hannah More's *Strictures On Female Education* two years later had more of the same: "the imposing term of *rights* has been produced to sanctify the claim of our female pretenders, with a view not only to rekindle in the minds of women a presumptuous vanity dishonourable to their sex, but . . . an impious discontent with the post which God has assigned them in this world." In tone, both books would have been as perfect a guide for Mary's mother, Elizabeth Wollstonecraft, as they would be for Victorian young ladies. "Wives, submit yourselves in all things unto your husbands as unto the Lord," quoted Gisbourne. Hannah More was perhaps more subtle: "But *they* little understood the true interests of women . . . nor . . . her true happiness, who seek to annihilate distinctions from which she derives advantages."[11] This was the carrot-stick argument of the new century, and it continued until economic change created a class of women for whom it had no meaning. It was decades before the rights and wrongs of women became a substantive issue. And even then many feminists shunned Mary Wollstonecraft as a prototype, fearing they would be accused of advocating sexual license.

Of Mary Wollstonecraft's friends, Jane Arden wrote Godwin in early 1799 offering him the early letters of "the beloved friend of my youth," for she had kept them and believed Mary to have been a genius. She later published them in a book called *English Exercises.* Jane married a Mr. Gardiner, ran a school in Beverley for several years, and died in 1840. Joseph Johnson died in 1809 and left Godwin a bond for £200 to be used for Fanny Imlay. Fuseli wrote his epitaph. Fuseli died full of years and honors in 1825; Mary's *History of the French Revolution* was among his books auctioned by Sotheby after his death. Fuseli's biographer used Mary's letters to the painter to ridicule her. Imlay's career after he and Mary parted is obscure, but he was buried on the island of Jersey in 1828. His long, peculiar tombstone inscription began: "Stranger intelligent! Should you pass this way / Speak of the social advances of the day."[12]

As for Mary's family, Edward John Wollstonecraft died at Laugharne in 1803. His will, which had been written in 1791, left nothing, but requested Mary to settle his debts. Ned died in London in August, 1807, almost simultaneously with his wife and apparently suddenly, for he left no will. His son, the fourth Edward, was granted administration of the estate and eventually emigrated to Australia, where he became a successful developer. James Wollstonecraft sold his share of his father's houses on Primrose Street in 1799 and by the end of that year was asking Godwin for a loan of £25 ("Have avoided troubling you before, fearing to offend"). James seems to have gotten money from Johnson as well, and left England for Hamburg in 1800 without repaying either of his sister's intimates. He reentered the navy and died on shipboard in the West Indies the same year as Ned. His will, made July 17, 1795, left everything to "Elizabeth Bishop and Everina Wollstonecraft of Dublin . . . Joseph Johnson sole executor." Charles, after his calico printing enterprise with Rowan in Wilmington, Delaware, failed, became a Captain in charge of Ordnance in the War of 1812, and died at a ripe old age, seemingly wealthy, but tangled in speculations.[13]

Eliza and Everina joined forces to run a day school in Dublin.

Godwin saw them and Skeys there in 1800 and continued to be the conduit for the sisters' share of the family rents and remittances, the only occasion for their brief, bitter correspondence, for Godwin and Everina disliked each other more intensely than ever after Mary's death. Everina was described in middle age as tall and formidable, Eliza as winning and gentle, given to passing candy around to her pupils and teachers to stifle arguments. After Eliza's death about 1827, Everina came to London. She died there in 1834.

Godwin was left with the memory of Mary's gift of a happiness, as he said, "so much more the exquisite, as I had a short time before had no conception of it"; an injured reputation; and two young daughters who, he wrote Mrs. Cotton, he knew he was "totally unfitted" to rear.[14] He did his best for them, but he was hard pressed for money, preoccupied with work, study, and friends; two years after Mary Wollstonecraft's death Coleridge remarked on the cadaverous silence in which her children were being raised. Godwin remarried in 1801, but young Mary Godwin hated her stepmother, and Fanny found her fatally unsympathetic.

The most tragic victim of Mary Wollstonecraft's death was Fanny, whose health Mary had been so proud of but who had been traumatized from birth by her mother's torment over Imlay and at three and a half by her death. Although Godwin gave Fanny his name and treated her as his own, she was a melancholy girl, apparently haunted by her origins. She killed herself with laudanum at twenty-two, and her unsigned suicide note began, "I have long determined that the best thing I could do was to put an end to the existence of a being whose birth was unfortunate." She was wearing corset stays, marked "M. W."; they were her mother's. But Godwin did not claim the corpse.

Mary Wollstonecraft's posthumous influence on her second daughter, and on those of her contemporaries who were rebels, was substantial. There could be no more apt symbol of the English Romantic Movement of the early nineteenth century than Percy Shelley, aristocrat, poet, and married man, and young Mary Godwin, child of radical moral philosophers, joining hands over the grave of Mary Wollstonecraft in St. Pancras churchyard before their elopement. As the next generation usually does, they took only what they wanted from her example, and rationalized her profound concern with morality to suit their own needs.

But after the poet's death Mary Shelley turned into a proper Victorian, and even kept aloof from the few early feminists who asked for the support of Mary Wollstonecraft's daughter.

Godwin lived for almost forty years after Mary Wollstonecraft's death. Dogged by humiliation and failure, without her to check his most unfortunate characteristics, he became a caricature of himself, even to those who remembered what he had been. For all those years Mary remained the paramount figure of his life. In spite of his second wife, who survived him, he asked in his will to be buried as near Mary Wollstonecraft as possible. When he died in 1836 her grave was opened for his interment with her, and Mary Shelley told Mary Hays her mother's coffin was found intact, "the cloth still over it—and the plate tarnished but legible."[15] Twenty-one years later, after Mary Shelley had died, a railroad line was laid through St. Pancras. Mary Wollstonecraft and Godwin's grandson, the son of Mary and Percy Shelley, reburied Godwin and Mary with Mary Shelley and Shelley's heart in St. Peter's graveyard at Bournemouth, although the old gravestone remains on St. Pancras property in London.[16]

Mary Wollstonecraft thus finally came to rest. The large, low, classic stone tomb is on a hillside sloping to the west in full sun. There are rhododendron, daisies, and fern about. The inscription for her is the same as that Godwin put on her original gravestone:

MARY WOLLSTONECRAFT GODWIN
Author of "A Vindication of the Rights of Woman"
Born April 27th, 1759, Died September 10th, 1797

The book, and even more the woman who conceived it out of her own life and then went beyond it, have been variously and heatedly interpreted. From her death down to the present Mary Wollstonecraft has been a warning to the fair sex, a misunderstood heroine, a feminist who either went too far or not far enough, as well as a historical figure. Apparently even now it is difficult to be comfortable with exceptional women unless they are queens of some sort, particularly if they are radical. Mary Wollstonecraft faced universal feminine and human problems, viewed them freshly, and assaulted them with insistent passion, originality, and optimism. Her essential insights have been rediscovered, often independently, and acted on in subsequent generations. Godwin's brief epitaph, confident of Mary Wollstonecraft's major achievement, speaks for itself. She once made a more personal affirmation, and it is characteristic of her that she wrote it just after she was dragged out of the Thames:

> it appears to me impossible that I shall cease to exist, or that this active, restless spirit, equally alive to joy and sorrow, should only be organized dust. Surely something resides in this heart that is not perishable—and life is more than a dream.[17]

Bibliographical References

MAJOR SOURCES

Letters of Mary Wollstonecraft and her circle, in the collection of Lord Abinger, Clees Hall, Bures, Suffolk; on microfilm in the Carl H. and Lily Pforzheimer Library, New York. *Abinger*

Letters of Mary Wollstonecraft and others, in *Shelley and his Circle*, edited by Kenneth Neill Cameron (Cambridge, Mass., 1961); collection of the Carl H. and Lily Pforzheimer Library. *SC*

Letters of William Godwin and Mary Wollstonecraft, in *Godwin & Mary*, edited by Ralph M. Wardle (Lawrence, Kansas, 1966). *GM*

Memoirs Of Mary Wollstonecraft, Written by William Godwin, And Edited, with A Preface, A Supplement, and Bibliographical Note, by W. Clark Durant (London and New York, 1927). *Mem*

MAJOR WORKS OF MARY WOLLSTONECRAFT

Thoughts on the Education of Daughters: with Reflections on Female Conduct, in the More Important Duties of Life (London, 1787). *T*

Mary; a Fiction (London, 1788). *M*

Posthumous Works of the Author of a Vindication of the Rights of Woman, in four volumes (London, 1798); reprinted in two volumes (Augustus M. Kelley, Publishers, Reprints of Economic Classics, Clifton, N.J., 1972). Contains:

The Wrongs of Woman: Or, Maria, in two volumes. *MM*
Cave of Fancy. *C*
Letters to Gilbert Imlay. *LI*

Letters to Joseph Johnson. *LJ*

Miscellaneous short pieces. *PW*

Original Stories from Real Life; with Conversations, Calculated to Regulate the Affections, and Form the Mind to Truth and Goodness (London, 1791); second edition illustrated by William Blake. *OS*

A Vindication of the Rights of Men, Introduction by Eleanor Louise Nicholes, facsimile reproduction (Gainesville, 1960). *VRM*

A Vindication of the Rights of Woman, printed as *The Rights of Woman* (Everyman's Library, London and New York, 1929). *VRW*

Letters Written during a Short Residence in Sweden, Norway, and Denmark (London, 1796). *LS*

Articles in *The Analytical Review*. *AR*

Notes to Chapters

CHAPTER 1

1. *Mem,* 8–9, 17. Godwin stated in his introduction: "The facts detailed in the following pages are principally taken from the mouth of the person to whom they relate; and of the veracity and ingenuousness of her habits, perhaps no one that was ever acquainted with her, entertains a doubt. The writer of this narrative . . . repeatedly led the conversation of Mary to topics [relating to her life] and, once or twice, he made notes in her presence."

2. Parish Registers of St. Botolph's, Bishopsgate; Christenings and Burials 1753–1779 (Guildhall Library MS 4517/2). When Edward Wollstonecraft was buried Feb. 5, 1765, his age was recorded as seventy-six; *SC* I, 40; *Survey of London,* General Editor, F. A. W. Sheppard, Vol. XXVII, *Spitalfields and Mile End Town* (London, 1957), 192; Eleanor Flexner, *Mary Wollstonecraft* (New York, 1972), 267; the will of Edward Wollstonecraft, Public Record Office, London.

3. *SC,* I, 39, note 1; M. Dorothy George, *London Life in the Eighteenth Century* (New York, 1925), 177, 371, 178–181.

4. The Wollstonecraft sisters spelled their mother's maiden name "Dickson." Godwin apparently wrote the name phonetically in the *Memoirs.* There is no record of the Dickson-Wollstonecraft marriage or the birth of Mary's older brother, Edward Bland, in St. Botolph's Registers; James Burgh, *Youth's Friendly Monitor* . . . (London, 1756), 11.

5. *SC,* I, 40.

6. Parish Registers of St. Botolph's.

7. William Buchan, *Domestic Medicine* (Philadelphia, 1797), 26; *Gentleman's Magazine,* XXIX, 243; James Nelson, *An Essay on the Government of Children* (London, 1756), 15–17, 45–48; *Mem,* 9–10.

8. *MM,* I, 157; *Mem,* 9.

9. *Gentleman's Magazine*, XXXIII, 514.

10. *SC*, IV, 569; Daniel Defoe, *A Tour Thro' The Whole Island of Great Britain* (London, 1742), 3; Letter to the author from K. C. Newton, County Archivist, Essex, May 8, 1972: "it seems very likely that the 18th Century 'Sun and Whalebone' public house in Latton was on the same site, or possibly is the same building, or partially so, as the public house you saw during your recent visit to Essex."

11. Daniel Lysons, *The Environs of London* (London, 1796), IV, 100–101; J. E. Oxley, *Barking Vestry Minutes and Other Parish Documents* (Colchester, England, 1955), 9, 46, 41.

12. *DNB*, VII, 926–927.

13. *Mem*, 9; *VRW*, 127.

14. *Mem*, 9, 11; *M*, 11–12; *MM*, I, 141–142; *VRW*, 213.

15. *T*, 12; *MM*, I, 90; *T*, 7; *Mem*, 10; *VRW*, 53.

16. *MM*, I, 143; *VRM*, 46–47; *MM*, I, 145; *VRM*, 156.

17. *VRW*, 38.

18. Ibid., 93; *Mem*, 10, 12.

19. *M*, 12.

20. *VRW*, 169; *T*, 7, 6; *VRW*, 172.

21. *C*, 131–133.

22. M. W. to George Blood, July 20, 1785, *Abinger; Mem*, 10–12.

23. Ibid., 11–12; *M*, 14.

24. *M*, 14–15.

25. M. W. to Jane Arden, *SC*, II, 965; "I suffered more than any of them"; *MM*, I, 144.

26. *VRW*, 47; Lloyd DeMause, "The Evolution of Childhood," *History of Childhood Quarterly*, I, No. 4, 540, 554; *MM*, I, 145; *VRW*, 48.

27. Thomas Marriott, *Female Conduct; being an essay on the art of pleasing, to be practiced by the Fair Sex before and after marriage. A poem in Two Books* (London, 1760), 17 *et passim.*

CHAPTER 2

1. According to local tradition; this, and information about the Arden family, were given me by their descendant, Mr. C. A. Arden, of Pond Cottage, Ferrensby, Knaresborough; H. E. Strickland, *A General View of the Agriculture of the East—Riding of Yorkshire* (York, England, 1812); Flexner, *Mary Wollstonecraft*, 22.

2. *Mem*, 15; "RULES for Beverley Assembly—Rooms, 1763," in the Beverley Public Library.

3. *Mem*, 14; H. N. Brailsford, *Shelley, Godwin and Their Circle* (London, New York, and Toronto, 1949), 192; John Gregory, *A Father's Legàcy to His Daughters* (Philadelphia, 1775), 40; Lady Mary Wortley Montague, *Letters, 1709–1762* (Everyman's Library), 454.

4. *The Girlhood of Maria Josepha Holroyd . . .*, J. H. Adeane, ed. (London, New York, and Bombay, 1896), 49; Hannah More, *Strictures On the Modern System of Female Education . . .* (Boston, 1802), 11; G. E. G. Catlin, Introduction to *The Rights of Woman* (Everyman's Library), xix; Rosamund Bayne-Powell, *The English Child in the Eighteenth Century* (New York, 1939), 42.

5. *OS*, 51, 160.
6. Buchan, *Domestic Medicine*, 26; *VRW*, 140.
7. *M*, 10, 13, 16, 30, 27–30.
8. Hester Chapone, *Letters On The Improvement Of The Mind* . . . (London, 1773), 48.
9. *T*, 47; *M*, 12; *C*, 134.
10. *SC*, II, 944–948. This and all other manuscripts from *Shelley and his Circle* are quoted by permission of the Carl H. Pforzheimer Library.
11. Ibid., 950.
12. Ibid., 951–952.
13. Ibid., 954–955.
14. *LI*, XII, XXXII; *T*, 12.
15. *SC*, II, 955–956.
16. Ibid., 956–959.
17. Johnson's Notes, *Abinger*.
18. *SC*, II, 958–959.
19. Ibid., 965.
20. *VRM*, 49–50.
21. *GM*, 28; *LJ*, VIII.

CHAPTER 3

1. Register of Apprentices of the Beverley Corporation, Beverley, Yorkshire. The verbatim entry found and given me by Mr. G. P. Brown, Local History Librarian of the Beverley Library: 620. "Marmaduke Hewitt of Beverley in the County of Yorkshire, Surgeon and Apothecary, produced an indenture of apprenticeship dated the 16th day of January 1775, wherein it appears that Henry Woodstock Wollstonecraft of Beverley aforesaid, gentleman, hath bound himself apprentice to the said Marmaduke Hewitt for the term of seven years. Which said indenture was witnessed by Hassell Moor and Thomas Burton"; Church Warden's Accounts, 1731–1781, St. Mary's Church, Beverley; *Mem*, 15; *SC*, II, 964, 982; *LI*, XV.
2. Walter Harrison, *New and Universal History, Description and Survey Of The Cities Of London and Westminster* (London, 1776), 545; James Morris Brewer, *London and Middlesex* . . . (London, 1816), IV, 278; Harrison, op. cit., 546; Arthur D. Morris, *The Hoxton Madhouses* (Cambridge, 1958).
3. *Mem*, 15–16, 20; *SC*, II, 966.
4. *LJ*, II.
5. *SC*, II, 966, 964–967.
6. *Abinger*.
7. "Saturday afternoon" (1783), *Abinger*.
8. *VRM*, 56–64.
9. *AR*, VI, 467.
10. *MM*, I, 28–29; II, 144.
11. *SC*, IV, 858.
12. *Mem*, 18–19.
13. *OS*, 45–47.
14. *Mem*, 19; *GM*, 109; Ralph Wardle, *Mary Wollstonecraft, a Critical Biography* (Lawrence, 1951), 44.

15. To George Blood, Sept. 15, 1789; June 18, 1786, *Abinger; M*, 34; *Mem*, 19; *M*, 18; *Mem*, 19.

16. *Mem*, 20; *M*, 20–21, 18–19, 21–23.

17. *SC*, II, 966; *Mem*, 15–16.

18. *SC*, II, 965.

19. John Malcolm Brinnan, *Dylan Thomas in America* (Boston and Toronto, 1955), 99, 104, 124.

20. *OS*, 141. Although Everina told Godwin of this bare acquaintance in a letter of Nov. 24, 1797 (*Abinger*), he described it in the *Memoirs* as a close friendship, one of several instances of his snobbery or desire to represent Mary as well connected.

21. *SC*, II, 964–966; Flexner, *Mary Wollstonecraft*, 25, 268.

22. *VRW*, 38; *T*, 82–83, 63.

23. *T*, 158; Eliza to Everina, Jan. 20, 1793, *Abinger*.

24. *T*, 69–74.

25. *M*, 34–36.

26. Chapone, *Letters*, 71.

27. *SC*, II, 965; *Mem*, 73.

28. *Mem*, 72; *T*, 61–62.

29. *T*, 73; George, *London Life*, 140–141, 427–429; *VRW*, 162.

30. *OS*, 137; *VRM*, 22, 28.

CHAPTER 4

1. *The Bath Chronicle*, XVIII, No. 916.

2. *Maria Holroyd*, 77; Jane Austen, *Persuasion* (Modern Library), 1300; Letter to the author from Warren Derry of Bath on "Masters of the Ceremonies." This Dawson, whose portrait is in the Bath Public Library, is apparently not the son of Mary Wollstonecraft's Mrs. Dawson; *The Bath Chronicle*, XVIII, No. 948.

3. *VRW*, 188.

4. *SC*, II, 968.

5. Ibid., 936.

6. Ibid., 964–967.

7. Ibid., 967; *Maria Holroyd*, 180–182; *SC*, II, 967–968.

8. Ibid., 971; *LI*, XXXII.

9. Elizabeth Nitchie, "An Early Suitor of Mary Wollstonecraft," PMLA, LVII (1943), 163–169.

10. *Annual Necrology, 1797–8*, 460; *Mem*, 74.

11. *T*, 88–89, 81.

12. *M*, 146–147.

13. *M*, 149, 151–152; *T*, 85.

14. *SC*, II, 977; *VRW*, 204.

15. Ibid., 141, 204, 140, 139.

16. *Mem*, 22; *T*, 70–71.

17. Ms. *Diary*, Berg Collection, New York Public Library. Even in her diary, Fanny Burney probably would not have recorded the real name of such a scandalous young woman. Miss Joyce Hemlow informed me that Fanny Burney at

a later time used the name "Miss White" as a pseudonym for Amelia Locke, later Mrs. Angerstein, in a letter to her sister. (10–11 October 1796).

18. *SC*, II, 975–977.

19. *Abinger.*

20. *SC*, II, 977–979.

CHAPTER 5

1. *Mem*, 22–23; *SC*, II, 981.

2. *On Dropsy* (translated from the Latin by Maria Wilkins Smith, Gladwynne, Penna. 1964); Original title *DeHydrope* (Philadelphia, 1771).

3. *MM*, I, 173; *M*, 15–16.

4. *MM*, I, 171–173.

5. *M*, 39–40; *MM*, I, 174; *GM*, 120.

6. Flexner, *Mary Wollstonecraft*, 289; *MM*, I, 174–177; II, 15, 23.

7. Undated, from Mitchelstown (1786), *Abinger.*

8. *MM*, I, 176; *T*, 149, 142; Eliza to Everina, Feb. 10, 1795, *Abinger.*

9. Fanny Blood to Everina, Feb. 18, 1784, *Abinger.*

10. *SC*, II, 982–983.

11. Skeys to Godwin, Dec. 1, 1797, *Abinger; Mem*, 24.

12. *M*, 44–45, 51.

13. *SC*, II, 983–984.

14. *Mem*, 30–31.

15. George Mills Harper, *Notes and Queries*, IX, No. 12, 461–463.

16. "Sunday" (fall of 1783), from London, *Abinger.*

CHAPTER 6

1. *VRW*, 72–73.

2. Eliza to Everina, Nov. 28, 1791; Dec. 4, 1793; Dec. 8, 1791; Nov. 1, 1791; Oct. 4, 1791; Godwin to James Marshal, Aug. 14, 1800, *Abinger.*

3. Worshipful Company of Shipwrights, Admissions Stamp Duty Book, 1727–1825 (Guildhall Library MS 4602/4) 35, 115; Register of Baptisms, St. Mary Magdalen Bermondsey (Greater London Record Office *MS* P 71/MMG/10A); *Kent's Directory* . . . 1778–1788; *Lowndes London Directory*, 1788, 27; Documents of Commissary Court of St. Katherine's Near the Tower (Guildhall Library MSS 9740/4, 9772/34); Marriage Register of St. Katherine's (Guildhall Library MS 9671). The premarriage records state Bishop was twenty-one "and upwards," which simply meant he was of age.

4. *VRW*, 129–131.

5. See Register of Baptisms above.

6. Unless otherwise noted all further letters in this chapter are from Mary to Everina. Although she did not date them by year, they are from sometime after mid-September, 1783, to mid-February, 1784, *Abinger.*

7. *T*, 101.

8. William Alexander, *The History of Women from the Earliest Antiquity, to the Present Time* (London, 1779), I, 324, 240.

9. Eliza to Everina, Aug. 17, 1786; Mary to Everina, Aug. 23, 1790, *Abinger*.

10. Mary to Everina, Oct. 9, 1786, *Abinger*.

CHAPTER 7

1. Everina to Godwin, Nov. 24, 1797, *Abinger*. All other letters in this chapter unless otherwise noted are those of February, 1784, to August, 1786, *Abinger*.

2. *The Bath Journal*, No. 1841, April 12, 1779.

3. *Mem*, 26; *SC*, II, 976.

4. Andrew Kippis, *Biographia Britannica* (London, 1784), 14; Burgh, *Youth's Friendly Monitor*, 11–12.

5. *Mem*, 27; *VRM*, 35–36; *VRW*, 214; *LS*, 164–165.

6. Richard Price, *Observations On the Importance of the American Revolution* (London, 1784), 3–5; *Observations On the Nature of Civil Liberty* (London, 1776), 4; *The Evidence For a Future Period of Improvement In the State of Mankind* (London, 1787), 55.

7. *Mem*, 37; *T*, 23–24, 71; Everina to Godwin, Nov. 24, 1797, *Abinger*.

8. *Mem*, 32–33.

9. *T*, 113; Claire Tomalin, *The Life and Death of Mary Wollstonecraft* (London, 1974), 28; *Mem*, 38.

10. *OS*, 31; *VRW*, 141.

11. *Mem*, 31–32.

12. *T*, 110; *Mem*, 36.

13. *The Journal of William Beckford in Portugal and Spain 1787–1788*, Boyd Alexander, ed. (New York, 1955), 61, 111; *M*, 77.

14. *M*, 119–127; *Mem*, 36–37.

15. Price, *Observations On . . . the American Revolution*, 50; Gregory, *A Father's Legacy*, 11, 53–55, 104; Chapone, *Letters*, 121.

16. *T*, 110, i–ii, 1–4, 7–8, 11–22.

17. *T*, 29, 33–34, 36–37, 42–43, 49, 52, 60.

18. Ibid., 62, 61, 63, 66, 75, 79, 82–84, 89, 91, 93, 99–101, 97, 101, 104, 107, 109, 113, 115, 121, 123, 128, 126–128, 131–132, 160.

19. Ralph M. Wardle, in his *Mary Wollstonecraft*, links these censored passages and the alias "Neptune," to Waterhouse. Flexner disagrees, as I myself do. (Margaret Crum of the Department of Western MSS, Bodleian Library, very kindly attempted to decipher censored passages from the Abinger letters when they were on loan at Oxford, but informed me that a complete text was probably impossible to recover. She could make out only a few isolated words, which tend to confirm the probability that George Blood or someone to whom he gave these letters expunged material damaging to the Wollstonecraft family.)

20. *Mem*, 25–26.

21. Flexner, *Mary Wollstonecraft*, 278.

CHAPTER 8

All letters quoted in this chapter, unless otherwise noted, are from the fall of 1786 to November, 1787, *Abinger*.

1. *VRW*, 176, 178–179.
2. Ibid., 162.
3. *SC*, IV, 842, 859.
4. *T*, 157.
5. *Mem*, 40; Lady Mount Cashell to Godwin, *Abinger*.
6. *SC*, I, 66–67.
7. Eliza to Everina, April 24, 1793, *Abinger*.
8. *LS*, 21.
9. Mary had spelled "satire" correctly in the same letter.
10. *M*, 147–149.
11. *SC*, I, 75.
12. *SC*, IV, 859–860, 856–858.
13. *SC*, I, 76.
14. Ibid., 77.
15. *OS*, 138–139.
16. *SC*, IV, 858.
17. *SC*, I, 75–76.
18. Ibid., 77.
19. *SC*, IV, 857–858.
20. *M*, 151.
21. *LJ*, I.
22. *SC*, I, 76–77.
23. *SC*, IV, 860.
24. *M*, ii–iv, 1, 4, 6, 10, 40, 60–61, 91, 94, 103, 108, 134, 164, 169–170, 185, 186, 187.
25. Ibid., 109–110.

CHAPTER 9

All letters quoted in this chapter, unless otherwise noted, are from September, 1787, to May, 1788, *Abinger*.

1. George Paston, *Sidelights on the Georgian Period* (London, 1902), 89; *DNB*, XIII, 688–689.
2. Paston, op. cit., 153.
3. *Mem*, 44.
4. *SC*, IV, 859–860.
5. *LJ*, II, III.
6. *OS*, iii, v; *LJ*, IV.
7. *OS*, 1–8, 10, 37, 52, 159–160, 43, 138, 30, 128, 122–124, 91–92, 101.
8. *AR*, II, 478–479.
9. *LJ*, V.
10. *C*, 99, 135–136.
11. *LJ*, IV, *VI*, VIII–XII.
12. Jacques Necker, *Of the Importance of Religious Opinions*, tr. Mary Wollstonecraft (Philadelphia, 1791), 256, 33.
13. *AR*, I, i–v.
14. Wardle, *Mary Wollstonecraft*, 346.

15. *AR*, I, 207; III, 221; V, 361; I, 333; II, 223; V, 488; IV, 226; V, 217–218; I, 457.

16. *LJ*; XV; XIV.

17. *AR*, II, 8; *Mem*, 28; *AR*, III, 48; IV, 225.

CHAPTER 10

Unless otherwise noted, all the letters quoted are from Feb. 28, 1789 to Sept. 10, 1790, *Abinger*.

1. Johnson's Notes, *Abinger*.

2. *GM*, 74; Harper, *Notes and Queries*, X, No. 12, 461; *LJ*, XV.

3. Information on Fuseli from John Knowles, *The Life and Writings of Henry Fuseli* (London, 1831), and Eudo C. Mason, *The Mind of Henry Fuseli* (London, 1951).

4. *VRW*, 76; *Mem*, 58, 60; *LI*, XXIII.

5. *VRW*, 135.

6. Knowles, op. cit., I, 163–164; *Mem*, 56; Mason, op. cit., 146.

7. W. C. Durant, *Supplement* to Godwin's *Memoirs*, 190; *OS*, 42; Knowles, op. cit., 165.

8. Knowles, op. cit., 380; Eliza to Everina, Jan. 29, 1792; Feb. 29, 1793; May 18, 1793; Dec. 4, 1793; Jan. 14, 1794, *Abinger*.

9. *AR*, V, 42; VI, 134, 130; VII, 44; VIII, 141; VIII, 250–251.

10. Wardle, *Mary Wollstonecraft*, 123–125.

11. *AR*, VIII, 246.

CHAPTER 11

All letters in this chapter, unless otherwise noted, are from early winter of 1790 through November, 1791, *Abinger*.

1. *Mem*, 51; *VRM*, 128.

2. Richard Price, *A Discourse on the Love of Our Country* (London, 1790), 34, 49–50; W. E. H. Lecky, *A History of England in the Eighteenth Century* (London, 1887), V, 454–455.

3. *VRM*, Intro. by Eleanor Louise Nicholes, xvi.

4. *Mem*, 51–52; *VRM*, 1–6, 28, 9, 7–8, 9–10, 11–12, 50, 43, 24, 142–144, 148–149, 56, 93, 81, 112–113, 68, 34, 78, 21.

5. *VRM*, 29; *Mem*, 51, 60.

6. Flexner, *Mary Wollstonecraft*, 276.

7. *VRM*, 140, 70, 72.

8. *VRW*, 29; *LI*, III.

9. *Mem*, 61; Knowles, *Henry Fuseli*, I, 164–165.

10. Claire Tomalin discovered and first reproduced this portrait, which Mary referred to in her Oct. 6, 1791 letter to Roscoe; Flexner, op. cit., 275. Because of the powdered hair, it is thought that Opie's first portrait was done before Mary left for France in 1792. The engraving by J. Chapman reproduced by Tomalin appears to me to be a caricature of Mary Wollstonecraft. It shows her in a man's hat, and bears no resemblance to any authenticated portrait except that the bust seems to have been from Opie's second portrait.

11. Durant, *Supplement*, 251; *Mem*, 56; *VRW*, 129, 53, 55.
12. Flexner, op. cit., 277.
13. Ibid., 275.

CHAPTER 12

1. *SC*, I, 61; *An Anthropologist at Work: Writings of Ruth Benedict*, Margaret Mead, ed. (Cambridge, 1959), 493.
2. *Mem*, 62–63.
3. *VRW*, 11–13, 5, 22, 18, 111, 164, 48.
4. Ibid., 31, 39–40, 24, 152, 189, 194.
5. Ibid., 23, 7, 34, 61, 67.
6. Ibid., 163, 161.
7. Ibid., 41, 39, 40, 111, 102, 41.
8. Ibid., 33, 214–215.
9. Ibid., 177, 35.
10. Ibid., 34, 110, 82, 36, 120.
11. Ibid., 184.
12. Ibid., 77, 194–195, 39.
13. Ibid., 212, 70, 207; *LI*, IV.
14. Flexner, *Mary Wollstonecraft*, 276.
15. G. E. G. Caitlin, Intro. to *VRM*, xiii; Eliza to Everina, June 10, 1793, *Abinger*.
16. James Boswell, *The Life of Samuel Johnson* (Modern Library), 1105; *Mrs. Delaney (Mary Granville) A Memoir 1700–1788*, compiled by George Paston (London, 1900), 86; *Letters of Anna Seward* (Edinburgh and London, 1811), III, 117; *Maria Holroyd*, 347; *Diary of Elizabeth Drinker*, March 6, April 22, 1799, Penna. Historical Society.
17. Eliza to Everina, Jan. 20, 1793, *Abinger*.
18. Flexner, op. cit., 277; Johnson's Notes, *Abinger*.
19. *Mem*, 65; *VRW*, 115.
20. Eliza to Everina, July 3, 1792; Mary to Everina, Feb. 23, 1792; Eliza to Everina, Nov. 7, 1794, *Abinger*.
21. Flexner, op. cit., 276; Mary to G. Blood, Jan. 2, 1792; Mary to Everina, Feb. 23, 1792; Eliza to Everina, July 3, 1792, *Abinger*.
22. *Four New Letters of Mary Wollstonecraft and Helen Maria Williams*, Benjamin P. Kurtz and Carrie C. Autrey, eds. (Berkeley, Calif., 1937), 14–21; Flexner, op. cit., 277; Mary to Everina, Feb. 23, 1792, *Abinger*.
23. Mary to Everina, June 20, 1792; Sept. 14, 1792; Eliza to Everina, July 3, 1792, *Abinger*.
24. Knowles, *Henry Fuseli*, I, 166–167; *AR*, XIII, 60, 271; *PW*, IV, 179–182, 186.
25. Carol H. Poston, Janet M. Todd, *Mary Wollstonecraft Journal*, II, No. 2, 28; Knowles, op. cit., I, 363; Mason, *Henry Fuseli*, 174; Knowles, op. cit., I, 167.
26. Johnson to Fuseli, Sept. 10, 1797, *Abinger*.
27. *Mem*, 66; Flexner, op. cit., 279.

28. Eliza to Everina, Feb. 29, 1793, *Abinger;* Knowles, op. cit., I, 168; Durant, *Supplement,* 175–176.

29. Mary to Everina, undated, from Dover, *Abinger.*

30. Flexner, op. cit., 279–280.

CHAPTER 13

1. Mary to Everina, Dec. 24, 1792, *Abinger.*

2. *T,* 150–151; *LJ,* XVI.

3. Eliza to Everina, Jan. 20, 1793; Jan. 30, 1793; Feb. 10, 1793, *Abinger; SC,* I, 121–132.

4. Joel to Ruth Barlow, March 18, 1793, Houghton Library, Harvard; *Mem,* 73, 71; Quoted by Eliza to Everina, Jan. 30, 1793, *Abinger; SC,* IV, 865–867.

5. Eliza to Everina, Feb. 29, 1793, *Abinger.*

6. *PW,* IV, 40–44, 50, 44–45.

7. Gilbert Imlay, *A Topographical Description of the Western Territory of North America* (London, 1793), Intro.; Ralph L. Rusk, "The Adventures of Gilbert Imlay," Indiana University Studies No. 57 (Bloomington, 1923).

8. Imlay, op. cit., 1, 2, 55, 207.

9. *Mem,* 68; *LI,* LX; *MM,* I, 42, 32; II, 125; J. or I. B. Johnson to Godwin, Derby, Nov. 13, 1797, *Abinger.*

10. *Annual Necrology 1797–8,* 425; Barlow letters, Houghton Library, Harvard; *Mem,* 70.

11. Gilbert Imlay, *The Emigrants,* facsimile reproduction of the Dublin (1794) edition (Gainesville, 1964), intro. by Robert B. Hare *et passim.*

12. *MM,* I, 52, 55–56, 60–61, 64.

13. Ibid., 70–71; *GM,* 40; *MM,* I, 71–72.

14. *LI,* LVIII; *MM,* I, 137; I, 24, 38; II, 125–127.

15. *MM,* II, 123, 127–128; I, 74.

16. Ibid., 75.

17. *Mem,* 74.

18. *LS,* 94–95; *LI,* IX, I.

19. *LI,* IV; *MM,* II, 140–144; Eliza to Everina, July 14, 1793, *Abinger.*

20. *LI,* II.

21. Letter from Mary Wollstonecraft to Ruth Barlow, dated "Friday." Gratz Collection, Penna. Historical Society.

22. *LI,* IV.

23. Ibid., V–VII.

24. Ibid., VI, VIII–X.

25. Ibid., XI.

26. Ibid., XIII–XVII.

CHAPTER 14

1. Kurtz and Autrey, *Four New Letters,* 40, 41.

2. *MM,* II, 138–139.

3. Kurtz and Autrey, op. cit., 41; *LI,* XVIII, XIX.

4. Eliza to Everina, Nov. 5, 1793; Mary to Everina, Mar. 10, 1794, *Abinger.*

5. Mary Wollstonecraft, *An Historical and Moral View of the Origins and Progress of the French Revolution; and the Effect It Has Produced in Europe* (London, 1794), 259, 7, 15.
6. Ibid., 17; 6.
7. Tomalin, *Mary Wollstonecraft*, 174.
8. Kurtz and Autrey, op. cit., 41–42, 43–44.
9. *VRW*, 156–157.
10. Durant, *Supplement*, 262.
11. *LI*, XV; LV, XXII.
12. *LI*, XX, XXI.
13. Mary to Everina, Sept. 20, 1794, *Abinger*.
14. Eliza to Everina, Aug. 15, 1794; Mary to Everina, Sept. 20, 1794, *Abinger*.
15. *LI*, XXIV, XXVI, XXV, XXIX, XXVII, XXIII, XXVI, XXVII.
16. *LI*, XXIV: Durant, op. cit., 247; Tomalin, op. cit., 132.
17. Durant, op. cit., 253–254, 255.
18. *LI*, XXIII–XXVII.
19. Eliza to Everina, Oct. 12, 1794; Imlay to Eliza, *Abinger*.
20. *LI*, XXVIII–XXXVI.
21. *LI*, XXXVII, XXXVI, LXXVII.
22. *LI*, LXXVII, XXXVIII; Durant, op. cit., 293.
23. *LI*, XXXIX.
24. Eliza to Everina, March 4, 1795, *Abinger; LI*, LXXVI; Eliza to Everina, April 29, 1795; May 8, 1795, *Abinger*.
25. Document, *Abinger*.
26. *Mem*, 82; *LI*, XLIV, XL.
27. *LI*, XLIV; *MM*, II, 162–163.
28. Ibid., 164; *LI*, XLIV.

CHAPTER 15

1. *LI*, XLII, XLV, XLIV, XLVII, L.
2. *LI*, XLV.
3. *LI*, XLVI, XLIV; *LS*, 117; *LI*, LI.
4. *LI*, XLVII, XLIX, L, LI.
5. *LS*, 10, 8.
6. *LI*, LII, LIV.
7. *LS*, 20, 39.
8. *LI*, LV–LVIII.
9. *LS*, 49, 51–52, 62, 66.
10. *LI*, LIX.
11. *LS*, 93, 72, 95, 102, 115–116.
12. *LI*, LX–LXIII.
13. *LS*, 132, 117, 133, 136, 138, 136–137, 143, 156, 168, 169, 170, 174.
14. *LS*, 208–210; *LI*, LXIV.
15. *LI*, LXV; *LS*, 214, 241, 252; *LI*, LXVI.
16. *LI*, LXVII, LXVIII.

17. *PW*, II, 175; *LI*, LXIX. The *Gentleman's Magazine* reported steady rain or "rain at night," Oct. 17, 24, and 27–31. Mary had learned to row in Scandinavia, but it would have been difficult as well as conspicuous to row herself upriver, since the tide was adverse. Godwin says "she took a boat and rowed." Mary Hays says she was rowed by a boatman whom she questioned about bridge traffic. It is unlikely a professional boatman would rent his craft to anyone.

18. Tomalin, *Mary Wollstonecraft*, 187, found a report of Mary's rescue in D. Lysons' *Supplement To The First Edition of the Historical Account of the Environs of London* (London, 1811), 260.

19. *Mem*, 89–90; *LI*, LXX, LXXI, LXIII; *GM*, 140; *LI*, LXXV, LXXVI.

20. *LS*, Advertisement, 97.

21. Durant, *Supplement*, 306–307; *Mem*, 84–85; unsigned letter to "Mrs. Imlay," *Abinger*.

22. Durant, op. cit., 300–301; Knowles, *Henry Fuseli*, I, 168.

23. C. Kegan Paul, *Mary Wollstonecraft, Letters to Imlay* (London, 1879), li.

24. *LI*, LXXVII.

25. *Mem*, 92–93.

26. *MM*, I, 4; *LS*, 242.

27. *LI*, LXXVIII. It is typical of Godwin that he gives no detail about Mrs. Cotton, but records the name of her genteel neighbor, Sir William East. The Berkshire County Record Office can find no trace of Mrs. Cotton in or near Sonning.

CHAPTER 16

1. *GM*, 108.
2. *Maria Holroyd*, 324; Durant *Supplement*, 301, 303.
3. Flexner, *Mary Wollstonecraft*, 233.
4. *GM*, 107–108.
5. *MM*, I, 69–70.
6. *Mem*, 61; *MM*, II, 28–31; I, 140–141.
7. *Mem*, 98.
8. C. Kegan Paul, *William Godwin: His Friends and Contemporaries* (London, 1876), I, 154.
9. Ibid., 74; M. Ray Adams, *Studies in the Literary Backgrounds of English Radicalism* (Lancaster, 1947), 272; Paul, op. cit., 74; *The Essays of William Hazlitt*, Catherine MacDonald Maclean, ed. (New York, 1950), 8.
10. Ford K. Brown, *The Life of William Godwin* (London, Toronto, and New York, 1926) 3 *et passim;* Paul, op. cit., 6, 9–11, 14.
11. Ibid., 38–40, 67.
12. Ibid., 78; Malcolm Edwin, *Lord Byron's Wife* (New York, 1962), 258.
13. *The Complete Works of William Hazlitt*, P. P. Howe, ed. (London, 1930–1934), XI, 17; *New Letters of Robert Southey*, Kenneth Curry, ed. (New York and London, 1965), I, 79.
14. *Mem*, 131; Paul, op. cit., 13; *Southey*, I, 213.
15. *LS*, 118.

16. *SC*, I, 22; David Bonnell Green, "Letters of William Godwin and Thomas Holcroft to William Dunlop," *Notes and Queries* (October, 1956), 442.

17. *Southey*, I, 246. John Dryden, *Fables, Ancient and Modern, translated into Verse* . . . (London, 1700), 105–106.

18. *Mem*, 99.

19. *MM*, I, 43; *GM*, 4–5, 8–9, 10.

20. *Mem*, 42; *GM*, 11–13, 16, 14–19, 22, 23.

21. *Mem*, 102; *GM*, 28.

22. Ibid., 24, 26, 21, 22, 26, 24, 27–29, 30, 35, 30–32, 41–42, 58–59, 33, 34, 37, 39, 40, 42–46, 48–51.

23. *Southey*, I, 184; Alderson to Godwin, September, 1796, *Abinger;* Brown, op. cit., 117–118; Hazlitt, *Essays*, 280–281; *GM*, 46.

24. *AR*, V, 64; *GM*, 29, 31; Alderson to Mrs. Imlay, Aug. 28, 1796, *Abinger*.

25. *MM*, II, 25, 17, 145.

26. *GM*, 53–58.

27. *Mem*, 103; *MM*, II, 141, 147; *GM*, 59–61.

28. Mary to Everina, March 22 (1797), *Abinger; GM*, 61, 64, 68; Wardle, *Mary Wollstonecraft*, 358, Note 60; *GM*, 69.

29. *Memorials of the Life of Amelia Opie* (Norwich and London, 1854), 61–62.

30. *GM*, 74, 73; Paul, op. cit., 235–236, 237–238, 240, 278.

31. *GM*, 75, 76, 74–75, 73, 108.

32. *Southey*, I, 389, 166, 215; II, 349.

33. Hazlitt, op. cit., 8, 280–281; Knowles, *Henry Fuseli*, I, 363.

34. *Mem*, 108–109, 33–34; *GM*, 82–83.

35. Paul, op. cit., 361; *GM*, 76–77, 107, 80, 106–107, 83, 111–112, 115, 118.

36. *SC*, IV, 888; *PW*, IV, 175; *GM*, 119.

37. *Mem*, 125; *GM*, 82, 89.

38. *Annual Necrology, 1797–8*, 455.

CHAPTER 17

1. *PW*, II, 185–186, 195–196.

2. Alderson to Mrs. Imlay, Aug. 28, 1796, *Abinger; PW*, IV, 56–57.

3. *GM*, 119–120.

4. *Mem*, 112–123; *SC*, I, 188–196.

5. Paul, *William Godwin*, I, 276; Eliza Fenwick to Everina; Johnson to Fuseli, Sept. 10, 1797; Johnson to Godwin, Sept. 12, 1797, *Abinger*.

6. Knowles, *Henry Fuseli*, I, 170; Godwin to Carlisle, Sept. 15, 1797, *Abinger*.

7. *Mem*, 6; Everina to Godwin, Nov. 24, 1797; Skeys to Godwin, Dec. 1, 1797, *Abinger*.

8. *Mem*, 5; Adams, *English Radicalism*, 308; Wardle, *Mary Wollstonecraft*, 317.

9. *DNB*, XI, 156–157; Tomalin, *Mary Wollstonecraft*, 60; Everina to Eliza (1798), *Abinger;* Australian *DNB*, 620.

10. *New Letters of Robert Southey*, I, 213.

11. Thomas Gisbourne, *An Enquiry into the Duties of the Female Sex* (London, 1797), 19, 227; Hannah More, *Strictures On The Modern System of Female Education* (Boston, 1808), 167.

12. Jane Arden Gardiner to Godwin, Jan. 15, 1799, *Abinger;* Peter Tomory, *The Life and Art of Henry Fuseli* (New York and Washington, 1972), 236; Durant, *Supplement*, 246.

13. Johnson and Wollstonecraft wills, London Public Record Office; J. Wollstonecraft to Godwin, *Abinger;* Flexner, *Mary Wollstonecraft*, 282; Reports on Supply of Ordance at Fort St. Charles signed "C. Wollstonecraft." March 13, March 22, 1813, Penna. Historical Society.

14. Godwin to Mrs. Cotton, Oct. 24, 1797, *Abinger.*

15. *The Love Letters of Mary Hays, 1779–1780*, A. F. Wedd, ed. (London, 1925), 247.

16. Tomalin, *Mary Wollstonecraft*, 256.

17. *LS*, 97.

Index

adolescence and youth (*see also* names, places, subjects), 24–28
affection, 46–7
childhood need of, 12–14
need for priority in, 14, 27–33, 337–9
Alderson, Amelia, 314–18, 325–6, 332, 334, 342
America, 218–19, 235–6
Charles in, 219, 224, 296, 303, 321
American Revolution, 96–7, 194
Analytical Review, The, 171–2, 179, 181, 218, 235
Wollstonecraft, as editorial assistant on, 171–5, 178, 186, 192–8, 216, 221, 304, 335
reviews by, 38, 172–4, 178, 187–9, 192, 216, 221, 326
Anderson, George, 179
Ann (niece of second Mrs. Skeys), 201, 205, 218, 224
Anti-Jacobin Review, 329, 351
appearance, 57, 185–6, 203–4, 217, 326, 340
Arden, Jane, 35–6, 40–8 *passim*, 53–6, 59, 62–7, 74–6, 80, 93–4, 352
heyday of friendship, 22, 26–34
Arden, John, 22, 31, 32, 46, 48, 53
art appreciation, 184, 187
Austen, Jane, 52, 154, 306
author (*see also Analytical Review, The*; titles), xiii–xiv, 107–8, 151ff., 160, 176ff., 198–9, 204ff., 329–30
reaction to writings of, 163, 214–18, 295, 329
authority, parental, 13–15, 19–20, 28, 48

Babeuf (Baboeuf), 264, 336
Barbauld, Anna, 23, 108, 118, 130, 153, 179, 333
Barking (England), 10–21
Barlow, Joel, 218–19, 231–3, 237, 244–6, 253
Barlow, Ruth, 218–19, 237–8, 244, 251–3, 256–9
Bath (England), 51–63
Benedict, Ruth, 207
Beverley (England), 21–37, 279
Bishop, Elizabeth, *see* Wollstonecraft, Elizabeth (Eliza)
Bishop, Elizabeth Mary Frances, 80–1, 89, 99
Bishop, Meredith, 79–90, 92, 99, 158

Blake, William, 163, 179–80, 182, 185–6, 188, 193, 198, 215, 223
Blenkinsop, Mrs. (midwife), 342–4
Blood, Mr. and Mrs., 73–7, 83, 92, 101, 136–7
  supported by Wollstonecraft, 98, 103, 105–6, 114
Blood, Caroline, 73
Blood, Frances (Fanny), 99, 131
  Skeys and, 41, 45–6, 74–5, 100–5
  Wollstonecraft and, 39–47, 54–5, 63–5, 73–7, 92, 99
    daughter named for Fanny, 256
    death of Fanny and effect on, 59, 104–7, 113, 115, 129, 164, 177–8, 284–5
    reflected in writings, 39–42, 45, 74–5, 144–6, 164, 166
    school, 93–5, 98–9
Blood, George, 73, 87, 120, 156, 170, 205
  affection of Mary for, 101–2
  Everina and, 142, 155–6, 200
  in Ireland, 106, 116–17, 120, 123, 131–2, 155–6, 177
  letters to, 101–4, 106–7, 114–18, 129, 136, 164–5, 170, 176–8
Bonnycastle, John, 179, 181, 183, 200
Bregantz, Mrs. and School, 176, 186, 189, 199–201, 229
Brissot, 235, 241, 246
Bristol (England), 142–8
Browne, Warren, 326
Buchan, William, 108
Burgh, James, 6–7, 95, 96, 108
Burgh, Sarah, 95, 98, 103, 118, 120–1, 132, 141, 155, 158, 160
Burke, Edmund, 37, 193–8, 308
Burney, D., 187
Burney, Fanny, 20, 53, 61–2, 153–4
Burr, Aaron, 215
businessmen, attitude toward, 9–10
Byron, Lord, 335

Caleb Williams (Godwin), 297, 312, 321
Canova, Antonio, 182
Carlisle, Anthony, 325, 342, 344–6, 348
Carter, Elizabeth, 23
Cave of Fancy (Wollstonecraft), 26, 43, 158, 171
Chapone, Hester, 46, 108, 109, 154
character and temperament (*see also* Friendships and attachments; Love; Marriage; etc.), 15, 31, 46–7, 57, 99–100, 202–3, 264, 338–4
  self-image, 4, 26, 29, 36, 47, 128–9, 148, 167
    in *Mary*, 143–8
    in *Original Stories . . .*, 24, 186
    Vindication of the Rights of Woman and, 213–14
Chesterfield, Lord, 209
Child of Woe (Norman), 172
childhood, 3–24
  reflected in writings (*see also* names of persons, titles of books), 11ff., 17, 110, 144
  typical, of period, 19–20
children, *see* Godwin, Fanny Imlay; Shelley, Mary Wollstonecraft
Christie, Jane, 231
Christie, Thomas, 171–2, 206, 231–2, 245, 292
Christie, Mrs. Thomas (Rebecca), 231, 236, 291–3, 298–9
Church (nephew of Sarah Burgh), 95, 98, 101, 103, 141
Clare, Mr. and Mrs., 35–6, 38–9, 41, 54, 88, 94, 101, 187
Clarissa (Richardson), 19, 182
Clarke, John, 345
Cockburn, Mrs., 120, 130
Coleridge, Samuel, 308, 312, 325, 336, 351
companion to Mrs. Dawson, 48, 51–68, 112
Cooper, Thomas, 310–11, 337
Cotton, Mrs., 299, 345, 347, 353
Cowper, William, 152

Cristall, Joshua, 177, 331
criticalness, 98–101
Curran, John Philpot, 336

Darwin, Erasmus, 24, 153, 182
Dawsons, companion in family of, 51–68
Dawson, Sarah, 48, 52–3, 55–6, 59–60, 63, 66, 68, 112
Day, Thomas, 173
death, 71, 346ff.
  grave and epitaph, 354–5
de Genlis, Madame, 209
Delane, Betty, 107, 124, 131–4, 143, 178
Denmark, 288–9
de Staël, Madame, 171, 209
Dickson, Lucy, 142
Dicksons, 5, 131
Drinker, Elizabeth, 215
Dublin, 106, 123, 131–42, 148, 156
Dyer, George, 215
Dyson, 323, 325, 329, 345

editor, *see Analytical Review, The*
Edgeworth, Maria, 153
education
  France, 206–8
  of Godwin, 309–10
  sex, 24–5
  typical, of period, 22–4, 59, 108–9, 122–3
  Victorian, 351
  of Wollstonecraft, 3, 22–5, 35–6, 48, 95–7, 123, 184–5
  Wollstonecraft and (*see also Original Stories . . . ; Thoughts on the Education of Daughters*), 59, 78–9, 97–8, 108ff., 130, 132, 218, 323
    of daughter, 263, 341–2
    emotions, control of, 111–12
    family relationships and, 12
    as governess, 127–8
    translation of Salzmann book, 188
    vocational education, 210–11
    women's rights and, 173, 206–11
Elements of Morality (Salzmann; tr. Wollstonecraft), 188, 198
Emigrants, The (Imlay), 238–41, 258, 288, 328
Emile (Rousseau), 139, 143
Emmeline (Smith), 172–3
emotionality (*see also* Affection; Love), 29, 138–9
  adolescent, 25ff., 46
  control necessary, 111–12
  Mary as expression of, 143–8
Enquirer, The, 321
Epping (England), 9–10
Eton (England), 121–3
Evelina (Burney), 154

Father's Legacy to His Daughters (Gregory), 108–9
Faulkner, B., 38
Female Conduct (Marriott), 18–19
Female Reader (ed. Wollstonecraft), 175
Fenwick, Eliza and John, 343–5, 347–8
Fillietaz, M. and Mme., 229–30, 241
finances, 95, 103, 105, 176, 178, 183
  Blood family, 73–4, 98, 103, 105–6, 114
  family
    Charles, aid to, 177, 185, 219
    childhood and youth, 5–7, 10–11, 15, 32–3, 43–5, 71
    father, support of, 98, 176–7, 185, 217, 272
    James, aid to, 200, 201
  sisters, contributions to, 98, 115–16, 142–3, 151, 164, 170, 176, 185, 273
  Godwin and, 331–3
  generosity, 98, 331
  Imlay and, 292, 294, 321
  indebtedness, 107, 114, 117, 120, 141–3, 151, 178, 189, 205, 217, 294, 321
  Johnson and, 143, 164, 189, 205, 266, 321, 331
Fitzgerald, Mrs., 125–6, 130–3, 142–3

Fordyce, George, 179, 209, 332, 342, 344–5
France, 171, 218–20, 296
  Everina in, 164, 170, 176, 186
  Imlay and, 235–6, 293–4, 298
  Revolution and its aftermath, 113, 180, 184, 192ff., 220, 223–4, 230ff., 237, 241ff., 335–6
    education, 206–7
    English reaction, 171, 193ff., 215, 262–4
    Girondists, 231, 241
    Louis XVI, 229–30, 232
    Terror, 244–5, 255
    war with England, 231–2
    writings of Wollstonecraft and (*see also* titles), 193, 195–9, 207ff., 231, 234–5, 242, 246, 252, 254–6
  Wollstonecraft in, 223–5, 229–72
Frankenstein (Shelley), 4, 312
friendships and attachments (*see also* names), 39ff.
  with men, 58–9, 134–7, 146–7, 187, 199, 202–3
  with women, 218, 326–7, 337–8
  youthful, 22, 26–33, 46
Fuseli, Henry, 179–87, 193, 219–20, 333, 336, 342, 351
  death, 352
  Wollstonecraft and, 183–7, 190–1, 198, 200–6, 208, 213–14, 216, 220–4, 233, 239, 272, 297, 303, 350
    death of Mary, 223, 347
    ménage à trois suggested by Mary, 222–3
Fuseli, Mrs. Henry (Sophia), 182, 185–7, 203, 210, 220, 222–3

Gabell, Henry, 123, 131, 135–38, 140, 143, 147, 156–8, 187, 189–91
Gabell, Mrs. Henry (Ann), 190, 191, 199, 210
Gascoyne, Joseph, 11
Geddes, Alexander, 179, 183–4
genealogy, Wollstonecraft, 4–7
George III, 37, 63, 65, 194, 197
Germany, 289
Gisbourne, Thomas, 351
Godwin, Fanny Imlay, 256–7, 261–3, 270–2, 277–90 *passim*, 296, 298–300, 304–5, 344, 352
  care and education of, Mary and, 257, 259, 263, 341–2
  death, 333
  Godwin and, 320–4 *passim*, 334, 337–8, 346, 348, 353
Godwin, Mary, *see* Shelley, Mary Wollstonecraft
Godwin, William, 14, 33, 74, 76, 79, 155, 192, 216–17, 274, 290, 304
  appearance, 309
  author, 297, 311–12, 321, 351
  character and life style, 307–14
  death, 354
  on Fuseli, 181, 198
  political philosophy, 297, 309–14
  precocity, 309–16
  remarriage, 353–4
  Wollstonecraft and, 16, 57, 97, 208, 242, 314–18, 321ff., 329–30, 339–40
    death of Mary, 346ff.
    finances, 331–3
    lovers, 318–26
    marriage, 332ff.
    meetings, early, 186, 204, 297–8, 307–8
    Memoirs [*see also Memoirs* . . . (ed. Godwin)], 4–5, 315, 331, 336–7, 348–50
    pregnancy and delivery, Mary's, 337–8, 341–6
  women other than Wollstonecraft and (*see also* names), 317, 326–7, 338–9
governess, for Kingsboroughs, 118–48, 155, 158, 350
Grattan, Henry, 336
Gregory, John, 23, 108–9, 209

Haydon, Benjamin Robert, 183

Hays, Mary, 57, 224, 237, 297–8, 304, 326, 345, 347, 350, 354
Hazlitt, William, 326, 336
health problems, 129–30, 132, 138–9, 141, 164–5, 189, 271
Herder, Johann von, 181
Hewlett, John, 101, 107, 114, 121, 127, 130, 132, 165–6, 179, 185, 187, 198, 347–8
Hewlett, Mrs. John, 125
Historical and Moral View of the Origins and Progress of the French Revolution . . . (Wollstonecraft), 255–6, 352
Holcroft, Thomas, 308, 312, 325, 333, 335, 346, 348
Holroyd, Louisa, 56
Holroyd, Maria, 23, 52, 215
Hoxton (England), 34–42
humanitarianism, 19
Hurdis, James, 179

Imlay, Fanny, *see* Godwin, Fanny Imlay
Imlay, Gilbert, 29, 214, 218, 221, 235, 352
  author, 234–5, 238–41, 264
  debts, 294, 321
  in London, 262–93 *passim*, 298–300
  name used by Mary, 296–7, 305, 308, 321
  in Paris, 293–4, 298
  Wollstonecraft and, 239–300, 323, 329
    differences, 247–50, 253, 256, 258ff.
    end of relationship, 300, 304–7, 315
    England, Imlay in, 262ff.
    England, Mary's return to, 272
    indebtedness, financial, 294, 321
    Letters Written . . . in Sweden (Wollstonecraft) and, 294–6
    love affairs, Imlay's, 267–70, 274, 290, 292
    Maria (Wollstonecraft), as reflection of, 236, 239–43, 253, 275, 279, 299, 305–7
Imlay, Gilbert, Wollstonecraft and (*cont'd*):
    marriage, 245, 262–3, 332
    pregnancy, 246–58 *passim*
    reconciliation, Mary's attempts at, 265ff., 277ff.
    Scandinavia, Mary's trip to, 274–8, 294–6
  sex relationship, 239–44, 253–4, 260, 264, 285–6, 296
  suicide attempts by Mary, 274–5, 290–2, 336
Inchbald, Elizabeth, 308, 314, 317–18, 322, 326, 331, 333–4, 337–8, 342, 346
independence, search for, 35–6, 44–8, 51ff., 72ff., 78, 93–8
infant care
  typical of period, 8
  Wollstonecraft and, 257–8, 342–3
insanity, concern about, 37–8, 90, 138–9, 197
intellectualism, 139–40, 179ff.
Ireland, 74, 92, 116–43, 148, 156
  Charles Wollstonecraft, 177
  Eliza (Elizabeth) Wollstonecraft, 303, 350, 352–3
  Everina Wollstonecraft, 201–2, 303, 350, 352–3
  George Blood, 106, 116–17, 123, 131–2, 155–6, 177
  Mary Wollstonecraft, 118–48, 350

Johnson, Joseph, 107, 114, 151–3, 177, 186, 215, 221
  Analytical Review, The (*see also Analytical Review, The*), 171–2, 198
  coterie of intellectuals, 132, 171, 179ff., 193, 208, 218, 303
  death, 352
  illness, 199–200
  politics, 262–5, 303
  Wollstonecraft and, 31, 33, 36, 130–1, 140–1, 151–2, 154, 157–9, 165, 169–75, 177, 187, 197, 344

Johnson, Joseph, Wollstonecraft and (*cont'd*):
death of Mary, 223, 347–8
finances and, 143, 164, 189, 205, 321, 331
manager and mentor, 155, 158–9, 174, 224, 335
publisher of works of, 118–19, 132, 154, 160–1, 194–5, 207–8, 214, 216, 221, 254, 295–6
Johnson, Samuel, 24, 97, 165, 174, 214–15, 221

Kemble, John, 326
Kingsborough, Lady, 123, 125, 127–8, 131–5, 137–8, 140, 142–3, 164
Kingsborough, Lord, 118, 123–5, 135, 137, 143–4, 146, 350
Kingsborough, Margaret, 126–8, 132–3, 147–8, 161, 164
Kingsboroughs, Wollstonecraft governess for, 118–48, 155, 158, 350
as reflected in *Original Stories,* 161–3
Knowles, John, 183, 185, 186, 221, 233, 347

Laugharne (Wales), 43–4, 71–2, 352
Laveter, Johann Kaspar, 181
Le Havre (France), 245–62
"Letter on the Present Character of the French Nation" (Wollstonecraft), 234–5
Letters on Education (Macaulay), 188, 207, 214
Letters on the Improvement of the Mind, Addressed to a Young Lady (Chapone), 46, 109
Letters Written during a Short Residence in Sweden, Norway and Denmark (Wollstonecraft), 281–2, 286, 288–9, 294–9, 304–5, 314
Lisbon, 74–5, 100, 102–6
London
Imlay in, 262–93 *passim,* 298–300
Mary Wollstonecraft in, 151, 155,
London, Mary Wollstonecraft in (*cont'd*):
157–224, 272–4, 290–9, 303–8
Wollstonecraft family in, 5–9
Louis XVI, 229–30, 232
love (*see also* Friendships and attachments; Sex and sex relationships; Women's rights and roles), 44–5, 112–13, 140–7, 164–6, 169–70, 202–3, 209, 212–13
marriage and, 80, 209, 212, 265

Macaulay, Catherine, 23, 52, 154, 188, 192, 198, 207, 214
Mackintosh, James, 43, 308, 314
Marguerite (nursemaid), 263, 272, 288, 304, 321
Maria (Wollstonecraft), 322, 325, 348–9
family life in, 17
father in, 12, 69–72
Imlay relationship reflected in, 236, 239–43, 253, 275, 279, 299, 305–7
insanity in, 38
mother in, 12–13, 69–70
Rousseau and, 315
sisters reflected in, 328
sons, 13, 71
marriage (*see* Sex relationships; Women's rights and roles)
Godwin on, 315, 331–3, 351
Imlay on, 238, 241
of Wollstonecraft
to Godwin (*see also* Godwin, William), 332ff.
to Imlay (*see also* Imlay, Gilbert), 245
Wollstonecraft on, 33, 80, 112–13, 222, 331, 245, 258
breakup of Eliza's marriage, 84–91
education and, 108–9
family relationships and education of children, 12
love, 80, 209, 212, 265

Marriage, Wollstonecraft on (*cont'd*):
polygamy, 222
rejection of, 146–7, 169–70
Marriott, Thomas, 18–19
Marshal, James, 307, 325, 332, 334–5, 344–6, 348
Mary: A Fiction (Wollstonecraft), 153–4, 163, 165, 170, 239–40, 343, 348
emotionality of, 143–8
Fanny Blood reflected in, 40–2, 45, 74–5, 144–5, 164, 166
father in, 12, 15, 69
Gabell reflected in, 135–6
genius and morality, 134, 140
Lisbon voyage, 106
mother in, 69–70
religion, 25, 105
self-portrayal in, 25–6, 143–8
setting, 43
son in, 13, 144
Waterhouse reflected in, 58
Mason, Miss, 98, 103, 120, 161
Memoirs of the Author of a Vindication of the Rights of Woman (ed. Godwin), 4, 43, 348–50
childhood, 4–5, 8–9, 11–14, 22
on companion role, 60–1
education, 23, 41
Eliza's marriage, 89
Fanny Blood, 38–9, 75–6
father, 4–5, 8, 12, 35
French Revolution, 237
Fuseli, 183–4
Godwin, 42, 308, 315–16, 331, 336–7, 346
Henry, 7, 36–7
Imlay, 236–7, 291, 295, 299, 305
Johnson, 303
Kingsboroughs, 127
Lisbon voyage, 106
mother, 4–5, 8–9, 68
politics, 198
reaction to, 350
religion, 174
temperament, Mary's, 46–7, 99–100
Montagu, Basil, 325, 338, 345–6, 348
Montagu, Elizabeth, 153
Montague, Lady Mary Wortley, 23
Monthly Magazine, 335
More, Hannah, 23–4, 153–4, 214, 351
Moore, Miss, 131, 133–4

Necker, Jacques, 167, 170–1, 174, 255
Nelson, James, 8
"Neptune," identity of, 115, 136–7
Neuilly (France), 241–51
Newington Green (England), 95–119
Norman, Elizabeth, 172
Norway, 283–7

Ogle, George, 126, 131, 134–5, 137–40, 143, 145, 147, 180, 187
Ogle, Mrs. George, 131, 135
"On Artificial Tastes" (Wollstonecraft), 335
Opie, John, 203–4, 217, 304–5, 326, 328, 330, 340, 344, 346–8
Original Stories from Real Life . . . (Wollstonecraft), 160, 163–4, 170, 198, 341
Blake illustrations, 163, 180, 185–6
Fanny Blood basis of character in, 39
Kingsborough experience reflected in, 161–3
self-description in, 24, 186
setting, 43

Paine, Tom, 193, 198, 208, 215, 218, 231, 236, 245, 248
Paris, 223–5, 229–41, 262–71, 293–4, 298
Everina in, 164, 170, 176
Parr, Samuel, 308, 350
Pendarves, Mrs., 215
Pinkerton, Miss, 338–9
Pitt, William, 96, 193, 312
poetry, essay on, 335, 339
Poignard, Louis, 343–5
Political Justice (Godwin), 297, 311, 315

politics and political philosophies (*see also Vindication of the Rights of Men; Vindication of the Rights of Woman*), 95–7, 303–4, 335–6
  Godwin, 297, 309–14
  Imlay, 236
  Johnson, 262–5, 303
  liberalism, 95–7, 108, 171–2, 303–4, 351
  French Revolution (*see also* France), 192ff.
Portugal, 74–5, 100, 102–6
Posthumous Works of the Author of a Vindication of the Rights of Woman (ed. Godwin), 350–1
Pozzi, Madame, 209
pregnancies, 246–58 *passim*, 330–2, 337, 341–6
Price, Richard, 19, 95–7, 103, 108, 113, 121, 171, 179, 187, 193–4, 196, 198, 311
Priestley, Joseph, 96, 97, 153, 179, 198
Prior, Mr. and Mrs., 121
publishing business (*see also* Johnson, Joseph; names, titles), 151–4

radicalism in England (*see also* Politics and political philosophies), 303, 309–13
Rasselas (Johnson), 165
rationalism, 96–7, 311–14, 335–6
Reflections on the Revolution in France . . . (Burke), 194–8, 308
religion
  Godwin, 309–10
  Wollstonecraft, 25–6, 62, 96, 171, 174, 185, 212, 239, 303, 335
  in writings, 25, 111, 113–14, 146, 187–8, 196
Reveley, Maria, 314, 326, 330, 343–4
Richardson, Samuel, 19, 153–4, 182
Rights of Man (Paine), 198, 215
Robinson, Mary ("Perdita"), 314, 326–7
Rogers, Samuel, 96
Rogers, Thomas, 96
Roland, Madame, 213, 231, 237, 246
Roscoe, William, 201, 203–6, 216, 223, 225, 239, 333
Rousseau, 18, 139, 143, 181, 184, 209, 315–16
Rowan, Alexander Hamilton, 264–5, 272, 296, 304
Rowden, Miss, and school, 142, 155–7, 164
Rutson, Elizabeth Ann, 5–6, 10

St. Leon (Godwin), 351
St. Paul's Churchyard group, 193
Salzmann, Christian Gotthelf, 188, 214
Sanford and Morton (Day), 173
scandal
  Godwin marriage as, 333–4
  Memoirs and, 350–1
Scandinavia, 274–8, 294–6
school (Newington Green), 93–8, 103, 106–7, 114–15, 117
Schweitzer, Madeleine, 233, 244, 264
Scotland, 262
self-pity, 11–12, 100–2, 106–7, 115–16, 126–7, 143–4, 339–40
Sense and Sensibility (Austen), 306
Seward, Anna, 215
sex and sex relationships (*see also* Love; Marriage; Women's rights and role), 46, 138–9, 207–14, 221, 339
  double standard, rejection of, 209
  education and, 24–5, 209–11
  Fuseli, 185–6, 203–5, 214, 216, 220–2
  Godwin and, 318, 339
  Imlay and, 239–44, 253–4, 260, 264, 285–6, 296
  puritanism, Mary's, 25, 58–61, 137–8, 147, 185–6, 188–9, 203
  violence and, 16–17
Shelley, Mary Wollstonecraft, 4, 40, 96, 341, 353–4
  birth of and death of mother, 343–8
Shelley, Percy, 4, 96, 255, 354
Siddons, Sarah, 52, 304–5, 318, 333

Skeys, Hugh, 103, 353
Bishops' marriage and, 83, 87, 90
Fanny Blood and, 41, 45–6, 74–5
marriage, 100, 102
pregnancy and death, 102–5
remarriage, 137, 201
niece of wife cared for by Mary, 201, 205, 218, 224
Wollstonecraft and, 74, 83, 102, 105, 116, 120, 136–7, 178, 205
death of Mary and *Memoirs*, 347–9
Skeys, Mrs. Hugh, *see* Blood, Fanny
Smith, Charlotte, 130, 172–3, **223**
social life
adolescence, 27, 43
as companion, 56ff.
Godwin period, 325–6, 335–6
as governess, 126, 131ff.
London, 179ff.
Paris, 231
typical, of period, 21–2, 51–3, 59–62, 122
Southey, Robert, 309, 313, 314, 326, 335–6, 351
Stone, John Hurford, 239
Strictures on Female Education (Gisbourne), 351
suicide attempts, 274–5, 290–2, 336
Sweden, 281–3, 287–8, 294–6

Talbot, Catherine, 23
Talleyrand, 206, 208, 217
Taylor, Thomas, 76, 178
Thoughts on the Education of Daughters (Wollstonecraft), 108–14, 117–19, 130, 132, 144, 155, 164, 341
adversity, benefits of, 113
authority, parental, 15
class prejudice, 113
love and affection, 44–5, 110, 112–13
men, relationships with, 58, 187
moral discipline, 110–11
mothers, role of, 109–10
reassurance, need for, 29
Thoughts on the Education of Daughters (*cont'd*):
religion, 113–14
restraints, needless, opposed, 12–13
temper, and self-control, 26, 111, 163
on useless women, 125
Tooke, John Horne, 153, 312, 336
Topographical Description of the Western Territory of North America, A (Imlay), 235–6, 255, 264
translator, 165, 167, 170–1, 174–5, 188, 192
Trimmer, Sarah, 159–60, 173
Twiss, Mr. and Mrs. Francis, 304–5, 317, 333, 335

Victorianism, 351–2
Vindication of the Rights of Men, A (Wollstonecraft), 48, 72–3, 108, 148, 195–9, 202
Vindication of the Rights of Woman (Wollstonecraft), 3, 17, 33, 205–17, 221, 225, 238–9, 327, 354
education, 206–7, 209–11
expectations, societal, 210–11
infant care, 258
inferiority of women in general, 211
insane, care of, 37–8
love and reason, 44
marriage, 212, 245, 258
reactions to, 50, 214–18
sex roles and behavior, 209–14, 222
Von Schlabrendorf, Gustave, 204, 237, 245–6, 264, 304, 315

Wales, 42–4, 71–2
Eliza in, 201–2, 214, 220, 266
Walpole, Horace, 182
Waltham Green (England), 73–7
Walworth (England), 44–8
Waterhouse, Joshua, 53, 56–9, 115, 136–7, 145, 147, 187
Wedgwood, Thomas, 331–4
Williams, Helen Maria, 231, 236, 239, 245–6

Windsor (England), 63–7
Wollstonecraft, Charles, 21, 48, 65, 71–2, 142, 160, 165, 177, 201, 216–17, 248, 262, 352
  aided by Mary, 177, 185, 199, 219
  in America, 219, 224, 296, 303, 321
Wollstonecraft, Edward (grandfather of Mary), 5–7, 10
Wollstonecraft, Edward (Ned) (son of Edward Bland Wollstonecraft), 177, 350, 352
Wollstonecraft, Edward Bland (Ned), 7, 10, 18, 36, 48, 55, 77, 80, 93, 98, 117, 177
  Charles and, 177, 201, 217
  death, 352
  Eliza and, 73, 78–80, 85–6, 90, 93–5
  Everina and, 73, 78–80, 98, 115–16, 121, 142
  father, support of, 98, 176–7, 217
  favoritism, mother's, and Mary's resentment of, 8–9, 13–14, 17, 70, 72
  finances, 10, 43–4, 71, 117, 141, 217
  as head of family, and struggle with Mary, 176–7
  reflected in Mary's writings, 13, 15, 70–1, 144–7
Wollstonecraft, Mrs. Edward Bland (Elizabeth), 78–9, 352
Wollstonecraft, Edward John, 4–20 *passim*, 24, 34–5, 40, 48, 55, 64, 80, 90, 98, 176–7, 201
  attachment of Mary to and search for surrogate, 33, 43–4, 187
  death, 352
  fondness for family, 14–15
  gentleman farmer, 10–11, 42
  illness and death of wife (Elizabeth), 9, 71
  improvidence and financial failure, 11, 15, 32–3, 43–5, 54, 71, 201
  marital relationships, 14–16, 33, 69
  marriage, second, 69, 71–2, 201
  profession, 4–7, 9–11
  rages and brutality, 16–17, 19, 26, 32–3, 43, 54, 201
Wollstonecraft, Edward John (*cont'd*):
  reflected in Mary's writings, 12, 17, 41, 69–72, 144
  supported
    by Mary, 176–7, 185, 199, 217, 321
    by son (Ned), 71, 176–7, 217
  temperament, 6, 9, 11, 16–17
Wollstonecraft, Mrs. Edward John (Elizabeth Dickson), 4–26 *passim*, 44, 55, 64–5
  disciplinarian, 13–14
  illness and death, 68–73
  marital relationships, 14–16, 33, 69
  need for Mary, 48
  partiality toward son, 8–9, 13–14, 17, 70
  reflected in Mary's writings, 12–13, 25, 41, 69–70, 144–7
Wollstonecraft, Elizabeth (Eliza) (Bess), 7, 36, 44, 48, 55, 93, 116, 142–3, 155–60, 164, 190–1, 210, 223–4, 353
  aid, financial, from Mary, 98, 115–16, 151, 273
  attachment, mutual, of Mary and, 79, 121
  breakdown, 37–8, 80–83
  break with Mary, 200, 273, 321, 347
  at Bregantz's school, 176, 186, 189, 199–200
  character and temperament, 79, 99, 115, 142, 156, 176
  death of Mary and *Memoirs*, 347, 349–50
  father, remarriage of, 72–3
  Fuseli, Mary and, 186, 205, 220, 233
  governess in Wales, 201–2, 214, 220, 266
  and Imlay affair, 243, 262, 266–7, 272–3
  Ireland, 128, 303
  letters to, 64–5, 102, 123, 125, 127–8, 142–3, 189, 232
  living with brother, 71, 78–9
  at Market Harborough, 116, 118, 121, 157, 164

Wollstonecraft, Elizabeth (Eliza) (*cont'd*):
- marriage, 75, 79–92
- reflected in writings of Mary, 109–10, 197, 328
- school in Newington Green, 93–5, 99–100, 106–7, 116–17
- strained relations with Mary, 99–100, 102, 199–200, 217–18
- on *Vindication of the Rights of Woman*, 214, 217–18

Wollstonecraft, Everina, 10, 44, 48, 55, 64, 72, 89–90, 93, 155, 157–60, 164, 176, 190–1, 217, 353
- aided by Mary, 98, 142–3, 151, 164, 170, 176
- break with Mary, 200, 321
- at Bregantz's school, 186, 189, 199–201
- character and temperament, 99, 155–6
- death of Mary and *Memoirs*, 347–50
- Edward (Ned) and, 71, 78–80, 98, 115–16, 121, 142, 156
- France, 164, 170, 176, 186
- George Blood and, 42, 155–6, 200
- Godwin and, 332
- governess, 201–2, 332
- Ireland, 128, 131, 201–2, 303
- letters to, 36–7, 77, 81–8, 92–4, 102, 121–42 *passim*, 147, 158–9, 189–91, 205, 214–20 *passim*, 229, 233, 243, 254, 262, 266

Wollstonecraft, Everina (*cont'd*):
- reflected in Mary's writings, 328
- at Rowden's school, 142, 155–7, 164
- school in Newington Green, 98, 103, 106–7, 114, 116
- strained relations with Mary, 99–100, 102, 199–200

Wollstonecraft, Henry Woodstock, 7, 18, 36, 303
- apprenticeship, 34, 36
- breakdown, 36–8, 48, 90, 138–9
- reflected in writings of Mary, 145, 147, 197

Wollstonecraft, James, 18, 48, 71, 177, 200, 202, 217, 224, 251–3, 303, 352

women's rights and role (*see also* Education; Love; Marriage; Sex and sex relationships; *Vindication of the Rights of Woman*), 205–17, 329, 351–2
- employment, 47–8
- Imlay on, and influence of Wollstonecraft, 238–9
- typical of period, 3, 7, 18–20

Wordsworth, William, 153, 182, 193, 313

Wrongs of Women, The (Wollstonecraft), *see Maria* (Wollstonecraft)

Young, Arthur, 137

Youth's Friendly Monitor (Burgh), 6–7

DATE DUE	BORROWER'S NAME	ROOM NUMBER

1. All pupils in the school are entitled to use the library and to borrow books.
2. Reference books, such as encyclopedias and dictionaries, are to be used only in the library.
3. Reserved books may be borrowed for one period, or at the close of school, and should be returned before the first class the following school day.
4. All other books may be retained for two weeks.
5. A fine is charged for each day a book is kept overtime.
6. Injury to books beyond reasonable wear and all losses shall be paid for.
7. No books may be taken from the library without being charged.